OXFO

Menander,

and Terence

OXFORD READINGS IN
Menander, Plautus, and Terence

Edited by
ERICH SEGAL

OXFORD
UNIVERSITY PRESS

OXFORD
UNIVERSITY PRESS

£2.99

Great Clarendon Street, Oxford ox2 6DP

Oxford University Press is a department of the University of Oxford.
It furthers the University's objective of excellence in research, scholarship,
and education by publishing worldwide in

Oxford New York

Auckland Bangkok Bogotá Buenos Aires Cape Town Chennai
Dar es Salaam Delhi Hong Kong Istanbul Karachi Kolkata
Kuala Lumpur Madrid Melbourne Mexico City Mumbai
Nairobi Paris São Paulo Shanghai Singapore Taipei Tokyo Toronto
and associated companies in Berlin Ibadan

Oxford is a registered trade mark of Oxford University Press
in the UK and certain other countries

Published in the United States
by Oxford University Press Inc., New York

© Oxford University Press 2001

The moral rights of the author have been asserted
Database right Oxford University Press (maker)

First published 2001

British Library Cataloguing in Publication Data

Data available

Library of Congress Cataloging in Publication Data

Oxford readings in Menander, Plautus, and Terence / edited by Erich Segal.

p. cm.

Includes bibliographical references
1. Classical drama (Comedy)–History and criticism. 2. Meander, of Athens–Criticism
and interpretation. 3. Plautus, Titus Maccius–Criticism and interpretation.
4. Terence–Criticism and interpretation. I Segal, Erich, 1937–

PA3028.O88 2002

872'.0109—dc21 2001036504

ISBN 0–19–872192–7   0–19–872193–5 pbk.

10 9 8 7 6 5 4 3 2 1

Typeset by J&L Composition Ltd, Filey, North Yorkshire
Printed in Great Britain
on acid-free paper by
Biddles Ltd, Guildford & King's Lynn

To Hilary and Philip
with love and gratitude

CONTENTS

IV   Terence

INTRODUCTION

Towards the end of the fifth century BC, Old Comedy, that peculiar entertainment which was the particular province of Aristophanes and his then-extant contemporaries, had already begun to decline. *The Frogs*, with its resurrection of a dead poet, may well represent the last gasp. Was the simultaneity of the fall of the genre and the fall of Athens mere coincidence? A defeated people is in no mood for fantasy.

Yet the beginning of the 'new era' in comic drama is a moveable feast. Scholars like Hellmut Flashar and Kenneth Dover have viewed the history of classical comedy as a continuum, with the New as the natural evolution of the Old.[1] At the end of his career, Aristophanes himself produced what some might well regard as New Comedy. His *Ecclesiazusae* (*Assemblywomen*) eschews fantasy and emphasizes ordinary citizens and their economic woes. It anticipates such Hellenistic elements as the scene set in a public square before two houses, the relationships between man, wife, and courtesan, and other essentially domestic problems.[2] The last of his plays that has come down to us, the *Ploutos* (*Wealth*)—all too extant in no fewer than 150 manuscripts—presents the old master, if not leading the parade, at least following it. Here we find the pursuit of riches an overriding obsession. Where else in Aristophanes is money the be-all and end-all?

Some even argue—as Bernard Knox does in this volume—that the father of *nea kômôidia* was in fact Euripides, citing *Ion* (*c.*413/2) as the landmark play. Others point to Aristophanes' lost *Kokalos* as the first exercise in the new style by an old master. For, according to one

---

[1] K. J. Dover, 'Greek Comedy' in *Fifty Years (and Twelve) of Classical Scholarship* (Oxford, 1968), 147. H. Flashar, 'Zur Eigenart des Aristophanischen Spätwerks', in *Poetica I* (1967), 154–75, ed. by Hans-Joachim Newiger (Darmstadt, 1975). See also E. Segal, 'The *physis* of Comedy', *Harvard Studies in Classical Philology*, 77 (1973), 129–36.
[2] See Eric Handley, *Cambridge History of Classical Literature*, vol. 1, ed. P. E. Easterling and B. M. W. Knox (Cambridge, 1985).
[3] *Vita Aristophanis* 28. 65 (Dübn.)=Test.1.49–51 K-A.

ancient critic, it contained 'rapes and recognitions and all the other things Euripides loved'.[3]

At the same time, Heinz-Günther Nesselrath has recently redeemed the notion of a 'Middle Comedy'—a term coined by the third century BC scholar Aristophanes of Byzantium to refer to the plays produced in the sixty-year period between the end of Aristophanes' career and the beginning of Menander's. But what remains is merely the confetti of small quotations, and it is impossible to evaluate in detail except for a few generalities. It seems to be characterized by mythological travesties, the increasing role of the courtesan, and the marginalization of the chorus, all of which set 'Middle Comedy' apart from the antipodes of the two more familiar genres.[4]

Moving on in time, Geoffrey Arnott puts forth strong arguments that Menander is, if not the father of New Comedy, then certainly its most important innovator.[5] On the other hand, there are those who argue that true 'modern' comedy only began with the works of Terence.[6]

No one is right and no one wrong. All we can say for certain is that New Comedy is definitely *not* Old Comedy. The latter was wild, bawdy, and virtually plotless, dealing with men who were at once flesh and blood as well as virtual abstractions. Aristophanes dealt with issues, not people. With the possible exception of Socrates and Strepsiades in *The Clouds*—feminist historians might add Lysistrata, who was almost certainly modelled on the priestess Lysimache[7]—one does not readily recall any characters from his plays.

New Comedy was as markedly chaste as Old Comedy was bawdy. Aristotle contrasted the *aischrologia* (obscenity) of the old to the *hyponoia* (innuendo) of the New.[8] The phallus, once flaunted, was now operating more discreetly from inside the actors' clothing. Ploutos, the god of wealth, all but upstaged Phales as the presiding divinity.

[4] Heinz Günther Nesselrath, *Die Attische Mittlere Komödie: Ihre Stellung in der antiken Literaturkritik und Literaturgeschichte* (Berlin, and New York, Walter de Gruyter, 1990)

[5] There is an excellent introduction to Menander in G. Arnott's edition and translation for the Loeb Classical Library (Cambridge, Mass., 1979–2001).

[6] The argument that follows is fully developed in E. Segal, *The Death of Comedy* (Cambridge, Mass., 2001).

[7] Alan H. Sommerstein refers to this in his introduction to his excellent edition of the play: 'not only is this name strikingly similar to that of Lysistrata both in form and in meaning, but in the play itself (554) the heroine expresses her confidence that "one day we will be known among the Greeks as *Lysimachai*".'   [8] *Nic. Eth.* 128a.

But this does not mean the plays lacked an erotic dimension. The significant difference is that whereas in Old Comedy the girl is the reward of the protagonist in the finale of the play, in New Comedy the first sexual encounter has generally taken place eight and a half months *before* the play begins. The Aristophanic finale is usually a riotous uninhibited party, and there is no tomorrow for the characters. By contrast in New Comedy, in the words of Shakespeare's Don Armado, 'the catastrophe is a nuptial'.

Aristophanes' plays took place anywhere in the universe—in heaven, in hell, and exotic venues in between. By contrast, New Comedy was metropolitan—indeed 'cosmopolitan', to use a term which first appears at this time. New Comedy represents the *embourgeoisement* of the comic dream.[9] It brings Old Comedy's flights of fantasy down to earth with a thud. As the fourth-century critic Donatus describes it, the *nea* deals with 'private people living in town'.[10] Instead of conquering the world, the hero's highest ambition is merely to win a girl and a dowry.

Such was the genre as typified by—to adapt Horace's trio of Old Comedy poets to the new—Menander, Philemon, and Diphilus. Although Plautus seems to have given Menander a wide berth, he certainly relished the other two in the triumvirate.[11] By contrast, Terence concentrated on Menander and one of one of his disciples, Apollodorus of Carystus. Perhaps Plautus found Menander too subtle for his audience's taste. Philemon and Diphilus were more boisterous—hence Philemon's greater success in his own day.

After an indifferent career—only a handful of victories[12]—

---

[9] But see D. Wiles' contribution in this book, which takes issue with Eric Handley's view (which coincides with my own) in *Cambridge History of Literature*, 425.

[10] Donatus *De comoedia*, Kaibel, *CGF*, p. 67 (*Comoedia est fabula diversa instituta continens affectuum civilium ac privatorum*), rendering an earlier Greek definition which is also given.

[11] See *Mostellaria*, 1149–1150: *Si amicus Diphilo aut Philemoni es,* | *dicito eis, quo pacto tuos te servos ludificaverit:* | *optumas frustrationes dederis in comoediis* ('If you're a friend of Diphilus and Philemon, tell them what happened and how brilliantly your slave made fun of you today. You'd give them the best material for their trickery comedies').

[12] Quintilian, *Inst.* 10. 1. 72: 'A depraved taste caused his contemporaries to prefer Philemon over Menander' (Apul. *Flor.* 16; Aul. Gel. *NA* 17. 4. 1). As Gellius reports, Menander was often defeated by Philemon—whose dramatic skill it is difficult to assess from his fragments—because of intrigue, favouritism, and partisanship. When one day they met in the street, Menander accosted his rival: 'Tell me, Philemon, aren't you really ashamed when they picked you over me?' The reply is not recorded.

Menander received a great deal of posthumous praise which retroactively elevated him above all his rivals.[13] He was praised for his simple eloquence and psychological insights, for managing to 'suit the action to the word, the word to the action'. (Hamlet would have been pleased.) Aristophanes of Byzantium ranked him second only to Homer himself, and praised his realism with the famous 'O Menander! O Life! | Which of you has copied the other?'[14] And Plutarch, while dismissing the Old Comedy playwright as boorish, vulgar, and obscene, praised the matchless style of Menander: 'what other reason would a cultivated man have to go to the theatre?'[15]

But later ages did not share this enthusiasm. In the wake of seventh-century Arab invasions and Byzantine indifference,[16] his plays completely disappeared. Thereafter he was extant only in scholars' commonplace books and anthologies of quotable quotes like 'whom the gods love dies young'.[17] Thus, when distinguished minds praised him—Goethe, for example, celebrated the playwright's 'unattainable charm', while George Meredith rhapsodized about 'the two great comic authors', Menander and Molière—they were talking about a name which no longer had a face. Indeed, a statue erected to Menander in the Theatre of Dionysus at Athens is today a symbol of what happened to the playwright himself—for the sculpture lacks a head.[18]

Then magically, like the discovery at the end of one of his own comedies, a manuscript containing substantial parts of five Menandrian plays suddenly materialized in 1905. Now the scholars had more than *hors d'oeuvres* to chew upon. Half-a-century later, under mysterious circumstances, a complete copy of the *Dyskolos* was suddenly unearthed and published—appropriately enough for the romantic playwright, in 'love-town'—the Egyptian city of Aphroditopolis.

---

[13] Subsequent history shows, that critical opinion came to support Quintilian's assessment of Menander (*Inst.* 3. 7. 18), that posterity would vindicate the playwright's true worth: *quidam sicut Menander, iustiora posteriorum quam suae aetatis iudicia sunt consecuti* ('Just like Menander, about whom critical judgement was better in subsequent ages than his own time').   [14] Test. 170 K.-A.

[15] Plutarch, *Moralia* 852–4.

[16] Menander fell foul of the stylistic fashion that swept over the Greek world for re-creating classical Attic; he was too late and his language—as Phrynicus Arabius vehemently asserts (*Epit.* 418, 433)—'was incorrect'. (Byzantine schoolmasters, unlike the Victorian, were less afraid that Aristophanes would corrupt their students' morals than that Menander would corrupt their Greek.)

[17] The phrase occurs five times in the fragments.

[18] Pausanias, *Description of Greece* 1. 21. i; *Inscriptiones Graecae* 2. 1370.

Menander was at last on his way to becoming an Oxford Text—as well as a critical cottage industry. As Eduard Fraenkel remarked, the scholarly world was afflicted with 'Dyscolitis'.[19]

But this 'rebirth' occasioned a bit of post-partum depression. Menander seemed to be a kind of Johnny-one-note—all his plays appeared to be on the same theme. And yet this disappointment was dispelled by the realization that from the point of view of influence, Menander is arguably the most influential figure in the history of western comedy.

Unlike Aristophanes, Menander and his New Comedy colleagues are not overtly political.[20] In an oft-quoted phrase, Gilbert Murray distinguished between the matter of Old Comedy as *res publica* and that of New Comedy as *res privata*.[21] In fact, the transition from Old to New may be epitomized as a journey from the topical to the typical. There is a delimited cast of familiar characters: cranky old fathers, hyperventilating young lovers, blustering soldiers, and scurrying slaves. The women belong to either one of two distinct groups: virgins or prostitutes. Hardly a nuanced view of the opposite sex, it is nonetheless a social dichotomy of fundamental importance. One group is suitable for partying, the other for parturition.

In either case, Menander's quintessential plot is motivated by love—almost always at first sight. Though we have evidence that not every one of Menander's plays ended in marriage,[22] we have Ovid's testimony that this was Menander's favorite subject: 'Never did charming Menander write a play without love in it.'[23]

A sample plot might go as follows: During one of the Athenian fertility festivals, under cover of night, a well-bred young man, intoxicated by wine and the spirit of the *kômos*, 'forcefully seduces' a well-bred young girl. In his haste to decamp, he neglects to notice that he has somehow lost his ring. Sometime later, in the daylight, he falls

---

[19] Cited by Hugh Lloyd-Jones, 'Ritual and Tragedy', in *Geburtstags-Symposium für Walter Burkert, Castelen bei Basel, 15. bis 18. März 1996*, hrsg. von Fritz Graf (Stuttgart, Teubner, 1998), 271–95, at 271. For the history of the Menandrian finds, see A. W. Gomme and F. H. Sandbach, *Menander: A Commentary* (Oxford, 1973), 2–4.

[20] But see Timothy P. Hofmeister's subtle evocation of the political scene in Menandrian comedy ('*Hai Pasai Poleis*: Polis and *Oikoumene* in Menander', in *The City as Comedy: Society and Representation in Athenian Drama* (Chapel Hill, NC, 1997) 289–342, and David Wiles in this volume.

[21] Gilbert Murray, *Aristophanes* (Oxford, 1933), 251.

[22] There is no evidence of a marital ending to the *Epitrepontes*. The *Hecyra* of Apollodorus, later adapted by Terence, ends not in marriage but with the estranged couple's reconciliation.   [23] Ovid, *Tristia* 2. 369.

in love—'at first sight'—with the same girl, unaware that she had
been his victim. But then, learning that she is pregnant, he refuses to
wed her. Finally, after much ado, all is resolved in Act 4 (Menander
canonized the five-act format, which Horace insisted upon for all
dramas in his day[24]) when he spies her souvenir, acknowledges his
property and culpability, and they live happily ever after.

Menander and his contemporaries tell this same rape-and-
recognition story again and again with what seem merely cosmetic
changes. This very subtlety may have accounted for his relative
unpopularity in his own lifetime. The playwright's small number of
plots reveal many diverse *situations* and clever modifications of stock
figures and motifs. T. B. L. Webster employed the language of Lévi-
Strauss to describe Menandrian drama as 'a common armature,
union of youth and girl in spite of obstacles, clothed in sixty different
ways'.[25] There is a famous anecdote which bears this out. When a
friend chastised Menander about not having completed his comedy
for the upcoming festival, the poet replied 'The play is finished. Now
all I have to do is write the words'.[26]

To all but a small coterie of connoisseurs, New Comedy is little more
than suburban Euripides. Philemon, a contemporary of Menander,
might have been speaking for himself when he has one of his characters declare that he would hang himself if he thought he would meet
Euripides in the next world.[27] Yet for all these similarities, Euripides had
still presented his plays of uncertain genre at the *tragic* festivals. His
characters, though often verging on the bourgeois, are nonetheless
kings, queens, and princesses. It was left for the poets of New Comedy
to bring their dramatic focus from Homer to home sweet home.

The plays of the *nea* can best be described by distinguishing what
they are *not*. Greek tragedies conclude with an Aristotelian *anagnōrisis*,
the hero's painful discovery of his true identity.[28] The analogous
moment in comedy is most often described (at least since Northrop
Frye) as the *cognitio*—simply a Latin translation of Aristotle's term.[29]
Even the *Oedipus Rex* is amenable to comic treatment—as was report-

---

[24] Horace, *Ars Poetica* 189–90.

[25] T. B. L. Webster, *An Introduction to Menander* (New York, 1974), 22, p. viii.

[26] Plutarch, *Moralia* 347e (=K-A test. 70). See Eric Handley's discussion in *The Dyskolos of Menander* (London, 1965), 10. There is a similar anecdote about Ravel, who is said once to have quipped that he had already composed his new symphony—and only needed to write the notes.   [27] Philemon, frag. 118 K-A.

[28] *Poetics* 1452a16.

[29] Northrop Frye, *Anatomy of Criticism* (Princeton, 1957), 163

edly done in antiquity by the Middle Comic poet Eubulus.[30] For at the comic conclusion Oedipus need only discover that he is, in fact, the real son (not the adopted son) of the King and Queen of Corinth. Thus parricide and incest instantly vanish and the hero can marry the lovely widow Jocasta. It all can be explained by the oxymoron *Schadenfreude*: whereas tragedy evokes the *Schade* ('there but for the grace of the playwright go I'), comedy inspires the *Freude*. This is a substantial reason for the appeal of Menander's stereotyped drama.

If Aristotle's discussion of character in the *Nicomachean Ethics* (1112a2–13) did not directly influence Menander, Theophrastus (371–288)—Aristotle's successor as head of the Lyceum, and Menander's teacher—certainly did.[31] Among this polymath's voluminous writings was the *The Characters*, a Hellenistic forerunner of Wilhelm Reich's modern classic *Character Analysis* (1933).[32] Theophrastus' vignettes seem like sketches for Menandrian men and women. The *Dyskolos* ('The Grouchy Man'), for example, bears many of the traits of Theophrastrean *authadeia* (stubbornness) and *mempsimoiria* (resentment). For this reason scholars have tended to link philosopher and playwright in a kind of spiritual collaboration. Both were engaged in a growing area of inquiry in the Hellenistic age, the *dramatis personae* of the human comedy. One of Menander's famous utterances—'how humane is a human being when he acts humanely'[33]—is the essence of his celebrated *philanthropia*. How different from cartoonist Al Capp's famous dictum that all comedy is based on 'man's delight in man's inhumanity to man'.

Because Menander's characters are reduced to types, the playwright's young heroes (as with Molière) are unmemorable because they are interchangeable. Masks hardly encourage individual characterization.[34] Moreover, it was standard practice in New Comedy to give the characters *redende Namen* ('speaking names'), which identify not the person but his personality. As Donatus declares: 'Strictly speaking, the names of persons in comedy should have both meaning and etymology.'[35]

[30] Athenaeus, *Deipnosophistae* 6.239a.

[31] The relationship between Theophrastus and Menander is established by Diogenes Laertius 5.36–7 (= K-A, test. 8).

[32] The long literary tradition is studied by J. W. Smeed, *The Theophrastan 'Character': The History of a Literary Genre* (Oxford, 1985).   [33] Frag. 707K-A.

[34] Yet as we will see below, Terence begins to add new subtlety to these 'masks'.

[35] *Nomina personarum in comoediis dumtaxat habere debent et rationem et etymologium*, Donatus *ad* Ter. *Ad.* 1 (p. 12 Wessner).

This practice was also common in Aristophanes, who abounds in charactonyms like Dikaeopolis ('Righteous City') and Pheidippides ('Horsethrift'), the prodigal son of Strepsiades ('The Twister'). It was still more evident in his *Ploutos*, where the old man is called Chremylus, 'Mr McMoney', while his friend Blepsidemus was 'John Q. Clearsight'—in obvious contrast to the title character, the blind god of wealth.

But Menander and his contemporaries went beyond these colourful coinages, which indicated a specific character's agenda within the play. Rather, they use appellations which, although in some cases real names, tend to bespeak general personality types. Cleostratus and Straton, for example—'Sergeant Hero' and 'General Martial'—are pompous soldiers descended from Lamachus in the *Acharnians*. Smicrines ('Mr Stingy'), who appears in several Menandrian plays, is a perfect caricature of the miserly old man, recalling the Theophrastean *aneleutheros* ('tight-wad') and *micrologos* ('penny-pincher').

Whereas the people of Aristophanes are fantastical—descending to the underworld, consorting with Clouds, or flying to Olympus on dung-beetles—Menander's Everyman lives right next door. In fact the scene is usually on the same city street. And the dialogue is chaste. Vulgar language or outrageous coinages are rare, and explicit sexuality rarer still. It is particularly noteworthy that, although it was still a familiar part of Athenian life, there are few examples of homosexuality (the cooks are the rare exception[36]). Menander has few songs, and only simple metres—mostly iambs, which, as Aristotle noted,[37] are closest to human speech. He has precious few jokes and puns, avoiding all kinds of verbal acrobatics.

And yet in other ways Menander is more closely allied with the traditional elements of comedy than is often recognized. As with his Old Comedy predecessor, the occasions for performance were still seasonal, coinciding with the celebration of Greek fertility rites. Since these festivals play a key role in the New Comedy plots, in a real sense the genre had not gone far from its roots. Like Aristophanes—but with far more polish—Menander provides an anodyne for the painful

---

[36] See e.g. *Dyskolos* 892, and the two cooks' banter on lines 280–8 of Plautus' *Aulularia*. The type has persisted to our own day and may be seen in the 'Gourmet Night' episode of *Fawlty Towers*, written by John Cleese and Connie Booth. This series also featured Manuel, a running servant (*servus currens*), and The Major, a windy veteran who owes as much to Southern English folklore as to the classical *miles gloriosus*.

[37] *Poetics* 1449a 23–6.

realities of everyday life. He dares not say all's right with the state, because manifestly it was not. He can but offer the temporary reassurance that a happy ending is still possible in the private life of the spectator.

Ever the comic poet, Philemon died of over-laughing.[38] The year was 263 BC, and the date is conventionally regarded as the end of the era of New Comedy. Diphilus and Menander had left the scene much earlier—the latter in 292 at the age of 52—when, according to tradition, he drowned while swimming in the harbour of Piraeus.[39] We are told that Philemon composed more than one hundred comedies.[40] Although he began at the precocious age of 20 and lived—according to some reports—almost a century, this was still a prodigious output. Not all of his plays could have been produced in Athens. It is very likely they were performed in one of the many new theatres that were burgeoning in Attica, and in what used to be called the 'provinces'— albeit in this case high-paying ones like Sicily and Magna Graecia— either by 'touring companies' or local guilds of players.[41]

But none of these colonies could have been more enthusiastic than Tarentum (Greek Taras), inside the heel of Italy, which already had its own native comic tradition in the *phlyax* farce which we find depicted on so many vases.[42] This lively town gave birth to the first 'Roman' playwright, the bilingual scholar Livius Andronicus, a former slave who—after being relocated to Rome—rendered into Latin a Greek

---

[38] At least two biographical sources describe this merry death: ps.-Lucian, *Macrobiois* 25 s.v. Philemon (test. 5 K-A); *Suda*, s.v. Philemon (test. 1 K-A). For similar jolly demises of comic poets, see Mary R. Lefkowitz, *The Lives of the Greek Poets* (London, 1981), 105–16, esp. 112–13.

[39] Schol. on Ovid *Ibis* 591–2 (test. 17 K-A). There is some scholarly disagreement over the exact dates of both poets' deaths. Those interested in pursuing this should begin with W. G. Arnott, s.v. Philemon. in *The Oxford Classical Dictionary,* 3rd edn. (Oxford, 1996); also id.(ed.), *Menander,* (Cambridge, Mass., 1979–96), vol. 1, p. xiv; S. Schröder, 'Die Lebensdaten Menanders', *Zeitschrift für Papyrologie und Epigraphik,* 113 (1996), 35–42.

[40] Figures vary. See Aulus Gellius 17. 4. 5 (test. 46 K.-A.); *Suda*, s.v. (test. 1 K-A); Anon. *De com.* 53 (test. 3 K.-A.).

[41] Oliver Taplin, *Comic Angels* (Oxford 1993), 12–20, describes the evolution of the audience for plays beyond Athens. On the touring companies see also Niall Slater, 'The Fabrication of Comic Illusion', in *Beyond Aristophanes: Transition and Diversity in Greek Comedy*, ed. Gregory W. Dobrov (Atlanta, Ga.,1995), 41.

[42] For more details about comic activities in Tarentum specifically, see Taplin, *Comic Angels*, 14 with n. 10, and J. R. Green, 'Notes on Phylax Vases', *Quaderni ticinesi di numismatica e antichità classiche*, 20 (1991), 49–56, esp. 55.

tragedy and comedy for the harvest festival (*ludi Romani*) of 240 BC.[43]
This set the pattern for centuries: Latin plays 'with a plot',[44] based on
Greek models—such comedies were known as *palliatae*, 'in Greek
dress'. As the third century neared its close, many more performance
dates were added at other festivals.[45] The Romans were stage-struck.

A puritan folk, at once fascinated by and suspicious of the theatre,
for centuries they soothed their ambivalent psyches by having their
productions performed on a makeshift wooden stage which was dis-
mantled after each festival.[46] Even when Pompey the Great built the
first permanent venue in 55 BC, he had to dedicate it as a temple to
Venus Victrix, the stairs of which doubled as seats on theatrical occasions—and could hold some 40,000 spectators. As an agelastic, the-
atre-hating church father said: 'Thus he deceived discipline with
superstition.'[47]

Rome had also long enjoyed a native type of improvisatory comedy,
the so-called *fabulae Atellanae* or Atellane farces, named after the
Campanian village where the genre probably originated.[48] This crude
entertainment presented little skits with stock low-life characters, like

---

[43] Livy 7.2. The circumstances of Livius Andronicus' 'transfer' to Rome are the subject of much debate among historians. Those wishing to investigate the matter should
begin with the earnest discussion of Cicero (*Brutus* 18. 71–4), who did not rate the trail-
blazing poet's dramatic gifts too highly. See also G. Duckworth, *The Nature of Roman
Comedy*, 2nd edn. (Princeton, 1952), 39–40.

[44] Livy 7. 2. 8: *ab saturis ausus est primus argumento fabulam serere* ('From mere
improvisations he was the first who dared to write a play with a plot'). Friederich Leo,
'Varro und die Satire', *Hermes*, 24 (1889), 67–84, astutely noted that the similarities
between Livy's account and Aristotle's description of the development of comedy in
the Poetics were too great to be merely coincidental. See also G. L. Hendrickson, 'The
Dramatic Satura and the Old Comedy at Rome', *American Journal of Philology*, 15: 1
(1894), 1–30.

[45] These were the *ludi Plebeii* (November), *ludi Apollinares* (July), and *ludi Megalenses*
(April). See Lily Ross Taylor, 'The Opportunities for Dramatic Performances in the Time
of Plautus and Terence', *Transactions of the American Philological Association*, 68 (1937),
284–304; Duckworth, *Roman Comedy*[2], 76–9.

[46] See e.g. Tacitus, *Ann.* 14. 20. Early performances also took place at the Circus
Maximus (Livy 41. 27; Polybius 30. 22). See further Dwora Gilula, 'Where Did the Audience Go?', *Scripta Classica Israelica*, 4 (1978), 45–9, esp. 47–8 with n. 9.

[47] Tertullian, *De Spect.* 10. 4–6. For the *theatrum Pompei* see further Cic. *Off.* 2. 60;
Hor., *Carm.* 1. 20. 3–8; Pliny, *NH* 7. 34, 158, 8. 20–1, 36. 115 (number of seats); Tacitus,
Ann. 3. 23, 3. 72, 13. 54, 14. 20; Suet., *Cal.* 21, *Cl.* 21. 1, *Nero* 46. 1; Vell. 2. 130. 1; Aulus
Gellius *NA* 10. 1. 7–9; *CIL* 6. 1191. The theatre has left its impression in the curving outline of the piazza di Grottapinta. There were other attempts to build a permanent
theatre from as early as 179 BC but these were all aborted by patrician disapproval. See
inter alios Duckworth, *Roman Comedy*[2], 79–80.

[48] See the discussion of W. Beare, *The Roman Stage*, 3rd edn. (London, 1964), 137–48.

Bucco the babbling fool, Pappus the foolish old codger, Dossenus the hunchbacked buffoon, and Maccus, another type of simpleton.

It was from these lusty, popular entertainments that, scarcely a generation after Livius, the first true genius of Roman literature literally took the stage. Horace recalls the artist's roots in the native tradition: (*Epistles* 2.1. 170–17)

> Adspice Plautus
> quo pacto partis tutetur amantis ephebi
> ut patris attenti, lenonis ut insidiosi,
> quantus sit Dossennus edacibus in parasitis,
> quam non adstricto percurrat pulpita socco.
> Gestit enim luculos demittere, post hoc
> Securus cadat an recto stet fabula talo

> Look at Plautus—how he
> portrays the characters of lovestruck youth,
> of stingy father and of cunning pimp,
> How much of Dossennus is there in his hungry parasites,
> when he scampers around the stage in sloppy slippers!
> All he cares about is collecting his cash. After that,
> He doesn't give a damn if the play succeeds or falls on its face

Titus Maccius Plautus (*c*.250–184 BC) is very likely a theatrical pseudonym, for what kind of parent would call a child 'Dick O'Fool McSlapstick'?[49] What little we know of this poet's life does not help to explain how he rose from humble origins in the north Italian town of Sarsina, to become what Aulus Gellius would later praise as the 'Glory of the Latin Tongue.'[50] The imperial scholar also preserves Plautus' 'biography,' which states enigmatically that the playwright made a fortune in some kind of 'show business.'[51] It is pleasant to imagine our author in a band of strolling players. That would certainly help explain his unique instinct for pleasing the Roman crowds.[52]

---

[49] 'Titus' is Roman slang for phallus, 'Maccius' an allusion to the fool in Atellane farce, and 'Plautus' may be a contraction of Planipes, meaning 'Flatfoot', a mime player. See J. N. Adams, *The Latin Sexual Vocabulary* (Duckworth, London, 1982), 32; A. S. Gratwick, in the *Cambridge History of Latin Literature* (Cambridge, 1982), ii. 809; and the same author's 'Titus Maccius Plautus', *Classical Quarterly* NS 23 (1973), 78–84. See also *Plautus' Menaechmi*, ed. Gratwick (Cambridge, 1993), 3.

[50] Aulus Gellius, *NA* 19. 8. 6, *linguae latinae decus.*

[51] Ibid. 3. 3. 14, in *operis artificium scaenicorum.*

[52] See further E. Segal, *Roman Laughter* (Cambridge Mass., 1968), 1–7.

'Roman Comedy,' however, is a misleading term. For, unlike Aristophanes and Menander, none of the Roman *palliata* playwrights (see below) produced entirely original compositions. Rather they were, to a greater or lesser extent, based on Greek models. The very art of their dramaturgy lay in the manner in which they rendered the Hellenic originals. What Plautus and his colleagues created in their adaptations of Menander *et alii* was nothing short of revolutionary.

But as in the case of Aristophanes, either merit or capricious fate (Tyche perhaps?) has allowed only a single playwright to survive and represent the entire Roman genre, while his contemporaries—who seem to have written in much the same style—left only fragments. (Terence, as we will see, wrote a completely different type of comedy.) Thus, we should caution ourselves that Plautus may only be the tip of an iceberg of laughter.[53] But, since Livius Andronicus, Naevius, Caecilius, Accius, *et alii* have all melted away, we must, in Vergil's words, *crimine ab uno | disce omnis* ('From the crime of one learn that of all').[54]

Like his contemporaries, Plautus appears to have used the Greek models as a mere springboard, a process which he called *vortere* ('convert, adapt'), a term still recognized by Terence and, perhaps obliquely, by Horace—and surviving in the English 'version'.[55] As the playwright describes *Trinummus*: 'Philemon wrote it: Plautus made the "barbarian" version.'[56]

But Plautus is much too modest. His method transformed the Greek works into something entirely 'rich and strange'. He seasoned the bland fodder of the Greek models with the piquant sauce of native Italian farce, refurbishing the sedate originals into brash musical comedies by using his innate operatic sense to recast simple Greek dialogue into eminently singable, polymetric Latin songs (*cantica*).[57]

That he knew Greek well is unquestioned. That he translated faithfully is out of the question. Indeed, like the Old Comedy poets of

---

[53] The point was made by Eduard Fraenkel, *Elementi Plautini in Plauto* (Florence, 1960), revised ed. of *Plautinisches im Plautus* (Berlin, 1922), 324. John Wright, *Dancing in Chains: The Stylistic Unity of the Comoedia Palliata* (Rome, 1974), has contributed much to our understanding of Roman comedy by demonstrating how all his contemporaries, except of course the later Terence, wrote in 'Plautine' style.

[54] Vergil, *Aeneid* 2. 65–6.   [55] Terence, *Eunuchus* 7; Horace, *Ars Poetica* 268–9.

[56] *Trinummus* 19, *Philemo scripsit: Plautus vortit barbare.*

[57] In lyricizing his models, rather than simply translating them, he was anticipated by both Ennius and Accius. See Thomas Cole, 'Opera in Ancient Rome', *Ventures* (Magazine of the Yale Graduate School) (Spring, 1967), 35–6.

Athens, Plautus' language is so colourful and idiosyncratic that there can be no doubt that he took great liberties. Plautine style became synonymous with verbal virtuosity and neologisms. Despite his criticisms of the playwright elsewhere, Horace invokes the master as a precedent for his own poetic coinages.[58] Like Shakespeare and Molière, Plautus begs, borrows, and steals from every conceivable source—including himself. But once the play begins, all literary debts are cancelled and everything is 100 per cent Plautus.

Until the mid-twentieth century, a precise comparison between a Plautine text and its Greek model was not possible. And then in 1968, a long fragment was discovered from Menander's *Dis Exapaton* (*Double-deceiver*) which had been the playwrights' model for the *Bacchides*. In his memorable inaugural lecture at University College, London, Eric Handley presented the exciting results of his study of both texts.[59] Plautus had combined what were two separate speeches in Menander, changed the rhythm, and added several snappy jokes, as well as a distinctly Roman attack on the usually revered moral notion of *pietas*. This was hardly translation. Handley in fact substantiated many of Eduard Fraenkel's imaginative conjectures about the verbal techniques of early Roman comedy.

In the same vein, the characters onstage can eat foods normally forbidden to Romans, delicacies prohibited by the strict puritanical 'blue laws'.[60] In the *Menaechmi*, for example, the would-be errant husband asks his mistress Erotium to prepare a meal for their assignation which would give the audience a vicarious thrill:

> MEN. Iube igitur tribus nobis apud te prandium accurarier,
>   atque aliquid scitamentorum de foro opsonarier,

---

[58] Horace, *Ars Poetica* 46–55.

[59] Published as Eric Handley, *Menander and Plautus: A Study in Comparison* (London, 1968).

[60] Pliny (*NH* 8. 209–10) specifically refers to the 'sumptuary laws' of Plautus' age which restricted the consumption of items which outraged the stern Cato—*abdomina, glandia, testiculi, vulvae, sincipita verrina*. These are some of the very dishes featured in Menaechmus' menu. See further Emily Gowers's discussion in *The Loaded Table: Representations of Food in Roman Literature* (Oxford, 1993), 66–76, who argues incisively that 'not only did the ban help to redefine the structure of weekday and festival in the Roman year: the limited proportions of the everyday human or animal body, the meagre fowl on the table, also supplied a model for the proper limits of the Roman state's consumption' (p. 75).

> glandionidam suillam, laridum pernonidam,
> aut sincipitamenta porcina aut aliquid ad eum modum

> MEN.–Please arrange a feast at your house, have it cooked for three
>   of us.
> Also have some very special party foods bought in the forum.
> Glandiose, whole-hog, and a descendant of the lardly ham.
> Or perhaps some pork chopettes, or other things along these lines.[61]

This is gastronomic delinquency on the husband's part, as all these foods were normally forbidden by puritanical sumptuary laws. Even if one cavils that these laws were passed after Plautus' death and were already dead letters, such food would nevertheless be *prohibitively* expensive to the average Roman.

But the real rule-breaker is Plautus' consummate creation: the clever slave. Though anticipated in previous comedy, Plautus presents the bondsman in his ultimate apotheosis. This is not mere metaphor, for the *servus callidus* is as boastful as the Romans are never supposed to be, and is even not loath to compare himself to a god. He is the 'architect of trickery' (*architectus doli*[62]) who acts out his young master's worst fantasies, for example by swindling the lad's own father for the money to purchase the young man's girlfriend. What was hinted at in Aristophanes' Xanthias and sketched in Menander's Daos is fully drawn by Plautus in living colour. The bold faced bondsman acts as an alter ego for the young man's love pangs, 'disobediently' flim-flamming father while the *adulescens* remains in the shelter of ostensible *pietas*. It is only in Beaumarchais' *Figaro* that the slave and hero are fused into a single comic character without class distinctions.

Yet in Plautus love is anything but a fine romance. His heroes seek fun, not its polar opposite—marriage. The finale to *Trinummus* provides a typical example of his view of matrimony. Here the remorseful *adulescens* stoically accepts the punishment for his misbehaviour (1183–1184):

> SON. I will marry, father. Her and any others that you want me to
> FATHER. No—though I was infuriated with you
>   One wife is punishment enough for any man.

---

[61] Menaechmi 208–12; cf. *Captivi* 902–5. A closer translation of the foods he is ordering would be 'pork sweetbreadettes, hamletty fat bacon, pork half-heads'.

[62] *Miles Gloriosus* 901–3, 919, 1139.

Plautine comedy can best be viewed as a 'Saturnalian' inversion of normal values. Everyday life is turned on its head, everyday values topsy-turvy. The slave, the lowest man on the totem pole of life, emerges triumphant—and grandiloquent—over his esteemed Roman master (occasionally even a distinguished senator). And yet, in reality, every master had in his everyday power the ability to put a slave to death for this kind of audacity. Only during the Saturnalia was this right waived. What Plautus presents is, in the truest sense, a Roman holiday.[63]

Is it better to be Salieri or Mozart? Such was the relation of Plautus to Terence—at least during the younger playwright's lifetime. Plautus, the first as well as most successful *professional* dramatist, had no dark *Clouds* or angry *Mother-in-Law* in his career. His name was magic. The mere mention of it could turn a drunken, rowdy mob to total silence: you could hear a pun drop. At the end of a Plautine comedy the audience would often stand up and cheer for more. By contrast, at the *beginning* of a Terentian performance they might stand up—and turn their backs.[64] At least, this is what occurred twice with his *Mother-in-Law*.

Like Menander whom he so admired, Publius Terentius Afer (c.195–159 BC) became a classic only after his death. Plautus, though wildly popular in his own day and performed until the Dark Ages, began to languish thereafter in decaying manuscripts, unread and unproduced. Even by the late Republic, Plautus was already regarded as disdainfully as Ben Jonson treated Spenser, when he carped that the poet 'writ no Language'. Cicero tended to favour Terence in his quotations, as did Horace, who at times was almost hostile to the talents of the elder playwright.

Of course Terence's victory—if one may call it that—was not entirely owing to his comic merits. Julius Caesar, leader, Latin stylist *par excellence*, and influential opinion-maker—the Churchill of his day—belittled Terence's dramaturgy, drawing attention to his lack of *vis comica* or *comica virtus* ('comic verve' or 'comic power'[65]) and calling him a 'mini-Menander' (*dimidiate Menander*).[66]

---

[63] See further Segal, *Roman Laughter*, 7–14 *et passim*.
[64] The interruptions in the *Hecyra* came in the first act (*Hecyra* 39).
[65] Depending on which word the poet intended to modify with *comica*.
[66] *Carm.* 1 (=Seutonius, *Vit. Ter.* 7, p. 9 Wessner).

But the playwright was widely admired for other reasons. Caesar also praised Terence for being *puri sermonis amator* ('a lover of pure speech'). The imperial critic Quintilian referred to his style as *scripta elegantissima*.[67] Aulus Gellius, who coined the superlative *Plautinissimus* to describe a really novel passage,[68] never needed to label a verse *Terentianissimus*. This explains the huge number of quotable quotes we find in his plays.

It was this superb oratorical quality that made the playwright an ideal school text.[69] Student editions of Terence date back as early as the first century AD and continue unabated throughout the Middle Ages—when the scribes and artisans produced beautifully illuminated manuscripts.[70]

Yet like all post, humous fame (remember Achilles' bitterness at being a dead hero as expressed to the live hero of the *Odyssey*), the playwright's Mozartian standing in the Latin canon would be cold comfort to him since in his lifetime—with one notable exception—he seems to have met with only indifferent success.[71]

His background is interesting. Born in Carthage, he was taken as a slave to Rome by a senator, Terentius Lucanus. Enthused by the young man's mind (*ingenium*)—as well as his outward beauty (*formam*)—the lawmaker had him educated and then freed. At his manumission the young man took the *nomen* Terentius from his benefactor, while his *cognomen* 'Afer' suggests roots on the African continent.[72] It is true that this name is attested for other Roman families,[73] but Subtonics' description of him as 'dark-skinned' (*fuscus colore*) makes it likely that Terence was the first black author in the classical world.[74]

His approach to adaptation (*vortere*) was diametrically opposed to

---

[67] Quintilian, *Inst.* 10. 1. 99.   [68] Aulus Gellius, *NA* 3. 3. 4. 6.

[69] Sander Goldberg, *Understanding Terence* (Princeton, 1986), 40–60, has demonstrated the playwright's debt to contemporary oratory.

[70] There is, for example, the splendid Terence in the Lessing J Rosenwald collection in the Washington DC National Museum. See the article by E. Segal in *Vision of a Collector: The Lessing J. Rosenwald Collection in the Library of Congress* (Washington, 1991), 172–3.

[71] This view is strenuously disputed by Holt Parker, 'Plautus vs. Terence: Audience and Popularity Re-examined', *American Journal of Philology*, 117 (1996), 585–617.

[72] Suetonius, *Vit. Ter.* 1 (p. 3 Wessner).

[73] As noted by F. H. Sandbach, *The Comic Theatre of Greece and Rome* (New York, 1977), 135.

[74] The case is argued convincingly by Frank Snowden, *Blacks in Antiquity* (Cambridge Mass., Harvard University Press, 1970), 270, who also points out that in the Vergilian *Moretum* 32–3 the Negroid Scybale is described as *afra genus* and *fusca colore*.

that of Plautus, Naevius, Caecilius, *et al.*, who were never loath to shatter the Greek illusion for the sake of a Roman joke.[75] Terence aimed to bring the masterpieces of New Comedy to a Roman audience in their pristine Greekness (or so his prologues protest). He has been justifiably praised for the skill with which he glossed obscure allusions into Latin. And yet the scene remained essentially Greek— without any cheap asides or Roman anachronisms. For this he won Cicero's high praise for 'conveying and replaying Menander in a Latin voice'.[76]

But these indisputable merits may have been lost on the typically drunk and obstreperous Roman festival audiences described by Horace.[77] Terence's plays were, in Hamlet's words, 'caviare to the general': they lacked the common touch, the *nescio quae mimica*—the farcical elements that Gellius criticized in another adaptation of Menander—which corrupted the Greek but delighted the audience. Terence himself admits that his plays tend to be more sedate (*statariae*) than lively (*motoriae*),[78] terms which the fourth-century scholar Euanthius glossed as *quietiores* and *turbulentae*.[79]

Terence does put a few new wrinkles on the baggy masks of traditional figures, often adding touches of originality and realism, creating such novelties as a *nice* mother-in-law and an *honest* prostitute.[80] Compared with his predecessors, the rebellious young man is markedly subdued. Instead of wishing father dead, as do so many Plautine youths, the Terentian lover shows far more filial respect (*Brothers* 518–20):

> quod cum salute ei(u)s fiat, ita se defatigarit velim
> ut triduo hoc perpetuo prorsum e lecto nequeat surgere.

> I wish as long as he stayed healthy that Dad would tire out
> And lie in bed for three whole days, unable to get up.

Many of his contemporary critics cast doubt on Terence's claim to authorship, suggesting that the comedies were written by various aristocratic intellectuals. After all, how could a young African slave write such sparkling Latin? This view was still held as late as

---

[75] On Roman jokes see Gordon Williams, *Tradition and Originality in Roman Poetry* (Oxford, 1968), 285–96.
[76] *Conversum expressumque Latina voce Menandrum.* From his commonplace book *Limon,* as recorded by Suetonius, *Vit. Ter.* 7.   [77] Horace, *Ars Poetica* 225.
[78] *HT* 36. Northrop Frye, *The Anatomy of Criticism* (Princeton, 1957), 17.
[79] Euanthius, *Exc. de Com.* 4.4 (p. 22 Wessner).   [80] See Donatus, ad *Hec.* 774.

Montaigne.[81] But genius defies all cultural descriptions, especially linguistic, and the Roman theater itself can boast other 'foreigners'—like Seneca the Spaniard, or Caecilius, who was said to have been a slave from Gaul.

Terence marks the ultimate stage in the development of classical comedy and became an unchanging—classical—paradigm ever after. His contribution was, quite simply, the invention of suspense. This he accomplished in several bold strokes. First, he completely abolished the expository prologue. Menander and Euripides before him almost always had a speaker, usually divine, offering to the audience details of the drama they were about to see—and most important—reassuring them that the outcome would be happy. Until this point in history, the audience's concern was not *what* would happen, but *how*. This may seem obvious to modern sensibilities, accustomed as we are to this technique. (And yet how many people still begin a novel by reading the last page?[82]) But it was a bold innovation, for which Terence may have sacrificed a certain amount of popularity.

In the prologue to *The Brothers*, whose opening scene the learned Varro actually preferred to its Menandrian original,[83] Terence officially informs the audience that his dramatic technique has been permanently altered (22–4):

> de(h)inc ne expectetis argumentum fabulae,
> senes qui primi venient, î partem aperient,
> *in agendo* partem ostendent.

> Don't count on hearing all the plot from me right now.
> The oldsters who are entering will tell you part of it
> And *in the acting of it*, by and by, you'll learn the rest.

---

[81] Montaigne, *Essays*, I. 40 (trans. M. A. Screech): 'And if a perfect mastery of language could contribute anything worthy of a great public figure, Scipio and Laelius would certainly not have allowed the credit for their comedies, with all their grace and delightful language, to be attributed to an African slave—for the beauty and excellence of these works are adequate proof that they are really theirs, and Terence himself admits it. I would be deeply displeased to have that belief of mine shaken.'

[82] The old Chambers' Dictionary refers to such a reader as an end-dipper, one who turns to the end 'to see if she got him'. G.K. Chesterton inveighs splendidly against this bean-spilling ('The back of the cover will tell you the plot').

[83] Suetonius, *Vita Terenti* 2. Although the extant prologue announces Diphilus as the prime source, this playwright contributed only a single scene.

The absence of explanatory prologue allows the spectator to enjoy a special tension, a certain deliberate amnesia so that he can be 'surprised' by the happy ending. The playwright is in a position of power, and he leads the spectators by the nose, trailing crumbs of exposition in his wake. This is suspense.

Terence worked hard at developing this artful, gradual exposition, which in his skilled hands became what the *in medias res* beginning was for epic. For lack of a better term we may refer to this practice as the *in agendo* ('in the acting of it') technique. The warning of Terence' prologue became an *ars poetica*: 'from now on don't expect to hear the story of the play from *me*.' At each twist of the plot the spectator discovers something he has not known before. And in the now-traditional *cognitio* he has the pleasure of having his instincts confirmed. Indeed, when there is wish fulfillment without prediction the audience feels more personally involved, as though they themselves helped to bring about the happy ending. As Northrop Frye has aptly noted, the endings of comedy come 'from the audience side of the stage'.[84]

One might well wonder how the audiences of these plays could bear to watch essentially the same thing again and again. Yet could one not ask the same question about modern comedies? It seems we will never tire of boy-meeting-girl, parents objecting, villains being thwarted, hurdles being overcome, and ultimately boy and girl walking down the aisle to become man and wife. What we discern in the comedies of Menander, Plautus, and Terence is nothing less than the evolution of the form that would dominate the stage for two thousand years.

[84] Frye, *Anatomy of Criticism*, n. 29. 171.

I
Greek Antecedents

I

Euripidean Comedy

BERNARD KNOX

'The most tragic of the poets', Aristotle called him (whatever he may have meant by it), and succeeding ages have agreed; the great Euripidean tragedies, *Hippolytus, Meda, Bacchae, Trojan Women*, show us a world torn asunder by blind, disruptive forces, which affords no consolation, no compensation for suffering, no way to face it except resigned endurance, a world which reduces man from the status of hero to that of victim. But Euripides had another side to his genius: he introduced to the theater of Dionysus new forms of drama, the *Iphigenia in Tauris*, the *Helen*, the *Ion*, plays which critics and scholars have labored in vain to define. They are clearly a radical departure from Euripidean tragedy (from any of our notions of tragedy, for that matter), but the search for a term which adequately describes them has resulted only in a confusing assortment of vague categories: they have been called romantic tragedy, romantic melodrama, tragicomedy, romances, romantic comedy, *drames romanesques, Intrigenstücke*, to list only the most influential attempts at nomenclature. One cannot help suspecting that what everyone would really like to call these plays (at least the *Ion*) is comedy (though no one, to my knowledge, has taken the plunge). There are, of course, good reasons for such hesitation. But I should like to suggest that they are not good enough, that provided the word 'comedy' is understood in modern, not ancient terms, Euripedes, in these plays but especially in their culmination, the *Ion*, is the inventor, for the stage, of what we know as comedy.

One reason for stopping short of this word is of course the certainty that Euripides himself would have repudiated it with some indignation. 'Comedy', he would have said, 'is an entirely different kettle of fish: it is what my friend Aristophanes writes.' In fifth-century Athens the two genres were rigidly separate, and comedy—a high-spirited combination of unbridled personal lampoon, literary burlesque, indecent buffoonery, brilliant wit, and lyric poetry of the highest order—had its own recognizable conventions of plot, language, dance, and meter, which were quite distinct from those of tragedy. When at the end of a long night of revelry, drinking, and conversation, Socrates in Plato's *Symposium* proposed and defended the thesis that the same man could be capable of composing both tragedy and comedy, we are left in no doubt that his hearers, a comic and a tragic poet, are reluctant to accept this surprising idea. 'They were being forced [*anankazomenous*] to this conclusion,' says Plato, 'but they could not follow his argument too well, for they kept drowsing off—Aristophanes went right off to sleep first, and Agathon went the same way just as dawn was breaking.' Only Socrates could have proposed such a paradox; for the fifth-century Athenian, tragedy was tragedy and comedy comedy, and never the twain should meet.

But Aristophanic comedy has had no descendants, and comedy for us is something different. It comes to us from the Greeks all right, but not from Old Comedy; it descends through Plautus and Terence to the Renaissance dramatists from Menander, the Athenian comic poet of the fourth century, and his plays in turn derive from those plays of Euripides in which the prototype of modern comedy is to be found. In this, as in so many ways, Euripides is prophetic, the poet of the future; what he invents is the prevailing drama of the next century, the domestic comedy of manners and situation, of family misunderstandings (between father and son, husband and wife), of mistaken identity and recognition, of lost children reclaimed and angry fathers reconciled to spurned suitors finally revealed as long-lost sons of wealthy friends—the comedy of misapprehension, recognition, and restoration, of Menander and Philemon, which is also the main tradition of modern European comedy from Shakespeare to Oscar Wilde.

Of course, the mere fact that these Euripidean plays have a happy ending is not enough to justify the term 'comedy'. Aristotle preferred tragedies which end in misfortune, but his statement clearly implies that some sort of happy ending was far from rare and did not disqualify a play as tragedy. And this would have been clear even without Aristotle, for the *Oresteia* of Aeschylus and the *Philoctetes* of Sophocles, to take only two examples, do not end in misfortune, and yet no one has ever thought of them as comedies. Such a term for these Euripidean plays could be justified only by the appearance in them of a treatment of situation and character differing sharply from the tragic norm. And Euripides does indeed in these plays (and, for that matter, in others) introduce to the tragic stage an entirely new attitude to human nature and action. It has been called 'realistic', but it is not hard to show that the term is inadequate. To avoid begging the question, it is perhaps better to demonstrate the nature of Euripides' untragic tone, not from one of the plays in question, but by reference to the opening scenes of a play which, taken as a whole, clearly belongs to the tragic canon, the savage *Electra*. It is a shocking play. What in Aeschylus was the just punishment of a father's assassins by a god-driven son and in Sophocles the crowning achievement of a heroic daughter's lonely endurance becomes in Euripides a pair of sordid murders: Aegisthus ignominiously butchered by the guest he had invited to the sacrificial feast, Clytemnestra lured to her death through her solicitude for her daughter's feigned pregnancy. These actions are of course the climax of the play and are written in Euripides' grimmest mood. But the opening scenes are a surprising contrast.

The prologue speech is delivered by an unnamed character, a small farmer, who gives us the astonishing news that he is Electra's husband. Not that he has presumed to exercise his marital rights, he goes on: he has too much respect for Agamemnon's line (lines 43 ff.). The situation is piquant, to say the least, but we have no hint yet of a real departure from the heroic mode which has always been appropriate for this particular story—except one. Aegisthus, the farmer tells us, forbade Electra's marriage to a noble suitor, for fear of a son who would avenge Agamemnon (22 ff.). But then he decided to kill her anyway because of a fear 'that she would bear children to one of them secretly' (26). This slight hint of scandalous possibilities is all we are given to prepare us for the shock provided by Electra's entrance. She comes on stage as no tragic heroine we know of ever did before— balancing a jug on her head in the immemorial fashion of Greek village women on their way to the spring. 'O dark night,' she sings, 'keeper of the golden stars, in which carrying this jug balanced on my head, I go to fetch water from the river' (54 ff.). Perhaps, we think, we are meant to be moved to pity at the depths of poverty to which this princess has been reduced: this is one more pathetic prop—like the rags of Telephus, Oeneus, Phoenix, and many other Euripidean hero. But Electra goes on: 'Not that I have reached any such degree of poverty—it is so that I may show the gods the savagery of Aegisthus' (57–8). Just in case we don't get the point, her husband asks her why she goes to all this trouble, 'even though I tell you not to' (66). She replies that she wishes to repay his kindness by helping him, by sharing his labors. 'You have work enough in the fields. It is *my* duty to

prepare everything inside the house. When the workman comes
home, it is pleasant for him to find everything shipshape inside.'
'Well,' says her husband, 'go ahead, if you insist. The spring is not far
from the house in any case' (71 ff.). And in any case, Electra has a servant with her. 'Take this jar off my head and put it down', she commands later (140), as she sings her solo aria recounting the sorrows of
her life. Quite apart from the extraordinary visual detail of the water
jug, the tone of this scene is unmistakable. It is *domestic*: we are being
invited not to identify ourselves with the passions and destinies of
heroic souls but to detach ourselves and observe the actions and reactions of ordinary human beings in a social situation with norms and
customs we are only too well acquainted with. And this domestic
realism, which might have served simply to deepen the pathos of the
heroine's situation, is made, by ironic comment and juxtaposition, to
expose not merely the sordid details of Electra's misery, but also her
pretenses and affectations.

This scene is only the beginning; there is much more to come. To
the chorus which invites her to accompany them to the great festival
of Hera, Electra replies not only with a recital of her wrongs and a
repetition of her determination to mourn Agamemnon's death forever, but also with a more mundane excuse. 'Look at my hair; it's
dirty. Look at these rags of clothes. Are they fit for Agamemnon's
royal daughter?' (184 ff.). These sentiments are couched in faultless
glyconics but they still mean nothing more than 'I haven't a thing to
wear', and in case we had any doubt the chorus offers to lend her
something. 'Borrow from me fine-woven dresses to wear and these
golden ornaments to go with them—do please accept' (191–3).

Fewer than two hundred lines later, Electra is standing at the door
of the house talking to Orestes and Pylades (she does not yet know
who they are) when her husband comes back from his work (for his
lunch presumably). He is certainly a patient husband, but even he is
upset. 'It's disgraceful—a wife standing around with men.' 'Dearest,'
replies Electra, 'don't get suspicious of me.' The strangers are emis-
saries of Orestes come to see the sorrows of her life. 'Well,' says her
husband, 'some of them they can see, and I'm sure you are telling
them the rest': he is, of course, quite right. He invites the strangers
into his house. Orestes, in a long speech, admires his nobility, but
Electra takes a different view. When husband and wife are alone
together, she proceeds as follows: 'You rash fool, you know how poor
your house is; why did you invite in these strangers who are of a

higher station than you?' 'Why not?' says the farmer reasonably. 'If they are as noble as they seem, they will be as content in humble circumstances as in high.' 'Humble's the word', says Electra. 'You made a mistake. Now go off and find the old man who used to look after my father . . . tell him to bring some food for my guests.' 'All right,' says her long-suffering husband, 'I'll go. Now you go inside, and fix things up. You know very well that a woman, if she wants to, can always find something extra to piece out', *prosphorēmata*, a word which occurs nowhere else in Greek literature. And in the next scene the old man, complaining about his bent back and wobbly knee, comes in loaded with food and drink (487 ff.). 'Here, daughter, I've brought you a newborn lamb from my flocks, and garlands for the guests, and cheeses I took out of the buckets and this wine—vintage stock of Dionysus—such a bouquet—not much of it, but sweet stuff—just pour a cup of this into some weaker brew . . .'

The comic effect of much of this is unmistakable; but the play of course does not continue long in this vein. True, there is still the burlesque of Aeschylus' recognition scene to come, with the old man pleading for one after the other of the three traditional recognition tokens, only to have them all contemptuously dismissed by Electra as foolishness. But Orestes finally *is* recognized by the scar on his forehead, and after that, brother and sister plan and carry out the two treacherous, brutal murders. The effect of the domestic atmosphere of the first half of the play is to strip every last shred of heroic stature from Electra and Orestes, so that we see their subsequent actions not as heroic fulfillment of a god's command, but rather as crimes committed by 'men as they are', to use Sophocles' description of Euripides' characters, by people like ourselves. After we have seen a shrewish and snobbish Electra scold her husband for not knowing his place in society, we are not likely to see her murder of her mother as anything else than what it is, an unnecessary act of paranoiac jealous hatred.

The comic tone is used here for a purpose which has nothing to do with comedy. But as social comedy the opening scenes of the play are brilliant, and since they are the first extant appearance of such scenes on the tragic stage, they invite careful examination. The most novel and incongruous element in them is the repeated emphasis on the everyday details of domestic life, on meals and their preparation, the need to carry water and bring food, not to mention wine. This is a new note. In Greek tragedy before this (what we have of it), references

to food and drink are scarce, short, incidental, and frequently negative; certainly no tragic heroines before Electra balance water pitch-
ers on their heads, quarrel with their husbands about whether there
is enough food for the guests, ands end them off to procure cheese,
lamb, and wine. All this smacks of comedy, where people eat and
drink with gusto, prepare enormous meals and drink gigantic quan-
tities of wine, where menial tasks (from pouring gravy on a pancake
to feeding a giant dung beetle) are the order of the day. But such
matters also bulk large in satyr plays, and, although Euripides did
not write comedies in the ancient sense of the world, he did, like
Aeschylus and Sophocles, write satyr plays. In the only specimen of
this extraordinary genre which has survived complete, the *Cyclops*
of Euripides, food, drink, and domestic chores are very much to the
fore. 'Here I am at my work,' says the prologue speaker, Silenus, 'filling sheep troughs and sweeping floors. I wait on that godless
Cyclops at his unholy meals. And now I must follow orders, and
scrape out the cave with this iron rake.' Odysseus arrives; thinking
he is in Book 9 of the *Odyssey*, he beings in heroic style, but breaks
off at the sight of the satyr chorus. Soon he is exchanging his
wine for the Cyclops food—meat, cheese, and milk. And so it goes
on, including, before the climax (the blinding of Polyphemus), a
drunken symposium, with Silenus stealing the drunken Cyclops'
wine, which ends as Polyphemus, announcing that Silenus is his
Ganymede, carries him off protesting into the cave.

We have, of course, one other Euripidean play which, if not strictly
satyric, was at any rate performed fourth after three tragedies, the
Alcestis. It has no chorus of satyrs, and, though it has a contrived
happy ending it is a poignant and bitter play. In fact, the only thing
which reminds us that this is a substitute for Silenus and the 'fore-
heads villainous low' of the satyr chorus is the scene in which, after
the servant describes the difficulty of waiting on Heracles at table (he
is an importunate guest who, not content with what is offered,
demands more, and a hard-drinking guest as well), the hero himself
emerges to berate the servant for his gloomy looks and expound his
philosophy of eat, drink, and be merry in almost the same terms
Cyclops uses to Odysseus. Here we are for a moment, and we cannot
help wondering what the Athenian audience thought of this Euripidean experiment, the first of many. What he has done in *Alcestis* is to
present a satyr play completely transformed by the introduction of
tragic situation, character, chorus, and stle. And if he could do that,

why could he not do the opposite? In the *Electra*, I suggest, he has completely transformed the first half of the tragedy by the introduction of situation, character, and style proper to a satyric play.

This transformation of the tragic atmosphere by the introduction of domestic detail did not, of course, escape the keen eye of Euripides' constant critic. Aristophanes, in the *Frogs*, puts into his mouth the boast that he had improved tragedy by 'bringing in household matters, things we use and live with', *oikeia pragmat' eisagōn, hois crōmeth' hois sunesmen* (959–60), and taught the Athenians to 'run their houses better than before.' Dionysus' reply to this claim dots the i's and crosses the t's:

> So now the Athenian hears a pome
> of yours and watch him come stomping home
> to yell at his servants every one
> 'Where oh where are my pitchers gone?
> Where is the maid who has betrayed
> my heads of fish to the garbage trade?
> Where are the pots of yesteryear?
> Where is the garlic of yesterday?
> Who hath ravished my oil away?

In the opening scenes of the *Electra*, the domestic, light tone prevails, but they are an introduction to the grim horrors of the denouement. It is in such plays as *Iphigenia in Tauris* and *Helen*, which present not tragic catastrophe but hairsbreadth escape from it, that the new spirit achieves its full expression and dominates the whole play. These two plays are generally admitted to be a new departure. They are the ancestors of a whole genre of western melodrama in which captured white adventurers avoid a gruesome death by playing on the ignorance and superstition of the savages. They have a neat formula: part one, the recognition; part two, the escape by trickery (in both plays the woman provides the brainwork). But the only thing that puts these plays in the tragic category is the fact that they were entries in the tragic competition at the festival of Dionysus.

What Euripides has done in them is to eliminate from tragedy what previously had been its essence: *to anēkeston*—'the incurable' (it is Aristotle's word, and Nietzsche's). He has suppressed the action which cannot be recalled, which allows no escape from the consequences—the meeting of the hero and the absolute situation and his decisive act which changes, 'incurably', his world. If Iphigenia had actually sacrificed Orestes, that would have been incurable and could have been tragic. If all three of the protagonists had been recaptured and killed, that would have been incurable and possibly tragic. But Athena intervenes, they all get away, and furthermore the chorus of captured Greek girls get to go home, too.

The essence of this new dramatic form is that the characters are set to walk on the thin ice which separates them from the dark tragic waters; though they may crack the surface, they never quite break through. The genre is a virtuoso exercise in the creation of suspense, which ends with a happy escape from the incurable tragic act and suffering. But this new dramatic purpose is still expressed in and to some extent hampered by tragic form. There is still a chorus, for example (which has to be rescued *en masse* in *Iphigenia in Tauris*). But if the main purpose of the dramatist is to generate excitement from the danger and eventual escape of the protagonists, how can the chorus do what it has always done? How can it illuminate the deeper meaning of the action, trace its roots in the mythic past, explore its wider significance as a paradigm of man's condition, his relationship to his city and his gods? What has it to sing about? Nothing. And that is what it does sing about, very beautifully, with late-Euripidean lyric elegance, but it is still singing about nothing at all. 'Why should I dance the choral song?' the chorus of *Oedipus the King* asks. That question raises the main issue of the play and is answered in unmistakable terms by the outcome of the action. But this is a question which the choruses of the *Iphigenia in Tauris* and *Helen* had better not ask; it would only remind us that their choral songs are on the way to becoming mere musical interludes, the *embolima* of Agathon, which could be put anywhere in the play or, for that matter, in any play.

The chorus is not the only awkward impediment to Euripides' new dramatic design; there is also the myth. The end of the road on which he has taken the first step, suppressing the dignity and terror of the tragic action, is the abandonment of myth altogether. This was of course the achievement of his younger contemporary, Agathon, who produced the first tragedy based on invented characters. But Euripides puts his new wine in the old bottles, and though he chooses his myths carefully for their outlandishness (among Taurians, Egyptians, and, in the *Andromeda*, Ethiopians) and for their unfamiliarity to the audience (both Iphigenia and Helen have to explain their situation at length and with precision), the mythical figures and their associations keep suggesting that there are greater dimensions to the action—a suggestion which true tragedy can exploit, on which, in fact, it relies, but which now saddles Euripides with an incongruous element, a hint of seriousness clashing with the bright swiftness of his plot and the wit that distances us from his characters. In the *Helen* the heroic aspects of the Trojan myth are played down as much as possible except where they are used to pose a comic contrast; Menelaus, ordered off by an old gatekeeper woman who talks to him as if he were a beggar, recalls with regret his 'famous armies', only to be told: 'you may have been an important figure *there*, but you're not *here*' (453–4). And in the *Iphigenia*, Euripides allows the myth to add a sort of false profundity to the action, false because unrelated: the themes of Greek versus barbarian ideas of morality, of human sacrifice and divinity, and so on, like the antiquarian disquisitions on the Athenian Choës or the Artemis cult at Brauron, are grace notes, not a tragic bass.

Though these two plays briliantly exploit the new tone and techniques, their exotic setting works against too heavy an emphasis on the domestic detail, the everyday round. But this is well to the fore in the *Ion*, a play which, in a sense still to be defined, is full-fledged comedy—a work of genius in which the theater of Menander, almost a hundred years in the future, stands before us in firm outline.

Like the *Iphigenia* and the *Helen*, its plot depends on ignorance of identity, *agnoia*, and recognition, *anagnorisis*. A man comes from ignorance to knowledge, solves the mystery of his birth, and knows for the first time who he is. That is the plot of the *Ion* and also of Sophocles' *Oedipus the King*. The resemblances between these two plays are, in fact, remarkable. Both turn on oracles of Apollo, both contain a mother who exposed the child which she has now every reason to think is dead (but is alive); in both the hero fears that his unknown mother may turn out to be a slave (but in fact she is a queen); Oedipus killed his father and Ion threatens to kill his (supposed) father Xuthus. But between the two plays there is all the difference in the world. For the recognition, which is the catastrophe of the one, is in the other the happy solution of the potentially tragic deadlock. *Oedipus the King* presents the tragic spectacle of man's recognition of his real status, not god but man, not ruler but ruled, blind, not all-seeing. But the *Ion* presents a similar situation in fundamentally different terms: the recognition, the hero's realization of his identity, is not a tragic climax but a happy ending—what made Oedipus the King an outcast makes Ion the slave a king.

The play begins with a prologue spoken by a god, Hermes. But this is not the dread Hermes, conductor of the dead, invoked by Orestes in the *Choëphoroe*: he introduces himself as 'manservant of the gods', *daimonōn latrin* (4), as he recounts the background events in which he played a part—the part of 'manservant' to his elder brother Apollo. He carried off the child of Apollo and Creusa (whom the mother had abandoned) and 'doing my brother a favor', as he puts it, left the child on the steps of the temple at Delphi, where he was rescued by the priestess and brought up as a temple servant. Creusa (who returned to find the child missing) was later married to a foreign prince, Xuthus. But the marriage is childless, and they are on their way to Delphi to consult Apollo, Xuthus hoping for a son of his own to be born to Creusa, while she hopes that in some miraculous fashion Apollo will restore to her the vanished child. And that, Hermes tells us, is just what Apollo plans to do; he will give Ion to Xuthus as his own son (Hermes does not tell us how this delicate operation will be performed—Euripides holds that in reserve), Creusa will be told the truth when she gets home to Athens, Creusa's (and Apollo's) indiscretion will remain concealed from the world (and especially from Xuthus), and everything will be for the best. But here comes the boy himself, Hermes tells us: 'I'll step aside into the laurel grove here, to find out what happens to him.' And he does, as Ion, a temple slave equipped with a broom made of laurel branches (103), some kind of water container (105–6), and a bow and arrows (108), comes out of the temple.

This is a very unusual beginning. Gods as prologue speakers are no strangers to the Euripidean stage, but this Hermes is a world away from the menacing Aphrodite of the *Hippolytus*, the vengeful Dionysus of the *Bacchae*, the august figures of Poseidon and Athena, who in the *Trojan Women* prologue plan the destruction of the Greek fleet. For one thing, unlike all these deities, who have urgent personal motives for appearing, Hermes has no business here at all. 'I have come [*hēkō*] to Delphi', he says, echoing similar formulas used by Poseidon and Dionysus, but unlike them, he does not tell us why; the only reason suggested (faintly) is curiosity about the outcome, 'to learn what happens to the boy' (77)—an interesting statement in view of the fact that Apollo has planned everything down to the last detail. But even this suggestion is a mere dramatic pretext, for like his successors in New Comedy (Pan in the *Dyscolus*, for example, and Tyche in the *Aspis*) Hermes has no part in the action and promptly vanishes from the play. His sole function is to explain the situation,

and for that purpose, since the situation involves rape (11), concealment (14), and deceit (71), no better spokesman could be imagined
than the 'manservant of the gods'—*latrin*, 'a word which Aeschylus'
Prometheus (966) used to insult him, but which this Hermes compla-
cently applies to himself.

Ion's monody opens with a brilliant evocation of sunrise at Delphi
whch is justly famous, but as it proceeds we learn that his duties,
which he is performing, are to sweep the approach to the temple,
water down the dust, and keep the birds away from the statues. He
even sings a lyrical address to his broom (112 ff.), in which phrases
like 'O fresh-blooming instrument of service made of beautiful laurel
. . . with which I sweep the floor of Phoebus all day long' remind us
irresistibly of Aristophanes' merciless parody of Euripidean monody
(*Frogs*, 1331 ff.), the point of which is precisely the ludicrous effect
produced by the combination of high-flying lyric form and earth-
bound content. The resemblance of all this to Electra and her water
jug and still more to Silenus and his rake is only too clear, and the
dythyrambic grace of Ion's warnings to the various birds he threatens with his arrows does not disguise the obvious fact that if he fails
to keep them away from the statues he will soon be cleaning up bird
droppings just as surely as Silenus is raking out sheep dung.

It might be expected that the entry of the chorus would at last
strike the solemn note appropriate to tragedy, but this chorus, maid-
servants of Creusa, reinforces the holiday mood which has so far prevailed. Delphi was a tourist center in the ancient world as it is in the
modern, and the girls are sightseers, excitedly calling each other's
attention to the pedimental sculptures, identifying the figures for all
the world as if one of them had a *Guide Bleu* in hand. Finally in an
inspired bit of by-play, they ask the museum attendant, Ion, if they
can go inside, and like so many of their modern counterparts, get a
short negative answer.

Creusa and Ion feel an immediate sympathy; he admires her
nobility of appearance and she his courteous manner. She tells him,
in answer to his questions, the story of her marriage to Xuthus, a foreigner (he expresses polite surprise, 293), and of their childlessness;
Ion, questioned in turn, confesses that he has no name, no known
parents, and is a temple slave—his mother must have abandoned
him. This reminds Creusa of a friend of hers, who abandoned her
child, he would now have been about the same age as Ion, and his
father—well, his father was Apollo. Suddenly the real purpose of her

presence here is revealed: while Xuthus is off making preliminary inquiries at the oracle of Trophonius, she has come to make a secret inquiry about the child—her friend's child—and asks Ion to take the matter up with the Pythia. He points out that such a request would put Apollo in an awkward position, and no servant of the god will run the risk of doing that. As Xuthus comes on stage, Creusa hurriedly begs Ion not to say a word about the matter; Xuthus might not approve, and the thing might get out of hand. She is afraid that 'the story might develop along lines other than those we have pursued' (396–7)—an admirably diplomatic formula.

Xuthus goes in to consult the oracle and comes out wild with excitement to meet Ion, whom he rushes forward to embrace, for, as we learn later, he has been told by Apollo that the first man he meets will be his own true son. The ensuing dialogue, in racing tetrameters, here for the first time employed in tragedy for undeniably comic effect, is one of Euripides' most brilliant scenes. One feature of it which has not been sufficiently emphasized (in fact it has often been suppressed) is the ambiguity of the word Xuthus uses to address Ion in the opening lines, *teknon*. It can mean 'son' but it can also mean simply 'child' or 'boy'. Since in the dramatic circumstances it cannot possibly occur to Ion that it means 'son', the only explanation of Xuthus' conduct likely to recommend itself to him is that this middle-aged man is making vigorous sexual advances to him. This too is the only valid explanation of the violence of Ion's reaction (524). If an older man rushes towards you asking to kiss your hand and embrace you, you might well think him crazy and push him away if he also addresses you as 'my son,' but it is only if he calls you 'boy' that you will threaten him with a weapon. The ambiguity is essential to an understanding of the opening lines, and yet it is ignored in most commentaries and suppressed by translators, who consistently have Xuthus hail Ion as his son in the opening line. There is no excuse for this; it was clearly explained by Wilamowitz long ago, and he is certainly right; no one conversant with fifth-century Athenian ways can doubt it, and the art of the period is rich in apposite illustrations, from the red-figure vases on which bearded men court boys with gifts of tame birds and unmistakable gestures, to the self-satisfied smile on the face of the terra-cotta Zeus at Olympia as he carries Ganymede off in his arms.

But let the scene speak for itself. The rough translation which follows, far from exaggerating the comic element, falls far short of it for

want of a modern English tragic style to accentuate the contrast
between form and content:

> XUTHUS. Boy be happy. That's the only formula that fits the case.
> ION (*retreating*). I'm quite happy. You be quiet and we'll both be better
> off
> X. Let me kiss your hand, enfold you in my arms in fond embrace.
> I. Are you in your right mind, stranger? Has the god deranged your
> wits?
> X. Right mind? I've just found my dearest. Why not rush into his
> arms?
> I. (*still retreating*). Stop it! Don't you paw me. You'll destroy Apollo's
> laurel wreaths.
> X. I *will* touch you. I'm not stealing; you're my dearest, found at last.
> I. (*picks up bow and arrow*). Get your hands off me or you'll get arrows
> in those lungs of yours!
> X. Why do you repel me? Don't you recognize your dearest love?
> I. One thing I *don't* love is putting crazy foreigners in their place.
> X. Kill me, burn me, then, your father, that's who you'll be murdering.
> I. You my father? How can that be? You my father? What a laugh!
> X. Wait. If you'll just listen to me I'll explain my point of view.
> I. What have you to say?
> > X. Your father—
> I'm your father, you're my son.
> I. Who says so?
> > X. The god Apollo brought you up, but you're my
> son.
> I. Don't you need another witness?
> X. Just Apollo's oracle.
> I. You misunderstood some riddle.
> X. Not if I can trust my ears.
> I. Exactly what *did* Phoebus tell you?
> X. That the first man I should meet—
> I. Where and when?
> > X. Coming from the temple, from the oracle of
> the god—
> I. Well, and what's supposed to happen?
> X. —that man is my own true son.
> I. Yours by birth or a gift in some way?
> X. A gift, and yet my very own.
> I. And I'm the first one you ran into? No one else?   X. Just you,
> my child.
> I. That's a curious combination.
> X. Yes. I'm overwhelmed myself.

I. Yes, but, in that case, who's my mother?
X. There you have me, I don't know.
I. Phoebus did'nt tell you?   X. I was so delighted I didn't ask.
I. Earth must be my mother.   X. Hm. The earth does not bear
    children, though.
I. How *can* I be yours?   X. I don't know. I refer it to the god.
I. Well, let's try investigation.
X. Anything you say, my son.
I. Did you have an affair with someone?
X. Yes, when I was young and wild.
I. Before you married Erechtheus' daughter?
X. Naturally. I've since reformed.
I. That was when you got me, was it?
X. Yes . . . the times *do* coincide.
I. In that case how did I get to Delphi?
X. I don't have the slightest clue.
I. It's a long way from Achaea.
X. Yes, that's what is puzzling *me*.
I. Did you ever come here to Delphi?
X. Yes, for Bacchus' festival.
I. And you stayed with one of the locals?
X. Yes. There were some Delphian girls . . .
I. He introduced you to their circle?
X. Yes, and to their Bacchic rites.
I. And you, how were you, drunk or sober?
X. Well, I wasn't feeling pain.
I. That's *it*—the hour of my conception!
X. Fate has found you out, my son.

Ion rather reluctantly accepts his new father, but when told he is to come to Athens, he speculates gloomily on his status there as an outsider, the base-born son of a foreigner, and on the fact that his situation vis-à-vis Creusa will be, to put it mildly, delicate. But Xuthus has it all figured out (like Apollo). He will take Ion along with him 'as a sightseer', *theatēn* (656), and then, on some propitious occasion, he'll tell Creusa the truth. He's sure he can bring her around. He orders the chorus, on pain of death, to keep Creusa in the dark and rushes off to prepare a huge feast. But the chorus does tell Creusa, and there is nothing comic about the tormented aria in which she blurts out the whole story of her lost child and reproaches Apollo for his heartlessness. The chorus and the old man she has brought with her—the tutor of Erechtheus, a fierce guardian of the blood purity of the royal line—are appalled. But the old man, though he had trouble climbing the steep approach to the temple, is not slow to urge action ('I may be slow in the foot,' he says, 'but I'm quick in the head', 742), and he proposes revenge on the god who has acted unjustly. 'I am a mere mortal', Creusa replies. 'How shall I prevail against higher powers?' The old man's answer suggests that we are not to take all this too seriously. 'Burn down the holy oracle of Apollo!' 'I am afraid,' she says. 'I've got trouble enough already,' *kai nun pēmatōn adēn echō* (975). She rejects the suggestion that she kill Xuthus, for he was good to her once, but she accepts with alacrity the idea of killing the boy; Ion, the bastard son of a foreign interloper, shall never reign in Athens. The old man is sent off to poison Ion's wine at the feast Xuthus has prepared.

The attempt fails, the old man confesses, and Ion leads the hue and cry after Creusa, who takes refuge at the altar. The deadlock is resolved by the priestess who once found the child on the temple steps; hearing that Ion is leaving for Athens, she comes to bring him the cradle in which he was left—it may help him some day to find his mother. Creusa recognizes it and by describing its contents convinces Ion that he is her child. But it is not so easy to convince him that Apollo is his father; he knows that Apollo told Xuthus a different story. He goes toward the temple to resolve his doubts 'whether the god is a true prophet or a false' (1537). But this potentially embarrassing interview never takes place; Athena appears, to speak for Apollo, since, she says, the god himself thought it better not to face them, 'lest blame for things past should come into the open'. But all will be well. Ion will go to Athens, succeed to the throne, and become the ancestor of all the Ionians. Xuthus will never know the truth about Ion, but Creusa will bear him sons, Dorus and Achaeus, who will be the ancestors of the rest of the Hellenic nation.

This play is clearly a step beyond the plays of recognition in far-off lands and escape from the barbarians. The scene is Delphi, the background Athens and Athenian patriotic myth; the familiarity of the surroundings is emphasized by insistence on domestic detail. And the pattern of recognition followed by deceit has been transformed: here the recognition is delayed until near the end of the play, while deceit, used not by Greeks against barbarians, but by husband against wife, wife against husband, son against father, mother against son, and Apollo against them all, winds its complex threads throughout the entire play. There is only one reminiscence of the old pattern; in the end one character remains deceived—Xuthus, and he is, if not a barbarian, at least a foreigner.

It is time to document the claim that this extraordinary play is the prototype of comedy in the modern sense of the word. Definitions of comedy are notoriously inadequate, and I do not propose to attempt a new one; I shall be content if I can demonstrate that the *Ion* is the first drama we know of which contains in combination those elements which characterize the standard comic form as we see it in Menander, Plautus, Shakespeare, Molière, and all the way to Oscar Wilde.

First and foremost is the undeniably comic element of scenes which provoke laughter. No matter how ambitious or intellectual comedy may aim to be, it cannot dispense with this element; even *The Tempest* has its drunken butler and mooncalf, *Dom Juan* its Sganarelle, *Tartuffe* its Orgon. The *Ion* has not only its broadly comic Xuthus–Ion scene but a score of light touches here and there which must have caused, if not outright laughter, at least a smile. This laugh, even the smile, is something tragedy at its most intense dare not risk. There is no humor in *Oedipus the King*; one smile would have dissipated the almost unbearable tension on which Sophocles relies to sustain belief in the hopelessly improbable situation, and one good laugh would have shattered the illusion once and for all.

Second, the action is set in a context which emphasizes domestic realities—food and drink, clothing and shelter, cooking and cleaning, the normal human round. Ion's humble duties are emphasized not merely in the opening scene but throughout: the chorus identifies him for Creusa as 'that young man who was sweeping the temple' (794–95), and the play contains a long description of a feast (Ion's birthday party) at which the wine flows freely. This emphasis is constant in comedy: Caliban has to 'scrape trenchering' and 'wash dish', and his reply to Prospero's threats is 'I must eat my dinner'; Falstaff's tavern bill shows 'one half-penny-worth of bread to this intolerable deal of sack', and in *The Merry Wives* he is hidden in a laundry basket and covered with foul linen; Dom Juan is eating (and Sganarelle is trying to) when the statue knocks on the door, and no one is likely to forget the cucumber sandwiches of *The Importance of Being Earnest*.

These two elements of comedy, broad humor and the emphasis on mundane detail, are Euripides' most striking innovations, and their source is not in doubt; they are both regular ingredients of the satyr play. The next feature of this prototype of comedy, the hair's-breadth escape from catastrophe, appears also in the plays of recognition and escape, the *Iphigenia in Tauris* and the *Helen*. This close brush with the incurable tragic act—Ion and Creusa narrowly avoid the fates of Orestes and Medea—becomes a standard feature of comedy, which generates the excitement of tragic potentiality but spares us the pity and fear caused by its fulfillment. Hegio in Plautus' *Captives* is on the point of killing his son Tyndareus but relents and sends him off to the quarries to be recognized and welcomed later. Antonio and Sebastian are about to kill Alonso—'then let us both be sudden'—when Ariel intervenes. Tartuffe's triumph is complete, but the police official, to his surprise (and ours) arrests *him* instead of Orgon. Macheath is led off to be hanged, but the Player objects—'Why then, friend, this is a downright deep tragedy. The catastrophe is manifestly wrong'—and Macheath is spared. Tom Jones tumbles into bed with one Mrs. Waters and it turns out that she is probably his mother and Tom a sort of Gloucestershire Oedipus, but it's all right—she's not. Comedy skirts the edge of the tragic frontier but retreats just in time.

The next significant feature of the *Ion*, the presentation of the recognition not as catastrophe (*Oedipus the King*), nor as the prelude to the tragic action (the three Electra plays), or escape (*Iphigenia in Tauris* and *Helen*), but as the happy ending, seems to have no precedent in drama but becomes, from this point on, through Menander, Plautus, Terence, *Twelfth Night*, *Cymbeline*, *L'Avare*, and *The Importance of Being Earnest*, the stock comic solution, 'la fin d'une vraie et pure comédie', as Mascarille introduces the double recognition which ends Molière's *L'Étourdi*. The delayed prologue of Menander's *Perikeiromene* is delivered by a goddess who had neither temple nor priest—Agnoia, mistaken identity; she mercifully explains the extremely complicated situation for which she is responsible. In Greek society, exposure of unwanted children and enslavement of a slave girl as an heiress or a temple slave as a prince; in modern comedy the effect is usually obtained by disguise, as with Viola and Sebastian in *Twelfth Night* (they almost kill each other in a duel), or by robbing the cradle (as in *Cymbeline*). It takes an Oscar Wilde to have his hero left by the charwoman in a bag at the Victoria Station cloakroom. Of course, to bring about the recognition there must be some stage property left with the baby to be brought out at the crucial moment, like the cradle and the snake bracelet in the *Ion*, or, as in *Cymbeline*, 'a most curious mantle, wrought by the hand of his queen mother, which, for more probation, I can with ease produce' (Act V, Scene 5).

In the *Ion*, ignorance of identity is dramatically exploited in virtuoso fashion. The unknown identity is that of Ion—only Apollo and Hermes know it. Before the play is over, we have seen a false as well as a true recognition; Ion has been taken for the son of three different mothers and two fathers. The happy solution has an ironic twist: both Xuthus and Creusa accept Ion as their son, each one thinking (correctly, in Creusa's case) that the other is deceived. This ending is like that of *Tom Jones*. Is Tom a bastard or a true man? He ends up a squire, but he is still a bastard. Only, like Ion, he happens to be the bastard son of the right person.

The happy ending of comedy is, as in the *Ion*, a restoration of normalcy, an 'integration of society,' as Northrop Frye puts it, 'which usually takes the form of incorporating a central character into it.' Ion is restored to his proper station, in his family (son returns to mother) and his city (from slavery to freedom, indeed to royalty). This characteristic of comedy was long ago remarked by Euanthius ('illic prima turbulenta, tranquilla ultima'), and the restoration may take many forms: of individual to proper status, of balance between the sexes (*The Taming of the Shrew*), of order in the state (the return of the Duke in *Measure for Measure*), or a deeper spiritual restoration, as in the finale of *The Tempest*:

> In one voyage
> did Claribel her husband find in Tunis
> and Ferdinand her brother found a wife
> where he himself was lost; Prospero his dukedom
> in a poor isle, and all of us ourselves
> where no man was his own.

Further, this restoration of normalcy reaffirms, as in the *Ion*, the traditional values of society. Tragedy presents the hero overthrown, though he is magnificent in defeat; a world collapses in and with him, never to be restored. It is the rejection of all normal standards of success, of all comforting moralities, the naked exposure of the fault in things, a view of the abyss. But comedy leaves us with a sense that the standards of this world, though not perfect, are sound: there is no flaw in the universe, only misunderstandings, maladjustments; once restoration is achieved, all is peaceful, *tranquilla ultima*, and everyone gets his just deserts. 'Now everybody's pleased by this death,' says Sganarelle as Dom Juan goes down in flames 'heaven outraged, the laws scoffed at, girls debauched, families shamed . . . husbands humiliated—everybody's happy now.' The chorus closes the *Ion* with a similar assurance that justice governs the universe:

> In the end the good and noble all enjoy their just reward,
> but the low and evil natures never prosper in this world.

This uninspired jingle (translation for once offers no insoluble problem) is a far cry from the lines that end the *Bacchae*:

> Many are the shapes of divine dispensation
> many the unexpected decisions of the gods.
> What we expected is not fulfilled
> for what we never thought of the god found a way.

Furthermore, in comedy as in the *Ion*, the traditional values which are reaffirmed are those of an exclusive group—social, racial, or national. Comedy depends on a feeling (shared by the audience) of cohesion and exclusiveness, of a common identity which resents and repels outsiders; part of the pattern of restoration, in fact, is the expulsion of the intruder, balancing the readmission of the lost or disguised group member. This intruder is of course the most comic figure in the cast, the pretender, the *alazon*, and at the end of the play he is restored to his proper (lower) station—like Parolles, the 'gallant militarist', who is exposed as a 'past-saving slave'; Malvolio, who, believing that greatness is thrust upon him, is 'most notoriously abused'; and Falstaff, who cried, 'The laws of England are at my commandment!' but was greeted by his 'sweet boy', now king, with the words, 'fool and jester'. In the *Ion* this figure is, of course Xuthus, the only character who is presented in broadly comic vein; he is a foreigner in an Athenian society which jealously guarded the privileges of hereditary citizenship (therein lies the relevance of Ion's long speech about the trials that await him in Athens), and Xuthus' final deception is accepted as just return for his presumption—his plan to put what he thinks is his illegitimate son on the throne of Athens. Xuthus' foreignness is emphasized by Creusa, the old man, Ion, and by Xuthus himself, who quickly dismisses Ion's suggestion that the earth may have been his mother, though Athenian tradition (recited not once but almost *ad nauseam* in the play) claimed just such a birth for Erichthonius, Creusa's grandfather.

Xuthus, the intruder, the comic butt, has one more characteristic which is to become a standard ingredient of the comic recipe—his wife is the mother of someone else's child. The real father is a god, and of

course many tragic husbands found themselves in the same position—
Amphitryon, for example, in the *Heracles*. But Amphitryon knew that
he was the 'bed-fellow of Zeus' and was proud of it. Xuthus is ignorant
of Ion's true paternity, and, what is more, he is tricked by the real father,
who has an oracle at his disposal, into believing (though everyone else
in the play finally knows the truth) that Ion is his own flesh and blood.
Such a situation of blissful ignorance is a constant fear of the comedy
father, in Athens as elsewhere. 'We none of us know whose son we are,'
runs a fragment from Menander's *Carthaginian*; 'we just suspect or
believe.' And a fragment attributed to both Euripides and Menander
runs: 'The mother loves her child more than the father; she knows it's
hers and he just thinks it's his.' The Athenian marriage formula ran,
'for the begetting of legitimate children'—a formula which Molière
could not have known but which sounds very like Mascarille's prayer
before his marrage: 'que les Cieux prospères | nous donent des enfants
dont nous sommes les pères.' Around the head of Xuthus, the deceived
but happy husband, floats a prophetic aura of things to come; he is the
prototype of the farcical St Joseph of the medieval mystery plays and of
Machiavelli's Messer Nicia.

All this, taken together, seems to justify the claim that in the *Ion*
Euripides invented what was to become the master pattern of western
comedy. The ingredients of the comic mixture come from different
sources: from tragedy, from satyr play, from his own invention. The
real originality lies in their combination, and the success of that
combination can be judged from the fact that down through the centuries comic dramatists have returned to the formula time and again.

And yet Euripides did have a model, a predecessor, though he was
not a dramatist. As in almost every field of Greek poetry, the great
original is Homer. The *Iliad* is the model for tragedy (especially for
Sophocles), and the *Odyssey* contains almost all of the elements
Euripides combined to create dramatic comedy. The emphasis on
domestic routine and food is remarkable throughout; Eumaeus tends
swine, Eurycleia washes the beggar's feet, while Odysseus himself
announces frequently that man's hungry belly is what drives him on,
and as for the meals, Fielding called the *Odyssey*, not without justice,
the 'eatingest epic'. The hair's-breadth escapes are many and various,
though the crucial one stems from Odysseus' decision not to go
straight to the palace; he goes disguised as a beggar and mistaken
identity is followed by recognition, which is the happy ending—the
slaughter of the suitors and Odysseus' restoration as husband and

king. The suitors are upstart intruders, usurping the place of a hero
of the Trojan War, and they are very definitely put in their places,
though they are not treated comically. But there is an occasional
touch of broad humor, the most remarkable being the song of
Demodocus about Ares and Aphrodite trapped in the golden web, and
this even presents us with a deceived husband. Finally, the normal,
popular standards of justice are reaffirmed; everyone gets his just
deserts. And on this point Aristotle remarked: 'The poem has a double plot and also an opposite catastrophe for the good and the bad . . .
the pleasure, however, derived from this is not that of tragedy. It is
proper rather to comedy.'

There is, of course, one aspect of the *Ion* which I have neglected
entirely, an important one—for some critics, in fact, it is the most
important one of all. I mean the religious problem posed by the play:
what are we to make of Apollo? The play begins with a description
of a god's intention and plan, a clear, logical design. So does the
Hippolytus. But in that play the plan works inexorably through to its
hideous end. In the *Ion* it comes completely unstuck: everything goes
wrong. Mother and son come within an ace of killing each other, and
though this unforeseen calamity is avoided, the whole story of Creusa
and Apollo is published to the world, whereas its continued suppres-
sion, Hermes told us, was one of Apollo's principal objectives—*gamoi
te Loxiou kruptoi genōnta* (72–3). And in the end, when Ion goes to the
temple to demand the truth from Apollo, Athena prevents the confrontation: Apollo, for fear of 'blame for the past', does not appear.

Explanations of this treatment, unique in tragedy, of a major
Olympian figure fall into three main groups. Verrall and many who
follow his lead but avoid his excesses see Euripides the rationalist at
his most trenchant, exposing the absurdity not only of the myth but
also of the Olympian religion. Wilamowitz and many after him see
political factors involved; Apollo had predicted a Spartan victory in
the war and was a safe target. A modern school of interpreters,
stressing the emphasis on religious and mythical motifs in the play,
tries to reclaim it as religious in feeling; Apollo's divine benevolence is
almost foiled by human ignorance and folly.

These explanations remain unconvincing: each is a partial solution which only throws more emphasis on those aspects of the play it
fails to explain. But once we regard the play as an entirely new
medium, a tragedy written in the comic mode, the whole problem disappears. For in comedy the gods are neither attacked nor defended;

they take their place with human beings in a world where nothing too much is expected except that things shall turn out right in the end—*tranquilla ultima*. Aristophanes can present Dionysus in his own theater as a coward and buffoon (a blasphemous buffoon at that) or Zeus overthrown by a couple of Athenian tax dodgers in *The Birds*, without anyone's believing that he is trying to undermine religion. On the contrary, Aristophanes is always given full marks, not always deserved, for religious and political conservatism. Here again, Euripides seems to have taken a hint from the comic poets. Ironic, but also sympathetic, his new vision embraces gods as well as men: the acceptance of limitations, weakness, passions, and mistakes extends even to Olympus. To err may be human, but in the *Ion* it is also divine.

In a papyrus fragment, discovered early in this century, of a life of Euripides by Satyrus, the following headless sentence occurs: 'towards wife, and father towards son, and servant towards master and also the whole business of vicissitudes, raping of young women, substitutions of children, recognitions by means of rings and necklaces. For these are of course the main elements of the New Comedy, and Euripides brought them to perfection.' D. L. Page, with that confidence we cannot help but admire, once proposed a correction—'Menander' for 'Euripides'—but no one seems to have followed his lead. And Philemon, who in the fourth century puts into the mouth of one of his characters the lines:

> If I were sure of life beyond the grave
> I'd hang myself—to meet Euripides

was not a tragic, but a comic, poet.

II
Menander

2

The Convensions of the Comic Stage and Their Exploitation By Mendander

E.W. HANDLEY

Near the end of Act II of Menander's *Dyskolos*, the young hero, equipped with a borrowed mattock, sets off for a bout of hard work in the fields, hoping to meet and impress the misanthropic father of the girl he loves. The stage is left empty. Enter a cook, dragging after him a sheep, and cursing it as he goes. The sight of an angry man in a muddle with an animal is universal enough as a source of amusement to have its effect on audiences nearly two-and-a-half thousand years later, even if many of them have met the name of Menander for the first time when they decided to buy their tickets, and are not accustomed to being catered for by men who bring the meal on the hoof.

The classical scholar in the audience is in a different position. He knows that *chefs de cuisine* are quite a well-documented character-type in fourth-century comedy, thanks in part to the material collected by Athenaeus for his *Learned Banqueters*; back in *his* study, he can put a hand to a considerable bibliography of the topic, quoting parallels for the action and for points in the language, and perhaps invoking a visual aid or two from terracotta statuettes of men with animals. In such ways, in spite of our very fragmentary knowledge of Greek Comedy in the two generations between the last of Aristophanes and the first of Menander, it becomes plain from sheer repetition that certain elements in Menander's comedies are in some sense conventional or traditional. In other words, the very appearance on stage of a man with an animal who is recognizably a *chef de cuisine* creates certain expectations with which the dramatist must reckon.

The dramatist's reckoning may lead him in several ways. He may, for instance, attempt to outdo the convention by making his own treatment brighter and better, rather in the mood of Plautus, when he makes a slave boast that he has secured his young master a royal and golden fortune, and has no time for your Parmenos and Syruses with their frauds of two or three minas (*Bacchides* 645–50). Or he may exploit the convention more subtly, realizing that he can recreate an expected pattern of words or action with no great displacement of effort; and then, perhaps with equal economy, marking a point or two of difference from the image in the detail of his supposed own treatment. He may also want to link such a motif into a chain of expectation, giving the audience a hint in advance that such and such a thing is to happen, and then using it, when it does, to create further anticipation for something else. This seems rather more like Menander; for it is, perhaps, by infusing the apparently familiar with the tension created by context and structure that he achieves some of his most successful dramatic effects.

I should like to suggest recurrent motifs as one general heading under which we can consider conventions of the comic stage. Given New Comedy's links by descent from both the major forms of fifth-century drama, and the continuing influence of classical tragedy as well as earlier comedy, it is clear that exploitation of tragic as well as comic motif may enter into this. Equally clearly, one could consider Menander's use of conventional topics in speeches and dialogue under a related heading. All this, at one end of the scale, could involve, or lead into, discussion of his use of conventions of language, even of metre and metrical forms; at the other end, it might run into questions about his approach to character-portraiture and plot-construction. Although I shall suggest that the critic of ancient comedy should beware of drawing lines too firmly between different departments of the comic playwright's art, there does seem to be here a group of conventions which can go together for our purposes as literary conventions, and reflect the point that comedy is a species of literature.

A second class may be made of conventions which are to do with theatrical performance: conventions springing from the physical character of the theatre for which Menander wrote; the conventions of costumes and masks, in so far as we recognize them as established in his time; conventions in the use of a limited number of actors (however limited we think it was), and in the actual stage-management of action and spectacle in so far as we can reconstruct these visual elements from the available texts and illustrations left to us from Antiquity.

Thirdly, in a kind of drama which has had from Antiquity onwards a much treasured reputation for realism, there is a special sense of convention which comes in when we ask questions about the status of the comic representation in relation to real life; as when we ask how far events in plays are supposed to make sense in terms of real time and place, or how far the economic facts about characters' lives are 'true' facts, with precise counterparts in the world outside the play, as opposed to facts only acceptable in a fictional context and with a conventional sense.

It might be objected that so comprehensive a scheme would allow us to turn the discussion to anything in Menander. That is, in fact, the idea. Comic poets of the fifth century, one recalls, sometimes took conscious pride in their novelties, and decried stock jokes and themes, even, as it might be, in the act of using them. At the opposite pole, Terence (admittedly in the course of a literary controversy) asserted that the comic poet has no novelty left open to him. The same is sometimes said nowadays about plots for novels. Yet they go on being published in quantity. Thus, whatever value one wants to put on sheer innovation, the pleasures of familiarity are considerable; and if there were any danger of our underrating this, the immense development of certain forms of drama as entertainment for mass audiences through cinema, sound radio, and television would rapidly rescue us.

The very fixity of convention which can be exploited to hold the audiences for which it was created is also something which can make a whole genre acceptable in a quite new environment: thus the 'Western' idiom is known and liked by some large number of Europeans for whom the Old West of the United States is even more of a fictional entity than it must be for many of the present inhabitants of those lands. This is a factor which it may be interesting to remember when one considers the long life and the popularity of Menandrean comedy in places far removed from the Athens in which it evolved. And such analogies, however imprecise, could also lead us to reopen the discussion of Menandrean comedy—how closely drawn are its conventions of subject, in terms of the range of human experiences which it reflects?

Let us return to our cook with his sheep. Even a simple incident can be used to illustrate the basic point that a single event in a play can simultaneously involve a number of dramatic conventions, some of them latent, in that they are accepted without special consciousness as part of the normal means of communication between dramatist and audience; others not so, in that, on the given occasion, a special and conscious use is made of them. Thus both dramatist and audience neglect the fact that, being someone in a play, the cook is wearing tights like a comic actor and unlike a real cook. He is recognized for what he is on sight, so far as we know, by his mask, and perhaps his familiar knife or other standard details of costume.

This time the point does matter, and typically, it is reinforced by what he says, most directly in referring to himself as 'the *cuisinier*' and to the place where he is as 'the Nymphaion where we are to sacrifice' (399–401). Moreover, he is given a variant on one of the very familiar stock-in-trade jokes of cook scenes, the word for to chop or cut up (*koptō*), with its slang sense of giving someone a thoroughly unpleasant experience, as by hacking at him with criticism or battering him with sheer conversational boredom. This time, with all the struggle they have had, the notion is that the sheep has had the cook under the chopper: he is hauling it along 'like a boat up a beach'. Thus both visual and verbal conventions play their part simultaneously, and variants on both add, or seem to add, a spice of new interest.

Suppose we approach from another angle. The stage building, that place of many uses, is accepted as representing somewhere in a remote valley in the mountains of the Northern Attic borders for the very good reason that Menander has made it clear in advance that that is where the play is happening. The point is gently reinforced by making the cook say 'fortunately here it is' (he has come a long way, and his loaded companion Getas is trailing behind), and by inventing the notion that when carried over the shoulders, as animals commonly were and are in Greece, the sheep held up the march by reaching for leaves to eat on the way (400, 394 ff.).

Is one surprised to see a figure so commonly associated with town life in so remote a place? No: because we have already been told, in a context where the information had the air of an incidental detail, that Sostratos' mother is a woman who goes all round the district making sacrifices, and had sent Getas to hire a *chef de cuisine* for one of her pious excursions (259 ff.). Do we worry about where the cook came from, to be fetched to so remote a place in time to sacrifice and prepare a mid-day meal? No, the dramatist can expect to carry the audience with him in a little convenient stretching.

If the cook was supposed to live in or near Athens (where, not surprisingly, he boasts of having an extensive practice), Getas would be supposed to have had a journey of around 25 miles since early morning to fetch him and bring him back. The point of this meticulous organization of detail is not, of course, that it is some kind of private game between the dramatist and his more scholarly admirers, but that, if the audience is to be relaxed and properly attentive to the effect being created, they must be given just enough information to carry on their interest without irrelevant surprises; and loose ends which may distract them from the main business in hand must be tied in or tucked out of sight. A puzzled or distracted spectator is, for the moment, a lost one.

Perhaps we can now extend our analysis a little further and make some comparisons. The whole comic episode of the entry of the cook in the *Dyskolos* makes an immediate contrast with the mood of romantic resolution given by Sostratos' departure with his mattock for toil and hot sun. Similarly in the *Misoumenos*, the moment of Thrasonides' resolve to confront the father of the girl he loves is succeeded by the entry of Kleinias with a cook, giving instructions on a very familiar topic—the number of guests to be catered for, and on the need for speed; in the *Aspis*, the moment in the first act when Daos makes a stand against Smikrines' determination to have his rights over the girl and the estate that goes with her is brought sharply up against—not the arrival of a cook, but the departure of one, from the household which was to celebrate a wedding and is now plunged in sorrow. Once again, familiar topics appear: theft, in the form of reproach to his assistant for failure to capitalize on the situation by filling the oil-bottle on the way out, rivalry between cook and *maître d'hôtel*, and, once more, a form of the *koptō* ('cut') joke.

Now one effect of these three scenes, placed as they are, is to bring the action down from a high point to which it has developed, and carry the act to a swift close on a new note: six lines are spent on this in *Misoumenos*; thirty-four in *Dyskolos*; the same, perhaps one or two more, in *Aspis*. The pattern of introducing a new development towards the end of an act is a recurrent one in Menander, and, naturally enough, the development is often brought by the arrival of a character new to the play, or new at least to the preceding sequence. For example, *Samia*, Act I, at 96, say about thirty lines from the end, Moschion has resolved to steel his nerves and go off and rehearse the social and ceremonial business for the wedding of which he is so nervous. Enter the two old gentlemen Demeas and Nikeratos, with their travellers' talk of the Black Sea, from which they turn, apparently casually, to the topic of the wedding which their return home has brought to mind. Or *Epitrepontes*, Act II, at the end of the Arbitration, at 206, enter Onesimos, thirty-seven lines from the end of the act: a brief reference to the slowness of the cook (it is because things are so slow that he has time to step outside), and then he notices that the ring which is just being looked at and talked about is the one his master once lost. Or *Sikyonios*, Act III, at about 120, some thirty lines from the end, enter Pyrrhias with the vital news, and the evidence, of Stratophanes' true parentage, on which the next stage of the action is to turn. Or, from Act IV, *Dyskolos* 775, after the climax of Knemon's major speech and Sostratos' betrothal, enter Kallippides, required for the next stage, but at this moment with his mind on being late for the party, just nine lines from the end of the act; *Aspis* 491, some thirty lines from the end, enter Kleostratos who is thought by all but the audience to have died in battle by the river Xanthos in Lycia.

Thus if one function of the three cook-scenes which led us into this topic is to bring contrast and end the act on a lighter plane of comedy, the varied sample of instances we have taken from elsewhere suggests that their placing is unlikely to be an accident in the purely structural sense, but has something to do with Menander's use of the convention of act-breaks in relation to the progress of an action. We are, of course, exceedingly ill-informed about what happened in the breaks. Tradition enacts that the first entry of the chorus may have special treatment, even if it is almost or wholly disregarded as an entity elsewhere: thus, in Aristophanes' *Plutus*, in addition to providing that the chorus shall have some sort of performance before 325 (and probably, in composing the play, he had no need to think what sort), Aristophanes also devised a parodos for which the chorus is in character, and a special dance, parodying the *Cyclops* of Philoxenos, which they are to do with Karion before they come to their conventional break for a choral song.

This is the tradition which Menander preserves in his formulaic announcements of the chorus's first entry at the end of Act I, and we can digress to note two special variants: *Dyskolos*, where the drunken young men are given a special character, either as 'paean-singers', if, like myself, one is stiff-necked enough to hold on to the text; or as 'followers of Pan', by an easy and attractive conjecture; and *Aspis*, where they are not simply 'a crowd' but 'another crowd'—the audience has seen one crowd already in the procession of captives led home by Daos, and, it may be, Menander is not merely alluding to this, but marking the contrast of mood and spectacle which he has created in this play. What interests us here, however, is a particular kind of plot-planning in relation to the discontinuity given by the breaks. Such a break may simply be treated as an interlude between episodes. An extreme case would be the breaks between episodes at the end of the *Plutus*, after 958, for instance, if it is right to think that the chorus performed there. But the break can have more of a dramatic function if something is done by the shape of the action or the words of the dialogue to create expectation for what will come after it, and it may then be used to mark a lapse of dramatic time, as in the *Plutus* after 626, where a night passes during which Plutus incubates in the temple of Asklepios. With a play of integrated structure, such as the *Dyskolos*, the problem, I take it, is to use the breaks as part of the design, so that they give intervals in the continuous action, but not destructive ones.

The content of our three short cook-scenes takes on another interest when viewed in this light. Let us take *Misoumenos* first. If these six lines were a fragment, we should perhaps only dare to observe that someone was instructing a cook in a not very surprising way: 'There's one stranger to entertain, cook, and myself, and for third—a girl of mine—if she's come in, for Heaven's sake: I'm worried about that myself. If not, just him: I shall be after her all over town. But come on in, cook, and make your motto Speed.' We have enough to know that what we are getting, in the rather simpler visual terms of the cinema, is a quite different camera angle on two of the principals. The word *xenos*, which in the context of dinner-party means 'guest', has a particular function in this play in relation to Demeas, the stranger arrived from Cyprus. It has appeared prominently before; it will soon come in again, when, a few lines from the beginning of the new act, Kleinias asks Getas 'Has a *xenos* just come into your house?' and the verbal link helps the theme to take up again. One could offer a contrast with what must be a near-minimal use of cook-motif at the end of Act II of *Epitrepontes*, which we mentioned just now: there of course, the main interest is on the discovery which Onesimos is to make about the ring, and it is the ring which makes the verbal link with the next act; the cook is not only not silent, but does not even show his face. Even so, words are not wasted. In eight of them, Menander shifts the focus of attention to Charisios' side of the story, suggests a motive for his character's entrance, and (as with the progress of the sacrifice and party through the *Dyskolos*) uses the reference to the meal to keep a time scale of the action going. English can only match in syllables, not words. 'No-one ever saw a slower cook—this time yesterday they'd been having their wine for hours.' If this sounds, as it may, like a bad case of over-interpretation, the test is to put in some other form of words instead: 'I suppose I might as well go and sit on the porch for five minutes.' For many playwrights, that would have been quite good enough.

The effect of the new angle, as well as that of thematic contrast, is clear to see in the *Aspis* cook scene, and Menander's choice from the available store of conventional detail has clearly been made with that in mind. By putting the death of Kleainetos so prominently to the fore at the opening of the play, and by providing him with an uncle of extremely grasping unpleasantness, Menander sets himself a problem which could well be pondered by those who expect comedy be to all jokes. Accordingly, just as this essentially serious theme is handled with an eye alert for the relieving humour of the human weaknesses which show through, so also the predominantly comic tailpiece with the cook has links and contrasts with the serious themes to give them perspective. For Daos, the situation has brought grief at the loss of his master, and of his own prospect of a comfortable retirement in old age. Grief comes to Kleainetos' sister, who was about to be married with a beneficent dowry from the nicer uncle, and for the women of the household preparing for the wedding. Instead of having a brother who could have endowed her handsomely from the spoils of his campaigns, she is an heiress, which could be a most unenviable position for a young woman to be in. There is very perfunctory grief from Smikrines, as head of the family and with all the wealth now capable of being grasped. Now we are to have a cook's eye view: annoyance at losing his contract through the arrival of 'some corpse from Lycia', fury that the distraction of the women in their grief has not been exploited as an opportunity to steal oil; the thought the *maitre d'* will come in to cater for the funeral feast; then, whether from him as the manuscript has it, or from the cook continuing, the play on *koptō* ('cut'): the women are beating their breasts. 'I shall be cut off (*kop-tomenos*)—just like you—if I don't get a drachma.' Finally, there is contempt for the loyal Daos, who has brought all the wealth home and not made off with it. A Phrygian, is he? Thracians, especially Getai, are the real men, not half-men like that. The joke on the slave's nationality (without dramatic context a conventional one, even if nicely turned) has an extra point from the fact that Daos has just turned his nationality to a quite different use in declining to help

Smikrines' plans to get the estate: 'I am Phrygian', he argues (a people who proverbially saw things the wrong way round) 'and a slave:
you must not expect me to see things the same way as you do, or to
help you in legal affairs which are above my station.' We do not know
if the cook came back in the lost part of the play. He has served his
purpose well here. He leaves at the end of the act, as the chorus of
revellers appear, and the next act takes up from Smikrines' exit immediately preceding the incident.

A difference with the *Dyskolos* is, of course, that there the cook has
a substantial part. A good deal has been said about him elsewhere,
and we can take the remaining points we need from his entrance
scene very briefly. The detail of his opening speech we have already
considered. By the design of this play, two lines of action, each
touched off by Pan, converge in the neighbourhood of the
Nymphaion at Phyle. Sostratos has been made to fall in love with
Knemon's daughter; the rest of the family is brought as a result of a
dream in which Pan appeared to the young man's superstitious
mother. The cook and the household slave Getas, complaining about
their mission and discussing the omen which sent it, are part of the
mechanism for bringing the two lines of action together. They show
Sostratos' mother's superstitions in a different light from that which
we had from her son. They talk of her dream; dreams are by no means
a novel topic in drama, but this one has the excellent comic effect that
its apparently alarming content refers in fact to the bout of digging
for which the audience has just seen Sostratos leave. They talk of getting things ready, and their words, and the theme, will be echoed
when the action is resumed the other side of the act-break, though
not without the diversity of a sudden appearance by Knemon.

The topic of linking and transition over the act-break is one which
could well be pursued further. Before we move on to something quite
different, it will be useful to mention one passage as a control on our
observations, namely the Oxyrhynchus Papyrus of *Dis exapatōn*. The
pattern we have been considering is present. A very interesting
sequence of action (of which we have an idea from Plautus' *Bacchides*),
has put Sostratos in the position of being asked to reprove a trusted
friend for being involved in an affair with someone who, to the best of
his knowledge, is waiting for him. This turns him to the notion of
handing over to his father the money he had proposed to divert in
order to further the affair. Enter the father, some thirty-four lines
from the end of the act. They go off to transfer the money: choral

interlude. Re-enter the same pair, and the theme of the conversation re-opens. After twenty-seven lines of the new act, exit father. Sostratos returns to reflect on the girl and the friend who, as he thinks, have betrayed him. Eleven-and-a-half more lines of soliloquy, resuming with the aid of a verbal echo from where we left off, and enter the friend.

Now here it is much more difficult to get a clear idea of the function of the scenes on either side of the act-break, because much of the content is lost by damage, and we do not have the relevant part of the rest of the design except in the Latin play. It is, however, a point of some interest that Plautus, who had no concern to arrange the action round a break, eliminated the two scenes, had the transfer of money made in a rapid off-stage transaction, and refashioned the move between stages of the action by conventions of his own. There are occasions when something which should happen indoors is needed for public presentation to the audience, or when something important happens off stage and cannot be staged because to do so, rather than presenting it through narrative or dialogue, would be impracticable or uneconomical.

A very simple device which can be used to extend the stage momentarily to the inside of a house (if we may put it like that) is the device of having a character talk back through the open door as he is leaving. This convention is so common that it is normally completely latent (as we have called the cook's tights). So in the *Dis exapatōn* (102), Moschion, whom the audience cannot have seen for some time, enters from the house of the twin sisters saying 'So he's heard. I'm here—where on earth is he?' This is apparently enough for Menander's audience to reconnect with the situation. Plautus, adapting the passage and using the same device, evidently thought his audience should have more. It comes out as (*Bacch.* 526): 'I will put your instructions before everything else, Bacchis, to look for Mnesilochus and bring him with me to you. I am surprised indeed at his delay if the message from me has reached him. I will go to his house here and see if he is at home.'

Another example might be the case of the bibulous midwife, for which we depend in part on Terence's version of *Andria* 481, the midwife Lesbia comes out of the house giving instructions to an old woman Archylis at the door. The incident is known to be Menandrean, since we have the Greek for part of the instructions—Terence, not untypically, has simplified some of the detail. The primary dramatic point is to confirm to the audience that Pamphilus' baby son is now born. Simo, standing outside, remarks, 'she didn't say face-to-face what should be done with the girl after the birth, but after she'd come out, shouting back inside from the road. Oh, Davus, do you think so little of me? Do you really think I'm a man you can set about tricking so openly?' He thinks that the whole thing is a put-up job, purely for his benefit, to convince him that there is a baby when there is not.

Now if the midwife is to say anything at all that the audience hear, outside is where she must say it. The dramatist perfectly well could have let her give her instructions on leaving, and have made no more of it; but he chooses, in this instance, to play with the convention by making someone on stage give it a 'real-life' value. But once attention is drawn to the behaviour of the midwife, it needs some sort of naturalistic motivation, or the audience will share the viewpoint of Simo, and wonder why she is behaving like that. That, I believe, is why, when we first heard of the midwife, at 228 ff., she was given a character which is perfectly conventional for an old woman, but usefully relevant to the incident we are discussing: she is, we were told, 'imprudent and fond of a drop of drink', and the Archylis, with whom she has her doorstep conversation, we know of as a drinking companion of hers (232). It is partly because of this unostentatious preparation for the incident that I incline to think the design of it was Menander's rather than Terence's—a tentative view of a passage which has provoked plenty of diverse and interesting discussion.

The same principle of 'special use when needed' can be seen to apply to conventional details of setting or costume. The altar to Apollo Agyieus at the house door is an expected part of a setting which can be ignored if and when it is not wanted. But it comes into special use in the *Samia* at 444 ff., when Demeas appeals to his Apollo to help him carry through the wedding and sing a good wedding song in spite of himself and the feelings he wants to conceal. Or, in the *Dyskolos*, there is nothing surprising in the fact that a rich and elegant young man like Sostratos should go out hunting wearing a cloak. But in a country context, it makes him conspicuous for what he is, he is 'the man in the cloak' when seen by Gorgias at 257, and Menander still has more use of the point to make later.

A somewhat more difficult exercise with conventions is given in the *Dyskolos* by the staging of Knemon's major speech. The old man has been badly shaken by his experience in the well, and wants to call the family to his bedside for what is, in effect, his will and testament. He has himself carried outside. Menander does not attempt to motivate that naturalistically. Instead, he treats Knemon like a stricken hero of tragedy, perhaps underlining the point with an echo of Euripides' *Hippolytus* at the beginning of the scene, and alluding to the convention when Knemon asks to be 'wheeled in' at the end of it. If this case is valid, it belongs to the class of uses of tragic convention for special effects. That class, as has often been pointed out, is in itself a compound one; for certain kinds of borrowing from tragedy are by Menander's time so well established in the comic tradition as to be, in some sense, part of the fabric, while others seem to represent fresh inspiration.

Thus it is conventional in New Comedy, as earlier, for the tone to rise to that of high poetry when characters express specially strong emotions. and there is a whole range of effects from actual quotation through kinds of parody or adapted quotation to the much less pointed kind of effect which is given by a choice of elevated rather than strictly poetic words, or by the effect of tragic strictness in the verse—all of which effects could no doubt be underlined by voice and gesture. So much is common ground, though one may well argue about the nature of the tragic allusion in any particular context; we may discover that it is compounded of several elements, visual as well as verbal; and that Menander, on the whole, is less interested than Aristophanes in the purely laughable or satirical possibilities of the incongruity between the foreground comic situation and the background tragic one, and more interested in gaining an extra dimension to his comic action by referring it implicitly to a classic standard.

A slight, but I think possible case of the compounding of verbal and visual elements, which I have thought of as resembling that of Knemon in bed, would be the entry of his daughter at *Dyskolos* 189 in distress: 'O, wretched me for my misfortunes'. And carrying a water-pot, she recalls the Euripidean Electra. If the audience took the point, they will have had an extra dimension to the comic situation, and an extra touch of amusement when Sostratos says of her, 'She's a country girl; and yet she's somehow like a freewoman'. There is no such doubt about the allusion to the messenger speech of the *Orestes* in the long narrative by the man from Eleusis at *Sikyonios* 176 ff., for it is clearly given by reminiscence of Euripides' own words; but the function of the speech in relation to dramatic convention and dramatic effect is a much more speculative topic. The debate over the slave Dromon and the girl Philoumene was evidently to be a major feature of the plot. To stage it in full, even if resources in actors could have permitted that, would have taken a great deal of time and would have been uneconomical of effect. And so the scene is carried elsewhere in imagination by dramatic narrative, which has the great capacity of being able to select, and to call on the imagination to supply what the eyes do not.

An extreme case of the vivid and important, but unstageable, would of course be Daos' long narrative of the Lycian campaign and the death of Kleainetos at the beginning of the *Aspis*. But there are also vivid and impressive narratives of more domestic scenes, which might somehow have been presented in direct action. Such is Demeas' long narrative, beginning Act III of the *Samia* (706 ff.), in which he tells of the wedding preparations in his house, and how he overheard a conversation about the baby which has aroused a suspicion he will not voice. The further dramatic point here is that the personality of the narrator itself enters into the effect, and may in turn be illuminated by the way in which he tells his story. In the *Sikyonios* speech, Menander learnt from Euripides to let the narrator characterize himself at the start, so that we have some impression of the quality of our outside witness which we can test by what he says; precisely because he is in the position of an outside witness, his descriptions of the characters we know already give an extra dimension of interest, just as, on a small scale, the action we examined in the three short cook-scenes has an indirect value in relation to our other knowledge of the situation. A further variant on this technique of indirect presentation is given by the *Misoumenos*, when at 284 ff. Getas paces round the stage narrating to himself and turning over in mind the quarrel he has witnessed between Demeas and Krateia and his master Thrasonides. Here we have not only the extra dimension of a slave's eye view of the matter, but the further comic effect of a very puzzled Kleinias pacing after the slave and cutting in with comments on Getas' recollection.

Returning now to the *Sikyonios* speech, we can be clear that there is much more point to it than some kind of diluted Euripidean echo. I should like to think that the allusion does two things other than give the audience the pleasure of recognizing it. I should like to think that it points to the analogy of situation between the slave and the girl and the heroic Electra and Orestes; and that it does something to justify dramatically the very long uninterrupted speech, by placing it in a dramatic tradition of descriptions of assemblies of which the *Orestes* was a classic case, one which had already made its dramatic influence felt before Menander wrote this play, and continued to be remembered because the *Orestes* continued to be a popular classic.

The question then is, when Menander gives a hint that he is writing in a convention untypical of his usual manner, is this a sign that the normal criteria of realistic presentation do not apply? The point could be considered not only of scenes explicitly in the tragic manner, but of the ending of the *Dyskolos*, where several critics have wondered about the relation of the farcical ragging of Knemon to the carefully constructed and not wholly unsympathetic portrait of the character which the play has built up: part of the answer may be given by the change of convention which comes with iambic tetrameter lines delivered to flute accompaniment. An opposite problem of convention, perhaps, is presented by the opening of the *Aspis*: how can a death in the family be comic? Clearly it would not be if the opening were handled entirely naturalistically, and without the aid of any expectations created by convention. But just as the ending of the *Dyskolos* depends for its effect in part on the tradition of farcical revel at the ends of comedies, so the opening of the *Aspis* depends in part on the long tradition of surprise openings, of teasing the audience's expectations, as Aristophanes sometimes does, before explaining the truth in a prologue speech deferred until after the opening scene.

It is consistent with this tradition, perhaps, that the first event should be a spectacle, that of the procession of the old *paidagogos* carrying his master's shattered shield; the captives and booty; and—the diversifying element—Smikrines in attendance. One wonders if the effect was heightened by the implied comparison with tragic spectacle, and it may be worth remembering that, according to a scholiast on Euripides' *Orestes* 57, productions of the play of which he knew were augmented at the beginning by a procession in which Helen arrived with the spoils of Troy. The campaign narrative is also something with a respectable literary pedigree, and therefore a conventional value as well as its actual one: it is interesting that its counterpart in the *Amphitruo* (203 ff.) is treated in the grand martial manner by Plautus, and that Menander's narrative concerns the affairs of an ordinary soldier, not a king, and as seen by the elderly ex-tutor—which is the best approach to a military servant that can be made by this not-very-well-off young man who has become a mercenary in order to provide a decent dowry for the sister in his care. If consistently elevated in tone, or consistently natural, the opening would lack comic effect. Its working depends partly on the audience's built-in willingness to be surprised at the start of the play, and partly on the blend of conventions, with the added interest of the insincerity of Smikrines' grief gradually showing through and turning at the end of the scene into naked but disclaimed self-interest.

The prologue-speaker, Tyche, makes sure that true perspective is given, and she herself reminds the audience of the force of convention when she begins: 'If something unpleasant really had happened to them, I, a goddess, would not have been likely to follow': she would, perhaps, have removed herself from the scene of misfortune and grief, like a latter-day Artemis leaving the deathbed of Hippolytus (1437 ff.).

Beginning from what seemed to me some of the most obvious conventional material in comedy, I have tried to show something of the complexities which arise when we try to translate our observations of recurrent themes and stage-practices into an evaluation of dramatic effect. The overall result, if one can dare to suggest it from such a miscellany of instances, is that in Menandrean comedy it is not so much what happens that matters, but how. That is why, I suppose, plot-summaries such as one reads in textbooks often sound so extremely trivial and novelettish.

It is, of course, easy to say that his subject-matter is too closely confined to love-affairs and family relationships, but, whether rightly or not, these domestic affairs are things which a large part of mankind are preoccupied in for a large part of their time, and it is not necessarily reprehensible to weave them into amusing and sometimes, perhaps, genuinely enlightening patterns. What seems to distinguish the use of conventions such as we have been considering is not only the novelty that is given them by an unconventional selection, or an unconventional context, but the general sense of design which calculates the ingredients of comic appeal with an instinct both for immediate effect and for dramatic structure. Worlds apart in many ways, Menander might almost have said of himself with Pindar (*Pythian* 1. 81–3): 'Praise spoken in due season, theme after theme set down in quick succession, reaps less blame from men, for tedium dulls their keen attentiveness . . .' (trans. Nisetich).

3
Marriage and Prostitution in Classical New Comedy

DAVID WILES

The idea that a 'comedy' is a narrative which culminates in marriage can be traced back, via the Renaissance, to the Greek dramatist Menander. Though New Comedy was, on the face of it, a realistic form reproducing a specific and contemporary social milieu, it also constituted a kind of myth, a myth which was to satisfy the Graeco-Roman world over several centuries. The myth of romantic hetero-sexual love had found little place in pre-classical or classical culture, but within the Hellenistic world performances of New Comedy helped this myth to become a common currency.

All works of New Comedy (with one exception) tell the same basic story of how the amorous male tries to overcome the obstacle in his path in order to secure the female of his choosing. The male of the story is usually young, handsome, and freeborn. The obstacle may be familial, financial, or social. For example, the father may object; there may not be enough to pay the brothel-keeper, or the dowry; the couple may be kept apart by the social code that prevented marriage between citizen and non-citizen. These external obstacles may be bound up with psychological considerations. The female of the story, finally, may be at one extreme a virgin bride, at the other a professional prostitute.

A basic concern of New Comedy is the relationship between love and sexuality. Through eliminating the phallic costume and verbal obscenity of 'Old' Greek Comedy, the 'New' form set up a dichotomy between body and mind, between actions and feelings. Michel Foucault describes Greek sexual ethics in a way which pinpoints a central preoccupation of New Comedy. Friendship is reciprocal, and sexual relations are not reciprocal: in sexual relations, you can pene-trate, or you are penetrated . . . if you have friendship, it is difficult to have sexual relations.[1] If there was no true reciprocity in homosexual relations, which always distinguished 'lover' and 'loved', there was necessarily far less within heterosexual relations in a male-oriented Graeco-Roman world.

With the arrival of Christianity, the concepts of love and marriage become almost indisseverable. At the centre of the sacrament of marriage is a promise that the couple will love each other, and if there is no true love, there is no true marriage. The word 'love' in our culture forges erotic desire and a desire for the lasting companionship and well-being of the other into a conceptual unity. Within classical Greek language, the case is different. *Eros* and *philia* are conceptually distinct. *Eros* is desire, brought on by the arrow shot by the winged son of Aphrodite. *Philia* implies affectionate feelings, as do its synonyms *storgē* (particularly used of parent/child relationships), and *agapē* (the usual New Testament word for love, love which shows itself in external signs of respect). Another word, *hetaireia*, is usually translated as 'companionship': the word implies membership of a common political, social or military grouping. A *hetairos* is a male comrade, but a *hetaira*, because she was present at male social gatherings, is a prostitute.

Within Greek religion we find again no single concept of love. Sexual pleasure falls under the patronage of Aphrodite—homosexual pleasure as much as heterosexual. Marriage is the province of other goddesses: Demeter, goddess of fertility, Artemis, goddess of childbirth, Hera, wife of Zeus. In Athens, a virgin bride dedicated her weavings to Athena, she dedicated her childhood dolls to Artemis before marriage, and sacrificed to Artemis during pregnancy. As a married woman, she joined other married women in the worship of Demeter at the Thesmophoria. Aphrodite had only a transient association with marriage, but was the permanent patroness of courtesans. A *hetaira* dedicated herself to Aphrodite when she embarked upon her profession (*Palatine Anthology* vi. 285), worshipped Aphrodite annually at the Adonia, and might give her as a tithe one-tenth of her earnings (*Palatine Anthology* vi. 285, 290). Aphrodite Hetaira was one of the cultic names of the deity (Athenaeus xiii. 559, 571). We should not conclude that the procreation of children was entirely pleasureless, however. In vases which portray a wedding procession, the bride

---

[1] 'On the Genealogy of Ethics', in *The Foucault Reader*, ed. Paul Rabinow (Harmondsworth, Penguin, 1986), 345.

is shown accompanied by Eros. Aphrodite and marriage connected temporarily on the wedding night.

The Greek distinction between sexuality and marriage has to be understood in its sociological context. Citizen Athenian women were segregated from men. At home they occupied the women's quarters, and did not encounter male guests, who were entertained in the men's quarters. Religious ceremonial provided the one all-important occasion when women were allowed to appear in public and to some extent mingle with free men. Women had no legal or property rights, and were always in the wardship of their husband or closest male relative. A socially approved system of prostitution evolved in response to this segregation of citizen women. In the absence of wives and daughters and sisters, prostitutes were required to enliven private male gatherings. Since men did not normally marry until their thirties, for unmarried men prostitutes were, apart from close relatives, the only female society available.

Romantic love, with its connotations of strong emotion and voluntary reciprocity, could not easily flourish between males and females of equal status. Athenians of the classical period tended to idealize homosexual love because the passive partner, the freeborn youth, gave himself voluntarily to a mature man who pleased him, and he could not be bought for money. The mature male expressed dominance through the act of penetration, but preceded this with rituals of abject submission, and in this sense the relationship was reciprocal.[2] Free prostitutes were in a rather similar position. Unlike brothel slaves—*pornai*, 'women for sale'—free *hetairai* gave their 'companionship' voluntarily, in return for supposedly voluntary gifts of clothing and jewels. They could withdraw their affections when they pleased. There might also be a voluntary element in the relationship between a man and his concubine. A concubine was a non-citizen, she brought no dowry with her, and could not bear her partner citizen children. Having no dowry, she had no protection from being discarded. But in every other sense she was a wife, and the relationship of concubinage carried no social stigma. Here, where either party was free to withdraw from the relationship, affection was the principal bond that held the couple

---

[2] See K. J. Dover, 'Classical Greek Attitudes to Sexual Behaviour in the Ancient World', in *The Arethusa Papers*, ed. John Peradotto and J. P. Sullivan (State University of New York, 1984), 143–57, esp. 150.

together.[3] These alternatives to legal marriage—homosexuality, *hetaireia*, concubinage—were a far more natural focus for ideas of romantic reciprocated love than marriage could be.

The trick performed by Menander's complex plots, with their unexpected revelations of identity, is to make the husband love his legal wife-to-be while thinking she is, or treating her as, his prostitute or concubine. In all the extant Greek texts, the plots end with marriage. Aphrodite and marriage are in a sense reconciled. The idea that sexual attraction properly and naturally culminates in marriage is something new in Greek culture, and I shall try to suggest why this new concept emerged.

There is little that we can term romantic love in earlier Greek drama. In Aeschylus the problematic relationship between Aphrodite and marriage is confronted in the Danaid trilogy. In the first play, a chorus of maidens tries to evade marriage. At the end of the play one hemichorus dedicates itself to Artemis, and prays that no marriage come by compulsion of Aphrodite, while the other hemichorus acknowledges that Aphrodite is too powerful not to be honoured (*Suppliants* 1030–42). At the end of the trilogy, Aphrodite herself appears to argue that she is the basic creative principle which makes the wet sky choose to mate with the dry earth. This is basically the same argument as that used by the evil nurse in Euripides' *Hippolytus* (lines 447–50) when she persuades Phaedra to surrender to Aphrodite, and commit incestuous adultery. The chorus, women who have born children, pray to escape the bolts of Eros and Aphrodite (lines 527–33).

In Sophocles' *Antigone*, Haemon may seem to be a prototype romantic lover when he kills himself for love of his betrothed—but again the chorus roundly condemns the destructiveness of Eros. When the bride's eyes are filled with desire, they say, then Aphrodite the unconquerable is at her sport (lines 781–99). We are tempted to sympathize with Haemon because of our own cultural assumptions, but there is no sympathy in the chorus for a young man's infatuation. We find a similar language of love in Aristophanes. 'Aphrodite, why do you drive me mad?' asks the young lover in *The Assemblywomen*. 'Eros, I beg you to free me, and bring her to my bed' (lines 966–8). Love is a species of madness, a powerful external force that must somehow be controlled.

Menander's lovers have no sophisticated language in which to

[3] S. Humphreys, *The Family, Women and Death* (London: Routledge & Kegan Paul, 1983), 64.

express their new form of love. A vocabulary is lacking. To illustrate
the point, I shall quote the opening lines from one of Menander's
plays. A mercenary has acquired a girl enslaved in war, has given her
a measure of legal freedom, and has installed her as his concubine.
She refuses to submit voluntarily to his embraces, and he is unwilling
to assault her, as a man would normally do in this situation. The
speech idiom is borrowed from tragedy, and 'Eros' is the word which I
have translated as 'love':

O Night! you of all the gods have most in common with Aphrodite. *You* are the
occasion for most talking about it, most thinking about—love. Have you ever
looked on a man more distraught, a lover more doomed? I am standing now
before my own doorway, I walk up and down the lane, this way and that, and
you are almost halfway done. I could be asleep, in possession of the one I love.
She is in my house. I could, and I want to, like the maddest of lovers, but I don't
do it. This winter weather is preferable, as I stand and shiver, talking to you.

(*Misoumenos* A1–A14)

Menander's plays give us the actions of lovers, not their verbaliza-
tions of feelings. His theatre demonstrates what the lover does—
stands about in the rain at night, for instance—not why he does it.
The medium of theatre proves well suited to working out a new ethi-
cal/emotional orientation which could not as yet be articulated adequately in speech.

Although the soldier in this play has or has had legal power over
the woman, he wants something that she can only give voluntarily.
Eros could be satisfied with a slave, but the soldier here is looking for
free reciprocity. He develops the paradox that although the girl was
once his slave, she has now enslaved him (frag. 2). The situation is
resolved when the girl's father arrives, and her citizen status is established. The hero declares to the girl that he loves her with the verbs
agapē, philō (line 308). The father asks if the marriage is his daughter's
wish (lines 438–9) before bestowing her with the traditional legal formula: 'For the sowing of a legitimate crop, I give my daughter,
together with a dowry of two talents' (lines 444–6). Marriage is here
accompanied by *agapē* and *philia*, by the free choice of the wife,
because of the extraordinary circumstances of the plot—because the
hero has already lived with the woman as his slave and as his concubine. The trajectory of the play, from Eros to *philia*, and to a situation
which permits the procreation of legitimate children, is a feature of
all Menander's extant plays. Menander works out in theatrical terms

a problem which the Stoics of the next generation worked out in philosophical terms. Chrysippus the Stoic used this play to support his argument that *eros* is not the result of divine intervention, which is to say irrational, but is the result of *philia*, a wish to do good at the prompting of beauty (Diogenes Laertius vii.130).

In all Menander's plays, through miraculous coincidences and discoveries of unexpected paternity, the object of erotic desire is fused with the object of matrimony. Menander's plots are all centred on, or triggered by, a rape—that is, by a violent, apparently irrational, satisfaction of Eros. I must point out immediately, in relation to rape, that Greek attitudes were different to our own. For us, rape constitutes unpardonable violence, but in the normal Athenian view rape was less objectionable than seduction. The rapist succumbs to a momentary weakness, but the seducer, while in full command of his reason, threatens the state through corrupting the mind of a woman destined to be the guardian of a citizen's seed. We can divide Menander's plays conveniently into two groups. In the first group, the hero has at some point in the past raped a girl, without knowing her identity, and this girl, through a chain of circumstances, becomes the rapist's bride. In the second group, a man refrains from sex with a girl who does temporarily lie in his legal power.

Some examples may be helpful. *The Hero* is a play which falls into my first category. A woman before the play begins was raped and gave birth to twins. She disposed of the children and later married the man who raped her. The children have fallen into debt-slavery, and the daughter, now aged eighteen, has recently been raped by the hero of the play. When the girl's parentage is revealed, the young couple become free to marry. A play which falls between my categories is the *Perikeiromene* 'She Who Was Shorn'. A jealous soldier assaults his concubine asexually through cutting off her hair, giving her the mark of a slave. The girl's parentage is revealed, the man sees the error of his ways, and the couple marries.

The Arbitrants is a play which spans both categories. The hero once raped a girl, and does not know that this is the same girl as the one to whom he has been contracted in marriage. When he finds that his bride has recently given birth, he refuses to consummate the marriage. He hires a slave prostitute, but cannot bring himself to have sex with her. Finally the truth emerges, the hero sees that he has been guilty of double standards, and the marriage is saved.

In these, as in all Menander's other plays, the same inversionary pattern is found. The forbidden woman becomes permitted, the permitted woman becomes forbidden. An arbitrary social code, founded upon the institutions of slavery and endogamous citizen marriage is magically overturned. At the same time, a new ethical code for interpersonal behaviour seems to be articulated. The man must treat the woman as he would expect to be treated himself: i.e. with respect and understanding.

It would be unwise, however, to regard New Comedy as in some way advocating the cause of women. The interest of the playwright and of his predominantly male Greek audience is centred on the behaviour of the man, not of the woman. No new female role model is offered, no new system of marriage is envisaged. There is no external evidence to suggest that this theatrical genre coincides with any changes in Greek sexual or marital practices. There are nevertheless important artistic, scientific and political changes which can be correlated with the emergence of New Comedy.

Within the visual arts, the glorification of the naked female body connects very obviously with the cult of romantic love in the theatre. A generation before Menander, sculptures like Praxiteles' *Aphrodite of Knidos* and paintings like Apelles' *Aphrodite Rising From the Sea* established the female rather than the male nude as the idea of erotic beauty. Heterosexual love replaced homosexual love as an aesthetic aspiration. Menander's theatre, like the visual arts, above all celebrated Aphrodite. The salt of his comedies, Plutarch observed, 'springs from the same sea whence Aphrodite rose' (*Moralia* 854c). But both art and theatre played down the traditional association between the woman and productive deities like Demeter, goddess of the crops, or Athena, goddess of crafts.

Within the scientific sphere, the new biology of Aristotle is of interest. Popular tradition, enshrined in the teaching of Hippocrates, held that female secretions are seminal, and the female's pleasure in intercourse is linked to her ability to produce children. Aristotle, a generation before Menander, overturned this theory and threw out the idea that female pleasure is linked to procreation. Knowing nothing of ovulation, he portrayed the female as essentially a 'sterile male' (Aristotle, 'Genesis of Animals' 727a–728b). While Hippocratic medicine had traditionally seen pregnancy as an aspect of female health, Aristotle saw it as an affliction.[4] In science as in art, the function of the woman was now not to do but to be done unto, not to look

---

[4] Aline Rousselle, *Porneia* (Paris, Presses Universitaires de France, 1983), 59.

but to be looked at. Aristotle's scientific thought is linked to his political thought. The foundations of the state, for Aristotle, rest upon three natural relationships of authority: of father over son, of master over foreign slave, and of husband over wife (*Politics* 1253b ff.).

The role of women in Athens was a function of its system of government. We can only understand the changing historical position of women in Athenian life in the context of the whole democratic structure. Where the focus of feudal society was the household, the focus of democratic society was the market place, the assembly, the theatre, and other public places where women did not belong. Citizenship became both a privilege and a duty, and it was necessary to define with precision who were or were not citizens. If women lived secluded lives, no one could doubt that the children they bore belonged to citizen fathers. The legislation which restricted citizenship to children of citizen mothers as well as fathers was passed in 451 BC and followed naturally upon the triumph of democracy—male democracy, as I should rather call it. A related piece of legislation required that an heiress—that is to say, a woman who inherited property for lack of brothers or sons—was obliged to marry her nearest male relative. Two of Menander's plays deal with this law, one focussed upon the plight of the reluctant husband, the other on the reluctant bride. The purpose of this legislation was to prevent the disappearance of a household through marriage, and the concentration of wealth in the hands of an elite. For men as for women, the interests of the state were placed above those of the individual.

Citizen women were secluded, but not simply to preserve their chastity. A woman's participation in public life was restricted also because her appearance was associated with politically unacceptable displays of private wealth in the form of clothes, jewels, and chariots. Solon in the early days of Athenian democracy first legislated to minimise female participation in processions, funerals, and feasts. Lycurgus' attempts to revitalize Athenian democracy in the generation before Menander involved new restrictions upon women's participation in festivals (Plutarch, *Solon* 21; *Moralia* 842a). Under the Macedonian protectorate in Menander's own day, official 'supervisors of women' were appointed with the task of regulating female conduct in public, in matters of clothing, and so forth. One of Menander's plays refers to their covert methods of checking the number of guests at wedding banquets (frag. 238 K-T).

With this institution, we come to one of the unresolved contradictions in Athenian democracy. These supervisors of women were, on
the face of it, a restriction placed upon the rich who wished to be
ostentatious. But such officers were equally unacceptable to radical
democrats, since the poor were, as Aristotle puts it, forced to use their
wives in place of slaves. The wives of the poor could never be secluded
like the wives of the prosperous. The freedom of women in the
home—'gynecocracy', as he calls it—was seen by Aristotle as a characteristic of fourth-century radical democracy and a source of its
inherent weakness (*Politics* 300a). If Athenian attitudes were confused, non-democratic Sparta was at least available as a clear object
lesson. Aristotle shows us why Spartan women were thought in
Athens to have too much freedom. Their social freedom encouraged
the private display of wealth. Their freedom of movement was a hin-
drance in time of invasion. The possibility of alienating entire estates
through inheritance and over-sized dowries resulted, in the fourth
century, in a concentration of wealth, and in a drastic reduction in
the manpower of the Spartiate military elite (*Politics* 1269b–1270a).

It is too simple to see Menander's plays, with their domestic setting
and love interest, as clear evidence of *embourgeoisement*, as an asser-
tion of private as opposed to public values—though this is the usual
analysis that is made. The private and the political were deeply inter-
woven in Athens. A marriage was not simply—as it might have been
for Molière or Jane Austen—a personal and moral fulfillment for the
individual. A marriage was a contribution to the strength of the state.
In the fourth century, Plato advocated fines for men who did not
marry by the age of thirty-five (*Laws* 774). Philip of Macedon in the
third century and Polybius in the second both commented on the
weakness of Greek cities in their time through depopulation (Polybius
xxxvi. I 7.5–7). The marriages that end Menander's plays are—and
this is the definitive distinction between a wife and a concubine—
marriages that can provide the city with a new generation of sons. The
cult of romantic love in Menander is not a simple reflection of changing interpersonal relations in Athens. The magical trajectory of the
plays from erotic desire to marriage permits the reconciliation of many
basic oppositions and contradictions in Greek democratic life. I shall
describe briefly some of the levels on which the plays work.

There is an opposition between sexual licence and sexual prohibition. On the cosmic level, this can be termed an opposition between
Aphrodite and Artemis: the patroness of prostitution on the one

hand, the chaste moon goddess on the other who wounds the bride with her bow during childbirth. The scholiast on Theocritus ii.66b records that women in Menander call upon Artemis to forgive them for the loss of their virginity as they are being impregnated. Women in labour call upon Artemis at *Andria* frag. 3 K-T and at *Georgos* 112. There is a transition from anarchy to law when the rapist and the raped woman are reunited, when private violence gives way to marriage by contract. The rape usually takes place at a religious festival in honour of a savage deity such as Aphrodite, Artemis, or Dionysus. The plays thus bridge god and man, for the wedding is not sacramental but a civil manmade contract. The rape occurs because the god makes a man mad, but the wedding is undertaken through free choice. The human being who acts upon impulse is transformed into the citizen who acts rationally. In the rape, the man is enslaved to emotion, the woman is treated physically as if she were a slave, but in the finale the man and woman become free in both moral and status terms.

Foucault in his *History of Sexuality* requires us to see sexuality not as a drive but rather as a discourse. While Christian sexual ethics are concerned with purity, the main concern of the Greeks, for Foucault, was with self-control: 'The theme of virginity has nearly nothing to do with sexual ethics in Graeco-Roman asceticism. There the problem is a problem of self-domination. It was a virile model of self-domination, and a woman who was temperate was as virile to herself as a man.'[5] This concern with self-domination, so evident in the cult of homo-sexuality, is scarcely less evident in Menander, where homosexuality is conspicuous by its absence. The discourse is constant in Greek sex-ual ethics, and only the object of the discourse—the boy, the courte-san, the bride—changes. When the bride becomes the object of the discourse, however, questions of status immediately come into play, for marriage is only possible if the couple are both of legitimate stock.

What I wish to suggest is that Menander's plays are a way of talk-ing about self-domination—a necessary positive in the value-system of a slave society, where it matters to be free of soul as well as free of body. And the plays are also a way of talking about social status—about the restrictions which the institutions of the state placed upon people's freedom to act as they wished. It is this second theme that is new. Under the cosmopolitan Macedonian empire, the well-being of the city-state was no longer the ethical imperative that it had been in

---

[5] 'On the Genealogy of Ethics', 366.

the classical period. Menander's plays of romantic love provided a discourse capable of dealing with changing relations between the individual and the state.

If we can judge from the papyri that chance has extricated from the Egyptian desert, prostitutes play a relatively small part in Menander's plays. Though the idea of prostitution is important, prostitutes themselves do not dominate the stage. Important helping roles are played by a former *hetaira* turned concubine in *The Samian*, and by a slave *hetaira* in *The Arbitrants*. In two short papyri, the hero is in love with a *hetaira*, in the one case free, in the other a slave in danger of being sold to a nouveau-riche soldier, but we do not know how Menander resolved the plots. In general, young men in Menander undergo a change of character, young women undergo a change of status. The plays locate their heroines in a wide variety of different situations with respect to status, and prostitution is one possibility among many within the complex social system of democratic Greece.

I introduce the caveat 'if we can judge from the papyri' because we perceive a very different Menander if we come to him through the eyes of later Graeco-Roman culture. Ovid declared that Menander's work would survive for 'as long as the deceiving slave, the hard father, the shameless bawd, the persuasive prostitute' (*Amores* 1. 15). Athenaeus preserves for us a large selection of quotations from Menander on the theme of prostitution. And most important of all, Plautus and Terence chose to adapt for the Roman stage plays in which prostitution plays a central part in the plot. If we study Roman New Comedy as an independent form, and not as evidence for reconstructing a Greek form, then we see quickly that the focus of the Greek material upon rape and marriage is replaced by a new focus upon prostitution.

4

Love and Marriage in Greek New Comedy

P. G. McC. BROWN

Part of my purpose in this chapter is to advertise to an astonished world the variety of the plots of New Comedy. I shall then turn to some aspects of a related matter, the portrayal of prostitutes in Greek Comedy, starting from Plutarch's remarks about Menander at *Moralia* 712c. I do not offer a detailed account of the history, sociology or vocabulary of ancient prostitution, nor of the development of affairs with prostitutes as a theme of Comedy; I do not even have the space to give a full account of Menander's *Epitrepontes* and *Samia*, which portray a prostitute and an ex-prostitute respectively, or of other plays which may be (or have been) thought relevant. To some extent, this chapter represents a preliminary clearing of the ground, a task which has turned out to be larger than I expected when I began. But I hope that my discussion will shed some light on the ways in which prostitutes actually are portrayed in Greek New Comedy.

New Comedy as a whole has an undeserved reputation for monotony. It is symptomatic of the reputation of the genre that even scholars who know better are tempted to make false or misleading generalisations about it. No doubt at a deeper structural level the plots of New Comedy can be shown to display one basic pattern, in that love (of one kind or another) finally triumphs over obstacles (of one kind or another). What I wish to bring out is that there is greater variety on the surface than is generally allowed.

F. H. Sandbach's Oxford Classical Text of Menander includes eighteen plays of which more or less substantial remains have been discovered on papyrus, a selection of 'longer fragments preserved in other authors', some of which are attributed to a further fifteen named plays, and in addition papyrus fragments from seven Greek comedies of uncertain authorship. For many of these forty plays there is very little that we can say about their plots, in particular about the nature of the love-relationship. But at least nine of them probably or certainly show young Athenians in love, not with *hetairai*, 'freedwomen or slaves', but with women who are known or believed to be citizens by the world at large, and one possibly shows a Corinthian in the same situation. These include some of the best-preserved Menandrian plays (*Aspis*, *Dyskolos*, *Epitrepontes*, *Perikeiromene* and *Samia*). Of Plautus' twenty-one surviving plays, *Aulularia* shows an Athenian and *Cistellaria* a Sicyonian similarly in love with citizens, and four of Terence's six plays show Athenians in this situation.

Against these fifteen cases may be set perhaps as many as fourteen in which marriage with a girl is made possible only by the discovery that she is a citizen, six in plays by Menander, five by Plautus and three by Terence.

Apart from this simple statistical fact, there is the misleading impression that citizen parentage was enough to make a girl a suitable match, and that there were never any other obstacles to a love relationship in New Comedy than the (supposed) impossibility of a legal marriage. In fact there are cases in which a young man has promised to marry, or actually has married, a citizen girl of whom he expects his father to disapprove, although there is no dispute or ignorance about her identity. In others the girl is already known or believed to be a citizen, but a more precise identification removes the father's objection. We cannot always say why there is a difficulty at all in these cases, but whatever it was it was not the girl's legal status. Sometimes we know that the father has planned another marriage for his son, sometimes we may imagine the problem to be that the girl is poor, sometimes perhaps the young man is simply embarrassed to have to admit to his father that he has made her pregnant.

Furthermore, there are plays in which the obstacles to the course of true love are of a different kind altogether; in addition to plays in which the young man's problem is how to get his girl out of the hands of a pimp or a rival, or how to persuade *her* father, there are Menander's *Misoumenos* and *Perikeiromene*, where it is the relationship between the man and the woman themselves which has gone wrong and needs patching up. Davies rightly speaks of Menander's plots as showing an 'intense, even obsessive awareness of the status boundaries separating citizen from foreigner, citizen from slave, well-born from low-born, legitimate from illegitimate, wife from concubine, wealthy man from poor man from beggar'.[1] This is quite a number of different status boundaries, and it is not only status boundaries which cause problems for comic lovers.

It may be worth adding briefly some further examples of variety: Menander's *Heros* shows a slave in love, and Plautus' *Persa* is entirely devoted to this theme; in several plays the (or a) young man is recognised or identified; Plautus' *Amphitruo* shows the love of a god for a mortal woman, while his *Captivi* is not about love between males and females at all.

Some scholars believe that a legal marriage was essential for a happy ending in Greek New Comedy. This may not be altogether misleading, but it calls for further discussion. There are six plays of Plautus and three of Terence in which citizens continue affairs at the end of the play with girls who have not been recognised and identified as citizens and who have never been thought to be citizens; we do not have a clear case of this in Menander at first hand (the only complete final acts by Menander which we have are those of *Dyskolos* and *Samia*), but it is unlikely that either Habrotonon in *Epitrepontes* or the girl in *Kolax* turned out to be of citizen birth,[2] and it is quite possible that at least some of the nine Latin plays are faithful to their Greek originals in this respect.[3] However, *Epitrepontes* and the three plays of Terence contain more than one affair and do end with a marriage (or the restoration of a marriage) as well as with the continuation of an affair with a non-citizen girl; we cannot be sure that the same was not also true of *Kolax*, of whose plot we know very little. Is it significant that the only plays which certainly end without any focus on a legal marriage are Latin comedies by Plautus?

Wiles makes the following claim: 'If we study Roman New Comedy as an independent form, and not as evidence for reconstructing a Greek form, then we see quickly that the focus of the Greek material upon rape and marriage is replaced by a new focus upon prostitution.'[4] He acknowledges that prostitutes play a part in *Epitrepontes*

---

[1] J. K. Davies, 'Athenian Citizenship: The Descent Group and the Alternatives', *CJ* 73 (1977–8), 105–21, here 113.

[2] We do not know for certain that anyone continued an affair with either of these girls at the end of the play, but in both cases there are reasons for believing that they did so.

[3] Demeas and Chrysis continue to live together at the end of *Samia*, but Demeas is not a 'young man'.

[4] David Wiles, 'Marriage and Prostitution in Classical New Comedy', *Themes in Drama 11: Women in Theater* (Cambridge, 1989), 31–48, here 39. See pp. 42–52 of this volume.

and *Kolax*, and also in *Dis Exapaton*, the Menandrian original of
Plautus' *Bacchides*; and he mentions that Chrysis in *Samia* is a former
prostitute. But (quite apart from the fact that we only have 'a new
focus' if we can be sure that Plautus and Terence are not faithfully
reproducing the plots of their originals in the relevant cases—a difficulty which Wiles does not face up to),[5] he ignores a certain amount
of further evidence.

We know of Menandrian plays named after prostitutes (*Hymnis*,
Paidion, *Phanion* and *Thais* are probable or certain cases), his *Demiourgos*
included a prostitute, and a remark of Plutarch suggests that they
played a part in more comedies by Menander than we could have
guessed from the papyrus fragments which happen to have turned up
so far. This comes in a passage where Plutarch recommends
Menander's plays as suitable entertainment for married men at a
dinner party (*Moralia* 712c):

Even the erotic element in Menander is appropriate for men who when they
have finished drinking will soon be leaving to relax with their wives. For there
is no pederasty in all these plays, and the deflowerings of virgins end decently
in marriage. As for the prostitutes (*hetairai*), if they are audacious and bold,
the affairs are cut short by punishments of some kind or by repentance on the
part of the young man; but if they are good and return a man's love, either a
father is discovered for them who is a citizen.

In which case they will marry their young man—'or some extra
time is allowed for their affair, which brings a humane relationship of
respect'. Plutarch is arguing a case about the moral value of studying
Menander; he does not attempt to give a comprehensive survey of his
plots, and is not an adequate guide to them. But it is hard to believe
that he could have written this paragraph if prostitutes were not
found in quite a number of plays by Menander.

We thus cannot accept Wiles' claim that there is 'a new focus
upon prostitution' in Roman Comedy. Plutarch makes it clear that
not all Menandrian prostitutes were recognised as citizens and that
sometimes affairs with non-citizen prostitutes continued at the end
of a play by Menander, just as they do in Roman Comedy. It seems
likely that there was some satisfaction for the audience in seeing the
continuation of an affair with a 'good' prostitute. For the triumph of

---

[5] Few will accept the apparent implication (39 f.) that Terence has added the affairs
of Clitipho and Bacchis to *HT*, Phaedria and Thais to *Eun.* and Ctesipho and his girl to
Ad.

love which New Comedy shows us is not necessarily associated with marriage.

Caution requires me to add once again that it may (on our present evidence) have been peculiar to Plautus to end his plays with the triumph of this sort of love affair without also showing an affair which culminated in marriage. It is certainly striking (in comparison with the surviving Menandrian and Terentian material) how many of Plautus' plays are not concerned with citizen marriage. But I hope I have shown that, simply in terms of overall story-line, there is sufficient variety in the Greek material alone to discourage generalisations about it.

If we now turn to consider the portrayal of prostitutes in more detail, we may start by noting that scholars have sometimes tended to discuss characterisation in crude terms, putting women wherever possible into neat pigeon-holes, and thus (once again) obscuring the variety which is in fact to be found in the plays of New Comedy. An extreme instance of this tendency can be found in studies of Terence's *Self-Tormentor*, where for most of the play the prostitute Bacchis shows herself in her behaviour to be exactly as her lover describes her (227): 'overbearing, shameless, giving herself airs, extravagant, high and mighty.'

But there is one speech (381 ff.) which gives us quite a sympathetic insight into her feelings. Accordingly some scholars have suggested that in the Menandrian original of Terence's play Bacchis was more consistently portrayed in an unsympathetic light and that Terence has added her speech, or that in Menander's play she was consistently a 'good' prostitute and that it is Terence who has turned her into a 'bad' one. It is evidently hard for some to accept that Menander could have shown a prostitute as outrageously mercenary in her dealings with young men but reflective and self-aware in private conversation with another woman.

Plutarch's division of Menandrian prostitutes into two groups in the passage quoted above has perhaps not helped, nor the fact that Plautus and Terence speak of the 'wicked prostitute' as a stock character in Roman Comedy and Donatus praises Terence for presenting a 'good prostitute' who contrasts with the stock portrayal.[6] I shall suggest that we are more likely to do justice to these characters if we

---

[6] See Dwora Gilula, 'The Concept of the *bona meretrix*: A Study of Terence's Courtesans', *Riv. Fil.* 108 (1980), 142–65.

refrain from discussing them in such terms altogether. On the Greek side, the search for a 'good prostitute' has led some scholars to attach the label to women who are not prostitutes at all, here too obscuring the variety of the plots of New Comedy. I shall for the most part discuss Greek and Roman Comedy separately, and I shall start with further discussion of the Plutarch passage.

First, then, what sort of women is Plutarch talking about? *Hetaira* means 'female companion'. Fragment 21 K-A of Anaxilas (a little earlier than Menander) distinguishes a *hetaira* from a *pornē* ('common tart') and we also have a fragment of Antiphanes (210. 5–7 K-A), written at perhaps about the same time, which speaks of a *hetaira* with a 'golden disposition towards goodness', in contrast with the others who 'damage by their behaviour a name which is intrinsically a fine one'. Nonetheless, *hetaira* was also a general term for prostitutes, and *hetairai* were not always distinguished from *pornai*. We are told by Dionysius of Halicarnassus (*Ant.* 1. 84. 4), Plutarch (*Solon* 15. 2) and Athenaeus (13. 571D) that '*hetaira*' was simply a polite word for 'prostitute', and it did not necessarily convey a particularly close relationship. One striking fragment of Anaxilas (fr. 22. 1–7 K-A, from the same play as the fragment quoted above) describes the whole class of *hetairai* as surpassing in their monstrosity a she-dragon, a chimaera, Charybdis, Scylla, the Sphinx, the Hydra, a lioness, a viper and the Harpies; they are called *hetairai* in lines 1 and 31, but *porni* in line 22. Similarly, *hetaira* and *pornē* seem to be interchangeable terms at Diphilus fr. 42. 39 ff. K-A.

A variety of grounds is offered by some modern writers for distinguishing between *hetairai* and *pornai*, e.g. that the former were free, the latter slaves, or that *hetairai* were less promiscuous, or offered a longer-term relationship, or were better-educated or wealthier. Some of these distinctions doubtless held good in some circumstances, but I am not convinced that generalisations on these lines are very illuminating, and I have not seen a systematic study of the terminology (which would have to take account of the attitude of the speaker in many cases, as well as of any objective facts about the women's behaviour).

A *hetaira* (or a *pornē*) could be distinguished from a *pallakē*. The speaker of Pseudo-Demosthenes 59. 122, in a famous (and sometimes misrepresented) passage, distinguishes between *hetairai*, *pallakai* and wives: 'we have *hetairai* for pleasure, *pallakai* to care for the daily needs of our bodies, and wives (*gynaikes*) for the procreation of legitimate children and the trusty guardianship of our property.'[7] In the light of this, it may be disconcerting that Chrysis, the title-figure of Menander's *Samia*, a prostitute (or former prostitute) who is installed in the house of an Athenian citizen, is referred to as his *hetaira* at 130, his *pallakē* at 508, and his *gynē* (since *gynē* too is imprecise and can mean simply 'woman') at 561. But it is no doubt relevant that she was a *hetaira* in the past (cf. 21, 25); she may not have been installed in Demeas' house for very long, and her position there is not very secure, as the play shows. In other words, the transition from prostitute to concubine was not necessarily definitive and permanent, and it is not surprising that both terms can be used of her.

There is also no clear dividing line between a courtesan who is installed as one man's mistress, perhaps for quite a long period, and any other woman who happens to live with a man without being married to him (a line made harder to draw by the fact that payment in a commercial relationship can take the form of 'presents' rather than cash). But a *pallakē* had not necessarily been a prostitute and as far as I am aware it would not have been normal to refer to all *pallakai* as *hetairai*.

It would also be reasonable to include under this heading one Menandrian character who is not explicitly referred to as a *hetaira*, Habrotonon in *Epitrepontes*. She has been hired out as a harpist (*psaltria*) and is several times referred to as a *psaltria*. But *musiciennes* regularly provided sexual services for their customers, and Habrotonon clearly expected to do so in this case (cf. 431–41); Smikrines, who is hostile to her, calls her a *porne* at 646 and fr. 7.2 S. When someone says at 984 f. 'this is no *hetairidion*' (the diminutive form of *hetaira* presumably conveying 'no mere prostitute') he is probably speaking about her, and his remark suggests that it would be normal (though inappropriate in this case) to refer to a girl in her situation as a *hetaira*.

Once we allow that sexual pleasure could be associated in the minds of ancient Athenians with marriage as well as with other relationships, we shall perhaps be less tempted to lump those other relationships together. This is not to deny the interest of Menander's portrayals both of these girls and of their lovers; and it is perhaps possible that Plutarch did have cases like these in mind. If so, he used the term *hetaira* loosely and is to that extent unhelpful.

---

[7] The point is not that wives give Athenians no pleasure, but that only they can procreate children who will count as legitimate; the list is not exclusive but cumulative. This has been clearly stated (e.g. by W. K. Lacey *The Family in Classical Greece* (London 1968), 113) but is not always remembered.

In my view, Plutarch divides *hetairai* into two classes, as indicated
by his use of *men* ('on the one hand') and *de* ('on the other hand'); on
the one hand are the 'audacious and bold' ones, on the other those
who are 'good and return a man's love'. This latter class is further
subdivided into those who turn out to be daughters of a citizen father
and those who do not, but these are subdivisions of one class; the
description applies equally to both subdivisions. *Anterōsai* helps to
define *chrēstai*, the 'goodness' of this class of *hetairai* consists in their
returning a man's love rather than treating him with audacity and
boldness.

Plutarch is of course not suggesting that a citizen girl was in all circumstances expected to be in love with the man she married, but he
does suggest that if a prostitute in a play by Menander was going to
turn out to be a citizen she would be given a sympathetic characterisation and not portrayed as 'audacious and bold'. But it remains true
that such a girl has been functioning as a *hetaira* (even if her only
partner has been the man she is ultimately going to marry) and that
Plutarch calls her a *hetaira*. In any case it is simply untrue that
chrēstos is necessarily a social term.

The only other occurrences of the expression *hetaira chrēstē* known
to me (apart from the ironic use of *chrēstē* at Lucian, *Dialogi Meretricii*
12. 3) are at Alciphron 4. 3. 3, where the term clearly carries no social
implications, and in an anecdote of dubious historical value at
Athenaeus 13. 594d. According to this anecdote, Menander's contemporary, the comic playwright Philemon, once fell in love with a
hetaira and said in one of his plays that she was *chrēstē*; whereupon
Menander, who had fallen out with his mistress Glykera, retorted
that no *hetaira* was *chrēstē*. Whatever Philemon and Menander had
in mind in their use of the epithet, it is unlikely to have been the
social standing of *hetairai*.

The usage of *chrēstos* in Greek does not oblige us to believe that
Plutarch was aiming to distinguish three classes, and there is no
other reason to think that he was. Rather, as I have said, his second
class has two subdivisions, and the essential point about the girls in
this class is that they are genuinely in love with the man who loves
them. Also, by implication, they are not 'audacious and bold'.

If we look at other passages where favourable remarks are made
about *hetairai*, we shall find no very profound analysis. In Alciphron
the epithet *chrēstē* is not explained in any way. A character in
Antiphanes speaks of a *hetaira* with a 'golden disposition towards

goodness', but we do not know how this manifested itself. For the speaker in Anaxilas fr. 21 K-A, the true *hetaira* provides certain services *pros charin* to those who need them; this has been taken to mean 'free of charge'. But it cannot have been widely expected that a *hetaira* would make herself available to all and sundry for no financial return. In Alciphron 4.3, for instance, it is taken for granted that *hetairai* ask customers for money. Rather (unless the speaker is an eccentric character), *pros charin* means 'agreeably'; she provides her services in such a way as to give pleasure to her client, like the girl described in Ephippus fr. 6 K-A. At P.Koln 203, B 11 16 (published in *Kolner Papyri* 5 (Cologne 1985)) a girl is said to be 'sweet in her speech, a *hetaira* in her character', but this too tells us little.

'Audacious and bold' are not very informative epithets for the other class, but we can fill out the picture a little from Menander fr. 163 K-A, the one surviving passage from Greek Comedy where either epithet is applied to a prostitute. This is from the prologue to Menander's play named after the *hetaira* Thais:

> Then sing me, Muse, of such a one as she,
> a woman bold, but pretty and persuasive,
> who wrongs men, shuts them out, begs many gifts,
> loves none, but ever acts a loving part.

We need not doubt that this was the sort of behaviour that Plutarch had in mind.

If Plutarch is to be believed, then, Menander portrayed two types of *hetaira*, those who are 'audacious and bold' and those who are 'good and return a man's love'. This is too crude and schematic an account (not least because a *hetaira* must have been obliged by the conditions of her trade to make herself at least occasionally agreeable to her man, as is acknowledged by the speaker of Amphis fr. 1 K-A), but we can accept the basic point that not all of Menander's *hetairai* were portrayed in the same way. It looks as if Menander was working within established comic traditions in this, since earlier playwrights had spoken of *hetairai* in a variety of ways. We cannot say whether one type had previously prevailed over the other, or whether Athenian audiences had any particular expectations about the portrayal of prostitutes, in the way that they perhaps expected cooks and soldiers to be boastful.

It has been suggested that Menander in particular developed the portrayal of the *hetaira chrēsté*, and that he did so to characterise girls who were going to turn out to be citizens and eligible for marriage at the end of the play. But we cannot say much about the part played by *hetairai* in the plots of earlier fourth-century plays which are lost, and there is no reason to think that Menander reserved a favourable characterisation for those destined to be recognised as citizens—particularly not if Plutarch is accepted as in any way reliable evidence for his plots (and if I have interpreted him correctly).

It would be interesting to know whether the masks worn by the actors contributed anything to the expectations of Menander's audience. Pollux's catalogue of the masks of young women in New Comedy (compiled in the second century AD) lists separate masks for the *pallakē*, the 'full-grown *hetaira*', the 'little youthful *hetaira*', the 'golden *hetaira*', the '*hetaira* with a headband' and the 'little torch', as well as two separate masks for the *pseudokore*, who is sometimes taken (in spite of the etymology) to be a prostitute or concubine who will turn out to be of citizen birth. Pollux does not tell us what (if anything) these different masks were supposed to convey about the different women they represented; they are distinguished by their hairstyle or by varying amounts of adornment, and Pollux does not suggest that they were used to mark any differences in characterisation.

It is interesting that there is a separate mask for a *pallakē*, but we have no way of telling whether Chrysis in *Samia* would have worn this or one of the *hetaira*-masks—even if we accept Pollux's list as evidence for the range of masks available to Menander, which is debatable. It is possible that the choice of a particular mask aroused the expectation in Menander's audience that a character would be portrayed in a certain way; if so, our ignorance of which characters wore which masks deprives us of all important clues to the effect of the plays in performance. But I have argued elsewhere that this is unlikely. (On costume apart from masks we are even less well informed; nor can we say much about these matters in connexion with the Roman stage.)

Sadly, after these extended preliminaries, there is very little in the surviving Menandrian material that we can check against Plutarch's remarks about *hetairai* at *Moralia* 712C. Prostitutes do not play a large part in the plays which happen to have been rediscovered so far, and we do not have a single case where we know that an affair with an 'audacious and bold' *hetaira* was cut short at the end of the play. *Hetairai* played a part in *Kolax* and *Sikyonios*, but we cannot say how they were characterised; and most other plays which contained *hetairai* (such as *Thais*) are too fragmentary for us to discuss them. If it is accepted that the heroines of *Misoumenos* and *Perikeiromene* are not *hetairai*, we are left only with Chrysis in *Samia* and Habrotonon in *Epitrepontes*. But neither of these is in the situation envisaged by Plutarch of women having an affair with an unmarried young man (who is expected to marry a citizen girl sooner or later). Chrysis is living with an Athenian of the older generation who will presumably never marry, and Habrotonon is having an affair with a recently married man who must return to his wife to achieve the play's desired happy ending.

Furthermore, Plutarch's epithets for *hetairai* are beside the point in these two cases. Chrysis is certainly not 'audacious and bold' (in the sense in which Plutarch is likely to have meant these terms), and in her current situation as Demeas' mistress it would be surprising if she were. Whether she returns his love is something about which we can only speculate, she plays a much smaller part in the play than do Demeas and his adopted son Moschion. She is wrongly suspected by Demeas, and we are glad to see their relationship continue at the end of the play. But hers is not the sort of continuing relationship that Plutarch had in mind.

Similarly, Habrotonon cannot be described as 'audacious and bold' in her relationship with Charisios (although she does perhaps deserve these epithets in a more favourable sense); she does not get a chance to display these or any other qualities in her love life with him, since (although he has hired her) he displays a strange lack of interest in her. Thus she does not get a chance to 'return his love' either, and we might in any case not expect her to do this, since she has been hired out to him for a fee by her slave-owner. At the end of the play, it is generally believed that she was given her freedom and started up in a relationship with another man altogether; her relationship with Charisios is indeed 'cut short', but there is no point in trying to fit her into either of Plutarch's categories.

A scrap of evidence from the second century AD, first published in 1970, seems to suggest that at least one ancient reader of Menander was able to free himself from reliance on crude categories. This is a plot summary of a play by Menander (perhaps his *Demiourgos*);[8] the papyrus is in a fragmentary state, but it looks as if at one point a

---

[8] *P1 FAO* 3375=Menander, *Demiourgos* testimonium iv K-A.

woman is said to be 'bold but not bad', and that woman is perhaps most likely to have been a *hetaira*.

Since some scholars have regarded Habrotonon as entirely self-interested, it may be worth saying a little more about her. In the course of the play she pretends to be the mother of a baby which has been found exposed in the countryside. She does this as a way of establishing who is the father of the baby. She is quite explicit at 548 f. that she wants to obtain her own freedom as a reward, but this is at the end of a lengthy discussion which began with a clear indication that she wants to help both the baby and its parents (468–70). The discussion has been dominated by the laying of her plan; it is only at the end that her more selfish motivation is emphasised, and it is the slave Onesimos (who has no very high opinion of her motives) who first suggests it at 538–40. It is no criticism of her to say that she has selfish motives.

But one way in which she stands out as a character is by the contrast between what we know of her motives and behaviour and what other people say about them. As well as Onesimos, fr. 7 K-A of the play shows her being discussed by Smikrines in typically hostile terms: 'It is difficult, Pamphile, for a free-born woman to compete with a prostitute. She does more mischief, she has more tricks up her sleeve, she has no shame and is more wheedling.' In fact Habrotonon's merits stand out by their contrast with this generalised picture of prostitutes, as appears to be recognised by the speaker of 984 ff.

We may call these women 'good', if we like, in the sense that there is more to be said for them than other characters allow. But by now we have left Plutarch far behind.

5
Tragic Space and Comic Timing in Menander's *Dyskolos*

N. J. LOWE

Two lifetimes of continuous theatrical development separate the *Oresteia* of 458 BC and the *Dyskolos* of 316; we possess some forty complete scripts from the first half of this period and (perhaps excepting the *Rhesus*) none from the second. And yet, in the evidential void between the death of Aristophanes and our earliest extant Menander, something remarkable happens. The comic theatre that re-emerges to view with Menander's *Dyskolos* has adopted the basic stagecraft not of its ancestral fifth-century form, with its easy plasticity of space and time, but of late fifth century Attic tragedy—which purports, at least, to represent place and action realistically, and has evolved a sophisticated matrix of latent significance around the boundaries and oppositions constructed by its setting. There are fourth-century extensions and refinements—the development of asides, the three-door *skene*, the vastly elaborated system of entrance motifs—but even these are developments out of the performance conventions of Euripidean tragedy, rather than radical departures in the direction of a new theatrical grammar. This comic colonisation of tragedy's signifying space is fundamental to New Comedy's theatrical poetics: the structure it gives to the world it professes to mirror.

The *Dyskolos* is the earliest dateable text from which we can assess the New Comic stagecraft; but it has long been recognised, in this as in so much else, as an atypical specimen of its genre. Not only does it use all three of the available scene doors, where two seems to be much more Menander's norm, but it is unique in its dramatic location, and the abundance of topographic details with which the scene is fleshed out. Other plays had village settings (*Heauton Timoroumenos*, *Epitrepontes*, *Heros*, perhaps *Sikyonios*), but the only functional parallel for this remote country locale is the even more extraordinary North African seashore of Diphilus' *Rudens*. In any case, the *Dyskolos* is remarkable for its use of a real location, the Nymphaeum at Phyle in the foothills of the Parnes ridge. There are precedents in fifth-century tragedy and comedy for a known histori- cal building, always a sanctuary, as the backdrop to the action, but this is our only New Comic example. Why such a setting, and why does this comedy spend more attention on topographical detail than any other extant Greek play?

At the back of the stage there are three houses, the central one standing for the Nymphaeum (grotto of the nymphs), here conceived as a shrine on a village street rather than a cleft in the rocks. This is the door from which Pan emerges to speak the prologue, and into which he probably retires on the arrival of Sostratus and his parasite Chaereas at 49–50. The shrine is empty, save for its unseen divine inhabitants, but sooner or later everyone in the main body of the play will find themselves passing through that door. Inside is a spring, which will play a small but decisive role in the plot at 197. One of the two doors flanking the shrine, probably the left, is Cnemon's house, which he shares with his housekeeper Simiche and his unnamed daughter by his marriage to Myrrhine. As the action unfolds, this door will develop into a cumulative running gag and at the same time a dramatic symbol of Cnemon's misanthropic exterior, as character after character is innocently drawn to knock on its lethal facade.

The interior of Cnemon's house is drawn in some detail: there is an inner yard with a well and a large pile of dung, presumably for manur- ing, waiting to be moved when Cnemon has the time. Both of these details are dramatically functional, for the inner yard is the unseen location of a crucial intermittent background subplot, whose phases are artfully interleaved with the stage action. At first merely an amus- ing distraction, this chain of small calamities behind the scenes will gradually converge to the turning-point of the main story. On the other side of the Nymphaeum is the third house, inhabited by Cnemon's stepson Gorgias, the latter's mother, Myrrhine, and their household slave Daos. Thus the two households into which the divided family has split are mirror images, just as their houses are symmetrically located on either side of the stage: father, daughter, and female slave in the left, mother, son, and male slave in the right. The long-term strategy of the stage movement is to reunite these characters and these households on the neutral intermediate territory of the Nymphaeum.

This initial system of relationships, and its final spatial and social unification, is thematically paramount. These somewhat elaborate family structures are typical of Menander, who likes to focus on the subtle tensions and relational complexities generated by the comparatively widespread practice of remarriage, adoption, and (in other plays) concubinage among the propertied classes. It is not a gratuitous naturalistic detail that Gorgias should be Myrrhine's son by an earlier marriage. Cnemon, who has no male issue of his own, has never formally adopted Gorgias, a detail which has two important consequences.

First, Gorgias has no testamentary claim on Cnemon's estate. In the event of Cnemon's decease, his daughter will become *epikleros* (heiress) with the two-talent *chorion* or plot of land. In the absence of eligible male kin, she and the property must by law then pass outside the family. Gorgias, though a half-brother, is related only in the female line and cannot therefore qualify as her *kyrios* (guardian). This is a tense prospect for all involved: for Cnemon because the estate will be alienated, and for Gorgias and Myrrhine because it leaves them with no prospect of escape from their current burden of poverty. The play is carefully silent on Cnemon's other kin, if any; his isolation (*eremia*) has estranged him not merely from society but from the universal systems of kinship on which society and law are founded.

Secondly, Gorgias' status leaves his obligations towards Cnemon and the daughter ambiguously defined. Legally Gorgias is not acknowledged as Cnemon's heir; he is therefore not bound by the reciprocal requirement upheld in Attic law for a son to care for his natural or adoptive parents. The play is at pains to stress that Gorgias is under no obligation whatever to save Cnemon's life (724–9; contrast 239–46) and has no authority even to safeguard the honour of his sister—who has been left vulnerable, by Cnemon's stubbornly self-imposed lifestyle, to any predatory seducer or legacy-hunter who chooses the daytime, when Cnemon is away at his plot, to make his approach. Gorgias' intervention to protect her from Sostratus is an act of pure family feeling, the more admirable because it goes beyond any strict legal obligation, conflicts with his own need to secure a living by spending time in the fields, and fulfils a duty or protection that ought by rights to be filled by Cnemon. At the same time, it evokes an uneasy state of relations in which basic elements of the traditional family order have been cancelled or problematised. All these uncertainties are resolved at a stroke, as we know dramatically they must, when Cnemon formally announces (731 f.) *pooumai s'hyon*, 'I adopt you as my son'. But Menander has been characteristically careful to explore the human consequences with extraordinary psychological and ethical sensitivity in advance of that resolution.

Offstage left probably runs up into the Parnes foothills: the 'public road' of 115 and 162. Out of sight up the road—we perhaps should not take Pyrrhias's two miles seriously (118)—lie two plots of farmland. In what appears to have been the normal pattern of settlement in rural demes, the residential community is geographically separated from the main agricultural land; like Menedemus in the *Self-Tormentor*, Gorgias must trek out along the public road to work their fields, a journey that removes him from the village during the normal working day. The larger plot belongs to Cnemon, and is worth two talents: an absurd size of estate to farm single-handed as Cnemon does. The smaller estate, which abuts Cnemon's, belongs to the impoverished Gorgias. The play chooses not to explain this arrangement, but an Athenian audience alert to such matters might infer that Gorgias' plot once formed part of a single property with Cnemon's lands, presumably inherited through Myrrhine his mother, the bulk of whose land went in dowry to Cnemon. Whatever the reason, the family estates compose a divided space offstage mirroring the divided household onstage; and once again the two halves of the family property are spatially united following Cnemon's recantation. (Cnemon's own instructions (737 ff.) are that half the property should be given as dowry with his daughter; but Sostratus has long since (308) refused a dowry, and at 846 f. Callippides explicitly forbids further division of the *chorion*.)

Offstage right is the road out of Phyle, passing Callippides' three-talent country estate before dipping into the Cephissus valley to the populous deme of Cholargus and eventually south towards Athens. From this offstage source Menander releases artfully-timed waves of characters from Sostratus' family. First Sostratus himself comes north on a hunt with his parasite Chaereas and Pyrrhias his slave; then Sostratus' mother has an ominous dream from Pan, and unknown to her son sends her slave Getas to organise a cook while she assembles a sacrificial party to trek out to the shrine. By the time Sostratus comes looking for Getas at home, he and the party have both left by different roads, so that the order of arrival at the Nymphaeum runs (i) Sostratus; (ii) Sicon, followed closely by (iii) Getas; (iv) mother with main party, and finally and long anticipated (v) Callippides, the family head, all the way from Athens.

This opposition of stage exits, as already indicated, is a usage familiar from fifth-century tragedy. But though tensions between country and city are important to the *Dyskolos* (or more accurately to the character of Sostratus), it must be stressed that the class barrier between the families of Sostratus and his intended is considerably more subtle than a simple division between urban rich and rural poor. Though Sostratus himself is 'a city boy', *astikos tei diatribei* (41), his father Callippides is a country proprietor whose farm is evidently close enough to Phyle to be visited between acts. Callippides himself, though his estate is farmed by slaves, can still be described as 'a peerless farmer', *georgos amachos* (775), and (presumably in this capacity) known to Gorgias by sight (773). No irony seems intended, such as we do find at 754 f. when the *astikos* Sostratus is introduced as *georgos* on the basis of his morning's work in the fields.

On the other side, Cnemon's harsh and frugal way of life is a direct, and correctable, consequence of his misanthropic temperament, as are the hardships it visits on his kin. A two-talent estate is not uncommon among the clients of orators; Cnemon is by fourth-century standards a comparatively wealthy landowner, though clearly not in the same bracket as Callippides, whose estate of six talents or more would place him within the wealthier ranges of the speechwriters' clientele. As Gorgias observes at 327–31, Cnemon (unlike his stepson) is a labourer by choice rather than necessity.

Cnemon, in fact, is a social, as well as a human, aberration: like Euclio in the *Aulularia*, a self-imposed exile from human society whose wealth is witheld from his family by his own decision. Thus the social barriers in the *Dyskolos* are less divisions of class per se than of wealth, demography, and lifestyle, in which the familiar town/country polarities are subjected to a complex system of subversions and mediations.

For these reasons, the scenic setup has far more to explore than a traditional opposition between town and country, although this is undoubtedly an element. The hillward path does connect the scene with the hard country life, to which Cnemon has condemned himself and his family, while the Cholargus road leads away to the world of urban sophistication and leisured wealth from which Sostratus is gradually weaned and to which the shallow parasite Chaereas, an irredeemably urbane type, disappears never to return. But this horizontal axis of the play space also assimilates a second pair of oppositions of far more central concern to the dramatic movement.

The Cholargus road brings the *ochlos* or 'mob' that Cnemon so shuns: Sostratus and his hunting party, Sicon and Getas with the sheep, and finally the whole picnic party under Sostratus' mother.[1] Out in the hills above Phyle, however, human society ends. There alone Cnemon can find the *eremia* he craves; there is his personal *chorion* where no human, slave or free, is permitted to tread.

Not surprisingly, the play's attitude to this overlay of polarities is complex. Cnemon's stern nature and rustic isolation, condemned by Pan, paradoxically make his daughter more desirable for her naive and sheltered modesty (202): she is 'rustic (*agroikos*) in a ladylike *(eleutherios)* sort of way', the normally pejorative term *agroikos* covering qualities that an urban bachelor values highly in a bride. The words are closely echoed at 387–8, in a speech where Sostratus develops his earlier thought more fully: although Cnemon is 'wild' (*agrios*), he is also 'an enemy of vice' (*misoponeros*), as we learn from Cnemon himself in his remarkable *apologia* at 718–21.

Cnemon's misanthropy, it turns out, is motivated by a loss of moral faith in his fellow humanity—a faith that can consequently be restored by Gorgias' single refuting act of unselfishness. Down the Cholargus road, therefore, lie not only the urban life Cnemon despises but also and equally the communal vices of the human world on which he has tried to turn his back. Up in the solitary rocks of Parnes by contrast, Cnemon can find an ideal of rustic virtue in *eremia* and self-sufficiency. To the romantic *astikos*, such an idyll might hold a powerful attraction; but Menander resists it by counterpointing fantasy with grim reality. Those who, like Gorgias, cannot choose their lifestyle hold a less happy perspective on the smallholding life; those who, like Sostratus, give it a try find that the romance quickly palls under the weight of a humble mattock; while Cnemon himself, far from achieving a life of simple and exemplary purity, is so warped by his puritanical isolation that he can no longer recognise the good in his fellow human. To reconcile these intricate conflicts, the *Dyskolos* draws on a second major element in the visual semantics of the inherited tragic space: a dimension of meaning additional and perpendicular to the left–right axis of the contrasted parodoi. If Cnemon is provoked by violation of his *chorion*, *his* personal space in the opposition of urban *ochlos* to rural *eremia*, so much the more is he enraged

---

[1] The word *ochlos* comes six times in the play, always with a strong sense of irony and thematic placement (7, 8, 166, 405, 432, 932). Its adverse sense emerges more strongly in the verbal compound *enochlein*, 'pester', another keyword: so at 157, 199, 232, 374, 458, 491, 680, 693, 750.

by further violations of the boundary between the private space behind his door and the public space out there on the stage. The cumulative comic and thematic importance of the scenes at Cnemon's door has already been mentioned. At 81 Pyrrhias pelts onto the stage after outrunning the pursuing Knemon, and pauses momentarily in his flight to warn Sostratus (87) 'let's get away from that door there' with comic illogic, as he knows Cnemon is still behind him offstage. He knocked there once (97), and though he only found Simiche at home the door is now an ominous emblem for him. Sostratus seems to mistake Pyrrhias' advice because Cnemon enters to find him 'in front of the door' (167), and in response to Sostratus' weak excuse about having arranged to meet someone there he stakes his claim to the doorway as his own personal space more clearly at 174 ('in front of my door'). The next knock at the door is narrowly thwarted (247): 'if he catches me approaching the door' (says Daos) 'he'll hang me on the spot.'

The confrontation is averted in the nick of time by the unexpected reappearance of Sostratus, who now announces *he* is going to knock on the door (267 f.); but his knock too is frustrated, by the intervention of Gorgias with his magnificently off beam moralising. At the beginning of Act 3 (427), Cnemon tries to leave his house again, with instructions to Simiche , 'lock the door and open it to nobody'. The punchline anticipated by this long sequence of teasers is finally delivered when first the unsuspecting Getas and then the insouciant Sicon each knock in turn and are confronted by Cnemon in full blast. 'The women told me to knock at your door,' is Getas' hasty excuse (476 f.); 'I've done that.' 'I'll make an example for all about,' Cnemon announces at 483 f., 'of the next man to approach my door'; and then, as soon as the door is closed, enter Sicon to do just that. The door recurs as an object of terror at 586: 'now he's rattling the door', shrieks Simiche, in flight from the house as Cnemon emerges in pursuit.

But when the noise is next heard at 689 f., its significance is quite inverted: Cnemon makes his entry prone, apparently wheeled out on a mobile couch.[2] The inversion is completed in the final scene, where in a strangely sadistic musical finale Sicon and Getas avenge

---

[2] K. B. Frost, *Exits and Entrances in Menander* (Oxford: Clarendon Press, 1988), 58. A minority of editors (Jacques, Sandbach, Arnott) have argued for the *ekkyklema* in this scene; but its use in New Comedy remains very uncertain, and the preparatory dialogue lacks the interiority cue normal in tragedy: O. Taplin, *The Stagecraft of Aeschylus*: *The Dramatic use of Exits and Entrances in Greek Tragedy* (Oxford, 1977), 240.

themselves on the crippled Cnemon by carrying him out of his house unconscious, then torment him by pounding on his door (899, 922) to pipe accompaniment while Cnemon lies helpless to intervene. He finds himself stranded in the public space of the open stage, truly *eremos* at last, while his precious door is violated with loutish battering and his house threatened with burglary.

Yet the play does not end on this harshly farcical upswing. Throughout the play Cnemon's private interior is opposed by the other major indoor space of the play, the capacious sanctuary of the adjacent Nymphaeum. Pan, the god *par excellence* of isolated places and rocky country landscapes, has drawn each of the dozen major characters' plotlines to finish up together under his roof, and irresistibly his influence has intervened at decisive moments to draw the families together. It was the daughter's piety towards Pan that moved the god to set the plot in motion (36 ff.), and an act of piety that brought her out of doors as Sostratus was passing, for him to see her and fall in love (50–2). The garlands she hung then at the entrance to the shrine are presumably still visible at the opening of the play, a concrete token of her devotion. Pan has also sent a dream to Sostratus' mother (407 ff.) to draw the rest of the family to the site just when they will be needed for the betrothal; and Pan's spring supplies the opportunity for Sostratus and the girl to meet for the first time face to face (197 ff.). When the sacrificial party arrives, not only Sostratus' family but also the long-divided household of Cnemon is funnelled into the Nymphaeum, as what began as a propitiatory sacrifice becomes first a betrothal feast and then a full-fledged symposium with *kōmos*. Only Cnemon remains aloof from the festivities, pathetic and alone. His Act 4 recantation has changed nothing; he has lost his conviction of autonomy, but the *eremia* of his life persists in his self-pitying isolation from the party going on next door.

The misanthrope's reform will only be completed once Cnemon can be made to pass voluntarily through that door and inside the shrine to be voluntarily reintegrated into the social world and the newly extended family from which he can no longer withhold. He makes that long-delayed entry propped up by three torch-bearing slaves and forcibly supplied with a garland, a reluctant but consenting participant in the victory *kōmos*. 'We've won', says Getas at 958, and punctuates the point by dropping immediately back into trimeters for the last lines, an unusually apposite twist on the conventional appeal for victory in the dramatic contest.

But this map of the play's dramatic topography leaves out the essential extra dimension that turns a latently symbolic space into an organic theatrical process. All the spatial techniques discussed above are part of the heritage of fifth-century tragic convention: the thematic opposition of left and right, inside and out, the extension of the stage world into fictive offstage spaces, the use of exit and entrance as moments of special significance in the traversal of spatial and symbolic boundaries, the elaborate patterns of frustrated exits and repeated or role-reversed echoes of previous action. What is largely new in Menander, and particularly remarkable in this play, is the elaborate plotting of simultaneous on and offstage *time*, in the service of the kind of ironic synchronicity that New Comedy has bequeathed to the mainstream European comic tradition.

Excluding Pan, the chorus, and the non-speaking *ochlos* attending Sostratus' mother, there are twelve characters in the *Dyskolos*. This is only one more than in the *Phoenissae* and *Rhesus*; but the quantitative comparison is misleading, for Menander's characters lead vastly more complicated offstage lives. In the *Dyskolos*, up to ten offstage locations can be occupied at any time. Consider, for example, the moment of the first chorus at 232 f., reading north to south. Cnemon's field is now empty and will remain so for the rest of the play, but it remains the goal of his frustrated attempts to leave the house. Gorgias' field is currently occupied by Gorgias and the newly-arrived Daos, come to tell him he has just seen a man making eyes at Gorgias' sister. Cnemon's house is fully tenanted by Cnemon, Simiche, and the daughter, while Pan's shrine is empty for now and Gorgias' house holds his mother Myrrhine. Offstage right, Sostratus has reached his father's estate in search of Getas, only to find that Getas has gone in search of a cook and his mother has taken a party out to sacrifice somewhere. All these characters are already on their way towards the Nymphaeum, but their paths fail to cross twice, on Sostratus' way home and on his way back. (Menander is wisely not too explicit on the routes here, nor on the precise nature of the day's movements for Callippides.) Finally, we should not forget, although by this stage in the play we are supposed to, the townslave and parasite Pyrrhias and Chaereas, now on the long road back to the city after the unexpected turn taken by their morning's hunt.

Some of these invisible lines of continuity are simply there to serve the cumulative texture of naturalism, the illusion of a world that continues to exist outside the fragment made visible in the theatre.

Others, however, are more directly functional. We have already remarked on the unfolding significance of events in Cnemon's inner yard, which emerge to view at occasional moments, but link into a continuous thread of escalating chaos. During Cnemon's absence in the fields, the old housekeeper Simiche has inadvertently dropped the bucket down the well (190 f.). Before anything can be done, Cnemon returns home unexpectedly (178), having pursued Sostratus' trespassing slave Pyrrhias with missiles all the way home from the field. Not unnaturally, he asks for hot water (193), and his daughter, terrified of his anger when he finds out the truth, has to sneak out to draw water from the only other available source in the neighbourhood, the spring in the Nymphaeum (195–7).

Her natural hesitation offers Sostratus the opportunity of making her acquaintance by fetching the water himself (199 f.); this is the scene witnessed out of context by Daos, whose misinterpretation of the scene (212 ff.) requires Gorgias to be fetched home from the field, an event which in turn leads to Sostratus' fateful day's digging. Cnemon is then unexpectedly prevented from leaving the house again (442–55) by the arrival of the sacrificial party led by Sostratus' mother, and with the old man confined to housework the missing bucket becomes an increasing embarrassment. Between 215 and 575, Simiche attempts secretly to fish the bucket out with the mattock (*dikella*) Cnemon brought home with him. Unfortunately she only succeeds in dropping the mattock in as well (576–82), and when Cnemon in the course of his housework decides to shovel up the dung he finds his mattock has disappeared. After chasing Simiche round the stage and in again (588–601), he tries to climb into the well to retrieve mattock and bucket himself, only to slip and fall deep into the well (625–8); which requires Cnemon's rescue by his estranged stepson, and teaches him the futility of his dogged attempts at independence.

The early links in this chain of background mishaps are introduced with deceptive casualness, but they connect into a subplot of central narrative function and sly thematic significance. Cnemon's disaster is directly seen to be the fault of his own character: if the members of his household were less terrorised, they would have confessed the accident and the mattock would not have been lost in the first place. Lying as it does on the far side of Cnemon's terrifying front door, the backyard action makes Cnemon himself a victim and prisoner of the personal territory he has so aggressively defended.

Not all such offstage timelines are sustained with the same degree of dramatic care,[3] but it is remarkable nevertheless how far Menander is prepared to go in motivating and accounting for the offstage lives of his characters, particularly when an entrance or encounter is opportune for the characters and necessary for the plot. The movements of Sostratus are a particularly interesting case in point. Like other irresolute lovers in New Comedy, he spends a good deal of time wandering aimlessly back onstage, first at 260 and again after his transformation at 522. 'The business keeps dragging me back to this place', he remarks with fine irony at 545. *Pragma* ('business') is a favourite with Sostratus, who uses it specially of the 'business' of the plot (56, 180, 183, 186, 217, 392, 545, 860); while *topos* ('place') was the word used to identify the stage setting by Pan in the first line, and it is consistently so used of the miniature stage neighbourhood five more times in the play (43, 330, 508, 517, 609). Sometimes, as in 609, there seems a wordplay intended in the use of *atopos* or *ektopos*, 'extraordinary'. 'So you think I'm doing something out of place (*ektopos*) now?' is Sostratus' reply to Gorgias' key speech at 271–87. 'I'm extraordinarily (*ektopos*) fond of you,' Gorgias tells Sostratus (825) when offered the chance to marry out of his situation, 'but I don't want affairs (*pragmata*) too big for me' (825–6).

Sostratus, in fact, seems *particularly* sensitive to the metadramatic ironies of other people's timing. 'In a way,' he observes at 557–8, 'the sacrifice here has not been ill-timed' (*akairos*). When Cnemon falls conveniently down the well, 'By the gods,' is Sostratus' comment at 677 ff., 'I've never seen in my life a man more opportunely (*eukairoteron*) close to drowning.' 'I see my father approaching,' he says of Callippides' long-awaited arrival just as the plot seems to be wrapping up, 'with perfect timing' (*eis kalon*, 773). 'Have you finished eating?' asks Callippides. 'Yes,' says Sostratus, 'but we've kept a share for you.'

Yet Sostratus himself is ironically enough the character whose timing is most in need of adjustment. New Comic lovers are traditionally disabled from decisive individual action; they depend on the machinations of their slaves and friends to achieve their desires for them. But the *Dyskolos* flirts with this type of action only to dismiss it

---

[3] T. B. L. Webster, 'Menander: Production and Imagery', *Bull. of the John Rylands Library*, 4S (1962), 235–72, at 237–9; W. G. Arnott, 'Time, Plot and Character in Menander', *Papers of the Liverpool Latin Seminar*, 2 (1979), 343–60 at 349.

emphatically. A town slave and parasite are imported from the alien world of urban comedy only to fail dismally in the very first act. 'I've enlisted you for this *pragma*,' Sostratus tells Chaereas at 56, 'because I judged you particularly sympathetic and *praktikos*.' 'So I am,' replies Chaereas; and he describes two stereotypical plotlines from urban comedy in which he has a well-defined role to play: love-affairs with *hetairai*, marriages with free virgins in which the parasite's role is one of capable intelligence-gathering. 'Yes, wonderful,' says Sostratus; 'but that's not altogether what I want.' Chaeres is then banished from the play: 'a sense of timing is more *praktikos* for every *pragma*', he explains at 128 f., and announces that he will not be back that day, meaning we will not see him again in this play.[4] Left apparently resourceless, Sostratus decides to put the *pragma* in the hands of Getas, described as 'expert in all kinds of *pragmata*' (183 f.); but he finds on his trek back to the family farm that Getas is unavailable, and in a typologically extraordinary moment declares on re-entry 'I think I'll put aside these wanderings (*peripatoi*) and do my own talking on my own behalf' (266 f.). Only the intervention of Gorgias keeps him from a fatal knock at Cnemon's door—an action the more remarkable because Sostratus, unlike some others, is already acquainted with the likely consequences.

Sostratus has still to learn, however, that he must put aside his *peripatoi* in a more fundamental sense. *Astikoi*, as the aggrieved Gorgias points out at 294, are distinguished from *agroikoi* above all by their *scholē*, their freedom to use time as they wish. Cnemon's daughter, when first we meet her, has no free time (196) to dawdle onstage— unlike the loitering Sostratus, watching from aside. The connection between Sostratus' wealth and his leisure is central to the plot: 'if Cnemon sees you leisured and spoiled (356 f.) he won't even give you a glance.' In fact Cnemon and Sostratus have already met, and Cnemon has indeed identified Sostratus as a city idler, sarcastically demanding whether he has confused Cnemon's house with the famous Agora haunts of his class (193 ff.). But on their second encounter they meet as strangers.

The Sostratus Cnemon sees is no longer leisured and soft: at 755 he is presented, in a close echo of 356 f., as 'not spoiled or the sort of man

---

[4] For similar remarks, drawing point from the unity of time in New Comedy, cf. 71, 540, 571, 851 (with the supplement *aurion* following ed. pr.), 864; and see in general the discussion of Arnott, 'Time, Plot and Character'.

to wander lazily around all day'. Cnemon, like Getas before him, fails to recognise the tanned, cloakless labourer as the urbane dilettante he earlier banished from his door, and this time admits him to the heart of his *oikos* by accepting him for betrothal to his daughter. Timing has a special importance, however, to the lugubrious Gorgias, much the most complex and sensitively-drawn character in the play. 'I think', he announces at 271 f., 'that for all men, prosperous and stricken alike, there is some kind of limit (*peras*) and turning-point *metallagē*) to this fortune. . . Whenever someone is led by his riches into wrongdoing, he takes the *metabolē* for the worse.' This extraordinary outburst is announced as a 'rather serious speech' (269–70), and predictably sends Stobaeus reaching for the scissors oblivious to the deep ironic undercurrents. Circumstances have bred in Gorgias a pronounced tendency to moralise, not always to the point. We know even as we hear these solemn words that Gorgias has misapprehended Sostratus' intentions, and his diatribe at 289–98 is wildly off target, entailing a hasty and abashed apology as soon as the astonished Sostratus can get a word in to explain himself. Gorgias' suspicion of Sostratus is deeply rooted in his obsessive preoccupation with the injustices of wealth, and even after he has accepted the stranger's integrity he clings fiercely to his flat moralising insistence that honest poverty is ultimately rewarded while wealth and the wealthy are not to be trusted. He pours scorn on all Sostratus' plans to approach Cnemon, reiterating his glum resignation to the injustices of *tyche* (p. 340). The suggestion that Sostratus transform himself into a *georgos* comes not from Gorgias but in a spirit of mischief from Daos.[5]

Initially, dramatic interest seems to centre on the transformation of Sostratus. In a striking visual coup he exchanges the *chlanis*, badge of urban privilege, for the farmer's identifying *dikella*;[6] leaves by the hillward road, whey-faced and still tainted with urban overconfidence, and returns bent with exhaustion, tanned brown, and unrecognisable even to his favourite slave, let alone to Cnemon.[7] That he has absorbed Gorgias' sermon is apparent from his earnest oration at 797–812 contrasting the impermanence of wealth with the durability

[5] So, at least, in the papyrus; see Sandbach on 466 ff. for defence.

[6] For the *dikella* as a significant prop see Horst-Dieter Blume, 'Der Codex Bodmer und unsere Kenntnis der griechischen Komödie', in E.W. Handley and André Hurst (eds.), *Relire Ménandre*, Recherches et Rencontres 2 (Geneva: Droz, 1990), 13–36 at 29–31.

[7] A change of mask seems a strong likelihood; see E.W. Handley *The Dyskolos of Menander* (London, 1965), on 754.

of *philia*. This indeed is Gorgias' judgment as he returns to his theme of *metabolē* (769). You are a rich city youth, he tells Sostratus, and yet you were prepared to pick up a *dikella* and do an honest day's work: 'such a man will bear with dignity the turn of fortune' (*metabolē tychēs*).

Gorgias, however, has characteristically forgotten now the *metabolē* in the other (direction from poverty to prosperity. Yet Sostratus is already in fact plotting a *metabolē* for Gorgias, by giving him Plangon in marriage and thereby distributing Callippides' fortune evenly between the two families. When the suggestion of marrying up is put to him in Act 5, he digs in his heels (830 f.): 'I don't want to be rich on others' labours, but to have earned it myself.' The *autarkia* ethos of Cnemon's misguided life is mirrored in Gorgias' dogged refusal to be patronised by charity and his insistence that poverty is somehow ennobling. Just as with Cnemon, Gorgias' concessions in Act 4 mean nothing unless he can be persuaded to extend the lesson to his own life and accept a permanent transformation in his status.

The text at 835–41 is too damaged to allow confident reconstruction of the arguments by which Gorgias was persuaded to yield. No supplement of the difficult remains seems to yield a devastating clinch of reasoning, and editors have suspected that his rapid assent may be motivated more by generic momentum than by a missing masterstroke of argument or psychology. Perhaps Gorgias' abrupt acquiescence is in general terms prepared for by his equally sudden volte-face at 315–9, an earlier moment where his naive and blinkered stereotype of the rich finds itself instantaneously disarmed. Whatever the terms of resolution, however, there is a very delicate touch in Gorgias' reluctance to accept his long-awaited *metabolē* when its time comes round.

No other Greek play explores class divisions with such directness: the invisible barriers that exist between poor and rich, between rural smallholders and the leisured urban elite.

But Menander's interests lie ultimately in human natures rather than human societies, and what seems to attract him most in this scenario is not the barriers themselves but the characters' willingness to accept and even to reinforce them. Gorgias, like Cnemon, has to recognise the dissolubility of social boundaries, even here in practically the most isolated deme of Attica, the heartland of *agroikia* and rural *eremia*. To this end, territory and its violation, isolation and the *ochlos* are recurrent motifs both in the stagecraft and in the language of this play. Alone of the characters, Pan is not bound by the local rules of space and time, but can foresee and manipulate human events in collusion with the spectators outside. He lies both at the heart of the play and entirely outside it: a microcosmic *genius loci*, whose dwelling is the centre and end of the action, yet whose presence remains implicate and invisible to all but the theatre audience. Pan's benignly mischievous purpose is immanent rather than supervisory, a barely-personal metaphor for the self-conscious theatricality and strongly teleological movement of comic narrative itself. This is a momentum neither Cnemon nor Gorgias can hope to resist. Through Pan's unseen intervention, their human divisions are finally erased, and the fragmented world made whole again in the mediating house of the god.

III
Plautus

6

Plautus and the Public Stage

ERICH GRUEN

The fragments of early Latin literature invite groping in the dark. They stimulate imagination and give rise to attractive speculation. But the pieces are too few and isolated, the context too cloudy to permit clear vision. Livius Andronicus, Naevius, and Ennius remain shadowy and elusive. By contrast, the comedies of Plautus pull us from the dusky realm of the fragments to the radiance of literature. Twenty Plautine plays constitute the extant corpus, dwarfing the remains of poetic predecessors and contemporaries. The very richness of the material holds out promise of fuller insight into the relationship between artist and political society.

But the endeavor has its own hazards. A different set of obstacles stands in the way. Plautus' life and career are nearly a blank to us, thus blocking knowledge of the condition and associations that governed his work. Most or all of the plays themselves derive from Greek originals, adaptations of New Comedy that create grave difficulties in extracting the Roman elements embedded in the Hellenic texture. And more frustrating still to the historian, neither an absolute nor a relative chronology of the dramas can be established with any degree of precision. Hence, despite a plethora of material, the fundamental question remains open: what relationship did Plautine drama bear to the Roman public scene? Did the dramatist hold up his contemporaries to analysis—or derision?

The question is tough but not intractable. Much depends upon the methodology employed in approaching it. Efforts to ferret out the sequence and dating of the plays have exhibited considerable ingenuity, yet frequently fall into the trap of question-begging and circular reasoning. Historical events discerned in Plautine allusions owe more to the discerner than to the dramatist. Plautus, in fact, nowhere makes explicit and unambiguous reference to a contemporary event. Only conjecture can find correspondence, and the conjectures mount, building upon one another to create a shaky edifice without solid foundation. Individual suggestions are often acute and appealing, but the notion that scholarship has developed a reasonably reliable chronology of the plays is an illusion. Too much energy has been expended in identifying specific episodes and personages supposedly intended by Plautine allusions, as if the poet were some Roman Lycophron inviting readers to puzzle over recondite references. That approach misconceives Plautus' purposes. The absence of distinct pointers to contemporary incidents is deliberate—not surely to tempt readers into a guessing game, but because the specifics are irrelevant. Plautus' topicality has to be assessed on a broader level.

The existence of decidedly Roman elements in the plays that cannot have derived from Greek originals has long been recognized. Plautus regularly introduces Roman legal, political, and religious institutions, with conscious or inadvertent echoes of Italian usages and practises foreign to the Greek setting. These aspects have been much studied, with considerable profit. They provide invaluable enlightenment on Roman society in the late 3rd and early 2nd century, especially on matters like slavery, business relations, and private law. But they give only limited access to the disposition of the poet. And they do not address the critical question of comic drama's relationship to contemporary public life. A different angle of vision is needed. The present investigation proposes neither to mine the texts for information on Roman social history, nor to guess at particular identifications that might yield conjectural dates for the plays. Instead, a different method and purpose: to examine Plautus' presentation of issues and attitudes prominent on the Roman public scene, thus to gain insight into relations between contemporary developments and the comic stage. Relevant allusions in the plays are plentiful, not so much disguised as indirect. Plautus did not reproduce current events, but called attention to their implications.

The writer's own opinions are deftly masked. Comic characters and situations supplied convenient camouflage. Plautus could screen himself behind the conventions of the theater while simultaneously giving voice to matters of contemporary concern and discussion. But which was the poet's voice?

A reliable biography would help. But none issued from antiquity. The few details we possess are disputed and dubious, nothing to allow conclusions on character or attitude. Tradition located Plautus' birthplace at Sarsina in Umbria (Festus 274). That itself causes problems. Where did the poet learn Greek and gain mastery of Hellenic dramatic conventions? Hardly in Umbria. When and why did he come to Rome? And how did he establish a reputation? Unanswerable questions for the most part. But a clue resides in the peculiar tale preserved by Gellius and drawn from Varro's researches on the lives of the poets. Plautus, so it was recorded, earned a livelihood through employment associated with the theater, lost his savings in a commercial enterprise, and had to resort to work in a mill where he wrote his first comedies (Gellius 3.3.14). Assessments of the story range from complete acceptance to total rejection. The idea of Plautus as merchant entrepreneur is hard to swallow—not to mention the image of the poet laboring at a mill while scribbling comedies in his spare time. But the notice of work in the theatrical profession has some logic and plausibility. Just what kind of work invites hypothesis but escapes certainty. Gellius' language is vague: Plautus might have been actor, playwright, impresario, or stage-hand. Or, more probably, a combination of the above. A sharp differentiation of roles would not have been characteristic of the early theater. Livius Andronicus was both author of and actor in his own plays (Livy 7.2.8).

Experience in a dramatic troupe also provides the easiest answer to another puzzle: Plautus' acquaintance with Greek drama. That experience may already have been broad and deep before his arrival in Rome, with a reputation that preceded him. The travelling Dionysiac technitai perhaps offered opportunities and nourished his skills as playwright and producer. Precisely when Plautus reached Rome escapes record, but the later years of the 3rd century would be a safe estimate.

The atmosphere in Rome at that time was especially congenial to the theater. Livius Andronicus had given it respectability, and state encouragement allowed it to flourish. The Ludi Romani provided the initial setting for dramatic performances as part of national celebration, the occasion for Livius Andronicus' production in 240. In the last quarter of the 3rd century and the beginning of the 2nd century new festivals came into being and included theatrical performances as part of their offerings: the Ludi Plebeii, the Ludi Apollinares, the Ludi Megalenses, the Ludi Cereales. The number of days set aside for plays multiplied, increased still further by the practise of *instauratio*, the repetition of games called for by religious improprieties. Such circumstances markedly enhanced the desirability of popular playwrights. And official imprimatur was stamped on the profession c.206 when the guild of writers and actors gained public recognition, special privileges, and a conspicuous site in Minerva's temple on the

Aventine (Festus 446). The occasion honored Livius Andronicus, but the beneficiaries included all those engaged in the composition and production of drama. The climate was exceedingly favorable. Plautus' profession secured state sponsorship, and the playwright enjoyed public acclaim (cf. Plautus, *Casina* 11–20; *Men.* 1–4).

Did the favors of the officialdom and the public help to mold the creativity of the artist? Did the patronage of the powerful exercise an influence on the content of drama? In short, was there a political tinge to Plautine comedy? Numerous studies interpret the writer's inclinations in terms of factional or ideological conflicts prevalent in his day. The game is a seductive one, and it has led to a plethora of mutually inconsistent hypotheses. Plautus has been reckoned as an advocate of Scipio Africanus, as a sympathizer with Cato and adversary of Scipio, or as having moved from the Scipionic camp to the Catonian party, as supporter and then opponent of philhellenic movements in Rome, as adherent or critic of Fulvius Nobilior, or as antagonist of Flamininus. The suggestions rest more on ingenuity than on testimony. Plautus does not parade his political orientation. The playwright puts no contemporary figures on the stage, and makes no forthright comment on contemporary affairs. He wished to avoid the fate of Naevius, so it is commonly said: hence, the comments are veiled, the names unexpressed, the allusions indirect. That analysis misdirects inquiry. The dubious stories on Naevius' demise provide too shaky a foundation for hypothesis. Plautus deliberately chose a genre that avoided political embroilment: not the overt topicality of Aristophanic comedy which savaged the most prominent figures of the day but the drama's of ordinary life peopled by the stock characters of New Comedy. The conventions of the genre rather than the fate of Naevius governed this feature of the Plautine plays—several of which may have preceded Naevius' last years. The dramatist's choice itself must be given due significance: he elected to steer clear of engagement with political personalities, factions, and programs. To foist them upon him posthumously seems singularly misguided. The scholarly pastime of identifying public figures or current events lurking surreptitiously in Plautus' scripts violates his own purposes. A different approach is called for.

Not that the comedies are devoid of political meaning. Nor did their author strive to suppress personal sentiments. Plautus was alive to issues that engaged his contemporaries on the public scene in an age of overseas expansion and rapid internal change. The models of New

Comedy had little place for direct political commentary or a one-to-one correspondence between characters or events and their real-life counterparts. But the plays could serve as vehicles to address, promote, mock, or satirize items that held public attention or provoked public debate. At that level Plautus' topicality, neither Aristophanic nor Menandrian, takes shape. The subjects of public discourse, rather than particular persons or incidents, find an appropriate outlet on the stage. And the great popularity of comic drama gave that outlet a special importance. Plautus had a medium with which to expand awareness and augment discussion.

Numerous themes course through the plays, yielding insight into matters that captured Roman attention around the turn of the 3rd century. Only a selective sample can here be treated. But enough to give a sense of how the dramatist could both articulate and denigrate the issues that exercised his contemporaries.

The feats of the soldier dominated the era. The expulsion of Hannibal and conquest of Carthage gave the nation her finest hour, followed by dramatic expansion to the north, the west, and, most especially, to the Hellenistic East. It was a time of pronounced display of Roman power abroad, the influx of staggering amounts of wealth, and the opportunity for unprecedented authority by successful individuals.

Prime illustration of these developments comes over the quest for a triumph. The public celebration of one's military accomplishment had long been the most coveted of honors for Rome's leaders. Claims to a triumph and disputes over the legitimacy of those claims reached new levels of intensity in this period. The political stakes were high and the competition keen.

Evidence for contention over these matters abounds. Leadership and commons were regaled by disputes over the merits of *triumphatores*, the diversion of public funds to private use, and the appropriation of the prizes of war. The controversies began to be heard at the end of the 3rd century and gained in momentum during the first two decades of the 2nd—precisely the time of Plautus' prominence. If the dramatist paid any heed to current events, these debates should find reflection. The plays do not disappoint.

The clever slave Chrysalus in Plautus' *Bacchides* compares his successful deception with military victory. His words are pregnant with meaning for Romans attuned to public affairs in the early 2nd century. Chrysalus represents himself as marching along laden with booty—and *ovans*. The word was not selected at random. It refers to an *ovatio*, alternative to a triumph, an institution resorted to with greater frequency in these years to deflect claims on a triumph (1068–9). Allusion to debates over such matters is reinforced by the lines that follow. Chrysalus acknowledges that his conquest came through deceit but he has marched his army home intact (1070–1). Objection to triumphs, it will be recalled, sometimes focused on the general's inability to withdraw his army. And Chrysalus concludes by dismissing concern for a triumph: there were too many of them any- way, the institution had been cheapened by mediocrity (1072–3). One need not assume that Plautus pointed to a particular occasion. But the echoes of contemporary debates are unmistakable. Plautus' audi- ence could find in the scramble for triumphs a subject for amusement.

The vast sums accruing from foreign conquests and the repercus- sions they had upon the influence of the *imperator* also find reflection in the pages of Plautus. Distribution of spoils to soldiers as a means to popularity became more common and conspicuous. Amphitryon's victory at Thebes made beneficiaries of his soldiers: they acquired booty, land, and glory (*Amph.* 193). The expectation of material awards could now be assumed. Chrysalus in the *Bacchides* depicts himself as laden with spoils and announces a handsome reception for his soldiers (*Bacch.* 1069, 1074). The wily and resourceful slave of the *Persa*, Toxilus, also portrays his successful duplicity in military terms: victory allows him to carry off the spoils, to share them with his par- tisans, and to host them lavishly (*Pers.* 757–8). Closely comparable language appears in a heady speech of Pseudolus, boasting of his chi- canery: he will now pile on the booty for himself and his partisans (*Pseud.* 588) The phrases recall Cato's proud claim that he never dis- tributed plunder to his *amici*—thereby indirectly censuring contem- poraries who followed a different practise (fr. 203 *ORF*). The latter practise is strikingly illustrated in a Plautine line. The courtesan in *Truculentus* induces a youth to collaborate with her for purposes of profit, urging him *saltem amicus mi esto manubiarius*. The term *manu- biarius* is otherwise unattested, but the meaning clear enough: 'a friend in plunder', (Plautus. *Truc.* 880). It does not follow that Plautus acted as ally or sympathizer of Cato the elder. But he plainly under- scored contemporary uneasiness about the arbitrary disposal of for- eign spoils by Rome's generals.

The importance of the issue for Plautus manifests itself further in an indirect way: the great frequency with which he employs the term *praeda* or its equivalent as a metaphor for the object of schemes by crafty slaves and double dealing characters. The playwright does not announce his attitude. But the association of shady maneuvers and intrigues with the acquisition of spoils gave signals to an audience responsive to public affairs.

The comedies, in short, take definite notice of concern over the effects of expansion. Power in the hands of *imperatores*, intense competition for triumphs, opportunities to lavish favors upon partisans, the ambiguous character of public control over military spoils, the attacks on returning commanders, the tensions created by prosecutions or by fear of prosecution permeated the public scene at the beginning of the 2nd century. Plautus, to be sure, did not propose solutions. He was comic dramatist, not political reformer. But the plays had a contemporary resonance that reached beyond the fantasies of the stage. They mocked ambition, lampooned exaggerated claims, deflated conquerors, and likened the acquisition of plunder to the duplicitous guile of slaves. The medium of comedy itself and the popularity of Plautus served to keep these issues before a broader public.

The themes recur with some frequency in the scripts. Plautus, as usual, avoided the specific. He directed his aim not at a particular piece of legislation but at the fact of legislation. Lawmakers in the plays are busy and harried, but also foolish, with much ado about very little. Father and son in the *Asinaria* are both belittled as expending their labors in senate and legislative activity to no good purpose: the activity debilitates those who engage in it, and the legislation appeals to the debauched (Plautus, *Asin.* 599–602, 871–5). The parasite Peniculus in the *Menaechmi* vents his fury at public *contiones* which usurp the time of busy men and keep them from more important matters—like lunch (Plautus, *Men.* 451–9). In *Epidicus*, the *senex* duped by the slave berates himself and takes consolation only in the fact that his friend was equally bamboozled, despite a reputation for expertise in the fashioning of laws and legal principles (Plautus, *Epid.* 517–23).

The Plautine legislator, shallow and fatuous, wastes his own time and others. And the fruits of his labors are equally ineffectual. Plautus several times alludes to legislation that is ignored, unenforced, or violated with impunity. A character in the *Poenulus* makes reference to laws passed repeatedly by the people against the same offense—an offense committed again in the play. The statutes were obviously without force (Plautus, *Poen.* 725). Labrax, the pimp in the

Rudens, expresses contempt for *leges* designed to restrain his activities: he will pursue his operation in defiance of them (Plautus, *Rud.* 724–5). The parasite Curculio, himself hardly of the most distinguished occupation, excoriates pimps and bankers, lumping them together as practitioners of the most unsavory professions and levelling his harshest assaults upon the latter. Curculio blasts bankers for breaking every law passed to hold them in check. They can always find a loophole—like waiting for boiling water to cool down. Again it is the repeated passage of laws for the same purpose—and their futility—at which Plautus takes aim (*Curc.* 509–11). A slave's scorn rises to the level of indignation when he denounces laws which would only be obeyed by those who were themselves worthless and intemperate (*Asin.* 601–2). The most extensive tirade is placed in the mouth of another slave, Stasimus in the *Trinummus*, who laments the loss of *veteres mores*, replaced now by mores *mali* which sanction every form of deplorable behavior: contemporary practise runs roughshod over laws; *leges* are, without force, subservient to *mos*; whatever custom endorses is released from the authority of law (*Trin.* 1028–44).

Plautus underlines the inefficacy of legislation by having two characters in two separate plays propose transparently ludicrous bills. Eutychus at the close of the *Mercator* frames a measure prohibiting all men over sixty, whether married or single, from affairs with courtesans—and further debarring them from interference with their sons' wenching! A classic instance of the unenforceable law (*Merc.* 1015–24). Equally preposterous is the *lex* conceived by Saturio, the parasite in the *Persa*. Saturio denounces the practise of informing and suggests a remedy: a measure that requires the successful informer to yield up half his earnings to the public coffers and permits any defendant to sue his accuser for the same sum sought from himself, thus to appear before the *tresviri* on equal terms (*Pers.* 62–76). Implementation of such an ordinance was plainly unthinkable. The proposals perhaps parodied extant legislation that could command no obedience.

What type of legislation came under censure here? The dramatist, once again, refrains from explicit designation. But certain areas offer suggestive possibilities. Sumptuary laws, for example, warrant notice They did not lend themselves to easy enforcement.

The *lex Oppia* demands attention, a notorious and controversial measure. The assembly, on tribunician initiative, passed the bill in 215, while gripped by the intensity of the Hannibalic war. Its provisions prohibited any woman from having more than a *semuncia* of gold, from wearing colorful garb, and from riding in a carriage in Rome or any town within a mile. What was the purpose of the enactment and how effective was it? On the surface, it would appear to be a wartime measure designed to rally the community and rescue the treasury. If so, however, the provisions are most peculiar. Prohibition of fancy clothing and carriages would provide no material benefits to the war effort. And the restrictions on gold would be of only limited benefit. The state needed silver.

Nothing in the *lex Oppia* would provide it. The law, it has been suggested, would protect the less well-to-do by removing the need to compete or the shame of failing to compete. All would be put on an equal footing. Yet the measure could hardly wipe out distinctions of wealth or class. The war effort received a genuine transfusion in 210 when senators contributed gold, silver, and bronze to the common cause, each retaining only a token for his household. And three years later Roman matrons, to expiate ill omens, selected twelve in their number to draw on their own dowries for a gift to Juno. Does this imply that enforcement of the *lex Oppia* was lax from the start? Perhaps. But that conclusion depends on the premise that the bill was a confiscatory measure, a view shared by most commentators. The premise, however, is mistaken. The heated debate over repeal of the law in 195 nowhere breathes a hint that the wives are to receive back any cash—or that there is any to receive. Their demands concentrated only on the freedom to deck themselves out in finery once again. The Oppian law was a *lex sumptuaria*, not a means of economic relief. As such, its principal value was symbolic rather than pragmatic. The appearance of women, bedecked and bejeweled, in public would be offensive at a time of economic hardship and national crisis. The *lex* imposed a patriotic uniformity.

Retention of the measure after the end of the war, therefore, created an anomaly. Cato might argue that the moral welfare of the community would continue to benefit from an enactment which held women's extravagance in check. But the argument did not prevail for long. The women themselves engaged in vociferous demonstration in 195, gained support (or encouragement) in high circles, and generated heated dispute. The matter received considerable public visibility and issued in repeal of the statute. Its symbolic value had eroded away, once the constraints of the Hannibalic war were lifted. The vigorous complaints of its victims exposed the measure's hollowness.

Plautus' comedies contain recurrent references to female luxury and display. The oft-cited lines of the *senex* Megadorus in the *Aulularia* berate the arrogance and extravagance of wives who bring handsome dowries to their marriages. They parade about in polished carriages and purple finery, reducing their husbands to servitude (*Aul.* 167–9). The needs of their wardrobe and cosmetics keep an army of merchants in business (*Aul.* 505–22). Rich dowries encourage ostentation and allow wives to lord it over their spouses (*Aul.* 475–502). Those lines have traditionally served to date the *Aulularia*: Megadorus' strictures show close parallels to those of Cato, and the argument seems to mirror the debate on repeal of the law in 195: hence the play was produced in 194 or thereabouts. The conclusion is unverifiable and unpersuasive. Speeches for and against repeal of the law stem from Livy's narrative and his own composition. How near or far they are to the arguments actually expressed in 195 we shall never know. A case can be made for seeing them as reflecting the atmosphere of the Augustan age. Whatever one makes of that, it is methodologically unsound to employ the Livian text as a means of dating Plautus' comedy. The playwright, in fact, harps on the practice of luxurious living by women in numerous plays. That theme is not confined to a date or an occasion.

Pampered women appear with frequency in the comedies. Dowries support only a portion of them. Others are indulged by their husbands who provide maids, jewelry, linen, purple garments, and luxury items of all sorts. Nor are wives alone the beneficiaries of this generosity. Courtesans too sport jewelry and elegant raiment's supplied by lovers (*Curc.* 344). Their households include wardrobe mistresses, masseuses, bookkeepers, custodians of accessories, numerous flunkies, and every variety of garment—to the despair or ruin of their benefactors (*Epid.* 222–36). Special irony attaches to the remarks of the Carthaginian woman Adelphasium in *Poenulus*, who plays the part of moralist and censures her own sex for excessive devotion to luxury and pampering, thus causing endless trouble to men. The sentiments closely parallel those of Megadorus in the *Aulularia* (*Poen.* 210–31; *Aul.* 167–9, 475–522). To interpret this as Plautus embracing Catonian conservatism misses the mark. By placing analogous comments in the mouths of both *meretrix* and *senex*, the playwright surely parodies the moralism that frowns on luxury but is powerless to check it. Composition of these lines need not have awaited the specific debate over repeal of the *lex Oppia*. The very fact of legislation on the books that had outstripped its usefulness, antagonized its constituents, and contravened both public opinion and public practise provided a target for the playwright's wit. Plautus is neither moralist nor political partisan. The comic writer delights in the incongruity of rhetoric and reality.

Another type of legislation may also have prompted Plautine parody. Laws on usury made an appearance in the early 2nd century, with some frequency and reiteration. Livy speaks, under the year 193, of *multae leges* on the subject. They had curbed greed but also stimulated moneylenders to find loopholes and ply their trade in indirect ways. Hence the assembly promulgated still another measure in that year, closing one of the loopholes exploited by *faeneratores* and relieving the burden of high interest payments (Livy 35. 7. 2. 5). The bill engendered numerous prosecutions and the resultant fines paid for lavish public monuments. But the problem of usury did not evaporate. The moneylenders rechanneled their activities and found other means whereby to evade restrictions—or so it may be inferred from the passage of a new usury law, the *lex Juila de feneratione,* not long thereafter. Cato voiced opposition to the bill, perhaps as being insufficiently severe (Cato, fr. 56–7 *ORF*). It was, in any case, hardly more effective than its predecessors. Still another measure needed to be passed, the *lex Marcia,* perhaps in the 180s (Gaius, *Inst.* 4.23). Usury did not readily succumb to legislation.

The subject lent itself to comic treatment. Bankers, moneylenders, and usurers abound in Plautus' scripts. Nothing surprising in that, of course. The Greek models will account for most of them, essential as they are often are to the plot or intrigues of the play. But not always. Curculio's broadside against the whole tribe of *faeneratores* has a sweeping character that removes it from the realm of the plot. The assault matches pimps with bankers as objects of revilement: the first tear men apart with baneful solicitation and debauchery, the second with oppressive interest charges. Bankers, if anything, are worse: pimps at least conduct business in private, the *faeneratores* in the open forum. And, most important, the latter have scornfully violated a multitude of laws passed by the people against them; they count on ineffectiveness and escape-clauses (*Curc.* 506–11). The lines almost certainly have contemporary resonance—and deliberately so. They attack both the profession and the futile measures taken to curb it. An illustration of the loophole comes in the same play. The banker Lyco's initial entrance onto the stage brings a monologue in which he contemplates means of evading his own creditors: if they should put on too much pressure, he would seek a praetor's judgment, evidently confident in the outcome (*Curc.* 373–6).

The theme of bankers forever dunning their debtors but eluding their creditors recurs in the comedies. The prologue of the *Casina* presents it with word play. The *ludi* allow men to forget their debts, but the bankers have their own *ludus*: they dun no one at the games, and they repay no one after the games (*Cas.* 25–8). A conventional literary charge against *faeneratores*? Possibly. But a passage in the *Pseudolus* suggests something more topical. Calidorus complains that no loans are obtainable. Pseudolus concurs and explains: from the time that the bankers, having satiated themselves and closed up shop, called in their debts but paid none of their creditors, everyone is too cautious and distrusting to lend any money. The allusion has a concreteness that goes beyond the world of fantasy. Plautus may have in mind tight credit and straitened economic circumstances that prevailed in the aftermath of the Hannibalic war. Comparable allusions occur elsewhere in the texts—to economic hardship, to the high cost of living, to the cornering of the grain market. The playwright need not simply be copying out his Greek models here. Strictures against moneylenders have a ring of authenticity. A reputation for untrustworthiness clings to them. They are swift to find more moneys due from debtors. They are notoriously relentless in pressing for repayment. But if any cash is entrusted to them, they vanish faster than a liberated hare. No sure criteria distinguish the Plautine moneylenders who derive from New Comedy and those rooted in the Roman scene. But Plautus had an eye for the vexatious issues of his time. The troublesome circumstances of debt and tight credit, the greed and untrustworthiness of moneylenders, and the frustration engendered by inept and fruitless legislation all find place in the comedies, and touched chords familiar to Plautus' countrymen.

7

Traditions of Theatrical Improvization in Plautus: Some Considerations

GREGOR VOGT-SPIRA

Research into oral literature has so far paid little attention to the theatre. Several reasons might be adduced: an especially important one seems to be that extemporization lacks something specific, an 'oral' author to be deemed responsible for the whole. Another, directly connected, reason is that ad-libbing actors do not possess the dignity of an epic or lyric bard. In other words, the initial phase of the theatre lies outside our conception of poetic origins; it has found no way into the realm of natural poetry. The absence of revaluation for that initial phase in respect of drama—outside myth and ritual—has perpetuated the notion that the uncultivated spectator cares only for action.

However, the failure to discover additional value in primitive theatre may also be viewed from another angle. It all points back to the fact that the dramatic genre derives exceptional profit from the capacities of writing. The form, in which an action is directly represented by persons acting, requires—or shall we say permits—a highly complex organization of events. It is also because of this complexity that Hegel could declare drama to be the highest grade of poetry and of art as a whole.[1] Moreover, writing also plays a leading part: without it a dramatic author could not exist in the first place. To be sure, these considerations enable literality to become, all unnoticed, an essential property of the genre.

This state of affairs affects our view of Plautine comedy, which as written drama from the dawn of Roman literature has a position of exceptional interest in literary history at the point of tension between oral and written tradition. On the one hand comedy 'in Greek dress'

---

[1] C. W. F. Hegel, *Vorlesungen über die Ästhetik*, iii, ch. iii C iii.

(*palliata*) is defined by its relation to Greek Middle and New Comedy, which it translates or at least purports to translate. Nevertheless the Roman versions sometimes have features radically divergent from their originals, which belong to a quite different phase of literary culture: Attic New Comedy is a typical late product, behind which lies a long literary tradition. Analytical study of Roman comedy has been dominated by a negative view of these divergences: Fraenkel, for example, constantly declares that the Roman author took apart, nay perverted, his originals, offended against the rules of logical and probability, and so on.[2] Such judgements are the necessary consequence of a purely literary criterion; the question therefore arises how far they are appropriate to Plautus. Yet be that as it may, we must record as a general proposition that the view of drama as a fundamentally written entity has constantly hindered scholars from seeing Plautine procedures from the perspective of orality, that is, from principles lying close to extemporization.

There would be excellent grounds for doing so, for long before adopting the Greek scheme of literature Rome had an independent theatrical tradition. The famous chapter of Livy (7. 2) puts the institutionalizing of stage-plays in 364 BC, and records by way of subsequent development a partial transition to writing; this is before the turning-point when literary drama set in with Livius Andronicus in 240 BC. Whether Livy's description fits the facts has long been disputed; but since he had at his disposal registers of institutionally important information, such as the aediles' *acta*, the individual facts may be accepted as historically credible. Furthermore, there is important linguistic evidence for old Roman theatrical traditions, probably reaching back to the fifth century: the full development of metre of dramatic verse (in contrast, say, to the hexameter), seen in the earliest monuments of Roman literature is such as to show for certain that it had been in use for several centuries.

Extempore theatre did not die out in Rome with the introduction of the literary stage, but continued to be cultivated. One of its chief forms is the *fabula Atellana*, a popular farce originating in the Oscan city of Atella, which was not reduced to writing till the first century BC.[3] Another is the mime, cultivated at all times; Cicero finds fault with its sloppy structure, a typical feature of extempore plays (*Pro*

---

[2] See Eduard Fraenkel, *Elementi plautini in Plauto* (Florence, 1960), *passim*.

[3] A. S. Gratwick, 'Titus Maccius Plautus', *CQ*, NS 23 (1973), 78–84.

Caelio 64–5). If one keeps in mind that these extempore performances did not disappear at a stroke, the situation in which the *palliata* poets wrote becomes clear: the expectations of a majority of the audience were formed by the extempore theatre; they were not accustomed to refined literary late products, but more robust humour, hardly concerned with polished economy of plot or character-drawing.[4] The need for *palliata* poets to play to the crowd is shown by the twofold failure of Terence's *Hecyra*: the play was obviously too nuanced and soft-spoken, so that the audience twice escaped to the more attractive performances of boxers, rope-dancers, and gladiators. The prologue of Plautus' *Poenulus*, which portrays the lively bustle at the start of a theatrical performance, shows what gaudy, almost cabaret-like effects had to be created in order to quieten the undisciplined public.

The simple but far-reaching conclusion is that early Roman dramatic poets are not, in their theatrical practice, in direct competition with their Greek models, their *exemplaria Graeca*—this kind of explicit literary contest does not begin until the classical period. The Roman poets had to establish themselves against the other forms of drama already familiar to the audience. It is self-evident, then, that Plautus was unable, indeed unwilling, to dispense with the comic possibilities of the impromptu—to do so would have denied him success. His plays must therefore be regarded as a successful combination of two fundamentally different theatrical traditions, one high literary and the other originally oral.

Plautine scholars have often acknowledged this in principle, but in practice they usually pay most attention to the Greek side and regard divergence from it as destruction or distortion. In sum, they are still in thrall to the same classicizing literary and aesthetic categories as Gellius (*NA* 2. 23). In the present study I shall approach the question from the other side, focusing on the extent to which Plautus employs techniques of extemporization and transfers them to a written medium. Hopefully such criteria will make for a positive—and insofar as it is concerned with aesthetic affect—a more appropriate description of Plautus' mode of composition.[5] Nevertheless it would be wrong to equate Plautus with extempore drama. On the contrary, there are

---

[4] On the audience of Plautus' plays see E. W. Handley, 'Plautus and his Public: Some Thoughts on New Comedy', *Dioniso*, 46 (1975), 117–32.

[5] In the spirit of the 'undeniable fact' recalled E. Segal, *Roman Laughter: The Comedy of Plautus* (Cambridge, Mass., 1968), 7, that 'Plautus made them [the Roman groundlings] laugh. And the laughter was Roman.'

indications that he expressly distances himself from the extempore theatre. First, however, we shall consider the adoption of this theatre's traditions, taking as our guiding thread Aristotle's isolation of the various elements of tragedy,[6] which is no less valid for comedy.

Let us begin with phenomena of style and the development of ideas, and first of all with a scene from the middle of the *Asinaria*. The plot turns on the need of a young lover called Argyrippus for 20 minae in order to purchase a year's exclusive rights to the hetaera next door, Philaenium. Earlier in the play, two slaves, acting in the young master's interest, have relieved a merchant of precisely this sum. The scene begins with a pathetic parting dialogue between the lovers immediately before the reversal of fortune in which the slaves bring the necessary cash along. In this conversation we observe a first sign of oral origin: it is conducted in accordance with a catchword technique with the highest economy of ideas, being entirely sustained by a single motif, that the loss of the beloved means the loss of health and wellbeing, even of life. This idea has been stimulated by Argyrippus' parting formula *vale*, 'farewell', and as it were served up for further development (591–7).

> ARG. Why do you hold me back?
> PH. Because I love you and need you but you're going away.
> ARG. Farewell, farewell.
> PH. I should fare rather better if you were staying here.
> ARG. Keep well.
> PH. You tell me to keep well when by your departure you bring me death?
> ARG. Your mother has decreed my last hour and told me to go home.
> PH. It's a cruel funeral she'll give her daughter, if I have to do without you.
> . . . .
> ARG. Let me go, please.
> PH. Where are you off to? Why don't you stay here?
> ARG. I'll stay all night if you like.

The scheme of the dialogue is thus that the second speaker picks up a cue each time from the first, who does not answer, but starts anew. Philaenium's replies first take up the formulae *vale* and *salve* in the literal sense; then she returns the prompt intensifying the notion that

---

[6] *Poet.* 6 (1450a7–12). For reasons of space I treat only story, diction, and thought; in a larger framework character, spectacle, and music may be considered.

being thrown out by the mother represents for Argyrippus his last hour on earth. Finally, in the last exchange, it is the girl who takes over the initiative; Argyrippus' reply, so utterly plausible as it is, simply picks up her concluding verb 'to remain' and completely ignores the course of the dialogue up to now. The jest at once constitutes the end of the first round—how should the dialogue go on from here?— and allows the action to be interrupted at some length by exchanges on the theme of night-work between the slaves close by.

The entire dialogue is thus based on a competitive structure, even though the lovers wish for the same thing. It exactly complies with the rules of a specifically oral custom frequently admitted to Plautine comedy: the altercation. In another context the verbal exchange is technically known as *par pari respondere* ('to answer like with like', i.e. 'to give as good as one gets'), which originally denoted a legal principle. The ritual of answering back has been observed as an impromptu exchange of song in various cultures, and can be found even in our own day. In early Rome the *Fescennini* with their impromptu mocking verses used this form; we also find it in Greek, especially in bucolic poetry,[7] which exhibits the same basic rule obeyed by Plautine altercations.

The example cited above represents *par pari respondere* at a high level, being a genuine conversation. The principle often appears in the simplest conceivable reduced form, the duet of insults. When two persons meet, especially slaves, they often have fun at the outset by bestowing on each other such names as 'school of vice', 'warden of the gaol', 'cultivator of chains', 'delight of the birch-rods', and so on. This ritual trading of insults is called *velivelitatio*, 'verbal skirmishing' (*Asin.* 307). Fraenkel connects this 'genuine duet of insults' with pre-literary forms.[8] [The equivalent English, or at least Scots, term is 'flyting'—Ed.] It is extremely easy to ad lib provided the actors possess the right vocabulary, and was therefore a typical feature in the Atellane, whose distinctive element is said to have been 'rustic and jocular and comical words'.[9] This entertaining game is also attested for the Fescennines, not least through literary imitation in Roman satire.

We may now turn to a second characteristic element of improvization, which also falls under the heading of language and style. In

---

[7] Cf. R. Merkelbach, '*Boukolistai* (Der Wettstreit der Hirten)', *Rheinisches Museum*, NS 99 (1956), 97–133.   [8] Above note, 379–80 and n. 3.

[9] Fronto, *M. Caes.* 4. 3. 2 (57. 2–3 van den Hout[2]); he is referring to the written Atellane, but it can hardly have been fundamentally different in this respect.

the *Poenulus*, the young lover Agorastocles gushes over his beloved Adelphasium, provoking the slave Milphio to comment sarcastically (vv. 292–4):

> AG. But look, I've never rubbed (*limavi*) heads with her.
> MI. Then I'll run to some fishpond or pool and find some mud (*limum*).
> AG. What for?
> MI. I'll tell you: so I can muddy (*limem*) her head and yours.

There is a pun here on *limare* 'to file, rub' and *limare* 'to spatter with mud, dirt.' Such double-entendres are very common in Plautus; according to Quintilian (*Inst. or.* 6. 3. 47), they were also a favourite of the *Atellana*, and are in general a characteristic type of popular humour, besides being particularly favoured in the early stages of literacy. We are dealing with a mode of identification current in everyday speech, as in 'wine is life' (Petrouius, *Sat.* 34. 7.) or 'my father's a fly (*muscast meus pater*): you can't keep anything from him, there's nothing too sacred or too profane for him not to be there right away' (Plautus, *Merc.* 361–2).[10] Plautine wordplay may serve purely to raise a laugh, to satisfy a delight in wit, but may equally well also have a dramatic function, either as a stopgap during a pause in the action, or as a ploy to open a conversation. Thus the lovers' dialogue from the *Asinaria* cited above ends with Philaenium calling on Argyrippus to embrace her (v. 615). In theatrical technique this puts the lovers out of action, a clear signal that the initiative passes to the slaves standing to one side. But how do they come into play (vv. 619–20)?

> LE. Greetings, master—but is this woman you're embracing made of smoke?
> AR. How do you mean?
> LE. Because your eyes are watering, that's why I asked.

The turn of phrase refers to something present on stage and thereby makes the connection. This last functional aspect leads us beyond individual dialogue types to dramatic structures, what Aristotle calls the 'arrangement of events' (*Poet.* 1450ᵃ5).

Whether a play be conceived in writing or extempore, the central requirement is the continuity of stage action. In Plautine analysis scenes advancing the action are commonly distinguished from those

---

[10] [This was used by Fraenkel (n. 2 above; pp. 35, 374 f.) as a touchstone of Plautine style—the comparison of a character to another object or person, then expanded.—ED.]

which merely mark time. Let us look at a typical passage of the latter type. In the *Mercator*, the young Charinus has brought home from his trading voyage a beautiful girl whom he is keeping concealed on his ship. Unfortunately his father has inspected the ship and caught sight of the girl. This serious news is brought to his young master by the *servus currens* Acanthio, hitting every note of haste and urgency (vv. 123–5):

> My knees are letting me down as I run. Oh no! my spleen is rebelling,
> it's seized my diaphragm. Oh no! My breathing cycle's broken down;
> I'd make a pretty useless piper.

When he finally encounters Charinus, and immediately tells him he is done for, one might expect the dialogue to come straight to the point, on the grounds that the messenger wants to get his report delivered, and Charinus wants to know there and then what it is about. Quite wrong: Plautus' comedy is not an imitation of life. It takes almost fifty verses to get to the facts: first the meeting situation has to be played out, and that by two different techniques. The initial excitement of haste sets off the usual greeting by altercation, constructed on the principle of *par pari respondere* ('tit-for-tat'); then the power difference is exploited, in that one party possesses information that the other would desperately like to have, all the more interesting here for the Saturnalia-like role-reversal between master and slave.

Here we have a dramatic structure typical of extempore theatre: the action is directed towards a simple target immediately made clear to each other and to the audience by the parties involved, but within this framework a comic situation is played out. One might speak of a paradoxical reversal, for the transmission of information, the goal of the scene and critical for the whole plot, serves in the local context simply as the basis for a comic device. This can, rather like a soap-bubble, be extended or 'blown up' as long as the actors can think of something amusing. We ought therefore not to speak of a slowing down, since nothing is actually being delayed; rather, the progress of the action is temporarily unimportant. The carefully contrived balance between goal-directed plot and situation-bound comic business that is a defining achievement of New Comedy is broken down again by the Roman comic poets.

In improvised drama, where the broad outlines of the play are usually laid down in advance, the performers sometimes have to reach an understanding amongst themselves how the plot should proceed. If one examines Plautus' text from this standpoint, it becomes clear that it is full of signals for segmentation and transition in which communication between the actors becomes a component of the spoken text; these reflections of the dramaturgy of a non-literary theory have not yet been systematically examined. It may happen that two actors are drawing out a bit of business with too much relish and a third feels left out. He then sends out a signal that he wants to join in again, and demands a bridge to bring him back in play. This is just what happens in a scene of the *Asinaria*, when two slaves, trying to relieve a merchant of his moneybag, indulge in an exchange of insults that takes on a life of its own. The merchant, standing on the sideline, eventually gives a signal that he has had enough; at once they break off, and one of them says (vv. 449–50): 'Ahem! Kind sir, how long have you been here? Honestly, I hadn't seen you'—even though merchant and slave had had a conversation just a little while back! But it simply does not matter whether the link is in line with the previous action. The merchant immediately seizes on the offer, and a three-way dialogue ensues.

In such passages, scholars often speak of the characters' forgetfulness and accuse Plautus of carelessness. We should rather argue the other way around: it is in such passages, easily explicable by their function within the performance, that extemporization retains its privilege not to be bound by the norms of all-embracing verisimilitude, but to adapt itself entirely to the necessities or possibilities of the situation. In this connection we may take one last example of a typically Plautine structure of events, which again matches the dramaturgy of extempore theatre rather than New Comedy.

In the *Miles gloriosus* the soldier Pyrgopolynices is tricked into letting go his girl Philocomasium. The scheme is simple and proven: for the sake of a bird in the bush he is made to let go the two in his hand. The decisive scene is the arrival of Philocomasium's lover Pleusicles, who, disguised as a sailor, takes her away—purportedly to her mother and sister—to his ship, which is ready to sail. The scheming slave impresses in advance on the young lover that this is the final critical point for the plan's success (vv. 1150–4):

> Don't you know that when you're climbing upward in a well that's deep,
> You're in greatest danger of a fall when nearest to the top.
> We have almost drawn this from the well, but if he gets suspicious,
> We'll get nothing out of him—so now's the time to be our sharpest.

By the rules of psychological verisimilitude we should expect that in the abduction scene, when Philocomasium takes leave of the soldier with feigned tears, Pleusicles will behave as normally as possible. Wrong again. When the girl faints, he picks her up, and by his subsequent conduct provokes the soldier to comment (vv. 1334–7):

PY. Say—their heads are awfully close together. I don't like the looks
   of this. Hey, sailor—take your lips from hers!
PL. I just tried to see if she was breathing.
PY. Use your ear for that!
PL. If you'd like, I'll let her go—
PY. No, no—hold on!

The same game of nearly wrecking the intrigue is worked through a second time (vv. 1346–8). Additional risks and difficulties are loosely appended. The balancing act on the edge of the well, far from being reduced to a minimum, is prolonged as long as possible and exploited for all it is worth: the titillation of danger is relished and there is no getting free of it. Here too we have the inverse relation characteristic of the ad lib, in which the superordinate goal of the action serves mainly to act out comic business as inventively as possible. Nevertheless, the balancing act, however wanton, never signifies a real risk. Pleusicles could have behaved far more crazily; he'd still have got the girl in any case. For the outcome, that the soldier shall lose and the young lover win, has been abidingly fixed from the outset. While it would be a highly complex challenge to realistic comedy to make its characters behave in this stereotypical fashion without things' seeming any the less true to life, extemporization is free from such complexity: it possesses fixed types to each of which is attached a whole mass of established modes of behaviour and established outcomes of plot. A little of the resulting security retains its effect in the *Miles* passage and the many comparable 'balancing acts on the edge of the well'.

We have attempted to show how various elements of improvisation continue to be effective in Plautine comedy. Nevertheless, Plautus is not an impromptu 'author'. The *palliata* carefully distinguishes itself from the mass of pre-literary production and makes a point of not being an Atellane farce. The influx of Greek literary models raised its prestige, but brought about an all but unobserved and far-reaching change. In this transition from extemporized to pre-planned drama, from the oral to the written, there are occasional allusions and reflections that in a sense turn the fascination of the new into a theme, and make the most of it. Contrast the absence (so far as we know) in Middle and New Comedy of jokes about letters of the alphabet.

References to the change of medium fall into two classes. In one, writing and literacy themselves become the theme. Plautus has an astonishing abundance of examples. This is a reaction to a change in the world around him, in which literacy is becoming a phenomenon of general significance.[11] We thus encounter a large group of jokes based on the joy of acquiring a new cultural technique. The image of the school is strikingly frequent. Thus Sophoclidisca in the *Persa* complains of being thought a blockhead. She is in her fifth year of service with her mistress; if a sheep went to school for so long, it would certainly have learned to read long ago (vv. 172–4). In the *Truculentus* a lover is informed that he has completed the course: 'you've mastered the alphabet.' For his part, however, he seeks permission to memorize as before (vv. 735–6).[12] In the *Asinaria* young Argyrippus complains of being thrown out of his girlfriend's house like a 'half-taught school-boy' (vv. 26–7). The ability to handle the alphabet is another favourite theme. The *senex amator* Demipho announces at one point in the *Mercator* that today has been his first day at school: he already knows three letters, A M O (vv. 303–4). In the *Rudens* a slave asks a pimp if he is a doctor, *medicus*; the other replies that he is one letter more, from which the slave, sharp as a razor, infers that he must be a beggar, *mendicus* (vv. 1304–6). All this is not the most characteristic feature of the difference in composition between written and improvised comedy, but reflects with great exactness the general process of upheaval towards the end of the third century BC, being comprehensible only as reflecting the obvious novelty of the phenomenon. A culture in which literacy is fully established does not treat letters and reading like this.

Furthermore, there are metatheatrical reflections of the transition from extempore theatre to writtem drama, in which the author unmistakably distances himself from the world of the impromptu. They consist in frequent allusions to the fact that the actors must now learn their parts by heart, word for word. We may take two examples

---

[11] Cf. W. V. Harris, *Ancient Literacy* (Cambridge, Mass., and London, 1989), 158 ff.

[12] [This presupposes the traditional reading *commentari* and not Lindsay's *adcentare*, which fits this verse well but wrecks the sequel.— ED.]

from the *Poenulus*. At one point three witnesses need to be coached for their parts in the ensuing intrigue; one of them objects (vv. 550–4)

> We already know all that; it's the audience who need to be told. It's for their sake we're performing this play; you ought to instruct *them*, so that when you act they'll know what you're up to. Don't worry about us: we know the whole business, since we've all learnt it along with you so as to pick up your cues.

When shortly afterwards another of the participants is asked to say his lines in order to show that he is properly rehearsed, he replies with the same joke (v. 581): 'Look here, I'm better rehearsed than the tragic or comic actors.' Those are unmistakable allusions to the manner in which written drama is produced, and to the newly introduced position of author.

We may now attempt to draw some conclusions. For a long time the antithesis of 'Plautine' and 'Attic', though often criticized as inadequate, afforded the centre of gravity for analysing Plautus, especially in the German-speaking world. Nevertheless the idea that Italic extempore drama left traces in Plautine comedy and could help explain some of its features has been repeated so often as to be almost hackneyed. Indeed, as a matter of theatrical history this view is entirely plausible. It must necessarily follow that the conventional opposition between Plautine and Attic must be expanded by the third element, the Italic extempore tradition; for we ought to remember that concentration on the antithesis brings with it the danger of judging by classicistic canons, projecting back on to early comedy the contest between later Latin written culture and Greek literature. But if we take into account the time and place for which the *palliata* was devised, things appear in a different light. For the Roman theatrical audience around *c*.200 BC the standard of comparison was *not* New Comedy but Italian farce; its taste had been formed *not* by the likes of Menander, but to a large extent by extempore drama.

Yet nothing could be more wrong than to suppose that Plautus meant to present farces to his audience. On the contrary, he must be seen as superseding improvisation without giving up its comic qualities. It is against this background that we may explain the explicit allusions to written composition, as well as to the play's having been fully rehearsed in advance. Even naming his Greek models and their authors—which he was under no obligation to do—shows that the adaptation did not count as a lessening of his own achievement, a *furtum* (to use the accusation later thrown at Vergil), but as an enhancement. Literacy means elevation above the extempore theatre.

This is valid even at the level of technique and composition. The manifold resonances of extempore drama in Plautine comedy should not disguise the fact that his plays were written, and are stamped all through with the capabilities of writing. That does not result from the introduction of Greek models alone. Even when Plautus falls back on familiar oral forms and techniques, the use of writing leaves its traces. The farcical elements have passed through the filter of written composition. The 'comic' bits of business, without ever being too long, have a density and strictness of composition—judged not by verisimilitude but by optimization of effect—that is hardly possible in extemporization.

Thus at the same time Plautus' comedies render Attic New Comedy unliterary and extempore drama literary. As an author he stands at the point of tension between unscripted and literary theatre.

8
Plautus' Mastery of Comic Language
W. S. ANDERSON

Plautus establishes the verbal quality of his comedy in the opening words, whether of the prologue or, where that is delayed or abandoned, in the first scene. He and his characters, he shows, conduct a dialogue with the Greek originals and a conversation with the audience. For example, consider the start of *Mercator*:

> duas res simul nunc agere decretumst mihi:
> et argumentum et meos amores eloquar.
> non ego item facio ut alios in comoediis
> vi vidi amoris facere, qui aut Nocti aut Dii
> aut Soli aut Lunae miserias narrant suas:
> quos pol ego credo humanas querimonias
> non tanti facere, quid velint, quid non velint;
> vobis narrabo potius meas nunc miserias.
>
> (lines 1–8)

I have decided to do two things simultaneously now: I shall explain both the background and my love-life. I am not doing as I have seen others in comedies doing under the power of love, who set forth their wretchedness either to Night or Day or Sun or Moon: who I definitely do not believe make much account of human complaints, what they might wish or not wish; I shall set forth rather to you now my wretchedness.

The speaker is the young lover Charinus, who in the remainder of the play shows no particular understanding of himself or the comic genre. Here, he carefully analyses his behaviour and compares it with that of other comic lovers: they complain to the elements; he is going to address the audience. I consider this a deliberate intrusion by Plautus (not in the original Greek of Philemon) to force into the open the artificiality of the prologue and of the convention of apostrophizing aspects of Nature. Lines 3–8 break the dramatic illusion and, in rejecting as ridiculous one apostrophe, announce a different apostrophe to the audience, which would be problematic, too, except that

Plautus intends to maintain his relationship with the audience throughout the course of this comedy. After all, when the lover apostrophizes the Night or the Moon—it is doubtful that the list should include Day and Sun, except to suit the Latin love of words—what is he doing except indirectly addressing the audience? But when he does appeal to these elements of Nature, at least he seems to have a reason, namely, to ask for help; whereas addressing the audience accomplishes nothing within the dramatic frame, but wins attention for the play. Charinus declares his agnosticism in lines 6–7, further exposing his and Plautus' superiority to dramatic conventions of naturalism. In short, Plautus has used Charinus here as anything but the foolish, totally love-possessed young man he should be: he serves, rather, the Roman writer's purpose of wrecking the prologue and creating a connection with the audience apart from the drama.

Charinus does not exhibit any striking vocabulary, but he does show a fondness for words, repeating *facere* in lines 3 and 4, giving four 'deities' in a list connected with the polysyndeton of *aut*, repeating in line 7 *quid velint* in positive and negative form, and echoing *miserias narrant suas* + dative of line 5 at line 8. Now, after briefly identifying the Greek and Roman titles and writers of the comedy (lines 9–10), he starts on his story of love. In three lines, he quickly narrates how he went as trader to Rhodes and fell in love with an extraordinarily beautiful woman. But then he turns back to the audience (lines 14–15) to request its gracious attention. Note the potential contradiction here: Charinus has projected no personal character so far and thus earned no sympathy for his dramatic role or his love; yet as prologue speaker, playing with his opportunity to be within and outside the drama, he has aroused our interest.

In line 16, Charinus once again seems to distinguish himself from the usual lovers of comedy, but line 17, in which he might have clarified that distinction, has come down to us hopelessly corrupt. Then, he continues with a list of the faults that attend love (lines 18–23). Not content with that list, he proceeds to expand its contents with twenty-one more items, ending with *multiloquium, parumoquium* (lines 24–31). Both these Latin words seem to have been invented by Plautus here. The first captures our feelings about the verbosity of Charinus' lists and speech in general, and indeed he will soon (line 37) ask the audience not to be angered by his wordiness. The second serves as a surprise joke by which Plautus lets Charinus make fun of himself. What he calls 'brevity' or 'speaking in a few words' (*pauciloquium*, line

34: another neologism) turns out to be the lover's failure to be usefully eloquent for his suit (lines 35–6). But that kind of 'brevity' has fuelled his verbosity now for more than twenty lines and postponed the promised *argumentum*, which he started momentarily at line 11. Finally, at line 40 he resumes his sketch of the background and holds himself to it for the next sixty lines, until he comes back to the beautiful Rhodian woman he earlier mentioned. After telling us enough about her to indicate that she was a slave-prostitute and that he spent a night with her, he affects to come quickly to the point: 'What need for words? I bought her and yesterday brought her here [to Athens]. I don't want my father to know that' (lines 106–7). In that query, *quid verbis opus est?*, Charinus for the first time seems to consult brevity. But it is significant that he chooses to shorten the background narrative, whereas he has greatly expanded the 'business' with the audience and his 'dialogue' with the Greek play Plautus has adapted. Although this is not Plautus' longest prologue, it surpasses in length anything that we know from Menander.

The verbosity of Charinus, then, does not enhance his status as a character or enrich the dramatic power of the play; on the contrary, it creates an alliance between Charinus (who, by stepping outside his role, becomes a spokesman for Plautus) and the audience to stand apart and withhold sympathy from the Greek characters and composition of Philemon. In the course of Plautus' adapted comedy, Charinus continues to waste the sympathy that, I think certain, the Greek playwright generated for him. Instead of conveying some genuine feeling about his father, his Rhodian beloved, and his loyal friend Eutychus, he is made by Plautus to emote and rant and rage in the most extreme and extravagant manner. His two big scenes with Eutychus—first, when his friend reports the bad news that the girl has been taken away (lines 588 ff.) and, second, when his friend tries to get him to be reasonable about seeing the girl who has been located (lines 842 ff.), but cannot be approached just yet—give him the opportunity to overact, to overstate his misery, and thus to make himself ridiculous to the audience. Here are some of his responses to Eutychus in lines 601 ff.: 'Before you catch your breath, tell me in a single word: Where am I: here in life or among the dead? [Notice his impossible demand for an answer in one word, after all his loquacity.] ... I am dead; that statement has killed me ... Eutychus, you are committing a capital crime ... You have plunged your sword into my throat; now I shall fall dead ... Now you are hurling mountains of blazing evil against me. Go on, torment me, executioner, once you have begun.' Ringing the changes on various metaphors of death, Charinus keeps saying that he is dead and dying, but of course remains very much alive—comically so. The more he varies his images, the less credible he becomes. Thus, by expanding what may have been a single metaphor in the original, Plautus undoes the melodrama of the Greek.

Charinus is the most talkative character in his comedy, but Plautus uses his wordiness to make him an exaggerated and silly figure. As the typical lover, he cannot control his situation, and so his words emphasize his helplessness. Nevertheless, in the often spectacular imagery and ranting speeches that Plautus assigns him, Charinus has the premier role. We laugh at him, but we enjoy his verbiage, and the play acquires its unique Plautine character largely because of this talkative and silly lover.

In plays of Plautus' maturity, drastic changes are introduced to inherited love stories, and the typical lover gets shunted aside, upstaged by more enterprising characters who can act out Plautus' concept of comic heroism. These heroes revel in language; they are supremely articulate and love to use words to deceive and to boast of their exploits. Nothing like this has come down to us in Greek New Comedy, and the conclusion seems unassailable, that Plautus has introduced these verbal magicians and their boasting routines into his adaptations. In the *Mostellaria*, the lover Philolaches attracts much attention at the start, and he briefly stars in a lyric aria (lines 84–156), but by line 405 he has declared himself a client of his slave Tranio and yielded the stage to him for the rest of the play, and Tranio assumes the lead as the intrepid rogue. With one false story after another, he leads his master, the neighbour, and a loanshark a merry chase, doing it all with words, nothing more. In themselves, the lies are spectacular, and Tranio draws them out for our amusement, making his victims ridiculous. At one point, Plautus has him turn to the audience and chortle over his heroism and the folly of the others:

> Alexandrum magnum atque Agathoclem aiunt maxumas
> due res gessisse: quid mihi fiet tertio,
> qui solus facio facinora inmortalia?
> vehit hic clitellas, vehit hic autem alter senex.
> novicium mihi quaestum institui non malum:
> nam muliones mulos clitellarios

habent, at ego habeo homines clitellarios.
magni sunt oneris: quidquid imponas vehunt.

(lines 775–82)

They say that two men, Alexander the Great and Agathocles performed the greatest deeds. What about me as a third, who single-handed do deeds that are deathless? This old man here carries saddle bags, and this man does, too. I have invented for myself a new means of profit that's not bad at all: muleteers have mules carrying saddle bags, but I have human beings to carry them. They are great beasts of burden: they'll carry whatever you load on them.

Tranio here speaks behind his victims' backs, as he walks from one to the other, addressing us, calling our attention to his power and magnificent status. First, he links Alexander the Great, unquestionably a monumental figure, and Agathocles of Sicily, perhaps more familiar to his audience, but also of lesser stature. That might prepare us for the anticlimax of his claim to be a third 'hero,' because of his 'immortal and single-handed feats.' Then, instead of elaborating the military imagery, as other slave-rogues in Plautus often do, Tranio is made to emphasize the anticlimax by his sudden switch of images. His victims are not brave foes in battle (like those of Alexander and Agathocles), but human pack-animals; and his glorious achievement consists in outdoing conventional muleteers, who depend on mules! Thus, Plautus lets us enjoy Tranio's proud boasts, but also distance ourselves from his limited heroic horizons, as he tries to pull down the greatest generals to his level, whose proud image is that of a drover of old men.

Plautus finds it very easy to contrive grandiloquent and ranting soliloquies for his characters, both his heroes and his villains. Ballio the pimp, in *Pseudolus*, has a wonderful part; and other pimps and many fathers, when they have been cheated and made fools of, get some superb comic speeches to express their angry frustration. Euclio, the miser of *Aulularia*, takes over the comedy, almost entirely eclipsing the lover, Lyconides, and the love plot involving his daughter. He is Plautus' best comic 'villain' because of his torrent of excited, image-filled words and his volcanic energy racing around the stage. However, Plautus does not confine his verbal magic to soliloquies: he creates many scenes of verbal interchange, where words, not dramatic theme, dominate his interest and the audience's attention.

Midway through the *Bacchides*, as Chrysalus starts to recover from his young master's folly in returning the stolen money and prepares to cheat his old master again of the sum, Plautus stages his confrontation with old Nicobulus as follows: Nicobulus believes he is able to out-think the slave and his planned deception, and he scornfully taunts him, but Chrysalus taunts him right back and totally out-talks and -thinks him.

> NIC. propterea hoc facio ut suadeas gnato meo
> ut pergraecetur tecum, tervenefice.
> CHRYS o stulte, stulte, nescis nunc venire te;
> atque in eopse astas lapide, ut praeco praedicat.
> N. responde: quis me vendit? C. quem di diligunt,
> adulescens moritur, dum valet, sentit, sapit.
> hunc si ullus deus amaret, plus annis decem,
> plus iam viginti mortuom esse oportuit:
> terrai iam odium ambulat, iam nil sapit
> nec sentit, tantist quantist fungus putidus.
>
> (lines 812–21)

N. I am doing this precisely so that you can persuade my son to join you in Greek perversion, you triple villain.

C. You poor, poor fool: you don't even realize that you're up for sale now. You're standing on the very block, as the auctioneer starts to announce the proceedings.

N. Tell me, who's selling me?

C. 'Those whom the gods love die young,' at the peak of health, sensibility, and intelligence. If any god loved this man (pointing Simo out to the audience), he should have died more than ten, no, more than twenty years ago. Now he walks about, loathed by every person on earth, devoid of intelligence, devoid of sensibility, worth about as much as a rotten mushroom.

Nicobulus expresses his contempt for his slave by his sardonic tone and by the choice of verb and epithet in the second line: the verb, with its chauvinistic view of Greek depravity, could not, of course, have been in Menander's text, and we know that the epithet is unique here, hence also introduced by Plautus. Literally, it means 'triple-poisoner' and specifies Chrysalus' supposed villainy in a highly picturesque manner. Nicobulus implicitly wishes to execute this 'hardened criminal.' Undisturbed, however, by his master's confident irony, Chrysalus taunts him with his weakness and ignorance. He starts with the metaphor of a slave auction and claims that, unwittingly, Nicobulus is on the block, up for sale. This image points to a role reversal, and Nicobulus asks the obvious question: who has the power to sell him?

Although Chrysalus does not deign to answer him, we can understand (and this scene confirms the fact) that Chrysalus now has assumed mastery over foolish, gullible Nicobulus, a mastery that largely depends on his verbal superiority. By way of answer, the slave quotes a famous saying, which should serve as a consolation to parents of prematurely dead children: the gods take young men away when they love them and wish to spare them the misfortunes and misery of later life. We know that Menander used this saying, too, since he quoted it as a single trimeter, but his line comes down to us entirely divorced from its context, to frustrate any attempt to ascertain how it worked in the Greek comedy. I suspect that the way Plautus has divided the saying over two half-lines indicates his tactics of expansion and comic articulation. What may have been adequate for Menandrian irony in a single line, becomes, in Plautus' Latin, the basis for a highly amusing tricolon of interpretation. After analysing human life into health, feeling, and intelligence, Chrysalus proceeds to apply the tricolon in reverse order to his master, who lacks intelligence and feeling, he asserts, and has as much 'health' as a rotten fungus.

Thus, the slave has retorted to Nicobulus' confident insults with three distinct sequences of verbal mastery. Of these, I believe, only the saying about dying young was in Menander: Plautus has introduced both the image of the slave auction and the caustic elaboration of the Greek saying, which ends by reducing the master to a disgustingly decayed mushroom. To this, Nicobulus has no answer. Almost speechless in his anger, he commands that Chrysalus be dragged off and lashed to a column, to await further punishment. Slaves do not challenge their masters in this impudent manner in Menander; Plautus has created this kind of verbal confrontation, to give symbolic victory and 'mastery' to the articulate rogue. When, in line 818, Chrysalus stopped addressing Nicobulus directly and switched to the third person, he implicitly, probably explicitly, was addressing the audience and gesturing scornfully at 'this man' Nicobulus. It is Plautus' typical technique of letting his hero speak in his role and simultaneously comment on his performance for our delight. Thus, the words are mostly Plautine, not Menandrian here.

Critics often note the abundance of Plautine diction, especially in relation to the dictions of Menander and Terence. Plautine theatre makes lavish use of words: striking neologisms that exploit length and resonance, like *tervenefice* above; picturesque images, like being on the block or resembling a rotten fungus; series of verbs or nouns, in asyndeton or polysyndeton; wonderful stretches of alliteration and assonance that emphasize a key comic idea; resonant and significant names that substitute ridiculous overtones for the conventional Greek names of the originals, such as Pistoclerus and Mnesilochus for the two young men (originally Moschos and Sostratos) in the *Bacchides*. It takes normal situations of excitement, anger, despair, enthusiasm, which Menander and Terence keep strictly under control and subordinate to their dramatic themes, and they become occasions for histrionic performances, cameo parts for actors that use comedy to generate laughs. Terence will not let the 'running slave' (*servus currens*) take off and perform the glorious routine that Plautus leads us joyously to expect. Terence will not even let the angry father voice his rage in a long, satisfying rant against son and slave: all he is permitted to do is to say that he can barely control himself because of wrath, and then he quickly simmers down and takes rational steps to deal with the situation. Plautus wants us to enjoy and laugh at all kinds of energetic excitement and to distance ourselves from them, relishing them as performance. The more words he uses, the more he elaborates routines and situations, the less we identify with the supposedly deep passions that lie behind these great 'acts', the more we let ourselves just go with the flow of words and the verbal mastery that dominates.

Menander's characters seem to be straining to understand what it means to be a human being: they must learn to think, feel, and talk humanely, in order to live properly as men and women. It is significant that Cnemon, the 'inhuman human being', lets his rage get out of hand at first, and Menander can give him an opening speech in which he indulges his wild misanthropy by wishing he had the Gorgon's Head of Perseus, so that he could turn all mankind into silent statues. He must be 'humanized' during the play, to tone down his own speech and to accept the ordinary talk of his relatives and neighbours. In Plautus, however, we find an emphasis on the inhuman and the superhuman, and the extraordinary words he assigns his characters turn average situations—situations that his Greek sources kept in control to serve the humane theme—into fantastic, wildly unreal and hence thoroughly enjoyable scenes for the audience. If speech is the definitive feature of humankind, wildly improbable speech defines the comic beings that Plautus renders larger than life. And no small part of that largeness and grandiloquence is the versatile metre in which he embodies his words.

9

The *MENAECHMI*: Roman Comedy of Errors

ERICH SEGAL

Plautus wrote only one Comedy of Errors. His Greek predecessors wrote so many that *Agnoia* ('Errora,' or more literarily, 'Ignorance'), who speaks the prologue to Menander's *Perikeiromene*, (The Girl Who Gets Her Hair Cut Short), has often been called the patron goddess of New Comedy. The *Menaechmi* is generally considered to be early Plautus, and may well have been an experiment with a theme which proved uncongenial to the Latin comic poet. For the playwright usually prefers wit to ignorance, shrewd deception to naïve misunderstanding. Chance, *to automaton*, rules the world where things occur *apo tautomatou*, a condition which Plautus usually mocks as in Miles 287: *Forte fortuna per impluvium huc despexi in proxumum* ('On the roof, I chanced by chance to look down through our neighbor's skylight').

In a Comedy of Errors we 'automatically' laugh at the bumbling ignorance of characters who are nothing but puppets. And yet Plautus' real affection is for puppeteers, manipulators like Tranio, Palaestrio, Epidicus, and Pseudolus, men whose cleverness leaves nothing to chance, and who flourish in a world where the source of laughter is not automation, but machination.

The first man to translate it into English saw that the *Menaechmi* was different. Writing his preface in 1595, William Warner called the play: 'a pleasant and fine Conceited Comaedie, taken out of the most excellent wittie Poet Plautus: Chosen purposely from out the rest, as the least harmful, and yet most delightfull.' It is not 'harmful' because it lacks the very feature that was Roman comedy's prime legacy to the Renaissance: intrigue. It has none of *l'inganno* that was the staple of Italian *commedia erudita*, or the charming roguery that would characterize Jonson's *Mosca* and Molière's *Scapin* (not to mention Beaumarchais' *Figaro*, in a later age). Cedric Whitman refers to this special quality of cleverness in the Aristophanic hero as ponēria. Plautus celebrates it as *malitia*, as in the epilogue to the *Epidicus* (line 732): *Hic is homo qui libertatem malitia invenit sua.* ('Behold a man who won his freedom by being tricky'). Whatever it be called, it does not appear at all in the *Menaechmi*. Plaustus' comedy, though it deals in duplicates, has no duplicity, and, though its heroes are doubles, it has no double-dealing. There is only error, pure, simple . . . and harmless.

In other respects, however, the *Menaechmi* is a very Plautine creation. Much of it is in that musical comedy style which made its author famous and invited favorable comparisons with Aristophanes (Cicero was not loath to link the two names in praise). Terence, like Menander his paragon, has few—if any—real sons. And, while the *Menaechmi* lacks wit, it has in its place wish-fulfillment, in fact the greatest of all fantasies, that of the surrogate self, the alter ego with no superego, someone who can indulge his appetite for pleasure without concern for the consequences. Everyone yearns to be 'Jack in town and Ernest in the country', but this can only happen in dreams or in 'the twin brother of dreams'—as Freud once referred to it—comedy. Plautus presents this happy hallucination in an entertainment which might well be subtitled, *The Importance of Being Menaechmus.*

The two houses onstage represent the conflicting forces in the play. They are not unlike the statues of Artemis and Aphrodite which frame the setting of Euripides' *Hippolytus*. In both dramas, the action takes place in a magnetic field between personifications of restraint and release. It is no mere coincidence that the house of Menaechmus I stands at the exit nearer the forum. The Epidamnian twin is bound by innumerable ties, legal, financial, and social, as well as to a shrewish wife who is constantly 'on the job'. In fact Menaechmus I describes her behavior as excessive *industria* (line 123), a term which gives almost allegorical overtones to the actions of the comedy.

Across the stage, and nearer the harbor—whence visitors come—dwells a lady of pleasure aptly named Erotium. Plautus has an affinity for heroines with similarly delicious *redende Namen*, like Philocomasium in the *Miles* and Pasicompsa in the *Mercator*. Terence, on the other hand, seems content to name his ladies Pamphila in play after play. In contrast to the aptly titled Erotium, Menaechmus' spouse has no name at all; she is merely 'matrona.' Shakespeare reverses this in his *Comedy of Errors*, contrasting the wife Adriana and a *meretrix* referred to merely as 'courtesan'.

While Menaechmus I never seems to be in the right place at the right time, he at least knows the right words. His nickname for Erotium (itself a charactonym meaning 'pleasure') is *voluptas*. This word is not only an endearment, but *le mot juste* to describe the atmosphere in Erotium's domain, one which contrasts sharply with the *industria* across the stage.

Thus when he travels from one side to the other—or at least tries to—Menaechmus is 'acting out' the inner direction of the Comic Spirit. The two houses represent *industria* and *voluptas*, Everyday versus Holiday, or, as Freud would describe it, the Reality Principle versus the Pleasure Principle.

We are visiting the town of Epidamnus on a special day, one which Menaechmus has chosen for a festive release from the rules. Such occasions do not come often and, as the parasite Peniculus remarks, today's celebration is much overdue; there has been a long 'intermission' (*intervallum iam hos dies multos fuit*, line 104). According to the parasite, when Menaechmus does throw a party, it is a truly gala occasion:

> Ita est adulescens; ipsus escae maxumae,
> Cerialis cenas dat . . .
>
> (lines 101–2)
>
> Now here's the way he is: the greatest of all eaters,
> The feasts he gives are festivals of Ceres . . .

To Peniculus, his patron's entertainments are like those national Roman holidays when banquets are served in the Circus.

At this moment, the hero appears. And Menaechmus I is indeed the protagonist. Plautus focuses on the local twin, giving him the larger and more melodic role, whereas Shakespeare concentrates on the visiting brother. We first meet Menaechmus battling soldier-like against marital aggression; he is a military man fighting domestic restraint (cf. lines 127, 129). Now that he has broken through enemy lines he can celebrate: *Clam uxoremst ubi pulchre habeamus atque hunc conburamus diem* (line 152) Hidden from my wife we'll live it up and burn this day to ashes.

His aim, like that of so many Plautine heroes, is *pulchre habere* (or, as elsewhere expressed, *bene habere* or *bene esse*). It is hardly a coincidence that his domestic situation is later described as *male habere*, in fact his wife's behavior to him is *Semper male habere* (line 569).

Menaechmus' opening song describes his wife's restrictive actions in no uncertain terms:

> nam quotiens foras ire volo, me retines, revocas, rogitas,
>   quo ego eam, quam rem agam, quid negoti geram,
>   quid petam, quid feram, quid foris egerim.
>   portitorem domum duxi, ita omnem mihi
>   rem necesse eloqui est, quidquid egi atque ago.
>
> (lines 114–18)

> However often I try to go out, you detain me, delay me, demand such details as
>   Where I'm going, what I'm doing, what's my business all about,
>   Deals I'm making, undertaking, what I did when I was out.
>   I don't have a wife, I've wed a custom's office bureaucrat,
>   For I must declare the things I've done, I'm doing, and all that!

It is her behavior, her *industria*, which has driven him out of the house:

> malo cavebis si sapis,
>   virum observare desines.
> Atque adeo, ne me nequiquam serves, *ob eam industriam*
> Hodie ducam scortum ad cenam atque aliquo condicam foras.
>
> (lines 121–4)

> Watch out for trouble, if you're wise,
>   A husband hates a wife who spies.
> But so you won't have watched in vain, for all your
>   diligence and care,
> Today I've asked a wench to dinner, and we're going out
>   somewhere.

That the playwright himself understood 'holiday psychology' is demonstrated by the remarks of Menaechmus' father-in-law later in the play. When the wife sends for him to complain of her husband's vagaries, the old man does indeed get angry but at her. His infidelity is her fault:

> SENEX. Quotiens monstravi tibi viro ut morem geras,
>   quid ille faciat ne id observes, quo eat, quid rerum gerat.
> MATRONA. at enim ille hinc amat meretricem ex proxumo.
> SENEX. Sane sapit!
>   atque *ob istanc industriam* etiam faxo amabit amplius.
>
> (lines 788–91)

> OLD MAN. How often have I told you to behave yourself with him,

> Don't guard where he's going, what he's doing, what his
>   business is.
> WIFE. But he loves a fancy woman there next door.
> OLD MAN.   He's very wise!
> And I tell you, thanks to all your diligence, he'll love her more.

In this scene he repeats most of Menaechmus' complaints verbatim,
especially the charge of excessive *industria*.

But, just as the wife is 'diligence' incarnate, so the mistress is *voluptas*, Pleasure personified. When Menaechmus first spies her, his
exclamation emphasizes this contrast. The rhetorical structure of the
line defies adequate rendering into English, counterpoising as it does
uxor and *voluptas*, withholding the verb, and hence the entire meaning, until the last possible moment. When Erotium comes into view
he shouts: *Ut ego uxorem, mea voluptas, ubi te aspicio, odi male!* (line
189) ('Oh my wife, my joy, when I see you, how I hate *her!*'). The
antithesis is still more explicit. Just as Erotium is nothing at all like his
wife, so too the day Menaechmus will devote to her will be totally different from his ordinary agenda. Even the banquet he orders would
underscore—in a special sense for the Roman spectators—the fact
that the usual rules were being set aside. He asks Erotium for the following bill-of-fare:

> iube igitur tribu' nobis apud te prandium accurarier
> atque aliquid scitamentorum de foro opsonarier
> glandionidam suillam, laridum pernonidam,
> aut sincipitamenta porcina aut aliquid ad eum modum,
> madida quae mi adposita in mensam miluinam suggerant.
> atque actutum.
>
> (lines 208–12)

> Please arrange a feast at your house. Have it cooked for three of us.
> Also have some very special party foods bought in the forum:
> Glandiose, whole-hog, and a descendant of the lardly ham.
> Or perhaps some pork choppettes, or anything along those lines.
> Let whatever's served be 'stewed,' to make me hungry as a hawk.
> Hurry up and make it snappy.

The desire for 'stewed' delicacies is a normal festive impulse: to get
drunk, tie one on. But Menaechmus has been still more specific. For
all the delicacies on his menu and similar foods *ad eum modum* were
specifically forbidden to Romans by various sumptuary laws. Pliny
(*NH* 8. 78. 209) tells us that this legislation explicitly forbade the

eating of *cenis abdomina, glandia, testiculi, vulvae, sincipita verrina*. Not
only do these outlawed items figure prominently on Menaechmus'
carte du jour, but Plautus plays with them verbally, concocting such
comic dishes as *sincipitamenta* from *sincipita* and the absurd
patronymics *glandionida* ('son of glandules') and *pernonida* ('son of
ham'). Menaechmus can savor even the words which describe his
breaking-of-the-rules banquet.

In another passage Pliny also recounts how stern Cato—Plautus'
contemporary—constantly inveighed against gastronomic luxury,
especially the eating of certain cuts of pork (*NH* 8. 78. 210). In spite of
this, or rather because of this, Plautus' characters go whole-hog in
their infringement of these laws. In the *Casina*, there is a similar call
for 'inebriated' delicacies by Olympio, a slave about to be married
(744–8):

> propere cito intro ite et cito deproperate.
> ego iam intus ero, facite cenam mihi ut ebria sit.
> sed lepide nitideque volo, nil moror barbarico bliteo.

> Hurry up and go inside and quickly hurry up,
> I'll be right in. Prepare a drunken dinner for me.
> Something fine and fancy. Not your bland barbarian stuff!

Thus in the *Menaechmi* the comic escape from the rules (here dietary)
is emphasized by the playwright's calling attention to the very prohibition being violated.

Now that his un-Roman dinner is being swiftly prepared (he is very
insistent that they hurry), the hero strangely, inexplicably, heads for
the forum, not to return until the party is over. The stage is set for a
crescendo of errors. The moment that the local Menaechmus exits
towards the business district, his twin from Syracuse enters from the
harbor. By artful coincidence, the very first word which Menaechmus
II speaks is *voluptas* (line 226). He is little aware of the reverberations
which this word will have for him, and how apt a description it is of
the way of life in this town. For, with the exception of his brother's
house, Epidamnus is the ultimate in festive places. His slave Messenio
describes its denizens exclusively in superlatives:

> nam ita est haec hominum natio: in Epidamnieis
> voluptarii atque potatores maxumei;
> tum sycophantae et palpatores plurumei
> in urbe hac habitant; tum meretrices mulieres
> nusquam perhibentur blandiores gentium.

propterea huic urbei nomen Epidamno inditumst,
quia nemo ferme huc sine damno devortitur.

(lines 258–64)

Now here's the race of men you'll find in Epidamnus:
The greatest libertines, the greatest drinkers too,
The most bamboozlers and charming flatterers,
Live in this city. As for wanton women, well,
Nowhere in the world, I'm told, are they more dazzling.
Because of this, they call this city Epidamnus:
For no one leaves unscathed, 'undamaged', as it were.

The visiting twin will indeed encounter 'voluptuaries', especially the dazzling Erotium, but unlike an ordinary tourist on an ordinary day he will leave Epidamnus undamaged, since his brother will pay all the bills; *damnum* in its literal sense denotes financial ruin. The boy from Syracuse belongs to a great comic tradition: a lowly stranger who arrives in town, is mistaken for someone else of greater importance, and fulfills the comic dream—everything for nothing, specifically food, sex, and money. Xanthias in the *Frogs* is the first of such types in ancient comedy. True to this tradition is Klestakov, Gogol's lowly government clerk who is mistaken for the Inspector General and offered banquets, bribes, and a bride. Like Gogol's hero, the traveling Menaechmus has come to town nearly penniless (*Menaechmi* 255–7); what happens is too good to be true. A beautiful courtesan calls him by name and invites him to a lavish feast of all the senses, one which his brother has paid for. But, before going inside, he is careful enough to give his purse to Messenio—a final safeguard against *damnum*.

But what Menaechmus II experiences *chez* Erotium is quite the opposite of *damnum*. In fact, he profits in every imaginable way. Having revelled to the fullest and been given a fancy embroidered dress (supposedly to be taken to a seamstress for more improvements), he emerges drunk, garlanded, and totally amazed:

Pro di inmortales! quoi homini umquam uno die
boni dedistis plus qui minu' speraverit?
prandi, potavi, scortum accubui, apstuli
hanc, quoiius heres numquam erit post hunc diem.

(lines 473–8)

By all the gods, what man in just a single day
Received more favors, though expecting none at all?

> I've wined, I've dined, I've concubined—and robbed her blind.
> No one but me will own this dress after today!

He then receives some of Erotium's jewelry which, like the fancy garment, was originally stolen by Menaechmus I from his wife. More
damnum for the married twin, to pay for his brother's *voluptas*.

But what of our protagonist? Where has he been while the day was
'burned to ashes' for him? The moment Menaechmus II skips tri-
umphantly offstage, the married twin arrives, singing of his frustration. He enters with a barrage-in-song against the Roman patronage
system. The special 'Roman-ness' of this particular scene (lines 571
ff.) has often been remarked upon. But whether or not there is a reference to the *Lex Cincia* or any other aspect of *clientela* does not alter
the most basic dramatic fact, that just now in the forum, as he was en
route to Erotium's house, Menaechmus was stopped by a client who
forced him to act as his advocate. Molière based *Les Fâcheux* on a similar comic dilemma: a man trying to get to an amorous rendezvous,
delayed by a blocking character who constantly dogs him—like the
bore in Horace, *Sat.* 1. 9: *nil habeo quod agam et non sum piger: usque
sequar te* ('I've got nothing to do and I'm a good walker: so I'll follow
you all the way').

The fate of Menaechmus I demonstrates how inimical are the worlds
of business and pleasure. He vociferously regrets being a *patronus*, a
man with protective responsibilities towards others. From the Roman
standpoint, this was hardly a proper attitude. Polybius (31. 23. 11–12)
tells us that Scipio Aemilianus was considered 'un-Roman' by his
contemporaries precisely because he refused to argue court cases. It is
tradition, as Horace reminds us (*Epist.* 2. 1. 103 ff.), both a pleasure and
a duty (*dulce et sollemne*) for a solid citizen *clienti promere iura*. And it is of
precisely this solemn obligation that Menaechmus complains; he does-
n't want to be a good citizen at all (lines 588–9):

> sicut me hodie nimi' sollicitum cliens quidam habuit neque quod volui
> agere aut quicum licitumst, ita med attinuit, ita detinuit.

> I was just now delayed, forced to give legal aid,
>   no evading this client of mine who had found me.
> Though I wanted to do you know what—and with who
>   still he bound me and tied ropes around me.

Citizenship, like marriage, places certain restraints upon a man.
Which is why, according to Freud, marriage was the subject of the

first 'jokes'; it was one of the earliest restrictions placed on man. Menaechmus has been 'tied up' in the forum on business. To emphasize the 'tenacity' of these restrictions, Plautus employs three variations of the verb *tenere*. First *retinere* (line 113) in reference to the hen-pecking wife, and here *attinere* and *detinere* (line 589) to describe the clinging client. Both ties prevent Menaechmus from following his instinct, *agere quod licitumst*. In the famous *canticum* which follows—whose last four lines represent one of the few examples of near-rhyme in Classical Latin poetry—the protagonist realizes that his great mistake was even thinking about the forum on a day like this:

> di illum omnes perdant, ita mihi
> hunc hodie corrumpit diem,
> meque adeo, qui hodie forum.
> umquam oculis inspexi meis.
> diem corrupi optumum :
> iussi apparari prandium,
> amica expectat me, scio.
> ubi primum est licitum ilico
> properavi abire de foro.
>   (lines 596–600)

> By all the heavens, cursed be he
> Who just destroyed this day for me.
> And curse me too, a fool today,
> For ever heading forum's way.
> The greatest day of all—destroyed,
> The feast prepared, but not enjoyed,
> My love awaits, I know, indeed,
> The very moment I was freed
> I left the forum with great speed.

Plautus emphasizes the haste with which Menaechmus leaves the commercial center. From business in the forum, he rushes towards pleasure at its polar opposite, across the stage, at the house of Erotium. In this play, and at Rome, the first step in a holiday direction is always—as quickly as possible—*abire de foro*.

Forum and 'festivity' are also counterpoised in the *Casina*, a comedy which shares many characteristics with the one we are discussing. Here old Lysidamus, like young Menaechmus, has set aside this special day for merrymaking. But, again like Menaechmus, while he is en route to his banquet-of-the-senses, a lawsuit keeps him in the forum. When he finally returns, he has learned a bitter lesson:

Stultitia magna est, mea quidem sententia,
hominem amatorem ullum ad forum procedere,
in eum diem quoi quod amet in mundo siet;
sicut ego feci stultus: contrivi diem,
dum asto advocatus quoidam cognato meo;
quem hercle ego litem adeo perdidisse gaudeo.

(Lines 563–9)

It's folly, that's what I would call it, total folly,
For any man in love just to approach the forum,
The very day his love awaits, all fancied up.
That's what I've done—fool that I am. I've ruined the day,
While acting as attorney for a relative.
By Hercules, I'm overjoyed we lost the case!

His *faux pas*, in the most literal sense, was *ad forum procedere*. For, in Plautine comedy, the funny things can only happen on the way from the forum. This identical situation prevailed in Plautine Rome, since, on the days when his comedies were presented, there was no business at all: the theater was packed and the forum was empty. In fact the *Casina* prologue states this in no uncertain terms: 'the holidays are on . . . a halcyon quiet floats about the forum' (lines 25–6).

Thus, by whatever standards, Roman or Epidamnian, Menaechmus I has broken the cardinal rule of holiday: he has gone to business. Forum and festivity are polar opposites, two completely different ways of life. It is therefore understandable that Menaechmus I should be tied up with *industria* while his unattached twin enjoys the *voluptas*. Even when he finally breaks away from the forum and hastens to cross over to Erotium's house, the married twin encounters on stage the greatest *fâcheuse* of all: his wife. Having been warned by the parasite, the matrona now waits to ambush her wayward husband. *Industria* literally blocks the road to *voluptas*. Disaster!

What had promised to be 'the greatest day of all' has now turned out to be the very worst. The entire fabric of Menaechmus' existence seems torn to shreds. Everyone is angry at him. All doors are closed to him. Not only is he—to use his own term—*exclusissumus* (line 697), 'the most kicked-out man in the world', but he is then pronounced insane by a sort of psychiatrist *gloriosus*, ancestor to the quack doctors who appear in the Saint George plays, a professional whose questions are not unlike those which Socrates asks Strepsiades in the *Clouds*. And now several burly *lorarii* are about to drag him off for medical 'treatment'. Someone else has acted insanely, but Menaechmus I must suffer the cure.

How is it possible that one man could get all of the blame and yet none of the pleasure? This crucial question is finally answered when the brothers meet face to face. Messenio then sees the mirror-image of his master 'speculum tuum!' (line 1062), and proclaims the same apparent paradox which astounds the Duke in *Twelfth Night* (v.i. 208–9):

> One face, one voice, one habit and two persons!
> A natural perspective that is and is not!

Another of Shakespeare's characters, like Messenio in the Latin play, then cries, 'How have you made division of yourself?' In Shakespeare's comedy, as well as Plautus', the sudden discovery that the protagonist has a twin brother relieves a situation of potential tragedy. Indeed, there is an ambiguity to the phrase 'division of yourself'. In a tragic context it could mean, quite literally, schizophrenia. In a comedy, it means twins.

There is a special significance to the identity crisis in the *Menaechmi*. The hero, a married, responsible citizen, desires to go on a wild revel, to break the rules. In point of fact, someone named Menaechmus—someone who looks just like him—does savor all the forbidden delights. But this is another Menaechmus, who for one reason or another is not subject to the restrictions which bind the local twin. Without any consequences, Menaechmus II enjoys what is ordinarily illegal: *furtum, scortum,* and *prandium* (line 170), stolen goods, stolen love, and an 'illegal' banquet. The traveling twin bears no responsibility for the stolen property. After all, it was freely given to him. He is unmarried, so his fling with Erotium can occasion no domestic repercussions. And, since he is a foreigner, he can enjoy a *prandium* of forbidden delicacies without infringing any local legislation which would restrain his citizen-twin.

The local brother can derive some pleasure from this spree—he can enjoy being told about it (1141–4):

> MEN. II.   Prandi perbene
>   Potavi atque accubui scortum: pallam et aurum hoc abstuli.
> MEN I. Gaudeo, edepol, si quid propter me tibi eveniat boni.
>   Nam illa quom to ad se vocabat memet esse credidit.
> MEN. II.   Just terrifically, I've wined and
>   Dined and concubined—of dress and gold I've robbed
>   her blind.
> MEN. I. Wonderful! By Pollux I'm glad you had your little spree.
>   She invited you to dinner thinking you were me.

The married brother's joy can only be vicarious. But even here there is a consolation, at least it is completely guilt-free. While a certain Menaechmus, his mirror image, was reveling with Erotium, he was busy fulfilling his civic obligations in the forum—if it was anything like the business district in Rome, a place dominated from the north by the temple of Janus, that two-faced deity the Romans worshipped. Since the thought is not tantamount to the deed, Menaechmus I is, today at least, totally innocent.

Earlier in the play, at the height of the confusion, the married brother cries out that all these wild goings-on seem to him like a dream (line 1047). He does not realize how right he is. For this comedy is actually the *dream of Menaechmus* I, whose fantasies have conjured up a surrogate self to indulge in forbidden pleasures while he himself preserves the outward respectability of every day. In fact, as the recognition scene demonstrates, there is really only one Menaechmus: the married one. After this day of errors, this *folle journée*, everything will return to normal. Identities are properly distributed, and Menaechmus II must take back his original name—Sosicles. They both will return to Syracuse, and the family business. *Voluptas* today, but *industria* tomorrow. The play even closes with an auction announcement.

If nothing else, the finale of Plautus' one play of errors reminds us that Menaechmus II does not really exist. Such a man lives only in dreams or in comedy, when responsible citizens invoke an alter ego to let the world slip and succumb to the Pleasure Principle. Forgotten is the Reality Principle, which Freud describes as 'ever striving for what is useful and guarding itself against damage'. Today in Epidamnus, pleasure has prevailed. And so the brothers can leave this town of *voluptarii maxumi*, this festive spot like Shakespeare's wood outside Athens, where identities are scrambled and lunatics and lovers run rampant. They can depart with everything in order, for, unlike the world of the Reality Principle, there has been no damage. Comedy, which is in essence the triumph of the Pleasure Principle, creates that unique situation wherein joy comes *sine damno in Epidamno*.

10

Crucially Funny, or Tranio on the Couch: The *Servus callidus* and Jokes About Torture

HOLT PARKER

Even the casual reader of Plautus must be impressed by the frequency of jokes about the torture of slaves, the more so as this is a feature found very seldom in Greek New Comedy or in Terence. There is a certain amount of slave-beating in Old Comedy. The parabasis to the *Peace* includes jokes about beating runaway slaves as part of the old-fashioned material Aristophanes has banished (742–7), though he is not above using them in the prologue to the *Knights* (cf. *Wasps* 1292–3) and *Frogs* 616 ff., where Xanthias and Dionysus are beaten together. Compare the term *mastigias*, 'whipping-post', at Ar. *Kn.* 1228, *Frogs* 501, and even in Menander (*Dys.* 473, *Perik.* 134).

But there is nothing approaching the frequency, variety, and detailed vocabulary of torture that Plautus shows. The large number of the threats of torture, and their failure to be carried out, has been frequently noted by scholars, yet they have offered little in the way of explanation. Plautus is not a reliable source for Roman social history; yet to say that jokes are meant to be funny is not very illuminating. What a society finds funny and why can be very illuminating, and the Roman jokes about torture clearly do more in the plays than merely aid in characterization.

Erich Segal emphasizes the Saturnalian aspects of Roman comedy, the freedom for a day from the normal constraints—the threats are there precisely to demonstrate what will *not* be carried out.[1] They remind the audience of the real world and the flouting of conventional practice. Yet the main question has been left untouched. There are many aspects of normal Roman life and the life of slaves that

---

[1] E. Segal, *Roman Laughter* (Cambridge Mass., 1968), 144, 147.

could have served as a basis for comic reversal. Why is the torture of
the slaves singled out and singled out so repeatedly?

An answer, I believe, involves examining two separate problems.
The first question is why the threats are there at all: what comic purpose does the uttering of these threats of torture and crucifixion
serve? The second is why, once the threats are made, they are not carried out. I shall bring to bear on each of these questions certain well-
known facts of Roman social history, and operate within a Freudian
framework.[2]

Let us consider the first question: Why are these threats of torture
made at all? One principal source of comedy, as noted by Freud and
others, can be succinctly stated as 'We mock what we fear'. An object
of anxiety is brought forth from the dark places of the mind and
exhibited in the full light of the sun, for everyone to see and jeer at, on
the stage of the individual psyche or of the city itself. There under the
healing rays, it seems less terrible, and because it can be surrounded
by, and associated with, ludicrous objects or situations, it can be
flouted and so rendered less dreadful. In *Wit and Its Relation to Uncon-
sciousness*, Freud distinguishes Wit, Comedy, and Humour, defining
Humour as 'an economy of expenditure in feeling',[3] and notes,
'Humor is thus a means to gain pleasure despite the painful affects
which disturb it; it acts as a substitute for this affective development,
and takes its place'.[4] Freud notes the ease of application of this idea to
the grim jokes of gallows humour, and indeed most of his illustrations come from this genre.

In our own society, one may note the sharp increase in recent years
of 'horror jokes' (about AIDS, cancer, or terrorism). One of the reasons we all laugh at such subjects is that they allow us to dispel some
of our immense fear of random harm or death; they will thus be of
the greatest value to future cultural historians in showing exactly
what things we were most afraid of, perhaps unknowingly.

For the Roman, the free slave was the most terrifying of oxymora.
Seneca quotes the famous proverb 'You have as many enemies as you
have slaves' (*Ep.* 47. 5), and the speech Tacitus gives to Gaius Cassius,
following the murder of Pedianus Secundus by one of his slaves,

---

[2] Here I follow Amy Richlin in applying certain elements of Freudian analysis to
illuminate Roman Satire in *The Garden of Priapus* (New Haven, 1983).

[3] Sigmund Freud, *Wit and its Relation to the Unconscious*, in *The Basic Writings of
Sigmund Freud*, trans. and ed. with an introduction by A. A. Brill (New York, 1938);
hereafter cited as 'Freud, *Wit*'.   [4] Ibid. 797.

represents at least a portion of Roman sentiment (*Ann.* 14. 44): 'Such filth cannot be controlled except by force.' The Roman of Plautus' age had good reason to fear his slaves. Roman society had undergone and was undergoing profound changes.

During Plautus' lifetime Rome was engaged in a series of wars that resulted in a massive influx of slaves, and the transformation of the Italian countryside by the rise of the *latifundia*. Even after the Second Punic War, the number and percentage of adult male citizens under arms and away from their homes or even absent from Italy for periods of seven years or more (Livy 40. 36. 10) continued almost unabated. The absence of adult male citizens as soldiers and the massive influx of slaves made a rebellion a constant possibility.

This possibility erupted into reality on no fewer than four occasions during Plautus' adult life. The first we know of occurred in 217 (Livy 22. 33. 2), when twenty-five slaves were detected with the help of an informer in a conspiracy on the Campus Martius, and were crucified. Significantly, this is the first mention of crucifixion in the Roman historical record. In 198, there occurred a slave insurrection at Sestia, fomented by Carthaginian captives (Livy 32. 26. 4–18; Zonaras. 9. 16. 6). The notice in Livy is confused and it is not clear how far the rebellion spread or whether they were successful in capturing Sestia. The rebellion was crushed, the slaves fled, and some 2,000 were executed. Remnants of the conspiracy then attempted to seize Praeneste. They also were defeated and some 500 executed. There was considerable alarm at Rome. Patrols of the streets and prisons were increased and the captives were loaded with chains specified as weighing not less than ten pounds.

Two years later in 196, there was a slave rebellion in Etruria (Livy 33. 36. 1–3). Again the text is lacunose, but the conspiracy required a full legion to subdue it, and the leaders were flogged and then crucified. Finally, in 185 there was a rebellion among the slaves of Apulia, where the shepherds had taken to banditry (Livy 39. 29. 8–10). Some 7,000 were condemned to death, though many escaped.

It is against this background that the jokes about torture in Plautus must be seen. For all the laughable freedom of a disobedient Tranio or Pseudolus, the vast number of references to punishment constantly remind the audience of the absolute power of life and death it holds over these slaves. Further, it is the clever slaves themselves who say these comfortable words to the audience. The *servi callidi* go out of their way to point out that they have been punished yesterday (e.g. Sosia, *Am.* 446; Libanus, *As.* 551; Leonida, *As.* 564–5, Sagaristio, *Per.* 270–1) and will be tomorrow (e.g. Tranio, *Most.* 1178; Chrysalus, *Bacch.* 361–2). It is only today, while the Saturnalian spirit reigns, that they hope to get off.

A particularly fine example of the slaves' comforting the audience with reminders of the power it holds over them is *Cist.* 785: 'Whoever's messed up will get thrashed and whoever hasn't can get smashed.' This excellent bit of metatheatricality has been taken, perhaps uncritically, as indicating the servile status of all actors. While there is evidence that some actors at least in Plautus' time may have been citizens or freedmen, the point of these lines and the assumption that underlies them is unchanged. The troupe of actors consists of slaves and their master can beat them or not, according to how well they have acted. Thus the splendid paradox where an uppity slave may be punished for not acting enough like an uppity slave.

Two points need to be made about crucifixion specifically, as the summit of the range of possible tortures. Crucifixion is not just one more among the punishments with which a slave is threatened, including other ways of being put to death. Tranio for example is threatened with being burned alive and whipped to death (*Most.* 1114, 1167–8). Crucifixion is the *supplicium servile*, the slave's punishment *par excellence* (cf. Tac. *Hist.* 4. 11).[5] Barsby, citing some of the instances of wholesale crucifixion, writes: 'But these are cases of slave rebellions, not of domestic misbehavior, and it must be doubted that crucifixion was a real-life punishment for domestic slaves in Plautus' day.'[6] There is no doubt that the jokes about crucifixion are intended as exaggeration. The *senex iratus* huffs and puffs, but then a few lines later lets the slave off.

However, there is equally no doubt that behind these jokes lay a definite social reality. Until very late in the Christian era, the law placed few restrictions on the punishments that a master might inflict on a slave. Even then it is only certain specific modes of punishment (such as being sold to fight wild beasts: *Dig.* 18. 1. 42, 48. 8. 11) that are prohibited. Constantine upholds the right of a master to beat or whip to death a slave in the course of just punishment (*Cod. Theod.* 9.12.1). We

---

[5] But as John Crook points out not confined to slaves: *Law and Life of Rome, 90 B.C.–A.D. 212* (Ithaca, NY, 1967), 273; cf. Cic., *II in Verrem* 5.161–4. See M. Hengel, *Crucifixion in the Ancient World* (London, 1977), *passim*.

[6] John Barsby, *Plautus: Bacchides* (Oak Park, Ill., 1986), ad v. 365.

find Hadrian upholding the *SC Silanianum*, whereby all slaves under the same roof where their master has been killed must be executed (*Dig.* 29.5.28; cf. Tac. *Ann.* 14. 44).

For public contractors, we have a very precise decree specifying the details of crucifixion of condemned slaves.[7] There is no evidence for Plautus' own day for the crucifixion of domestic slaves, since the historians were only infrequently interested in household matters. However, Cicero's *Pro Cluentio* (185) vividly describes Sassia's torture, mutilation, and crucifixion of her slave doctor Nicostratus.

Secondly, crucifixion is a specifically Roman practice. It is not mentioned in Menander and is virtually unknown in the Greek world, where it was never used as a slave punishment. The Romans picked it up from the Carthaginians (Polyb. 1. 11. 5, Livy 22. 13. 9) and, as was pointed out, applied it first to rebellious slaves. Crucifixion is therefore another of the illusion-breaking Roman references and practices with which Plautus decorates his ostensibly Greek stage. This feature plays an important role in the functioning of the plays. The scene is Athens, the misbehaviour of the slaves is Athenian, for which they excuse themselves to the Athenian audience, as in Stichus' famous lines (*St.* 446–8):

> atque id ne vos miremini, homines servolos
> potare, amare atque ad cenam condicere:
> licet haec Athenis nobis.

> And don't be surprised that mere slaves
> drink, have love-affairs, and make dinner-engagements:
> we're allowed to do this sort of thing at Athens.

Cf. Donatus' famous comment on Terence *Eun.* 57: 'In the *palliata* [comedy set in Greece] poets are allowed to represent slaves as cleverer than their masters, which is virtually never permitted in the *togata* [comedy set in Rome].' As Gordon Williams notes:

In *fabulae togatae* Roman poets created a form of literature in which the slave-role was not merely a burlesque or a vehicle of boisterous comedy, as it normally is in Plautus, but may have had a more serious nature. This will have been forced on the poets by the fact that in writing *togata* they had to forgo the unreal world of the imagination, in which *palliata* operated, for a real and Roman world.[8]

---

[7] L'*Anuée Epigraphique* (1971), no. 88.

[8] Williams, *Tradition and Originality In Roman Poetry* (Oxford, 1968), 295.

The crucifixion jokes, therefore, confirm the Roman audience in its sense of superiority and power. They serve to remind the audience of the servile nature of the characters, as well as the actors who perform them, and of the absolute and everyday nature of the power that the audience wields over them.

Turning now to the second question: Why are these threats then never carried out? Why isn't the slave, who disrupts the social order, who humiliates and cozens the *senex*, whipped off the stage? After all, the Romans had no objections to public torture and execution in everyday life, much less mere beatings and only the mimesis of beatings at that. Nor did Romans of a later age object to actual crucifixion on stage (Suet. *Cal.* 57).[9] The question remains, why is beating an uppity slave not funny?

It is important first to note that not all threats are unfulfilled and that some beatings on and off the stage do in fact occur in Plautus, and second to note who gets beaten. In the absence of stage directions, it is impossible to be certain how realistically the language in these plays was interpreted, but as examples of slapstick one can point to Sosia (*Amph.* 370 ff.), the exchange of blows by Olympio and Chalinus (*Cas.* 405 ff.), and perhaps Milphio (*Poen.* 351). Others are Labrax (*Rud.* 656–62, 868–84), Dordalus (*Per.* 809 ff.), and Pyrgopolynices (*Mil.* 1402). The characters then who actually do get beaten are the good (i.e. cowardly or stupid) slaves, and the pimps and braggarts, that is, the enemies of the *servus callidus* and the *adulescens*. These are the figures whom Northrop Frye calls 'blocking characters' and whom Segal terms 'agelasts'.[10] It is these persons who are not integrated into society, who like Malvolio refuse the cakes and ale. For these characters, who refuse or pervert the blessings of the libido, punishment is fitting.

There is a deep connection therefore, as Frye and others have pointed out, between punishment and reintegration into the social order. It is simple to say that comedy as a genre requires a happy ending with a reconciliation. This clearly applies to the *servus callidus* in Plautus, since the social order is not disturbed, or rather, is disturbed only momentarily. The plays end, often through the very machinations of the slave, with marriage and legitimate children, the son and

---

[9] See now K. M. Coleman, 'Fatal Charades: Roman Executions Staged as Mythological Enactments', *JRS* 80 (1990), 44–73.

[10] Northrop Frye, *Anatomy of Criticism: Four Essays* (Princeton, 1957), 163–9; Segal, *Roman Laughter*, 70.

the father in harmony again, and the slave still a slave. In Plautus, the clever slave acts out of good will for the young master (e.g. *Epid.* 348) and from sheer love of mischief. He does not even desire manumission. Out of all the Plautine slaves, only a handful gain their freedom, a significant difference between Broadway and Rome. They are the clever Epidicus, to whom Periphanes enthusiastically grants his manumission unasked; the loyal Messenio in the *Menaechmi*; the stupid but lucky Gripus in the *Rudens*; and in that same play of remarkable reconciliation, with its Greek Romance setting, the clever Trachalio, who even gets the girl Ampelisca.

However, why should the clever slave be the one reunited and reintegrated into Roman society? His plots have not been directed only against the outsiders, the blocking characters, but against the father himself. As Duckworth says,

Of course, when the intrigue is directed against a pompous soldier or a rascally *leno*, the slave's machinations have the approval of the other characters and the sympathy of the spectators. Such trickery is successful and there is no question of punishment. It is different when the *senex* is the object of the deception.[11]

Yet even when he plots against the father the clever slave still goes unpunished. The reason for this is clear: the *senex*, of course, is also a blocking character, standing between the young man and his desires, sometimes a rival for the object of his desires. It is the slave who 'unblocks' him, and who for exactly that reason has the approval of the other characters and the sympathy of the spectators.

The reasons for our sympathy with the *servus callidus* are well illustrated by Aristotle. In analysing the superiority of the plot of tragedy to that of comedy, Aristotle argues from an impossibility (*Poet.* 13, 1452^{a}11–13):

The second best, which is called first by some, is the plot which has a twofold plot, such as the *Odyssey*, and ends in opposite ways for the better (*beltiosi*) and for the worse (*cheirosin*) people. It only seems to be the first because of the weakness (*astheneian*) of the theatre; for the poets follow the audience, acting according to their wish (*kat' euchên*). But this is not the pleasure of tragedy, but rather the characteristic of comedy: for there those who are the greatest enemies (*echthistoi*) in the story, such as Orestes and Aegisthus, become friends at the end, go off, and no one is killed by anybody.

[11] George E. Duckworth, *The Nature of Roman Comedy: A Study in Popular Entertainment* (Princeton, 1952), 288.

If the reconciliation of slave and master is not an impossibility, it is because they are not dire enemies (*echthistoi*). If the audience wishes (*kat' euchên*) for Tranio to be forgiven at the end of the *Mostellaria*, it is because it classes him among the better people (*beltiosi*). If we find him humorous, it is because we find him worthy of, and superior to, our sympathy (*astheneian*). Most importantly, the reason why we find the *servus callidus* sympathetic is that he is in large measure a figure for the *adulescens* himself.

Again, certain well-known facts of Roman social history can aid in supporting this idea. Unlike slavery in the Americas, no outward sign of race distinguished slave from free in Rome or Greece. Bondsmen were not even distinguished by dress (lest they see how numerous they were, according to Seneca *Clem.* 1. 24; cf. App. *BC.* 2. 17). On the farms, sons and slaves were brought up side by side, performing the same tasks. They differed less in their present circumstances than in their expectations. Several pieces of anecdotal information contribute to this picture. Plutarch (*Cato Major* 20.3) records how even Cato the Elder had his wife suckle and rear the slave children together with their son 'so as to encourage fraternal affection in them towards her own son'. Gaius Cassius (Tacitus, *Ann.* 14. 44) spoke of 'slaves, born in the same fields or houses, and who received right from the start affection for their masters'. Seneca, on an inspection tour of one of his country estates, sees a decrepit doorkeeper, who reminds him that they were brought up together, calling himself Seneca's *deliciolum*, 'playfellow' (*Ep.* 12. 3).

In particular, the relation between son and *paedagogus* was particularly close, and even the law acknowledged its special nature. So Gaius (*Inst.*1. 19) recognizes as a just reason for manumission a man freeing his natural children, a sibling, a foster-child (*alumnus*), a slave-girl for marriage, or his *paedagogus*, thus placing this relationship on a par with other familial ties. Cf. 1. 39, where the relations of father, mother, *paedagogus*, or 'someone who has been brought up with him' are reasons for manumission before the age of 30 or by a master under the age of 40. The relation between the *servus callidus* and the *adulescens* in Roman Comedy is that of an anti-pedagogue (as it were, a *paedoparagogus* or child-misleader) to his charge. The slave is the young man's confidant, adviser, friend, and especially his factotum. It is significant that the only slave explicitly to be identified as a *paedagogus*, Lydus in the *Bacchides*, is a blocking character, a spoilsport in the eyes of father and son alike. Like a pompous headmaster, he is a figure of fun. The clever slave, on the other hand, is responsible for ruining the son, leading him astray, allowing him to satisfy his desires, though always at the son's own command (cf. the accusation by Theopropides at *Most.* 1117–19). Indeed son and slave reverse position. The *adulescens* makes himself over to the slave as if he were a slave, since he is already a slave to love, leaving the *servus* to run the show (e.g. *Rud.* 1265–6, 1280, *Most.* 407, *Poen.* 145–6, 447, *Ps.* 119).

However, there is one aspect in which son and slave were most alike; this called forth comments from the Romans themselves. Gaius (*Inst.* 1.54–5), calls the father's power uniquely Roman. Son and slave were equally under the absolute power of the father, the *patria potestas*, which extended to the power of life and death (*ius vitae necisque*). It follows that a large number of those watching the *Mostellaria* might be under the *potestas* of the father. As Crook comments:

This lifelong power over children, however extraordinary it might seem (and it did to the Romans), was a reality and we must not water it down . . . In private life it mattered nothing that you might be forty years old or married or consul of the Roman people; if you were *in potestate* you owned nothing, whatever you acquired accrued automatically to your *paterfamilias* . . . One might well wonder how such a society can possibly have worked.[12]

Son and slave both had independence of action only under the legal fiction of the *peculium*; over both the *paterfamilias* had the right of life and death.

This fact directs us to another aspect of Freud's analysis of jokes. While Humour results 'from an economy of expenditure in feeling' (affect), Wit results 'from an economy of expenditure in inhibition' (repression). Freud uses the famous three-person analysis of how aggressive impulses are masked by wit, and notes its particular targets:

Tendency-wit is used with special preference as a weapon of attack or criticism of superiors who claim to be in authority. Wit then serves as a resistance against such authority and as an escape from its pressure.[13]

However, in Plautus it is not so much the aggression that is disguised but the aggress*or*. The Plautine slave can profitably be viewed as a theatrical device for splitting the son and so preserving the psychic peace of the audience. The slave, ironically, can do things the

[12] Crook, *Law and Life of Rome*, 109. See also his article, 'Patria Potestas', *CQ*, NS 17 (1967), 113–22.   [13] Freud, *Wit*, 803, 699.

son cannot. It is the slave who carries out the libidinous desires of the son, who dupes, detains, defies, deceives, deflates, and destroys the father. It is against him that the father turns all his wrath, leaving the son untouched. Cf. Epidicus' rhetorical question to Stratippocles (*Epid.* 139–40):

> Men piacularem oportet fieri ob stultitiam tuam
> ut meum tergum tuae stultitiae subdes succidaneum?

Is it right that I should be the expiation for your stupidity, that you can offer my back as a substitute because of your stupidity?

The son is thus left untouched by guilt. He can defy his father's wishes for his marriage, think impious thoughts (e.g. *Ps.* 122, *Bacch.* 505–8, *Truc.* 660–2, *Most.* 229), even desire his father's death (*Most.* 233–4), but emerge forgiven by the latter. His character is illuminated by Freud's remarks on the Comic, specifically the Comic of Naïveté.

The Plautine *adulescens* is naïve in his monomaniac pursuit of the girl. He has no inhibitions at all, and we in the audience can enjoy vicariously his evil wishes against his father and his ultimate triumph, while protected from guilt by our own sense of superiority.

It is here that Freud subsumes the older ideas of the comic as a perception of our own superiority and another's inferiority (Plato, *Phil.* 47–50, Arist., *Poet.* 1449a, Cic., *de Or.* 2. 58, Hobbes, *Leviathan*, 1. 6, etc.). Likewise, the Plautine *servus* is monomaniac in his pursuit of trickery as an end in itself. He too has no inhibitions, and we vicariously enjoy his evil deeds against the father. And yet it is the impudent slave who allows the youth to be naïve, by removing the intentionality. It is the slave who acts, plans, intends, does, and thereby takes on (and takes away) all the guilt that would have fallen to the son.

To the son falls the important task of interceding for his *alter ego* with his father. It has often been noted that the slave is forgiven far too readily. What is less often noted is that the son, or someone acting on his behalf, arranges for that pardon. Son and slave are pardoned together. Thus Callidamates intercedes for Tranio on behalf of Philolaches (*Most.* 1154 ff.), Bacchis for Chrysalus on behalf of Mnesilochus (*Bacch.* 1182 ff.), Stratippocles for Epidicus (721 f., though off-stage). The son's intercession for the slave is an even more marked feature of Terence. Thus Pamphilus intercedes for Davos (*And.* 955 ff.), Clitipho for Syrus (*Heaut.* 1066–7), and Aeschinus for Syrus (*Ad.* 960, with aid from Demea). The most remarkable case is the *Captivi*, a play that requires a separate chapter, where of course the slave is the son.

Thus the non-punishment of the slave is humorous for the audience on two different counts. First, the threat of punishment arouses sympathy, because the audience is on the side of the clever slave who wishes to rebel against the established authorities. The sympathy proves needless, however, for the slave is indifferent to the punishment and successful in his rebellion. The threats also arouse anxiety, again because the slave is incurring the guilt for enacting the wishes of the audience, but the anxiety is suddenly released when the punishments are removed at the wish of the *adulescens*. Secondly, the fears of the audience are obviated as soon as they are stimulated. The slave's rebellion is never on his own behalf. Even his freedom of action is always in the service, and for the pleasure, of his young master, recapitulating the relation of slave-actors to audience. The slave's actions are hemmed in and controlled by the very threats of punishment that provide the audience with a source of humour.

Thus the *servus callidus* allows the audience to have it both ways. The audience can identify with the young man, who is allowed to step outside the power of his father, even to make the Oedipal wish for his father's death, yet incurs no guilt and is reunited in the traditional order of family and property. That guilt is displaced onto the slave, who satisfies the son's anarchic and libidinous desires, yet is always controlled by the threat of punishment, but remains unpunished. Power is mocked, but mollified. Desire is satisfied, but without cost. The wish for rebellion is indulged, but the fear of rebellion is pacified.

11

Aulularia: City-State and Individual

D. KONSTAN

In the characteristic story-type of new comedy, a young man's passionate infatuation with a girl who is ineligible for marriage is fulfilled in a respectable way through a turn in the plot—a recognition scene, for example—which reveals the maiden's citizen status. It is discovered, then, that the wayward passion had all along aspired to a permissible object, and the original tension turns out to be illusory. In plays of this type, the prohibited passion drives outward beyond the limits of the community. Love fastens in its willful way upon a stranger, and thereby threatens to violate the exclusiveness by which the community is defined. But a special class of stories, relatively rare in new comedy, looks not so much to urges that push across the boundary as to figures who withdraw into isolation from their fellow citizens. These are the tales of the misanthrope and the misogynist, the miser and the prude. Their challenge to the community manifests itself as a secession, rather than as the pursuit of a forbidden relationship. Characters of this sort bear a certain affinity to the stern fathers who are typically the obstacle to love. By his withdrawal from society the misanthrope or miser may for example block a romantic alliance involving his daughter. Nevertheless, the differences between the two types are essential. In the amatory plays the 'blocking characters' prevent or oppose the romantic union, but they do so as representatives of the claims of marriage, that is, of legitimate social communion. The recognition scene is an essential part of a plot of this kind because it permits the fulfillment both of the erotic impulse and of the social requirement of marriage among citizens, which had seemed to be opposed in their demands. The misanthrope and the miser, on the contrary, have themselves severed their ties with society. It is they who will not marry or allow their daughters to marry, they who will not engage in commerce with their fellows which is the right use of wealth. Consumed as they are by a private passion, they are more akin to the lover than they are to the conventional morality of the blocking character. Where the lover threatens to defy the bound-aries of the community, the miser and the misanthrope dissolve its inner bonds and encyst themselves within society as internal exiles. They cannot be brought back into society by a dramatic coincidence or revelation. They must rather be made to realize the insufficiency of their isolation, so that they turn back of their own will to the com-munity of men. Hence such plays depend essentially upon a change in character. The recusant forgoes his specious autarky, recognizes his insufficiency and the insufficiency of the ideal or symbol which he had made the sole object of his desire, whether it is the miser's gold or the misanthrope's virtue and sincerity. In a word, he gives up his fetish, which, from the point of view of community, consists in the worship of an abstract value at the expense of the social relationship that its function is to mediate. This paradigm defines the general form of Plautus' comedy, the *Aulularia*.

According to one editor: 'The *Aulularia* stands alone among the comedies of Plautus as a character piece.' He continues: 'The charac-ter of the miser is developed in connexion with a simple plot dealing with middleclass life, but it is the picture of the avaricious Euclio that gives unity to the whole.'[1] I shall begin my analysis of the play by undoing its apparent unity to reveal the separate strands, woven together to compose a plot that in fact is double or complex. The ini-tial conditions of the drama are these. Euclio has discovered buried in his hearth a pot of gold, which his grandfather had concealed, and with it his native stinginess grows into a grand passion.

The Lar—the household deity who speaks the prologue and gives the mise-en-scène, explains that he has revealed the treasure so that Euclio may arrange a proper marriage for his daughter Phaedria, whose generosity and devotion have touched the god. The Lar also relates that the unfortunate Phaedria has been raped. The offender is Lyconides, the nephew of Euclio's wealthy neighbor Megadorus. Finally, the Lar declares that, to induce Lyconides to marry Phaedria, he will inspire Megadorus to propose to the girl himself. The prologue thus introduces two distinct components of the story, the avarice and the romantic theme. The discovery of the gold and the violation of the miser's daughter are not logically related events. Only the inten-tion of the Lar that the gold be used as a dowry for Phaedria (27) brings the themes together at this point.

---

[1] E. J. Thomas (ed.) *T. Macci Plauti, Aulularia* (Oxford, 1913) p. v.

In the first act, Plautus exhibits the character of the miser and the significance of his obsession as a withdrawal from social life. The action neatly lays bare the difference between the miser's passion for his gold and ordinary acquisitiveness or parsimony, which the Romans regarded as a virtue. Despite a paranoid anxiety for his gold, Euclio is obliged to leave it unguarded while he goes to the forum to receive a handout which the head of his *curia* or political unit has advertised. Now, Euclio does not want the dole, inasmuch as his trip to the forum puts his treasure in jeopardy, but he fears that if he did not go out to get it, the danger would be worse, since others would suspect him of harboring some hidden wealth. Because his hoard is secret, Euclio is caught in a double bind: If he stays home with his pot of gold he may arouse the curiosity of his neighbors, so he must, however reluctantly, engage in public life in order to keep up appearances. All of the miser's social activity is a sham—even commerce or, as here, a petition for a free bequest. The miser wishes not to make money but to have it, and to keep it out of social circulation. The irony in Euclio's behavior is that, in his obsession with his gold, he would reject, if he dared, even the minimal public commitment involved in receiving a donation.

Before he sets out, Euclio torments his old servant, Staphyla, with suspiciousness and orders her to extinguish the fire in his hearth, lest anyone enter his house to borrow a light (91–2). Perhaps he is particularly worried about the fire because the pot of gold, as we have noted, was buried in the fireplace. Nevertheless, the quenching of the hearth fire in Greece and Rome, as in all communities before the invention of matches, was a serious matter. More than this, Euclio also orders Staphyla to deny that she has any water. Now, the symbol of banishment in Rome was the *aquae et ignis interdictio*, the prohibition on the lending of water and fire. Fixated on his private treasure, Euclio has in effect estranged his society from himself. The scene abounds in farcical humor, and Euclio extends his interdiction to knives, hatchets, mortars and pestles, and jugs of any kind. But the, elements of parody or, exaggeration do not conceal Euclio's attempt, in abolishing the commerce in fire and water which define symbolically the mutual tie of community, to exile the whole community from himself.

The romantic theme introduced in the second act, when Megadorus bids and wins consent for the hand of Phaedria from her father Euclio. In anticipation of the wedding, Megadorus arranges for a troupe of slaves and retainers to prepare the festivities. Congrio, a cook, is dispatched to Euclio's house, because the old miser is too niggardly to provide for his daughter's marriage celebration. Euclio himself, who has been out shopping but has found everything too expensive except some incense and flowers, returns to find his house wide open and Congrio hollering for a larger pot (end of Act II). 'Pot' is all the miser hears, and he rushes in to drive the poor cook from his house under a storm of blows. Suspicious of Megadorus and everyone else, he decides at last to remove the pot of gold from the house and conceal it in the temple of Fides, good faith (end of Act III). While Euclio is in the temple, a slave of Lyconides marches on stage. He has been sent to reconnoiter the wedding preparations on behalf of his master, who, he tells us, is in love with Phaedria (603). Plautus does not explain Lyconides' sudden feeling for the girl he raped nine months earlier. Presumably he is anxious lest, thus violated, she should become his uncle's wife, and Megadorus' interest in her may also have awakened a slumbering passion of his own. The Greek original, if it at all resembled Plautus' play at this point, may have accounted more clearly for Lyconides' change of heart. However this may be, Lyconides' slave is on hand to overhear Euclio's injunction to Fides to preserve his gold. With a vow of his own to Fides, the slave enters the temple to search out the gold, but is violently driven out by Euclio, whom the cry of a crow had sent scurrying back to check on his treasure. Euclio thoroughly frisks and abuses the slave, who in fact is empty-handed. He then reenters the temple, repossesses his pot of gold and, charging that Fides has not kept faith and that it took a crow to save him, announces that he will hide it outside the city walls in a thick and lonely grove of Silvanus, the woodland god, whom he trusts more than Faith Herself (674–6). Lyconides' slave, quite angry now and determined to cheat the miser of his gold, has been eavesdropping. He beats Euclio to the grove, conceals himself in a tree where he can watch the old man bury the gold, digs it up himself, and steals home with it. The next words we hear are Euclio's after he discovers his loss: 'I'm dead, finished and done for' (713).

As to the plot alone, the concealment of the gold twice, first in the temple of Fides and then in the grove of Silvanus, is plainly a doublet, a redundant repetition of a single act. Lyconides' slave could as well have found the gold in his first attempt. But to the theme of the play, the pairing of the actions is crucial. It is in the character of the miser, we have said, to exempt himself from the bonds of community. For the Romans, the spirit of these bonds was represented above all in the concept of *fides*, which variously meant good faith, trustworthiness, and, most concretely, the warranty on a pledge. It was the basis of all contracts, the soul of all honest exchange. From this spirit of collective good faith, Euclio withdraws his confidence. We must observe that, despite Euclio's ingratitude, his gold had been kept safe in the temple of Fides. The miser's trust did not betray him; he thought more of a crow's cackle than the personified force of social ties and rejected the good faith of his community. Instead he went beyond the city walls, which for the Romans especially represented the sacred boundary of the civilized community where law and honor reigned, and trusted his gold to the uncultivated precinct of a god of the wilderness. Euclio has deliberately and explicitly abandoned the city and committed himself to the chance concern of nature. And there, beyond the rule of Fides, his gold is appropriated by cunning and theft. The miser endures the fate of the stranger.

Thematically, then, the theft of the miser's gold is a function of secession from society. At the same time, it exposes his lack of self-sufficiency and establishes the conditions under which he may elect to be reintegrated into the community, and thus to satisfy the dramatic demands of comedy. To return to the romantic component of the plot, the rape of Phaedria represents exactly the same kind of assault on Euclio as the stealing of his treasure. The twin principle upon which citizenship was constituted in ancient Rome was the *ius connubii et commercii*, the right of marriage and of commerce. These two rights have in common that both are based upon the sanctity of the contract and therefore rest upon the communal principle of good faith. Outside the citizen community, the rule of violence, of, *vis et violentia*, holds sway, except where special agreements may be mutually recognized. Where the *ius commercii*, the right of commerce, is abrogated, there robbery, a relationship of force alone, prevails. Similarly, rape is the mode of sexual appropriation where the right of marriage, the *ius connubii*, ceases to prevail. Because of his withdrawal, the miser is no longer sheltered under the laws of the community. Despite the absence of a causal connection between Euclio's obsession with his pot of gold and the rape of his daughter the two facts are intimately related: The rape is the expression in the sphere of sex of the miser's isolation, just as the theft is its expression in the sphere of property. The rape and the theft are all the closer, in that women were not in Roman society so far removed from other forms of property. Phaedria's dishonor will be her father's loss.

The love story is advanced through the proposal of Megadorus which, for reasons that Plautus' version does not make very clear, kindles or rekindles in Lyconides the desire for Phaedria. After his change of heart the young man tells his mother, Eunomia, of the rape, and begs her to intercede with her brother Megadorus, who apparently retracts his offer of marriage: He is not seen again in our text. In this brief scene of nineteen lines (682–700), Phaedria is heard offstage to cry out in the agony of her labor pangs, and Lyconides wonders out loud where his slave might be, possibly a reminder of the connection between the theft and the rape. In the following scene, the slave appears with the stolen pot of gold, and in the next, Euclio bursts in with the vehement lament over his loss. Lyconides hears the howling, recognizes Euclio, and concludes that he has found out about the birth of Phaedria's baby (729). After a moment's hesitation, he decides to confess outright to the crime. An extraordinary exchange for some twenty-five lines follows, in which Euclio mistakenly believes that Lyconides has admitted to the theft of his gold. Without giving details of the misunderstanding, which accommodates even Lyconides' plea that love (*amor*, 745) was the cause of his offense, we note that the scene demonstrates the essential equivalence, from Euclio's point of view, of the rape and the robbery. Both are violations of his proprietary rights.

When Euclio at last dispels the ambiguity with an explicit mention of his pot of gold (763), Lyconides vigorously disclaims any part or knowledge of the theft. Then, just when he has persuaded Euclio of his innocence, he discloses the rape. Finally, he mollifies the old miser, who by now is utterly overwhelmed, by reaffirming his wish to marry the girl, which the laws require (793), and he assures Euclio that thanks to him the old man can attend the wedding as a grandfather.

From this point on, the play moves into the phase of reintegration. Lyconides learns what has happened to the gold from his slave, who expects a liberal reward but instead is ordered to return it to Euclio. Thus, the recovery of the treasure too is predicated upon Lyconides' change of heart, which was poorly motivated if we look only to the plot. Thematically, however, it is exactly right, and probably Plautus' dramatic instinct assured him it would work. For having refused the mutual exchange which is the basis of the communal bond, the miser has been humbled. He has been dealt with as an outsider, plundered and stripped without regard to the laws of fair dealing which he himself had set aside by hoarding. He has learned the lesson of his insufficiency, the same way Menander's misanthrope discovers his need of others when he falls down a well. In accord with the comic convention, he can now rejoin society, renew the rites of exchange that define the group. In a stroke, the violation of Phaedria and the plunder of the gold are undone. Made wiser by his losses Euclio is once more grant the chance of giving his daughter to marriage, and use of the gold as was intended, for a dowry. In the dowry, in fact, are symbolized and joined both terms of the *ius connubii et commercii*. In the relations of the community, the dowry is the exemplary use of wealth, for it represents the exchange of kin and property on which the solidarity of the several clans, of the society as a whole, is based. The giving of the dowry, Euclio's ultimate assent to the mutuality of the communal bond, must have been the culminating action of the *Aulularia*. Unfortunately, the conclusion to the final act has not survived.

Nevertheless, we may be quite certain about the disposition of the treasure. We know the Lar's intention in the prologue; the last line of an acrostic argument prefixed to the play reports the transfer of the gold; and finally, a fragment of our play preserved by the grammarian Nonius and undoubtedly to be attributed to Euclio reads: 'Night or day I was never at rest. Now I shall sleep.' The miser's hoard is at last restored to use, its abstract value is reembodied in the practical relations of social life.

I now turn to the discussion of Megadorus; no treatment of the *Aulularia* can be complete without an analysis of his role, which brings out some of the most complex and challenging aspects of its theme. Back in the second act, after Euclio's initial scenes, Lyconides' mother, Eunomia, appeals to her brother Megadorus to take a wife. Nothing in particular motivates her intervention, but we sense the influence of the Lar. When Megadorus learns what she wants, he replies: 'Aii! I'm dead!' (150). Megadorus may at once be recognized as a type: the inveterate bachelor, rich and contented with his lot, and loath to undertake either the responsibilities or the expense of a wife and family like Micio in Terence's *Adelphoe*. Megadorus also stands aloof from one of the bonds of community by neglecting the obligation to continue his line (cf. 147–8). He does confess, however, to a special passion for Phaedria, despite her poverty, and declares his intention to ask for her hand. Because Megadorus was already infat-

uated with Phaedria before Eunomia's intervention, her advice to her
brother serves no function in the plot, but again is a significant
contribution to the theme. The dialogue between Eunomia and
Megadorus underscores that Megadorus' interest is not, to marriage
as such, but has its source solely in desire. In terms of popular Roman
psychology, he is motivated by irrational passion rather than by cus-
tomary duty which, as Eunomia makes clear, would enjoin him to
contract an advantageous alliance.

Megadorus' desire thus resembles that of the young lover in the
amatory plots—so characteristic of ancient comedy—to which we
referred earlier. In those stories the erotic impulse usually attaches
itself to an object outside the limits of the community. The same is
true of Megadorus' passion, for Phaedria, because she has been
raped, is according to the conventional taboo in ancient comedy ineligible to marry anyone but the man who assaulted her, and so she is
removed beyond that circle of potential kin which defines the boundary of society. As we know, when he learns of the rape he will repu-
diate her. On the most general level, the stigma on Phaedria may be
regarded as a sign of Euclio's voluntary withdrawal from social relations which is implicit in the fetish of his secret hoard. Of course,
Megadorus is in complete ignorance of both the rape and the pot of
gold. But his motive, which is erotic rather than connubial, and the
relationship he is prepared to establish not between members of a
common group but as a personal tie beyond communal sanctions,
are reflected in the circumstances that Euclio and Phaedria are of an
inferior social order, and that Megadorus, whose name literally
means 'Great-Gift', is willing to remit the dowry.

When Megadorus approaches Euclio, the old miser immediately
suspects him of being after his gold. He distractedly mumbles threats
to his servant; when Megadorus asks him what he is grumbling
about, he claims it is his poverty that prevents him for want of a
dowry from marrying off his daughter (190–92). The connection here
is overt between the hoarding of wealth and the denial of conjugality,
the double abrogation of the *ius connubii et commercii* which isolates
the miser. After a further display of Euclio's paranoid antics,
Megadorus makes his proposal. Euclio, who has all along been leery
of this untoward regard of a rich man for a poor one, at first accuses
Megadorus of mocking him. Assured of his neighbor's earnestness,
he laboriously expounds his concern that for a poor man to join himself to a rich is like an ass consorting with bulls: His own order will

reject him, and Megadorus' will never accept him, the asses will tear him with their teeth while the bulls will attack him with their horns (226–35). Euclio's analogy between the different orders and different biological species points to the extreme separation of social classes in Plautus' Rome, whether or not the language goes back to the Greek original of the *Aulularia*. The wealthy and the poor constitute distinct communities within the society, not to be crossed by ties of marriage. Euclio then stipulates that there will be no dowry, lest Megadorus imagine that he has found some hidden treasure, as he says (240), and at last the nuptial agreement is struck, even though Euclio's fears are not altogether allayed.

If we look to the theme of the *Aulularia*, clearly Megadorus' proposal cannot possibly resolve the tensions of the play. If the miser is to be reintegrated into society, his treasure must be revealed and put to use in an exchange that confirms the communal bonds among families. Thus the dowry is crucial, and for Megadorus to waive it is to block the redemption of Euclio and leave him estranged by his obsession. That marriage to Megadorus is no solution is made all the clearer by Phaedria's pregnancy, which Staphyla proceeds to lament. To put it another way, marrying off Phaedria without a dowry is no better than giving her away to a total stranger. This point is developed at considerable length in Acts II and III of the *Trinummus*, where the young, impoverished Lesbonicus expresses his anxiety to his friend Lysitcles that 'they will spread the report that I have given my sister to you in concubinage, rather than in marriage, if I give her without a dowry' (689–91). The dowry is the sign of the communal sanction. Without it, marriage is not a bond but an appropriation. We have seen that Megadorus' offer is prompted by an erotic impulse rather than by a sense of civic obligation, and that his class is socially discrete from hers. In the plot as a whole, Megadorus' involvement is not so much the cause of Lyconides' reversal as a foil to it. Where Lyconides is in a position to convert the rape of Phaedria to marriage and the stolen gold to a dowry, Megadorus can do neither. He reaches out but cannot mend the breach created by Euclio's self-imposed exile. The class distinction between Megadorus and Euclio only mimics the separation between the miser and his fellows and may thus be regarded thematically as a metaphor for Euclio's isolation. Structurally, Megadorus' appeal across the barrier of class is only another manifestation of Euclio's being beyond the pale, as the erotic nature of Megadorus' attraction also suggests, and thus at bottom his proposal but reiterates the theme, albeit in a more gentle way, of the rape and the theft. Megadorus' proposal, then, is not the answer; it is rather another aspect of the problem of the play.

In the context of the play's dominant theme, the difference in order between Megadorus and Euclio may be interpreted as a representation of Euclio's estrangement from society. Once it has been introduced, however, Plautus takes up the theme of class distinctions and develops it for its own value. We have already noticed indications of its seriousness in the first interview between Megadorus and Euclio. After the miser drives Congrio the cook from his house, a scene occurs with Megadorus and the miser in which many critics have seen the hand of Plautus himself at work.

Sandwiched between Euclio's hostile complaints against his neighbor's suspected machinations (462, 551 ff.), Megadorus delivers a soliloquy overheard and heartily endorsed by Euclio on the faults of the dowry system and the manners of contemporary women. Megadorus makes the following points: Dowries are the cause of discord between and among the social orders (481); they contribute also to the prodigality of women, who regard the money they bring into a marriage as their own to spend on luxuries as they choose (498–502); and finally, as a corollary of the preceding, women are becoming, thanks to the dowry, freer of the authority of their husbands (534). Scholars have in fact arrived at an approximate date for Plautus' *Aululria* by interpreting this speech of Megadorus as a protest against the repeal of the *lex Oppia* in 195 BC, which regulated the sumptuary expenses of women. The most important feature of Megadorus' soliloquy, however, is that this intrusive condemnation of dowries and above all of their corrosive effect on the solidarity and harmony of the community runs exactly counter to the role of the dowry in the entire play. We have to do here with an independent set piece, in which the divisive social forces are represented not as the withdrawal of the individual householder from a community of equals, but as a general disintegration of social ties consequent upon the corruption of the dowry system by the qualitative but unequal increment in the wealth of the citizen body.

The contrast may be put more pointedly: The extravagance of the aristocracy is precisely the opposite of the miser's retentiveness. To be sure, these contrary causes have a like effect, the weakening of the conjugal bond. But in the one case, this enfeeblement is due, as Plautus sees it, to the growing independence of moneyed matrons, whose subservience may be restored by the abolition of the dowry, while in the case of the miser the dowry is the substantial symbol of the communal relationship. What Plautus has added to the *Aulularia*, if indeed the scene is his own invention, is a piece of social criticism which violates the thematic coherence of the drama.

Yet on the deepest level Plautus' inclusion of Megadorus' complaint may not be misguided. After all, the archetypal story of the miser is, like all archetypes, abstracted from the realities of social life. The miser's gold is not real wealth, it is a pure symbol. Euclio's grandfather never bought a thing with it, but buried it, as he thought, for all time in the earth from which it had come. No more is the miser's withdrawal from society an expression of true autarky or power. In his helpless isolation, he is easily brought low and as easily regenerated. His is a docile defiance, perfectly suited to a moral tale exalting the ideology of community. No such character ever seriously threatened the solidarity of society. But what, then, is the real danger which the miser represents, and which is imaginatively overcome in the reconciliation with which the comedy must end?

At the heart of the miser's nature is the priority he assigns to money over the actual human relationships with other members of his community. In the creation of the mythic imagination, this character worships the inert form of gold, as may in real life occur with the pathological personality. But the truly destructive manifestation of this spirit is not miserliness but materialism, which dissolves the ties of traditional obligation and restraint and leaves in their place the naked aspiration to wealth and power. The ostentatious spending of the aristocracy and the weakening of the marriage relationship are early symptoms of this spirit. The dowry was its victim: It ceased to be the material token of the communal identity of the clans, and became mere money. In this aspect, the dowry was a sign not of social integration but of fragmentation, both within the aristocracy and between the orders. In attacking it, Plautus did what the comic temper and the ultimate theme of the *Aulularia* itself demanded. He disdained the consistency of the formal idea of the dowry and reaffirmed the claims of community against the real centrifugal tendencies of his day.

12

The Art of Deceit: Pseudolus and the Nature of Reading

A. R. SHARROCK

It is the poet's role and prerogative to deceive. A tradition ascribing specifically deceptive power to poets goes back at least to Hesiod (*Theog.* 27, Muses speaking), *idmeni pseudea polla legein etumoisin homoia* ('we know how to speak many false things as if they were true'); is turned against poets by Plato (*Rep.* 317D–403C); is manipulated by Callimachus when he prays *pseudoimēn aiontos ha ken pepithoien akouēn* ('may I lie/speak fiction in such a way as to persuade the listener', Hymn 1.64); and later will be turned on its head by Ovid pretending to try to claim that everything he says about his mistress should be taken as the lies of poets (*Am.* 3.12).

Plautus seems well aware of the tradition of lying poets and deceptive realism, when in Pseudolus' *poeta* simile (401–5) he describes the poet's work as *fac[ere] illud veri simile quod mendacium est* ('[to] make what is false like reality', 403). If, as is considered below, Pseudolus stands for Plautus himself, then his warning to all and sundry that he will deceive them (125–8, discussed further below) might contribute to constituting a claim to poetic as well as dramatic power on the part of the playwright. Such deceptive power is enhanced in the workings of comedy: both 'externally' in the construction of the dramatic illusion, and 'internally' in the ruse around which so many Plautine (and other comic) plays are structured. The one reflects the other.

Drama of its essence involves the playing of roles (and often of roles within roles), the assumption of identities not one's own, and the collaborative construction of a pseudo-reality in the imaginative space between playwright and audience. 'Deception', then, stands at the heart of drama. Moreover, ancient tragedy was to a greater or lesser extent predicated upon the confusion of identity, either within a tragic protagonist or in the form of a mistake about identity (in the broad or narrow sense) which in so many cases is crucial to the tragic plot and situation, Sophocles' Oedipus providing the classic example. In tragedy such mistakes and misunderstandings lead through chaos to destruction; in comedy through a creative, carnivalesque chaos into renewal and affirmation. Add to this the point that the comic trickster is a figure with a tradition ranging from early Greek myth to the modern day. In the late medieval and much of the modern period, these tricksters often get their comeuppance, but in antiquity and most of the middle ages they generally did not, for to trick was the prerogative of the comic hero. The essence of comedy is getting away with outrageous behaviour. Deception, then, is the most powerful signifier of the brand of comedy which Plautus espouses.

Tricksters imply dupes; tricksters and dupes require an audience. Since at least the fourth century BC, it has often been presented as an orthodoxy of the psychology of laughter that the humour of comedy derives from a sense of superiority engendered in the audience, who look down in indulgent but disdainful amusement on the follies of those poor characters who are unaware of the fact that they are part of a play. Even the clever rogue who thinks he knows he is in a play— and plays with that knowledge for the audience's entertainment—is in the end dependent on the response of the audience which allows him to speak to them across the divide. This superiority theory seems to have been particularly prevalent around the turn of the century during the genesis of modern psychology, when thinkers about humour seem to have felt that there was always something a little bit nasty and even demonic about laughter. Up until that time, humour had almost always been rationalized in moral/didactic terms, to the effect that it consists in laughing at the foibles of others in order to correct them in others and ourselves. It's okay to ridicule because it improves the world. When these ideas become psychologized rather than moralized they sound a lot nastier, but the theme of audience-superiority, however valorized, has remained part of the story throughout. It is indeed crucial to the workings of comedy, but it may not always be straightforward. This article will argue that Plautus deceives his audience, and that that's funny. It is hardly original to suggest that audiences or readers can be deceived, but in the case of Plautus, where the author's simplicity or incompetence has been an accepted doctrine, such a reading may serve to question the orthodoxy.

Just as deception is programmatic for comedy, so Pseudolus, slave and play, is programmatic for Plautine deception (and comedy), for

Plautus himself is constantly highlighted by the connections drawn between the hero and the playwright, who may have acted the part. This connection is most fully developed by Slater, but there have been other metatheatrical readings as well.[1] Not only Pseudolus, but also his protégé Simia and even the cook have been seen as reflections of Plautus himself. It is hardly surprising that that magnificent piece of Plautine *contaminatio*, the musical *A Funny Thing Happened on the Way to the Forum*, has as its hero (which the character 'Hero' so delightfully and pathetically is *not*) a slave called Pseudolus. As the quintessential Plautine trickster, Pseudolus is the perfect paradigm for comic deception.

The deceptive power of playwrights, as of all poets, depends on the power of words. The *Pseudolus* achieves its goals by word-power, while pretending to be trying to disguise a weak plot. Hence the apparent artlessness, hence inconsistencies, hence structural problems: they are all part of the wool Plautus/Pseudolus pulls over your eyes, for the big joke in the *Pseudolus* is to *look as if* it's a weak plot and play all held together by words. Furthermore, I suggest, this deception and this pose of improvisation are indicative of a peculiarly Plautine brand of comedy and therefore also constitute a statement of originality. One possible and attractive response to the charges of inconsistency (using that term as a shorthand for the various 'problems' for which Plautine incompetence is offered as a solution), is to say with Walt Whitman, 'do I contradict myself? Very well, I contradict myself. I am large; I can contain inconsistencies'. Difficulties in the text constitute a creative chaos, a deliberately 'weak' plot which is pretending to be improvised, where we are dazzled by the power of words.

At some level, the *Pseudolus* has a fairly simple plot almost entirely concentrated on the glorification of its hero. What is magnificent about the play is its grandiloquent self-presentation, more Aristophanic than Menandrian, and the outrageous apparent simplicity of the intrigue. It *is* also very complex, however, for it is hard to work out where all the *minae* go, partly because it sounds complex and partly because it is pretending to be improvised, thereby teasing the audience into feeling

---

[1] See N. Slater, *Plautus in Performance* (Princeton, 1985), 118–46, J. Wright, 'The Transformations of Pseudolus', *TaPhA* 105 (1975), 403–16, J. C. B. Lowe, 'The Cook Scene in Plautus' *Pseudolus*', *CQ* 35 (1985), 411–16, J. P. Hallett, 'Plautine Ingredients in the Performance of the *Pseudolus*', *CW* 87 (1993), 21–6, E. Gowers, *The Loaded Table* (Oxford, 1993), 93–108.

that it is being made up and that there is a 'real plot' which Plautus has up his sleeve but won't let out. Which of course, on another level, is true. In so much of what Pseudolus says it is necessary to respond on a metacompositional level as well as a theatrical and metatheatrical one. Pseudolus is (a) a character in a story (the theatrical level); (b) an actor playing with his audience (the metatheatrical); and (c) an author playing with his readers (the metacompositional).

The play gives the impression of having many possible plots: Pseudolus' first plan to play out the proper comic topos of 'touching father' is dropped when he discovers that Simo is suspicious (or is it? for in the end he does indeed get a crucial sum of money from the old man: was he dropping a plan, or pretending to?: see 422–6 but cf. 406–8); the chance arrival of Harpax (at 595, *Fortuna* and *Opportunitas* are apostrophized at 667–93) is good luck on the basis of which Pseudolus improvises, throwing his intermediate plan to the winds. But at a metacompositional level the 'chance' arrival of Harpax has already been written in and *of course* there never was any other plan, just as there are no rooms in the stage-houses whose fronts provide the backdrop to the action. Likewise, what Pseudolus 'knows' at any moment must always be subject to such a double-take. When Pseudolus pretends to be improvising, Plautine drama does indeed show its ancestry in improvised Atellan farce and its reliance on an Atellan-type mask which is always threatening to make up its own script. It is eminently probable that Plautine actors really did mess around with their lines—and that's particularly fun when the author acts the part of the controlling character: but what this play-text gives us is a *pose* of improvisation. This produces a paradoxical anti-realist realism, by making you think there is something 'real' behind the mask—which should here be taken to stand for all the conventions and workings of a play.

The hero of broad-brush comedy achieves his status by deception, while someone else must be deceived as the audience, feeling themselves 'in the know' along with the hero, look on in amused disdain at the dupes. In our play, the audience is indeed induced to appreciate the action by being manipulated into a sense of its own superiority. Pseudolus draws you in, tells you how to laugh with him at Calidorus the classic *amans et egens*, at Harpax the loyal (therefore stupid) servant, at Simo cheated out of his money as we knew he would be (what a fool not to realise that wearing that mask, playing the role of *senex*, he *must* be cheated—or rather, worse still, to realise it and nevertheless to fall for it!), at Ballio the pimp calling down comic nemesis on his own head. This is how Plautine drama works, by making it easy for the audience to laugh from their own comfortable position of superior knowledge. So the story goes. As audience and as readers, however, we must split our identity and see ourselves deceived also. What is remarkable about this play is the very knowingness of the dupes; they specifically reject the standard comic plot. Simo is already aware that something is afoot even before Pseudolus makes quite sure that the old man knows, with his oracular responses (483–8) and his overt warning. Then Ballio is put in the picture by Simo, in an informative act outside Pseudolus' control. Everything really is happening out in the open. The point of these knowing dupes is partly to enhance the triumph of the trickster, and also perhaps subliminally to increase the link between the dupes on stage and those in the auditorium (or study . . .).

Plautine prologues are supposed to tell us the story, the background and an assurance of the ending, so that we can enjoy the play in the comfort of our superior knowledge, but that is not what we get from Pseudolus. We get a two-line throw-away introduction telling the audience to stretch their legs now, as a long play by Plautus is about to start.

> Exporgi meliust lumbos atque exsurgier:
> Plautina longa fabula in scaenam uenit.

You'd better get up and stretch your legs: a long play by Plautus is about to come on stage.

This gives us a signal to begin, but nothing about the play, for a trick that is all done with words can hardly be explained beforehand.[2] The offhand, self-deprecating humour of such a prologue is classically comic: that is precisely what we have when Pseudolus refuses to explain to Calidorus about the token acquired from Harpax, on the grounds that to do so would make the play even longer and risk boring the audience (720–1)—an outrageous cheek given the level of redundancy in his own speech!

In a sense, however, the true prologue is the opening scene between Pseudolus and his young master Calidorus. The young man is so busy

---

[2] M. M. Willcock, *Plautus: Pseudolus* (London, 1987), 96, wonders whether there might once have been an expository prologue in place of or in addition to the two lines we have. K. Abel, *Die Plautusprologe* (Frankfurt, 1955), 15–17, defends the two lines as Plautine.

being mournful he cannot manage to articulate the source of his misery, so Pseudolus takes control of the situation and exposes the plot by exposing Calidorus. Pseudolus thus paradoxically places himself more firmly in control, more clearly outside, than he would by performing the same function in a prologue, which is after all generally seen as 'outside the play', for he is here acting on the metacompositional level even while maintaining his *persona* within the play.

Pseudolus, as is his wont, begins with far more words than are strictly necessary to meaning (3–12):

> Si ex te tacente fieri posseni certior,
> ere, quae miseriae te tam misere macerent,
> duorum labori ego hominum parsissem lubens,
> mei te rogandi et tis respondendi mihi:
> nunc, quoniam id fieri non potest, necessitas
> me subigit ut te rogitem, responde mihi:
> quid est quod tu exanimatus iam hos multos dies
> gestas tabellas tecum, eas lacrumis lauis,
> neque tui participem consili quemquam facis?
> eloquere, ut quod ego nescio id tecum sciam.

If from your silence I could find knowledge, master, as to what miseries so mournfully macerate you, I would gladly spare the effort of two men, me of asking you and you of replying to me; but now, since that cannot be, necessity forces me to ask you. Answer me: why is it that for many days now you have been mindlessly carrying writing tablets around with you and washing them with your tears, and not allowing anyone to enter your confidence? Speak, so that I may find out from you what I don't know.

This too is programmatic, for with its grandiloquent emptiness it acts in magnificent stylistic contrast to the comic lowliness of the first two lines (perhaps epitomized by *lumbos*), while also putting on display such Plautine linguistic features as alliteration and repetition, as if to say 'here's Plautus, larger than life'. Instead of asking 'what's the matter?', Pseudolus *talks about* asking, but the speech is self-referentially non-communicative, for while supposedly seeking information it discourses upon silence and knowledge.

In reply, all Calidorus can muster is a pathetic *misere miser sum, Pseudole*.[3] It transpires that the source of Calidorus' misery can be

---

[3] Slater, 119–20, helpfully exposes the interplays of comic and paratragic 'misery' in this scene. He too sees Pseudolus' manipulation of tragic, paratragic and generally elevated language as consciously programmatic. Plautus stakes his claim to comic ground, but on his own terms.

found in a letter, which he asks Pseudolus to read. The first action of the plot, then, and the founding moment of the play, depends on a text. Pseudolus is not the author of this text, as he is of the play as a whole, but its reader, its interpreter who takes control of its meaning and mediates that for the audience. The letter introduces a good range of comic ingredients, for it is a note from Calidorus' beloved, a prostitute, saying that she is about to be sold to a Macedonian soldier and that Calidorus must rescue her.

With these ingredients, the plot is laid out and we 'know' that Pseudolus will help Calidorus to get the girl, to the discomfiture of father, pimp, and soldier, and any other spoil-sport characters who may come along. Pseudolus forces the prologue by claiming not to know the situation, but at the metacompositional level he clearly does know for what are young men in comedy ever upset about? Love is a fixity of the comic text. Throughout this very funny scene, we as audience are encouraged to read along with Pseudolus and laugh in superior amusement at the folly of the young man, while appreciating Pseudolus' own manipulation of the text into material for humour. He is always in command of the meaning of what he says, and indeed even of what Calidorus says more than the young man is himself. The joke about the letters trying to procreate is an obvious example of Pseudolus' control of meaning.[4] It may prepare us for a more subtle suggestiveness under the farcical raising of Calidorus' hopes when Pseudolus says *tuam amicam uideo*—only to dash them with the explanation that she is lying, even sleeping, stretched out in the wax (35–6). There is an erotic naughtiness about the image which Pseudolus sends out to the audience at Calidorus' expense. Calidorus' response is paratragic (38–9):[5]

> Quasi solstitialis herba paulisper fui:
> repente exortus sum, repentino occidi.

Like grass in summer I was for a moment: suddenly I rose up, and as suddenly died.

Calidorus thinks he is playing the proper part of a suffering lover, but it would be a feeble audience which did not pick up a hint of sexual rising and failing in the lines Pseudolus/Plautus has fed to him. (Not

---

[4] 23–4 *ut opinor, quaerunt litterae hae sibi liberos: alia aliam scandit.* ('As I see it, these letters want to have children: one is piling on the other.') There might be a pun between *liberos* and *libros* here.   [5] See Slater, 119.

that Calidorus is supposed to realise it.) Pseudolus comes to the
scene supposedly not knowing what is going on or is going to happen,
but acts throughout as if he were the one with knowledge while
Calidorus is not, and for the moment we are privileged to share his
superior intellectual position. The trouble with Pseudolus is that you
never know when he is telling the truth. It is the metatheatrical game
of this text to show Pseudolus as claiming more knowledge than he
has, and its metacompositional game to pretend that Pseudolus has
more knowledge than he is showing—which, in so far as he is
Plautus, is true.

How do you know whether Pseudolus is telling the truth, whether
Pseudolus/Plautus is making it up as he goes along, except by the fact
that this—at the moment of your reading—is a fixed text? Although
it in fact costs Pseudolus very little effort to do the comically necessary (get the money, get the girl, triumph over authority), it is the fun
of the play that it all *looks* very complicated, so let's take this terribly
seriously and go through what actually happens as regards the trick.
The first thing to remember is that in this game, the exchange rate is
one girl equals twenty *minae*. The one stands quite happily for the
other. So: first of all Pseudolus offers to procure for Calidorus one girl
for twenty *minae*. This will do. We may reasonably assume that whoever gets to Ballio with twenty *minae* first will get the girl: the fact that
we have not heard previously of a deal between Ballio and Calidorus
is neither here nor there.[6] Next Pseudolus tells Simo he will get the
money from him if necessary. He then places a bet with his master,
apparently making the terms that Pseudolus will get the money from
Simo and cheat the pimp out of the girl, so that Simo will give him—
twenty *minae*, the value of one girl. Before examining that scene further, let us quickly follow the remaining movements of the money:
five *minae* are borrowed from Charinus; because Pseudolus has got

[6] See G. Williams, 'Some problems in the Construction of Plautus' *Pseudolus*',
Hermes, 84 (1956), 427, where this problem is analysed as an indication of *contaminatio*.
On the related subject of why Calidorus expresses surprise at hearing Ballio boast of
having sold Phoenicium to the Macedonian, when Calidorus must already know about
this from the letter, see W. G. Arnott, 'Calidorus' Suprise: A Scene of Plautus' *Pseudolus* with an Appendix on Ballio's Birthday', *Wiener Studien*, 95 (1982), 131–48, who
argues against *contaminatio* here, claiming that Plautus, being, in common with other
ancient playwrights, less concerned about realism than about dramatic effect, uses this
surprise as a device to convey to any of the audience who missed it first time the necessary but complex information about the prior sale. See also T. B. L. Webster, *Studies in
Later Greek Comedy* (Manchester, 1953), 190.

the girl (with these five and the letter from the Macedonian soldier), Simo must then give Pseudolus twenty *minae*; a further twenty *minae* are to be paid by Ballio to Simo; Ballio must also pay twenty (the original fifteen plus the five brought by the real Harpax) back to the Macedonian soldier; and finally presumably five *minae* will be paid back to Charinus.

Pseudolus promises Simo that he will pull off two outrageous stunts by his skill and cunning: get the money from Simia and the girl from Ballio. How come, then, Simo gives Pseudolus the money at the end, when only half of the bargain has been fulfilled? (The girl has been got but not the money.) But surely this bet precisely *is* the extortion of twenty *minae* from Simo. The act of gaining the reward is the fulfilment of the act of deception. Moreover, Pseudolus is cleverly vague about what precisely his side of the bet consists in, although quite clear about Simo's side. Of course, he *appears* to be being quite clear about his side (like all salesmen), when he promises that *effectum hoc hodie reddam utrumque ad uesperum* (530) And this he certainly fulfils. This is a magnificently simple way of extorting the money from Simo—all done by the power of words.

Perhaps what makes it so powerfully programmatic a trap is the fact that Simo is so well prepared for having his money taken from before his eyes without his noticing. Even before the confrontation between Simo and Pseudolus, the old man is suspicious about Calidorus' affair, and Pseudolus ' involvement, and is aware of the tricky nature of the slave. As he says to his friend Callipho, this man will tie you up in his words (464–5):

> conficiet iam te hic uerbis, et tu censeas
> non Pseudolum sed Socratem tecum loqui.

This man will finish you off with words, until you think you are talking not to Pseudolus but to Socrates.

Then Simo's suspicions are confirmed by Pseudolus playing the role of Delphic oracle, with his solemn, mock-impersonal response of *nai gar* ('yes indeed', or perhaps 'it is so') to each of his master's questions (483–8). Not only would the scene of a Roman pretending to be a Greek pretending to speak from the seat of wisdom be a great deal funnier than a Greek playing that role, but also the authoritative truthfulness which such Delphic responses convey within the 'Greek' world of the play become, in the 'Roman' world of the audience and of Pseudolus, a joke which shows the power and deceitfulness of the speaker. Pseudolus isn't conveying anything earthshattering here, but he really is the fount of all wisdom within the play. He is the only one who exhibits the most famous of Delphic virtues: know thyself. Simo thinks he has gained a triumph in forcing Pseudolus' confession (489), and to clinch the matter he passes judgement on the slave with the proclamation that no-one is to lend him a single penny (504–6: see further below). Pseudolus immediately counters with the overt threat to get the money from Simo himself (so he won't be asking anyone else). Then comes the great warning: *iam dico ut a me caueas* ('now I warn you to beware of me', 511), repeated a few lines later with the same in the form of his own proclamation: *praedico ut caueas. dico, inquam, ut caueas. caue. | em istis mihi tu hodie manibus argentum dabis* ('I proclaim that you should beware. I say again, that you should beware. Beware! You yourself will give me the money this very day with your own hands'). If Simo were not forewarned we would need a more complex plot in order to contrive the extortion. As it is, nothing need detract front the magnificence of Pseudolus.

Before this scene, Calidorus has been pushed out of the way by being sent to find a friend, Charinus, who turns out to be not what was wanted. While it would be fascinating to know whether and in what manner Plautus is alluding to a Greek play where such a friend was sought (and used? discarded?), we must be content with trying to see how Plautus has used his material creatively. I suggest three motivations, from plot, character, and metacomposition.

First, 'plot': Charinus, the friend, will provide both Simia, who will act as Pseudolus' deputy in the deception of Ballio, and the five *minae* which will enable him to play out his role. Pseudolus, when he sends Calidorus away to find a friend, 'doesn't know' that this is what he will need after Harpax has come along with the letter, of course . . . When Calidorus arrives with Charinus, Pseudolus has the letter and has changed his plans (or so he claims). We do need both Simia and Charinus: one for the trick, the other to provide the money.

Next, 'character': everything Calidorus does has to be useless: if he provided Simia himself—and the original request sounds very like what is actually required and what appears in the form of Simia— that would be far too helpful a role for the *adulescens* to play. Like everything else, he gets it 'wrong'. This is, after all, a play which exuberantly parades its comic stereotypes. Finally, 'metacomposition': since Pseudolus is—or pretends he is—making up the plot as he goes along, he thinks (at the compositional level) 'let's have the comic ingredient "helper"', and so this 'false start' in composition is only unmotivated in so far as to have such an unmotivated character is an integral part of a deliberately shaky plot. After the duping of Harpax, the plan is supposed to have changed, and 'as luck would have it' here is a man from whom one may acquire what is needed. I have used inverted commas here on words for 'luck' and 'knowledge' to indicate the metacompositional level of activity which, I suggest, should be read alongside the quasi-realist level of the 'inside' of the play. The interplay of these levels comes near the surface when Pseudolus refuses to explain what he plans to do with the *homine astuto, docto, cauto et callido* (385), even when asked by Calidorus (387–8):

> CA. cedo mihi, quid es facturus? PS. temperi ego faxo scies.
> nolo bis iterari; sat sic longae fiunt fabulae.

> CA. Tell me, what are you going to do? PS. I'll let you know later. I don't
> want to go through it twice; these plays are long enough as it is.

(Only Pseudolus can use the question-and-answer method of exposing the plot.) The metatheatrical joke about long plays also creates the illusion of quasi-realism on which Pseudolus' deceptive power rests, for we are tempted to think 'what was his plan at this time?' It turns out he didn't have one—or did he?[7] The play is, after all, only pretending to be improvised. Five *minae*, an actor and various props are borrowed from Charinus. How convenient . . .

Pseudolus then manages to procure the girl by means of the letter, Simia (dressed as Harpax), and the five *minae*. Meanwhile, Ballio and Simo engage in a bet: Ballio will give Simo twenty *minae* if Pseudolus manages to get the girl (1070–5). This is parallel first to the bet between Pseudolus and Simo, and also to the opening scene (114–16) where Pseudolus makes Calidorus ask him for twenty *minae* (equals one girl). Both 'underlings' take pleasure in having the social superior ask him for a favour, but, naturally, only Pseudolus gets away with it. Ballio, unfortunately for him, is so overconfident that he offers double the normal exchange rate: twenty *minae* and one girl (1075). 'If Pseudolus cheats me I'll give you twenty *minae*, and you can have the girl.' The dramatist's aim is not to tie up loose ends (which are only loose if you want them to be), but to create the theatrical effect of Ballio offering as a gift—which a pimp would never do—the girl he

---

[7] He claims not to have a plan at 366–400 and at 566–7.

has already lost. Only Pseudolus has the right to make offers with confidence, because only Pseudolus 'knows' the script. While it is true that no mention is later made of the gift of Phoenicium, there is the enigmatic response to the complaint of Ballio about Simo's demand that he hand over the money (1224–5). It suits Roman comic justice that the pimp should lose both.

The result of all this is that Simo has to give Pseudolus twenty *minae*. This would allow him to repay the debt to Charinus and have fifteen *minae* left over. There is no suggestion that Simo objects in principle to Calidorus having the girl, only to disreputable behaviour on the way—and to paying. This should leave Pseudolus and Calidorus with fifteen *minae* to play with. The fact that they do not expressly celebrate having this amount is an indicator that they are not quite so concerned with the arithmetic of the question as scholars have been. Rather, it is the thwarted characters, Simo and still more Ballio, who have to deal with the details of exact sums of money. Trying to sort out inconsistencies is part of the act of reading, but we have to accept the playwright laughing at us for our pedantry. Perhaps that is the greatest deceptive act of the play—sending the critic on this wild-goose chase through the *minae*.

And so the play ends in triumph for Pseudolus over the forces of authority and killjoy, while the audience join vicariously in his celebration.

13

The Theater of Plautus:
Playing to the Audience

TIMOTHY J. MOORE

si sine uxore pati possemus, Quirites, omnes ea molestia careremus; set quoniam ita natura tradidit, ut nec cum illis satis commode, nec sine illis ullo modo vivi possit, saluti perpetuae potius quam brevi voluptati consulendum est.

If we could get on without a wife, Romans, we would all avoid that annoyance; but since nature has ordained that we can neither live very comfortably with them nor at all without them, we must take thought for our lasting well-being rather than for the pleasure of the moment.

Q. Metellus Numidicus, censor, 102 BCE (Gell. 1.6.2)

Casina offers Plautus' most serious challenge to the assumptions of so many of his characters concerning marriage and wives. Elsewhere in his plays, the struggle between husbands and wives is peripheral to the main plot. In *Casina*, however, that struggle *is* the plot. At the beginning of *Casina*, both Lysidamus and his son are in love with Casina, the handmaid of Lysidamus' wife, Cleostrata. Lysidamus wants his bailiff, Olympio, to marry the girl, so that he himself can have sex with her. Lysidamus' wife and son seek to win the girl for the son by marrying her to the son's armor-bearer, Chalinus. After neither slave can be persuaded to give up his claim to the girl, the opponents agree to draw lots. Olympio wins, and Lysidamus conspires with his neighbor, Alcesimus, to use the neighbor's house for his liaison with Casina. Made aware of the plan by the eavesdropping Chalinus, Cleostrata, assisted by her servant Pardalisca and Alcesimus' wife Myrrhina, plots to undo the marriage. The women first cause confusion between Alcesimus and Lysidamus, then they persuade Lysidamus that Casina rages inside with a sword, threatening to kill her would-be husband and his master. Finally, they dress Chalinus as a bride and send him in place

of 'Casina' to Alcesimus' house, where he beats and humiliates both
Olympio and Lysidamus.

Scholarship on *Casina* has tended to concentrate on the character
of Lysidamus. As a *senex amator* (an old man in love), Lysidamus
belongs to a type seldom presented with much sympathy, and Plautus
makes him even more ridiculous and lecherous than other *senes ama-
tores*. However obnoxious Lysidamus may be, though, Cleostrata's
victory over him nevertheless represents a break from the rest of
Plautine comedy; for she becomes aligned with the spectators in spite
of her initial characterization as a stock shrewish wife. Both her characterization and her success thus undermine the assumptions made
about husbands and wives elsewhere in Plautus' plays.

The play's prologue both reveals the importance of the conflict
between husband and wife and suggests that that importance is to a
large degree the result of Plautus' reworking of the play he adapted
from the Greek playwright Diphilus. The *argumentum* begins with an
introduction of Lysidamus: *senex hic maritus habitat* ('a married old
man lives here', 35): the unnecessary epithet *maritus* is the first hint
that Lysidamus' status as husband will be important. Immediately
thereafter, the *prologus* reveals that the old man also has a son, that
both men are in love with Casina, and that each has assigned his slave
as surrogate. The spectators are thus prepared for a plot similar to
Asinaria or *Mercator*, where son and father struggle for one girl. As he
continues, however, the *prologus* reveals that this plot is to have a twist:

> senis uxor sensit virum amori operam dare,
> propterea una consentit cum filio.
> ille autem postquam filium sensit suom
> eandem illam amare et esse impedimento sibi,
> hinc adulescentem peregre ablegavit pater;
> sciens ei mater dat operam absenti tamen.
> is, ne expectetis, hodie in hac comoedia
> in urbem non redibit: Plautus noluit,
> pontem interrupit, qui erat ei in itinere.
>
> (58–66)

The old man's wife has figured out that her husband is after love, so she is in
agreement with her son. But after the old man realized that his son was in love
with the same girl and was getting in his way, he sent the young man away.
Aware of what is going on, his mother is helping her son out while he is away.
Don't expect the son to come back to the city during this comedy today: Plautus
didn't want him to, so he destroyed the bridge that was on his way.

The battle will be not between father and son, but between husband and wife: the son will not even appear in the play. 'Plautus didn't want him to' suggests that the son did appear in Diphilus' play: Plautus has removed him, making Cleostrata's role more central. In fact, Plautus appears to have removed from his source play not only the son, but also the *anagnorisis* that revealed that the son could marry Casina legally (he merely states in the epilogue that Casina will be discovered to be the daughter of Lysidamus' neighbor); and he may well have added part or even all of the deception that Cleostrata carries out on her husband in the last half of the play. He has turned a typical play of generational rivalry and *anagnorisis* into a farcical triumph of *matrona* over *senex*.

Though neither *senex* nor *matrona* appears in the play's first scene, that scene hints at a pattern that is to determine the relationship between characters and audience in what follows. Immediately after the prologue, Olympio enters, pursued by Chalinus, and he asks in exasperation:

> non mihi licere meam rem me solum, ut volo,
> loqui atque cogitare, sine ted arbitro?
>
> (89–90)

Can't I talk and think about my own affairs alone, as I wish, without you as witness?

After the two have exchanged a number of insults, Olympio exits, and Chalinus continues to follow him, saying, *hic quidem pol certo nil ages sine med arbitro* ('I tell you, you won't do *anything* here without me as witness', 143). Olympio's inability to speak without Chalinus hearing foreshadows his situation throughout the play. He will be at the bottom of the hierarchy of rapport among the play's major characters, managing only one half of one line aside to the audience without being heard (723). Nor does the foreshadowing apply only to Olympio: Cleostrata and her allies, including Chalinus, repeatedly overhear the monologues and asides of their opponents, Lysidamus and Olympio, and this ability to eavesdrop successfully will help considerably in aligning Cleostrata's side with the spectators.

Such an alliance will scarcely seem likely, however, when Olympio and Chalinus leave the stage and Cleostrata first enters; for Cleostrata is very much the stock comic shrew. She leaves the house commanding that the larder be locked up, for she refuses to obey Lysidamus' order that she have his lunch prepared; and she speaks of her husband in the most threatening and insulting terms (148–62). Aside from her tone,

Cleostrata's power in the household would seem to damn her. Why is she capable of keeping her husband out of the larder? According to Plutarch, substituting keys, along with adultery and murdering children, was one of the few reasons for which Romulus allowed a husband to divorce his wife without penalty (*Rom.* 22. 3). Though Romulus' law may be apocryphal, it reflects the importance early Romans placed upon a husband's access to his possessions. Even though no mention is made of Cleostrata's dowry, therefore, she has the characteristics of a stereotypical *uxor dotata*, appropriating power that should be her husband's.

Myrrhina then enters, presenting what looks at first like a clear contrast between the bad woman and the good. The entrances of the two women are closely parallel in staging: both enter talking back to their servants; both explain that they are going to visit their neighbor, in case their husbands should want them; and both, presumably, proceed toward the neighbor's house, meeting in the middle. The parallel staging serves to emphasize the apparent contrast between the two. Whereas Cleostrata entered with a refusal to do what the audience would see as her wifely duty, Myrrhina is in the middle of such duty: she has been spinning wool, and she asks that her distaff be brought to her as she goes to visit her neighbor. The difference in tone is conspicuous as each woman tells her servants that her husband can find her at the neighbor's. Cleostrata gives a harsh command, and she implies that exasperating her husband is one reason she is leaving the house:

> ego huc transeo in proxumum ad meam vicinam.
> vir si quid volet me, facite hinc accersatis.
>
> (145–6)

I am going over here to my neighbor's next door. If my husband wants anything of me, make him summon me from here.

Myrrhina is imperious to her slaves (163–5), but when she refers to her husband, she is more accommodating, and she makes clear that she is leaving so that she can do her weaving more efficiently:

> ego hic ero, vir si aut quispiam quaeret.
> nam ubi domi sola sum, sopor manes calvitur.
>
> (166–7)

I will be here, if my husband or anyone looks for me. For when I'm at home by myself, sleepiness makes my hands slow.

When Cleostrata complains to Myrrhina of her husband's behavior, Myrrhina responds with a joke at the expense of wives, much like those found throughout Plautus' plays. Told by Cleostrata that her husband is depriving her of her *ius* (what is rightfully hers). Myrrhina responds:

> mira sunt, vera si praedicas, nam viri
> ius suom ad mulieres optinere haud queunt.
>
> (191–2)

That's amazing, if you are telling the truth; for usually husbands can't get what is rightfully theirs from their women.

Cleostrata's insistence that Casina belongs to her inspires the following exchange:

> MYRRHINA.   unde ea tibi est?
>   nam peculi probam nil habere addecet
>   clam virum, et quae habet, partum ei haud commode est,
>   quin viro aut subtrahat aut stupro invenerit.
>   hoc viri censeo esse omne, quidquid tuom est.
> CLEOSTRATA. tu quidem advorsum tuam amicam omnia loqueris.
> MY. tace sis, stulta, et mi ausculta. noli sis to illi advorsari,
>   sine amet, sine quod lubet id faciat, quando tibi nil
>   domi delicuom est.
> CL. satin sana es? nam tu quidem advorsus tuam
> istaec rem loqueris.
> MY.   insipiens,
>   semper tu huic verbo vitato abs tuo viro.
> CL.   cui verbo?
> MY.   ei foras, mulier.
>
> (198–211)

MYRRHINA. Since when is she yours? For a virtuous woman should have no property of her own behind her husband's back, and the one who does have her own property got it in an improper way, stealing it from her husband or getting it through adultery. I think whatever is yours—everything—is your husband's.

CLEOSTRATA. Well! Everything you say you say against your friend.

MY. Oh, be quiet, silly, and listen to me. Don't oppose him, please; let him have his love affairs, let him do what he likes, as long as he doesn't do you wrong at home.

CL. Are you crazy? For really, you're speaking against your own interests!

MY. Silly! Always avoid hearing these words from your husband . . .

CL. What words?

MY. 'Get out of my house, woman!'

Myrrhina's opinions about a wife's property reflect the most traditional Roman type of marriage: marriage *cum manu*, in which a wife and all her property are legally in the power of her husband. Myrrhina's assumptions about the duties of wives toward their husbands would no doubt be shared by many in the audience. She is the prudent and obedient wife, whereas Cleostrata is the troublesome shrew, who, like a stereotypical *uxor dotata*, seeks to invert the proper power structure of her marriage. In what follows, however, the spectators' response to Cleostrata becomes gradually more complicated. Not only does Lysidamus become more and more outrageous, but Plautus manipulates the hierarchy of rapport between characters and audience, so that the spectators become aligned with Cleostrata and her allies.

Immediately following Myrrhina's reference to the divorce formula, Lysidamus enters, speaking the first long monologue of the play. He sings an encomium to love, which he says is superior to all things and should be used instead of spices by cooks. He offers his own love for Casina, which caused him to visit the perfume shops, as a demonstration of the maxim, and he curses his wife (217–27). Lysidamus thus assumes that he can confide in and win the sympathy of the audience. Yet his entrance is observed by Cleostrata. This monologue establishes the pattern of rapport that is to prevail throughout the play. Lysidamus speaks far more lines of monologue than any other character of the play. But his soliloquies and asides are repeatedly overheard by other characters, and from the very beginning Cleostrata knows Lysidamus' plans. Lysidamus thus assumes that he has rapport with the spectators, but in fact Cleostrata and her allies attain a higher position in the hierarchy of rapport.

The dialogue that follows reinforces this hierarchy, as Cleostrata overhears her husband's asides:

LYSIDAMUS.   quam ted anno!
CLEOSTRATA. nolo ames.
LY.   non potes impetrare.
CL.   enecas.
LY. vera dicas velim.
CL.   credo ego istuc tibi.
LY. respice, o mi lepos.
CL.   nempe ita ut tu mihi es.
      unde hic, amabo, unguenta olent?

LY.   oh perii! manufesto miser
    teneor. cesso caput pallio detergere.
    ut te bonu' Mercurius perdat, myropola, quia haec mihi dedisti.

                                                    (232–8)

LYSIDAMUS. How I love you!
CLEOSTRATA. I don't want you to love me.
LY. You can't stop me.
CL. You're killing me.
LY [*aside*]. I wish I were.
CL [*aside*]. I believe you in that.
LY. Look at me, my charming one.
CL. Sure, just like you're charming to me. Tell me, please, where's that smell
    of perfume coming from?
LY. [*aside*]. Oh! I'm done for! Poor me, I'm caught in the act. Quick, I'd better
    wipe my head with my cloak. May good Mercury destroy you, perfume
    salesman, for giving me this stuff.

Neither Lysidamus' use of perfume nor his aside to the audience
eludes Cleostrata. There is no sign, however, that Lysidamus overhears Cleostrata's aside.

After Cleostrata exits, Lysidamus calls attention to the fact that he
was unable to speak around her while she was onstage: *Hercules digne
istam perdant, quod nunc liceat dicere* ('May Hercules and all the gods
destroy her! I hope I can say that now', 275). He then curses Chalinus,
and he is again overheard:

LYSIDAMUS. qui illum di omnes deaeque perdant!
CHALINUS.   te uxor aiebat tua me
                                              vocare.

                                                    (278–9)

LYSIDAMUS. That man! May all the gods destroy . . . !
CHALINUS. You, your wife said, wanted me.

The joke in Latin depends on the fact that without the delayed *me
vocare*, the phrase *te uxor aiebat tua*, after the curse, means, 'Your wife
was saying that she wishes all the gods would destroy *you*. Another
hierarchy of rapport is established, and again Lysidamus is on the
bottom, for he has no idea Chalinus' words are a double entendre,
and that the end of his monologue has been overheard.

In fact, Lysidamus still assumes that he has the power to guide
the audience's reactions. After he fails to persuade Chalinus to give
up Casina, he indulges in another monologue, beginning with a

rhetorical question seeking sympathy from the audience: *sumne ego miser homo?* ('Am I not a wretched man?', 303). Fearing that Cleostrata will persuade Olympio to abandon his claim to the girl, he continues with a mournful plea for commiseration (305); and he melodramatically threatens to stab himself if he loses Casina (307–8). As Olympio enters, telling Cleostrata that he will not give up his claim to Casina, Lysidamus even manages some overhearing of his own; and he responds to what he hears with a joyful aside (312).

In the ensuing scene, Olympio, and Lysidamus pepper their dialogue with insults against Cleostrata like those used to abuse wives elsewhere in Plautus: she argues continually with Lysidamus (318); she is a bitch (320); Lysidamus wishes she were dead (Olympio turns this insult into an obscene joke as well, 326–7). The familiar insults further place Cleostrata within the category of the stock *matrona*. The manipulation of rapport, however, has made it less easy for spectators simply to agree with the insults and dismiss Cleostrata as an unsympathetic character. This dissonance between Lysidamus' assumptions and the alignment of the audience continues as Lysidamus overhears Cleostrata and Chalinus entering (353–5). This is the only place in the play where Lysidamus overhears words of his opponents not intended for his ears. Not surprisingly, his brief moment of greater theatrical power leads him to another joke at the expense of Cleostrata (356). What he learns from his eavesdropping, however, is that Chalinus and Cleostrata know something he would wish concealed, his own hostility to Cleostrata.

Given the fact that Greek dramatists almost always followed the rule of three actors, the ensuing lot scene almost certainly included only Lysidamus, Chalinus, and Olympio in Plautus' Greek original: Plautus added Cleostrata, thus continuing his emphasis on the struggle between husband and wife. As he did so, he made Lysidamus' inability to hide anything from Cleostrata still more obvious; for the old man commits a chain of what we could call Freudian slips, all of them noted by Cleostrata:

> LYSIDAMUS. atque ego censui aps to posse hoc me impetrare, uxor mea,
>   Casina ut uxor mihi daretur; et nunc etiam censeo.
> CLEOSTRATA. tibi daretur illa?
> LY.   mihi enim—ah, non id volui dicere
>   dum mihi volui, huic dixi, atque adeo mihi dum cupio—perperam
>   iam dudum hercle fabulor.
> CL.   pol to quidem, atque etiam facis.

LY. huic—immo hercle mihi—vah, tandem redii vix veram in viam.
CL. per pol saepe peccas.

(364–70)

LYSIDAMUS. Nevertheless, I thought that I would be able to persuade you to do this for me, dear wife, to give Casina to me to marry; and I still think I can persuade you.

CLEOSTRATA. To give her to you?

LY. Yes to me—ah, that's not what I wanted to say: when I wanted to say 'to me' I said 'to him', and since I really want her for me—now I keep on saying the wrong thing.

CL. You sure do, and you keep doing the wrong thing, too.

LY. For him—goodness no, I mean for me—ah! I still can hardly get it right.

CL. You really say the wrong thing a lot.

When Olympio wins the lot, all characters leave the stage except Chalinus, who delivers the longest monologue of the play thus far that is not observed by another character (excluding the prologue). In it he reveals that he, like his mistress, is suspicious of Lysidamus' motives (424–36). Before he left the stage, Lysidamus had emphasized to Olympio that he did not want to be overheard by Chalinus (423). The effect on relative rapport is thus all the greater when Lysidamus and Olympio next enter to plot strategy, and Chalinus eavesdrops on them (437–503). The audience learns along with Chalinus that Lysidamus plans to have Casina brought to the neighbor's house. The shared knowledge creates rapport between slave and spectators, and the rapport is reinforced as Chalinus comments aside repeatedly on what he hears and ends the scene with a long monologue (504–14).

When Cleostrata returns to the stage, she possesses without doubt all the knowledge she needs to condemn Lysidamus, and she is indubitably in charge. She frames the next scene, during which she inspires strife between Lysidamus and Alcesimus, with monologues (531–8, 558–62). She also seems to overhear Alcesimus' monologue, either remaining onstage or listening from behind the door (558); and she overhears another entrance monologue of Lysidamus. If there was some doubt as to how much of Lysidamus' previous monologue Cleostrata heard, this time Plautus makes the difference in rapport obvious. After eleven highly incriminating lines, Lysidamus finally notices his wife watching him:

LYSIDAMUS. sed uxorem ante aedis eccam. ei misero mihi.
metuo ne non sit surda atque haec audiverit.

CLEOSTRATA. audivi ecastor cum malo magno tuo.

(574–6)

LYSIDAMUS. But look! There's my wife in front of the house. Oh, poor me! I'm afraid that she's not deaf and she heard what I said.

CLEOSTRATA [*aside*]. I heard, all right, and you'll pay for it.

Again, Lysidamus' monologue is overheard, but Cleostrata's aside is not. Finally, Cleostrata speaks a brief exit monologue, unheard by Lysidamus, even though he is onstage (589–90). The normal pattern, of course, is for exit monologues to be spoken only after the other characters have left the stage.

After he has straightened out the confusion Cleostrata created with Alcesimus, Lysidamus gets to be an eavesdropper himself, but only because Pardalisca performs for him, pretending that she flees a raging Casina. This inversion of the knowledge surrounding eavesdropping places Lysidamus in a still lower position in the hierarchy of rapport. As Pardalisca then explains to her master what is allegedly happening within, she, like her mistress before her, overhears and responds to his asides (667–8, 681) and catches him in 'Freudian' slips (672, 703). Pardalisca intensifies her own alliance with the spectators, established at the expense of Lysidamus, by telling them in an aside exactly what she is doing:

> ludo ego hunc facete;
> nam quae facta dixi omnia huic falsa dixi:
> era atque haec dolum ex proxumo hunc protulerunt,
> ego hunc missa sum ludere.
>
> (685–8)

I'm playing a great trick on him; for everything I told him is false. My mistress and her next-door neighbor here came up with this deception, and I have been sent to trick him.

The alliances of the play are now unmistakable: the audience is aligned with Cleostrata and her onstage allies against Lysidamus and his allies. Significantly, the 'linking monologue' Lysidamus speaks between the exit of Pardalisca and the ensuing entrance of Olympio, lasts for only one line (720); and his status falls still further when he reports Pardalisca's news to Olympio. Unlike his gullible master, Olympio immediately realizes that the story of the sword-bearing Casina was nothing but the women's ruse (751–2).

The audience sees the next deception entirely through Pardalisca's

eyes: she reports how the cooks and the women have kept Olympio
and Lysidamus from getting any supper. Pardalisca then eavesdrops
on Lysidamus (780–9); and when she leaves the stage, the old man
again reminds the audience that his attempts to communicate with
them are being repeatedly foiled while others are onstage: *iamne abiit
illaec? dicere hic quidvis licet* ('Has she gone now? Now I can say whatever I want', 794). Even now that he is alone, he only manages one
line on the glories of love (795) before he sees Olympio and the *tibicen*
entering, ready for the wedding.

The climax of Cleostrata's plot follows, as Chalinus, disguised as
Casina, is led to Olympio's bridal chamber. Lysidamus, this time with
Olympio, again overhears what the women want him to hear, as
Pardalisca advises 'Casina' to be a domineering and deceptive wife:

> sensim supera tolle limen pedes, mea nova nupta;
> sospes iter incipe hoc, uti viro tuo semper sis superstes,
> tuaque ut potior pollentia sit vincasque virum victrixque sies,
> tua vox superet tuomque imperium: vir te vestiat, tu virum despolies.
> noctuque et diu ut viro subdola sis,
> opsecro, memento.

(815–21)

Lift your feet gently over the threshold, my new bride; make this journey
safely, so that you can always stand above your husband, and so that your
power will be greater, so that you will overcome your husband, and be the
victor, so that your word and your command will win the day: let your husband clothe you, while you strip him. And please, be sure to remember to
deceive your husband day and night.

Pardalisca parodies Roman wedding ritual and inverts Roman ideals
of wifely obedience. 'Casina', like the stereotypical *uxor dotata*, should
want power and luxuries. Plautus has now established an alliance
between the spectators and those who explicitly associate themselves
with the quintessential outsiders of Plautine comedy: wives who
want power over their husbands.

When Olympio and Lysidamus, after receiving several blows from
'Casina', have led 'her' into Alcesimus' house, Myrrhina, Pardalisca,
and Cleostrata enter to watch what happens. Myrrhina describes the
events to come in decidedly theatrical terms:

> acceptae bene et commode eximus intus
> ludos visere huc in viam nuptialis.

(855–6)

Now that we have been entertained pleasantly and well indoors, we are coming out here into the street to watch the nuptial games.

The women are now an audience, aligned with the real audience watching the discomfiture of Olympio and Lysidamus. They are also the playwrights responsible for the performance they will watch, as Myrrhina points out in the next lines:

> nec fallaciam astutiorem ullus fecit
> poeta, atque ut haec est fabre facta ab nobis.
>
> (860–1)

No poet ever made a more clever trick than this one we have crafted so skillfully.

Unaware of the women's presence, Olympio enters, fleeing his bride. He addresses the spectators explicitly (879), and he delivers a long and incriminating monologue, only to learn to his chagrin that he is being observed by the women (893). He then delights both onstage and offstage spectators with an obscene report of his misadventure with 'Casina': he was beaten when he tried to deflower 'Casina' before Lysidamus could get to her, and what he thought was a sword was actually 'Casina's' phallus.

Finally, Lysidamus enters, bruised and disheveled by his encounter with 'Casina'. Staging underscores the fact that Lysidamus has reached his nadir, for he is overheard now by no fewer than five eavesdroppers: Pardalisca, Chalinus, Cleostrata, Myrrhina, and his former ally, Olympio. He is in fact caught right between the eavesdroppers: when he later attempts to escape the pursuing Chalinus, he runs into his suite and her colleagues (969). This visual situation brings intense dramatic irony to Lysidamus' opening words:

> maxumo ego ardeo flagitio
> nec quid agam meis rebus scio,
> nec meam ut uxorem aspiciam
> contra oculis, ita dispirii; <om>nia palam sunt probra,
> omnibus modis occidi miser.
>
> (937–40)

I'm burning from the greatest shame, and I don't know what I should do for myself; nor how I can look my wife in the face, I'm so utterly ruined. All my vices are in the open, and—poor me!—I'm finished in every way.

Lysidamus will have to look his wife in the face sooner than he thinks, for she is watching him as he speaks: his vices are even more in the

open than he realizes. Nevertheless, Lysidamus still assumes that he
can confide in the audience. He even asks if any spectator will be beaten
for him (949–50). He also continues to assume that the spectators share
his hostility to his wife: forced to choose between running back to
Chalinus and running into the women, he says he chooses between
wolves and bitches, his wife and her female allies being the latter (971–3).
By now the inadequacy of such insults will be more than obvious.

Lysidamus' utter humiliation is further reinforced visually by the
wretched state of his dress: he has lost his staff and cloak. When he
tries to blame the loss on bacchants, he is rebuffed by Myrrhina:

> CLEOSTRATA.   quin responde, tuo quid factum est pallio?
> LYSIDAMUS. Bacchae hercle, uxor—
> CL.   Bacchae?
> LY.   Bacchae hercle,
>   uxor—
> MYRRHINA. nugatur sciens, nam ecastor nunc Bacchae nullae
>   ludunt.
> LY. oblitus fui, sed tamen Bacchae—
> CL.   quid, Bacchae?
> LY.   sin id fieri
>   non potest—
> CL.   times ecastor.
>
>   (978–82)

CLEOSTRATA.   All right now, answer me: what happened to your cloak?
LYSIDAMUS. By Hercules, dear wife, it was Bacchants—
CL. Bacchants?
LY. By Hercules, dear wife, it was Bacchants—
MYRRHINA. That's nonsense and he knows it, for goodness, now there are no
    bacchic revelries.
LY. I forgot; but just the same, Bacchants—
CL. What's that? Bacchants?
LY. Well, if that's not possible—
CL. My, but you are frightened.

With her theatrical double entendre, *ludunt*, Myrrhina reminds
Lysidamus that the women have gained power over the performance:
their play, not a performance with bacchants, is now being performed.

The reference to bacchants is also topical. Lysidamus alludes to the
contemporary controversy over nocturnal rites held by worshipers of
Bacchus, rites brutally crushed after a decree of the senate in 186 BCE.
One of the accusations made against the worshipers of Bacchus was

that female revelers made male participants have sex with one
another: Lysidamus, caught trying to have sex with his male slave,
offers the excuse that women worshiping Bacchus forced him to do it.
He cites an extreme example of women's power over men, an ideal
exemplum for those seeking to keep wives and other women 'in their
place'. Myrrhina's response reminds him and the audience that here
women's power is not a heinous aberration, but a positive force.

Lysidamus then begs his wife for forgiveness, and Myrrhina proposes leniency. Cleostrata agrees:

> MYRRHINA. censeo ecastor veniam hanc dandam.
> CLEOSTRATA.   faciam ut iubes.
>   propter eam rem hanc tibi nunc veniam minus gravate prospero,
>   hanc ex longa longiorem ne faciamus fabulam.
>
> (1004–6)

MYRRHINA. I think, really, you should forgive him this time.
CLEOSTRATA. I will do as you suggest. Here's why I'm forgiving you more willingly now: so that we don't make this long play longer.

Cleostrata's reason for forgiving Lysidamus is not personal but theatrical: again, Lysidamus and the audience are reminded that the
women control the play. As in *Mercator*, the self-deprecating joke
about the length of the play is ironic, for *Casina*, at 1018 lines, is even
shorter. Behind the joke lies an additional message: the inversion of
the expected roles of men and women has gone on far enough, and
the real issue of the marital relationship is not to be dealt with in a
comedy. Not surprising, then, is Lysidamus' response to Cleostrata's
mercy, using *lepidus*, with its connotations of excellent performance:
lepidiorem uxorem nemo quisquam quam ego habeo hanc habet ('Nobody
has a wife more charming than this one of mine', 1008).

Here, however, issues of husbands and wives are not as easily dismissed as they were in *Mercator*. Cleostrata's release of Lysidamus
and the audience from those issues leads to the epilogue, which
ostensibly returns to a narrow masculine perspective and wishes for
the spectators access to a prostitute behind their wives' backs if they
applaud enthusiastically. The epilogue's sudden association of the
spectators with Lysidamus, as they, like him, are assumed to want sex
behind their wives' backs, makes a great joke at the audience's
expense. It also reminds them that in most plays, they would in fact
be aligned with a man like Lysidamus against a wife like Cleostrata.
This play, however, has been a completely different experience.

In *Casina*, then, Plautus offered a daring plot, involving the triumph of a *matrona* who at first appears to match the characteristics of some of Plautus' least sympathetic characters. One of the ways he overcame potential resistance to this unusual plot was by establishing a clear hierarchy of rapport, with Cleostrata and her allies on the top and Lysidamus on the bottom, a hierarchy made still more powerful because through most of the play, Lysidamus thinks he is on top.

There is more at work here, however, than simply variety, topsy-turviness for its own sake, or moralizing about lust. Cleostrata's victory over Lysidamus represents a nightmare come true for those on the conservative side of contemporary debates about *matronae*. Yet in spite of their initial impression of her as an unsympathetic stock figure, the spectators find themselves aligned with Cleostrata against Lysidamus. Plautus thus encourages the audience to view from an entirely different perspective contemporary controversies about the proper role of married women.

14

The Theatrical Significance of Duplication in Plautus' *Amphitruo*

FLORENCE DUPONT

In the *Comedy of Errors*, which is based on Plautus' *Menaechmi*, Shakespeare makes the Duke address the Ephesian twins and their accusers thus: 'I think you all have drunk of Circe's cup.' Later, when all four twins are present, he says of the two Dromios:

> One of these men is *genius* to the other:
> And so of these, which is the natural man,
> And which the spirit? Who deciphers them?[1]

This Elizabethan reference to Circe, the sorceress of transformations, from within the Plautine tradition, will remind us at the outset that a Baroque theatrical device, which I should like to call that of duplication, already forms part of an early phase of Western culture. Ancient Rome supplied Baroque Europe with its language and its images, among the latter the Amphitryon story and the figure of Sosia. Thus Rotrou exploits Plautus' *Amphitruo* to write *Les Sosies*, just as Shakespeare reuses *Menaechmi*, and combines the game of mirrors with the exploration of a cardinal concept in our Western culture, that of representation. To be sure the Plautine tradition is not enough by itself to reveal the importance of his comedies, but it suggests a line of research, namely to trace across history, through the constituent texts of our culture, what might be called discourses on representation.

Roman comedy does not employ theatrical illusion: the comic stage does not claim to represent real life by making the audience think the characters are copies of themselves. On the contrary, the action often relies on playing games with the code, as when Mercury dances in like a *servus currens* with the words (986–7):

---

[1] v. i. 271, 334–6.

nam mihi quidem hercle qui minus liceat deo minitarier
populo, ni decedat mihi, quam seruolo in comoediis?

And why should *I*, a god for goodness sake, have less right to threaten the people if they don't get out of my way than a rubbishy little slave has in the comedies?

Plautus constantly uses such reference to the code, his characters constantly recall the conventions that fix them in their role of Old Man, Slave, or Parasite. For example Sosia, preparing to make up for his mistress Alcumena a report on a battle in which he did not take part, justifies his lying as follows (198): *si dixero mendacium, solens meo more fecero* ('If I tell a lie, I shall be acting in character as usual'). By lying he will be playing the part of the comic Principal Slave, *meo more*.

But this taste for metatheatrical quips may also be rooted in Plautus' personal life. Varro, as cited by Aulus Gellius,[2] preserves the memory of a man who before writing comedy had originally made his money 'in operis artificum scaenicorum', in other words as a scene-painter and stagehand. He had spent his days behind the scenery, and had even built it. He had been what Jupiter calls himself in *Amphitruo*, an *architectus*, a framer of illusion, at once powerful and ridiculous, and in the tragicomedy of *Amphitruo* he may be making himself his own material and putting a creator's point of view on stage, a comedy about comedy, a form notoriously important in Baroque aesthetics.

Here then is our thesis: the Greek tale of Amphitryon, exploited and developed by Plautus, became a comedy of duplication, as it were a comedy about the Roman theatre, because the transformation of gods into men, of Jupiter into Amphitryon, of Mercury into Sosia, is realized in speech and action throughout the play by means of theatrical disguise.

This play thus generates a new figure that has become part of the language [i.e. French *sosie*, 'double', 'lookalike'] and is at the same time a theatrical myth: the myth of Sosia. The Sosia–Mercury pairing was thereafter to afford a particular theatrical device that the ideologies of classicism rejected and even denied. It was to be seen above all in the Baroque, but cannot be limited to one historical period because it constitutes one of the threads in the weft of Western culture. It

---

[2] *Noctes Atticae* 3. 3. 14.

makes of the stage the place in which the identity and unity of the
subject are called into question. Of this device, inseparable from
opera and from the Italian stage resulting from Vitruvius' drawings,
Plautus' *Amphitruo* may well be the first trace, which is not to say the
origin.

The myth is well known: it tells how Heracles was born from Zeus'
dalliance with Alcmene, the wife of a Theban general called Amphitryon. In certain versions of the legend,[3] Zeus impregnated the young
woman in the form of rain; according to others,[4] in order to achieve
his ends he took the human shape of Amphitryon.

Before reaching the Roman stage, in comic guise with Plautus,
then in tragic with Accius,[5] the story had known some success in
Greece itself. Under the title *Alcmene* or *Amphitryon*, it had been the
subject of several tragedies.

Despite Hesychius' evidence, it is not certain that Aeschylus wrote
such a play; it is certain that Sophocles, Euripides, Ion of Chios, and
some Hellenistic authors did. Euripides' tragedy, of which fifteen fragments are preserved, has been reconstructed as follows with the help
of some representations of performances: Amphitryon accused his
wife of adultery and sought to kill her. She took refuge at an altar. He
piled up wood around it, to which he set fire. Zeus intervened by
unleashing a storm that extinguished the pyre.[6] He reveals the truth
and reconciles husband and wife. It is impossible to say whether, in
the tragedies, Zeus adopted the guise of Amphitryon. In any case the
whole business of pyre, rain, and thunder are enough to prove that
the tragic version must have been different from the comic one we
know. It must have been a mythological spectacular of the kind its
reviver Accius revelled in.

Indeed, the actual text of *Amphitruo* shows how comic spectacle
could be created on the basis both of the legend and the tragedy, by successive play of mirror and disguise. Characters and situations are
duplicated, action blends with the dialogue, in a comedy closely woven
out of parallel scenes (Jupiter–Alcumena, Amphitruo–Alcumena;
Mercury–Sosia and Jupiter–Amphitruo), of mistakings (Mercury–
Amphitruo; Jupiter–Alcumena), of mirror-like encounters where
each identity is at stake (Mercury–Sosia, Jupiter–Amphitruo). The

³ Pindar, *Isthmians* 7. 5–7 ('snowing gold').
⁴ Pindar, *Nemeans* 10. 15–17; Hyginus, *Fabulae* 30.
⁵ Otto Ribbeck, *TRF*, 169–71.   ⁶ Mentioned by Plautus, *Rudens* 86–7.

whole theatrical game based on the initial premiss is presented to the audience by the gods as their way of playing with mortals: *deludere* (980).

The first trick of disguise gives birth to Sosia, the product of dressing a tragedy as a comedy. Mercury's announcement in the prologue runs thus (51): *post argumentum huius eloquar tragoediae* ('Then I shall expound the plot of this tragedy'). The starting-point is indeed a tragedy, but (52–3):

> quid contraxistis frontem? quia tragoediam
> dixi futuram hanc? deus sum, commutauero.

Why did you crease your brows? Because I said it would be a tragedy? I'm a god, I'll change it.

The play is a mock-tragedy.

How can one move from tragedy to comedy? One way would be burlesque, keeping the tragic characters with their costumes and masks but giving them comic lines; or again, another way would be parody. Plautus rejects these methods (61–2):

> nam me perpetuo facere ut sit comoedia
> reges quo ueniant et di, non par arbitror.

For I don't think it right for me to make it a comedy from beginning to end, seeing that kings and gods come into it.

These procedures, which belong entirely to the comic stage, would make playing on the duplication impossible. Plautus, says the prologue, will therefore keep up both stage worlds: that of the gods will be tragic, that of the mortals comic, in other words it will use the costume, gestures, and speech of comic roles (63–4):

> quid igitur? quoniam hic seruos quoque partis habet,
> faciam sit proinde ut dixi tragicomoedia.

What then? Since there's even a slave in it, I shall make just as I said a tragicomedy.

But the gods, when they meet mortals, will leave tragedy to borrow comic roles; contrariwise Amphitruo and Alcumena in certain situations will be *reges*, royal characters of tragedy. Thus when Amphitruo is the victorious general he belongs to the tragic world, at least verbally: when Sosia recounts his exploits, it is in the tragic manner (203–61). But when he returns home and comes on stage, he is no more than a jealous *senex* (1072): *sed quid hoc? quis est hic senex qui ante aedis nostras sic iacet?* ('But what's this? Who's this old man lying like that in front of our house?'). says the aged Bromia when she catches sight of Amphitruo lying on the ground and does not recognize him.

Tragicomedy is thus more than a simple parody: it displays at one and the same time the heroic model and its comic travesty. *Amphitruo* is simultaneously the story of a deceived husband and of Hercules' nativity. Already in one version of the heroic legend Zeus had taken the form of Amphitryon to come down to earth. But on top of that in Plautus' play the human universe is twofold: it is both tragic and comic. And as in his comic aspect Amphitruo has a slave to accompany him, being a comic *senex*, so must Jupiter. Since there is no slave god, it will have to be a god liable to be at Jupiter's service, his son Mercury.

Thus the association of Jupiter and Mercury is motivated and constructed by the fact that their transformation into human beings follows the model of a characteristic comic pair, the master and the slave. That is exactly how Jupiter defines the role of Mercury (861–2):

> Ego sum ille Amphitruo quoii est seruos Sosia,
> idem Mercurius qui fit quando commodum est.

I am the Amphitruo who has a slave Sosia who also becomes Mercury when it is convenient.

This character Mercury, who has the duty of delivering the prologue, is by his nature a very suitable figure for the complex character of this tragicomedy. He says it himself when he associates his disguise with the dressing up of tragedy as comedy (116–18):

> Nunc ne hunc *ornatum* uos meum admiremini,
> quod ego huc processi sic cum seruili schema,
> ueterem atque antiquam rem nouam ad uos proferam;
> propterea *ornatus* in nouom incessi modum.

Now so you shan't be surprised at my costume, because I have come here like this got up as a slave, I shall bring you an old and ancient matter as new; that is why I have entered in a new style of costume.

His change of costume, *ornatus*, that is to say his own transformation into a slave, sums up the passage from the old story, *ueterem atque antiquam rem*, to the new, *nouam*, since it signifies at the same time the doubling of Sosia and the association of the comic world with the tragic.

When the gods are alone, that is, they address the audience, they regain their divine status and stop playing the human character whose costume they wear. These spoken (not sung or danced) scenes are their opportunity to reassert their omnipotence, since in them they inform the audience of the course of events and announce the tricks they will play on their human duplicates; thus Mercury (470–1):

> erroris ambo ego illos et dementiae
> complebo atque Amphitruonis omnem familiam.

I shall fill both of them with confusion and delusion, and indeed Amphitruo's whole household.

or again Jupiter (980–1):

> uolo deludi illum dum hac usuraria
> uxore nunc mihi morigero.

I want him to be deceived while I am pleasing myself now with this borrowed wife.

It is clear in these two passages that the exercise of divine power consists in *deludere*, 'playing with' mortals, in the different senses of the Latin word, 'trick' and 'make fun of', and in creating *ludi*, 'shows'. That is the metatheatrical point of view. But divine power also succeeds in making mortals mad, filling them *erroris et dementiae*, in blinding them to the difference between truth and lies, between reality and image. The gods are thus in the position of ringmaster, a classic position in Roman comedy occupied by the parasite or principal slave, but they are ringmasters with powers infinitely superior to those of a normal comic character in the same position, a slave or a parasite, and it is this omnipotence that lends the comedy its tragic dimension, making of it so to speak a 'supercomedy'.

All-powerful to make mortals mad, the gods are all-powerful too to make them sane again and restore their lost honour. But at that point they definitively abandon comedy, including their human disguise, and can at last address human beings in the manner of tragic deities. At the end of *Amphitruo* Jupiter thus appears in the *theologeion*, above the *frons scaenae*, perhaps wearing a tragic mask but with his body invisible. He speaks in iambic senarii, the metre common to tragedy and comedy (1131–41), with a gravity suitable to a tragic role. Opposite him, down below, a poor *senex* of comedy decides not to follow him into tragedy by consulting a seer straight out of *Oedipus* or

Troades or *Iphigenia*: he sends Tiresias away and once more becomes Amphitruo, the comic Old Man, who concludes the play by singing the trochaic septenarii expected at the end of every comedy and often performed by the *cantor* (1145–6):

> Ibo ad uxorem intro; missum facio Teresiam senem.
> Nunc spectatores, Iouis summi causa clare plaudite.

I'll go inside to my wife; I can do without old Tiresias. Now, audience, loud and clear for highest Jupiter's sake—now clap!

Amphitruo's sung finale counterpoints the *diuerbium* or spoken matter of Mercury's prologue. The 'clap now' *canticum* marks out comedy by opposing it to tragedy, for not only are trochaic septenarii the specific verse of tragedy but in taking on the *cantor*'s functions Amphitruo is no more than one of the devices that go to make up comedy, the one that makes the musical show just as the *diuerbium* makes the narrative plot.

Let us return to those divine monologues addressed to the audience in which the gods discharge their function of ringmasters. These monologues also serve to demonstrate their methods, which are those of the theatre. Plautus makes character and performer speak together: the disguised god thus becomes an actor who has changed costume.

We should read once more the four lines of Mercury's cited above (116–19). We had interpreted them as spoken by the character Mercury; but they may also be understood as coming from an actor who has exchanged the traditional garb of the tragic Mercury, winged helmet, staff, and caduceus, for the slave's red wig and short tunic and padded calves. The actor's change of costume and the metamorphosis of the god are stated in the same terms. The god describes his metamorphosis in the language of disguise, so that Jupiter's arrival on earth becomes the invasion of the 'real' world by simulations. The play shows us scenes in which men and simulations of men meet, and strangely enough in the duels that they fight it is always the simulations that win.

From the same perspective, let us look at some lines said by Jupiter *solus* introducing himself to the audience (863–6):

> in superiore qui habito cenaculo,
> qui interdum fio Iuppiter quando lubet;
> huc autem cum extemplo aduentum adporto, ilico
> Amphitruo fio et uestitum immuto meum.

... who live in the upper chamber; who sometimes become Jupiter when I feel like it, but when I bring my sudden appearance here, straightway I become Amphitruo and change my clothes.

These words may be understood in three different ways, uttered by three different speakers. First a comic Jupiter. He relates his adventure in a tone of parody and describes Olympus as an upper chamber; on this reading *huc* denotes the earth, the world of mortals. One may also find here the actor evoking his wretched garret on the top floor of an *insula*, which he leaves to play Jupiter and Amphitruo; *huc* thus becomes the stage in the theatre. A third speaker is possible, a tragic Jupiter, that god wedged into the tiny balcony for divine appearances above the stage wall, the *theologeion*, called here the *superius cenaculum*. The god's transformation is no more than the passage from tragedy to comedy.

In the same way, when he intervenes as ringmaster, Jupiter does the work of a dramatic poet: 'I come so as not to leave this comedy unfinished', *ne hanc incohatam transigam comoediam* (867). Once again, in coming down to earth Jupiter declares that he is staging a play, writing a comedy.

Finally the return to order, Jupiter's revelations, and Alcumena's giving birth, are brought about by spectacular means: thunder and the god's appearance in the *theologeion*.

The most obvious effect of this divine comedy, in fact, had been disorder, but a disorder based on more than the conventional fiction of gods' omnipotence: it is the gods' exploitation of the thoroughly human powers of the theatre. For example let us take the famous scene in which Mercury robs Sosia of his identity. The spectacle really happens. The resemblance is so perfect that if the audience had not been warned in the prologue that Mercury's hat bore a token that Sosia could not see, they too would have been caught in the trap. First of all, the comic characters are all got up appropriately to their roles with the respective *personae*, without individual features. Two actors playing the principal slave therefore look exactly alike. Furthermore, the Romans were fascinated even, outside the theatre, by the device of the mime; certain artists excelled at it. The epitaph of the *mimus* Vitalis is familiar:[7]

---

[7] *Anth. Lat.* 487ᵃ. 17–18 Riese (*magis* is textually dubious).

> ipse etiam quem nostra oculis geminabat imago
> horruit in uultus se magis isse meos.

Even he whom my portrayal rendered double to men's eyes shuddered that he had rather passed over into my countenance.

The disorder reigning among mortals in *Amphitruo* has nothing intrinsically divine, it is that which follows from all twinship in a world where everyone is individual. One may think of the terrifying consequences of these games if they ceased to be games in a world in which eyewitness is the supreme evidence of the truth. *Amphitruo*'s friends can no longer testify to his identity, he himself no longer knows which is the real Sosia.

This disorder is taken to extremes in the meeting between Mercury and Amphitruo. The false Sosia cheeks his supposed master from the rooftop, and the scene plays on Mercury's dual character, symbolized by his elevated position and his costume: superior as a god, inferior as a slave. The slave refuses to let his master enter his own house by pretending not to recognize him, he makes fun of him, calls him a fool. The god cannot be punished by a man.

Therefore, the gods are there to offer the audience a theatrical code slightly different from that of comedy, even if it is derived from it. That is the function of Mercury's prologue, before we are shown the workings of comic theatre at large; in one respect tragicomedy is an exaggerated comedy.

In the prologue Mercury constructs theatrical space out of the reversal of the man–god hierarchy, substituting for it the inverse hierarchy actors–men. He addresses the audience in slave's costume but introduces himself as Mercury, god of trade and courier of his father Jupiter. He speaks to the spectators as traders, he asserts his power over them by his promises: he will secure them good bargains (1–16). Neither he nor they are yet in the show proper. Then everything is topsyturvy: the god and his father beg the audience's good will (26–7):

> et enim ille cuius huc iussu uenio Iuppiter
> non minus quam uostrum quiuis formidat malum.

For indeed even he at whose command I have come here, Jupiter, is no less afraid of trouble than any of you.

They are just like everybody else in fearing misfortune. They have come to act in a play, *facere histrionicam* (90); they are actor gods, and that is why Mercury is dressed like a slave.

Thus within this first theatrical space constituted by the divine actors a second theatre is set up, but known only to the audience: Jupiter and Mercury have borrowed parts that have already been assigned, those of the Old Man and the Principal Slave.

What does Plautus get out of this transformation of the comic code, this exaggeration of its usual means—lies and disguises—by entrusting the gods with directing the comic action? We suggest the following hypothesis: besides demonstrating the tragic bounds of the comic game, Plautus is putting on stage the *licentia* of the games, that absence of social distinction characteristic of the society formed by the audience in the *cauea*.

The text appears to allude to it in the following way. At the end of his duel with Mercury, Sosia finds himself bereft of his identity, *imago*, and abandons his mission of reporting to Alcumena on the victorious Amphitruo's return, since another self denies him entry to the house. Before turning on his heel, the comic slave saves face by two jokes.

The first is an allusion to the custom among the *nobilitas*, when one of its members dies, of manufacturing an *imago*, a wax death-mask moulded on the dead man's face, identically reproducing his features. This *imago* is carried by a mute in the funerals of the great man's descendants; after traversing the *Vrbs* in procession, accompanied by all the *imagines* of the clan, he will hear his funeral eulogy in the forum (458–9):

> Nam hic quidem omnem imaginem meam quae antehac fuerat possidet:
> Viuo fit quod numquam quisquam mortuo faciet mihi.

For this fellow's got the whole of my previous *imago*; I'm having done for me alive what no one will ever do for me dead.

Here then is Mercury, doing for Sosia alive what no one will do for him dead, exhibiting his mask as if he belonged to a noble family. But as the text makes clear, Mercury's game goes further, since he displays Sosia's *imago* in his lifetime.

It will be the same with Jupiter, who in a similar scene later on, unfortunately lost, also does for Amphitruo alive what this time will also be done for him dead. But if one thinks about it, the *imago* of a Roman noble, which is the only social privilege attesting his membership of the *nobilitas*—the privilege of *ius imaginum*—associates with the commemoration of his glory in his descendant's obsequies the inscribing of his individuality in human memory. For an *imago* preserves only the dead man's pure identity, independent of all his traits of character; those were visible on his *uultus*, his living face, 'the mirror of the soul', in contrast to the *imago*, from which the *animus* had departed in company with life. Thus Jupiter robs Amphitruo of the emblem of his aristocratic individuality, deprives him of all claim to *nobilitas*.

If now with this first joke we associate the second, we shall see that the gods, in becoming mortals' duplicates, wreck the social hierarchy. Sosia adds (460–2):

> Ibo ad portum atque haec uti sint facta ero dicam meo,
> nisi etiam is quoque me ignorabit. quod ille faxit Iuppiter
> ut ego hodie raso capite caluus capiam pilleum.

I'll go to the harbour and tell my master how this has happened, unless he isn't going to recognize me either; may great Jupiter bring that to pass, so that today I can shave my head bald and put on the cap of freedom.

If his master does not know him, Sosia will find himself freed *de facto*, since he will no longer have a master. But the Latin is more powerful, for it alludes to the procedure of the *legis actio* by which a master freed a slave before the praetor, during which the master did nothing other than not recognize his slave as his own, remaining silent when the moment came to claim him.

Thus we see that on the one hand Jupiter's arrival among men as a theatrical god has the effect of creating *licentia*, that is of abolishing that *uerecundia*, that respect for distinctions by which the social hierarchy is maintained. There is no longer either slave or noble. Hence the disorders of *Amphitruo* reproduce the ritual *licentia* of the spectators at the games by dramatizing it. But what is a mere controlled parenthesis in social life, within the ritual of the games, becomes a disorder bordering on the tragic within the fiction of the stage. On the one hand Sosia's jokes are based on interference between the theatre and two other Roman usages that have a theatrical nature. The *imago* of the deceased takes part in the life of the living, since along with others it receives a *laudatio* that cannot be pronounced in its absence. The legal fiction of emancipation permits the proprietorial bond between master and slave to be dissolved, in a way because the master has played at no longer being the master.

If then there is a meaning to be found in this tragicomedy of *Amphitruo*, it is the reflection it engenders on ludic and social theatre at Rome. The efficacy of the image, whose divine omnipotence it celebrates, is not only a game played for its own sake, it is also at work in Roman society and its rituals of law and memory.

Of course, this interpretation of *Amphitruo* as theatre severs it from the Athenian theatrical tradition, and in particular from Middle Comedy. In recalling at the outset the ancestors of Plautus' play we mentioned only the tragedies, but we must also discuss the comedies.

Did Plautus rework a Middle Comedy? Or did he follow the author of a *phlyax* who came from southern Italy? This is important, since it permits further consideration of Roman theatre.

The very fact that tragic and comic performances at Rome are called *ludi Graeci* is enough to remind us that every Roman play in these games is based on a Greek comedy or tragedy. That does not automatically mean an Attic play. Although Plato Comicus' *Nux Makra* has been proposed as Plautus' original, nothing forbids us to imagine a hilarotragedy as the model of this tragicomedy, for the prologue is silent on the Greek source.

The evidence on this matter is as follows. Athenaeus attributes to Rhinthon, who lived at Taras from 328 to 285 BC, various parodies of Euripidean and Sophoclean tragedy, including an *Amphitryon*.[8] The *Suda* makes Rhinthon the inventor of *hilarotragōdia*, a dramatic genre defined by grammarians as 'making fun of things not in themselves funny' and 'making ridiculous travesties of tragic legends'.[9]

The new question to arise now is this: was Rhinthon's hilarotragedy a mere parody, such as Mercury rejects in the prologue, or did it contain the doubling that forms the foundation for the tragicomedy?

The scholarly battle has raged for several years: the latest statements of position are as follows. Oliver Taplin returns to the interpretation of the *phlyax* vases,[10] painted ceramic items dating from 400 to 330 BC and decorated with scenes from comedy. These vases, of which one shows Amphitryon with Hermes dressed as a mortal under Alcmene's windows, have traditionally been interpreted as representing elements of the *phyax* or hilarotragedy. Taplin would relate to Attic comedy from Aristophanes' time and put an earlier date on the appearance of written hilarotragedy. This view makes more probable a link between *Amphitruo* and Attic comedy.

In contrast Renato Oniga, in his excellent Italian edition of 1992,

---

[8] Athenaeus 3. 111 C, 14. 620 F.
[9] *Suda* s.n. 'Ρίνθων.
[10] Oliver Taplin, 'The New Choregos Vase', *Pallas*, 38 (1992), 140–51.

asserts derivation from Rhinthon. I am inclined in that direction, but without casting doubt on Taplin's proof. It is not enough to introduce gods in a comedy, as Aristophanes did, to create the mixed form of tragicomedy; the writing itself must also combine tragic elements, pertaining to tragic dramatic poetry, and comic elements, pertaining to comic dramatic poetry. Our ignorance of both Plato Comicus' and Rhinthon's poetry prevents us from deciding.

Thus Plautus made the story of Amphitryon into a theatrical 'myth', as Euripides had done with the Pentheus legend in *Bacchae*. Dionysus is the god of the mask, Jupiter the god of *delusio*, of play; the two gods appear as masters of illusion, who deceive mortals by making them confuse image and reality. Pentheus the tragic victim, Amphitryon the comic victim: both heroes attest the omnipotence of the theatrical image, for here the dramatic poets and producers are gods, and as such by convention omnipotent. The mythological fiction serves to take the theatrical illusion beyond the normal range, in order to display its effects when let off the leash in a play within a play. The audience are protected from the illusion, since they have the means of distinguishing Jupiter and Amphitruo, Mercury and Sosia, whereas the human characters for their part are played with, *deluduntur*, by the gods—gods who 'play' the comedy, *faciunt histrionicam*—until they go mad.

It will come as no surprise that in a Roman play Jupiter should be the god of the theatre and not Dionysus as in Greece, for it was to Jupiter that the most ancient *ludi scaenici* in Rome had been dedicated ever since in 364 BC the first theatrical performances were inroduced into the Ludi Romani, which up till then had consisted only of shows on the race-track, the Circus Maximus. Jupiter is present and with other gods attends the stage show, he is represented by the giver of the games, the magistrate, who in the costume of Jupiter Capitolinus has led the games' procession riding the god's chariot and now presides over them.

The disguising effect thus extends beyond the stage and touches the space of the audience; for the action on stage, in which a god is disguised as a general, inverts the ritual action of the games, in which a general is disguised as a Jupiter. Neither is more than a passing illusion. But the ritual disguise lacks the dangerous consequences of the theatrical, for the fiction of the *fabula* sets this process of disguise in motion, demonstrates its effects through the powers of the poet, which are those of a god—of course within the limits of the stage, where he is in charge of the game.

15
Amphitruo, Bacchae, and Metatheatre

NIALL W. SLATER

I propose to interpret many of the outstanding questions about the *Amphitruo* as an example of metatheatre—which I define as theatrically self-conscious theatre, aware of its own nature as a medium and capable of exploiting its own conventions and devices for comic and occasionally pathetic effect. It is this self-consciousness (alien to Greek New Comedy) which, in light of the connections pointed out half a century ago by Zeph Stewart in a penetrating article, links the *Amphitruo* directly to the *Bacchae* of Euripides.[1]

My method will be performance criticism. I will examine the play in its natural environment, the theatre, and in the only way it existed, through performance. Therefore the approach will be strictly linear, as was the performance. The dynamics of staging and stage pictures also create meanings that may not be explicit in text; these will be a constant concern as well.

Let us turn to the *Amphitruo* itself. Mercury appears, disguised as the human slave Sosia (1–152). His prologue opens with a sixteen-line contract between players and audience: he will help them in their business dealings, if they will give ear to his play (*ita huic facietis fabulae silentium*, 15). There is far more here than bombastic parody of the Roman language of contract. It is an induction, a flatteringly phrased invitation into the world of the play which acknowledges the audience's part in creating that world. The explicit language of contract here suggests that Plautus is more than usually concerned with his audience's expectations of his play. Jupiter is compared to a character in tragedies (41) and also called an *architectus* (45), which will remind any spectator familiar with Plautus of another Plautine role, that of the *architectus doli* in Plautus' many comedies with clever slaves.

---

[1] Z. Stewart, *The 'Amphitruo' of Plautus and Euripides' 'Bacchae', TAPhA* 89 (1958), 348–73.

Mercury himself first raises the question of genre (which will pre-
occupy us for some time), in a way that leaves us, the audience, confused as to what sort of play we shall see. He first announces a
tragedy, then pretends to change the nature of the play in the face of
a negative reaction from the crowd (51–5):

> MERCURY. post argumentum hujus eloquar tragoediae.
>   quid? Contraxistis frontem quia tragoediam
>   dixi futuram hanc? deu'sum, commutavero.
>   eandem hanc, si voltis, faciam <jam> ex tragoedia
>   comoedia ut sit omnibus idem vorsibus.

> MERCURY. I shall now explain the story of our tragedy.
>   What? Do you frown because I said this would be a
>   tragedy? Don't worry, I'm a God. If you'd like, I'll change it
>   to a comedy, and never change a line.

What sort of play, though, can be a tragedy or comedy with exactly
the same verses? It is this curious property, more than any ironic
scruples against gods appearing on the comic stage (not that Mercury
is more offended at his own slave role than at seeing Jupiter disguise
himself), which causes the play to be a *tragicomoedia* (59–63). What
impact would the use of this term have had on Plautus' original audience? Indeed the term once coined seems to be thrown away, and the
play becomes a comedy again (88; 97), but audience expectations
have nonetheless been unsettled by the discussion.

The theme of appearance and reality, so essential to the meaning
of this play, is introduced by the use of the term *imago* (121; 124; 141)
and developed by the description of Jupiters as *vorsipellem* (123),
which we should not translate as simple 'werewolf' but 'skin-
changer', for it implies not just a duality of shapes, but the polymor-
phous capability to put on any shape whatever. With these last few
hints (Mercury's final word, *histrioniam*, reminds us of the fictive
nature of the world we are about to enter), Mercury now yields the
stage to Sosia, but only upstage so he can comment ironically on
everything the slave says. Sosia is preparing to tell his mistress of his
master's exploits—preparing like an actor.

We need to understand the visual and theatrical dynamic of this
scene before we even being to examine its narrative content. As with
any eavesdropping scene, the form is that of the play-within-the-play,
here certainly in rudimentary fashion. Sosia is not really in direct
communication with the audience in this soliloquy. Between him and

the audience stands Mecury, whose comments aside interpret and color everything Sosia says.

Sosia's first few lines strike typical notes for the slave character: he boasts of courage (153) but soon displays fear of the nightwatch (153–63) and complains of harsh service under his master (166–75). Any sympathy we might feel for his condition is quickly turned to laughter by Mercury's aside (176–9):

> MERCURY. satiust me queri illo modo servitutem:
>   hodie qui fuerim liber, eum nunc
>   potivit pater servitutis;
>   hic qui verna natust queritur.

> MERCURY. It would be more appropriate for me, Mercury to grumble
>   about my lowly status.
>   Until today I've always been divinely free
>   and now my father's made a slave of me.
>   This chap's born a slave and still he's grumbling.

The humor, of course, lies in Mercury's double role, god and slave.

Sosia's reply shows us something about the style of Plautine playing as well. He picks up the term *verna* which Mercury has used opprobriously, and flaunts it like a badge of honor, at the same time wondering whether he should give thanks to the gods for his safe return (180–1):

> SOSIA. sum vero verna verbero: numero mihi in mentem fuit

> SOSIA. It's me who needs a whipping, really, 'cause I've just
>   remembered I'm the slave.

In what sort of play world does this exchange take place? Realistically speaking Sosia has not overhead Mercury's aside; he displays no awareness of the other figure on stage until line 292. Nor is this a verbal irony of which the speaker, Sosia, is unaware. It is a tiny skirmish to regain theatrical advantage, a struggle for audience attention and sympathy, in which the actors, without regard for the overall illusion of the story, engage. It is a style of playing we may term non-illusory, in that the action does not take place within a plane of illusion, but appeals directly to the spectator for approval.

If nothing else (and the speech has many merits in its own right) Sosia's battle soliloquy demonstrates his ability to improvise. Note that Sosia himself was not present at the battle, having been too busy hiding (198–9). He must therefore rehearse a fictional account of the battle before he delivers the same to Alcumena. This 'rehearsal speech' has been discussed as tragic parody before. We need only note how Sosia's preparation (200 *simulabo*, 201 *fabularier*, both verbs meaning 'to perform') indicate that he himself approaches it as a theatrical fiction, one whose (almost accidental) truth Mercury later confirms in an aside (248–9). After Sosia's battle narrative concludes, Mercury announces his plan to delude Sosia (265, *certum est hominem eludere*) and conquer him with his own weapon, *malitia* (269). There is a short delay, though, while Sosia, through staring at the sky, introduces both the *Nux Makra* motif and the theme of drunkenness, which is his explanation for the phenomenon: the god Nocturnus has gotten drunk and is sleeping off his hangover.

Sosia at last sees Mercury standing before the house (292), and the long-awaited confrontation is imminent. All of this time Mercury has in effect stood outside the play (which contains Sosia), remaining in close communication with the audience. Before stepping into the play world he hesitates long enough to acquaint us, the audience, with how he intends to play the scene: he will delude Sosia, of course (295 *deludam*), but by the seeming inversion of the scene just concluded. Mercury will still pretend to be ignorant of Sosia's presence and play the victim's role in an eavesdropping scene (300–1):

> MERCURY. clare advorsum fabulabor, auscultet hic quae loquar,
>   igitur magi' modum majorem in sese concipiet metum.

> MERCURY. Now I'll speak out loud so he can hear the words I say
>   and I'll bet that he'll really quake with fear.

Mercury thereby seems to surrender his theatrical power over the scene, but in fact he increases it through changing places with Sosia. With his claim to be the real Sosia, the actor here must now maintain and make clear to the audience three superimposed roles: he is playing Mercury playing Sosia playing victim in an eavesdropping scene. On top of this, as he explicitly acknowledges in ironic parallel to the emphasis on fictional creation in Sosia's rehearsal speech (198 *mendacium*, 200 *simulabo*, 201 *fabularier*), Mercury himself will create a fiction through speech (300 *fabulabor*). Mercury's bombastic threats and eagerness for a fight have their intended effect on Sosia, who nonetheless manages to make a joke of most of them.

The scene which follows is the *locus classicus* of the *Doppelgänger* (double) theme. Mercury not only by physical resemblance, but far more importantly by detailed knowledge of Sosia's life, succeeds in causing Sosia to doubt his own identity. The only metatheatrical irony in the scene is the exchange of oaths.

Sosia reteats in disarray. The comedy of the scene is undeniable, but the undertone of fear is very strong as well. There is real pathos in Sosia's use of tricolon in his parting speech (455–7):

> SOSIA. Abeo potius. di immortales, opsecro vostram fidem,
>   ubi ego perii? ubi immutatus sum? ubi ego formam perdidi?

> SOSIA. I'd better go. O gods above! Please come and help me. Tell
>   me where in heaven I've lost myself. Where was I
>   transformed? Where did I misplace my face?

Dreams and drunkenness are no longer a sufficient explanation for these phenomena; it is now a mad world, my masters—precisely Mercury's plans for both master and man in his ensuing soliloquy (470–1 *erroris ambo ego illos et dementiae | complebo,* 'I'll befuddle both of them and make them crazy').

As Jupiter and Alcumena now come out of the house, Mercury through his asides to the audience once again interprets and comments on the scene. His joke about Juno's jealousy (510–11) reminds us of Jupiter's double role as Amphitruo. When Mercury does choose to enter the scene, he changes his role from that of the slave to parasite. Having failed in the role of the parasite, Mercury will now have to return to his slave role.

Alcumena, somewhat placated by the gift of the golden cup which will figure so prominently in proofs of identity later in the play, departs, leaving the stage to Jupiter and Mercury. Jupiter commands an end to the long night and follows Mercury off.

Visually and verbally, Jupiter and Mercury's exit and Amphitruo and Sosia's entrance form a *chiasmus.* On the divine level it is the slave who is taking the lead and the master who follows (550 *supsequar*). On the human level, Amphitruo is in complete control at the scene's beginning, and it is the unfortunate Sosia who tags along behind (551 *sequor, supsequor te*). Amphitruo cannot believe the confused and confusing report of events at the house which Sosia has given him and suspects drink (574) or disease (581) as the cause of the disorder. Madness is also hinted at: 585 *dictis delirantibus* ('crazy words'). At the heart of Amphitruo's rage lies the suspicion that Sosia is playing him for a fool.

Apart from drink, madness, and disease, Amphitruo can now think of only one more natural explanation for Sosia's confusion: he must have dreamt it all. Sosia eloquently denies this (621–4):

AMPH. ibi forte istum si vidisses quendam in somnis Sosiam.
SOSIA. non soleo ego somniculose eri imperia persequi. vigilans vidi,
   vigilans nunc <ut> video, vigilans fabulor,
   vigilantem ille me jam dudum vigilans pugnis contudit.

AMPH. Why then perhaps what you have seen is in a dream of yours
   perhaps?
SOSIA. I never sleep when on the job. Totally awake I was as I am
   wakeful now while we are talking, and I was wholly wide awake
   when he kept punching me a while ago.

Alcumena's soliloquy which follows is a study in miniature of
tragicomedy. Visually almost grotesque in her pregnancy, she
nonetheless conveys a touching affection for her husband. Once
again the comments of an eavesdropper, here Amphitruo, help shape
audience response: she is the virtuous, loving wife.

Amphitruo's strange questions and manner when he appears
make Alcumena suspect she is being made fun of (682), and she play-
fully threatens to tease him (694). She is indeed too kind-hearted to do
much of this, even if Amphitruo did not begin to bluster and confuse
the issue even more. Once again Amphitruo offers the same naturalistic explanations: she is mad (696) or dreaming (726). Sosia is the
first to suggest a supernatural explanation with his implied comparison of Alcumena to a bacchant (703). Indeed, Sosia is often a step
ahead of his master, whether with advice or explanation. He is the
first mortal, for example, even to hint at the real state of affairs, when
he suggests that all now have been doubled (786). Amphitruo's suspi-
cions of his wife's chastity, aroused by her tale of a previous visit by
himself, will admit of nothing but an examination by witnesses, and
he goes off to seek his fellow voyager, Naucrates, as proof of his own
version of events.

Jupiter now returns for yet one more prologue. The plethora of prologues provided to explain (and excuse?) the action is perhaps indicative of the improvisatory nature of this play on the divine level. He
begins with a playful restatement of who he is (861–6):

JUPITER. Ego sum ille Amphitruo, quoii est servos Sosia,
   idem Mercurius qui fit quando commodumst,
   in superiore qui habito cenaculo,
   qui interdum fio Jupiter quando lubet;
   huc autem quom extemplo adventum adporto, ilico
   Amphitruo fio et vestitum immuto meum.

JUPITER. I am that Amphitryon who has a slave named Sosia,
who sometimes when it suits him turns into Mercury.
But I am the Amphitryon who lives 'upstairs'—and
when I'm in the mood I change to Jupiter again.
But when I'm in this neighborhood I change my clothes
And dress up as Amphitryon again.

Jupiter announces that he will take up his guise as Amphitruo again in order to extricate Alcumena from her difficulties. Like a typical divine prologue he looks at the play from the outside and shows his concern that the audience will find the play complete and satisfying.

Alcumena requires some soothing before she will respond to Jupiter's overtures. The king of the gods begs (932) Alcumena to forgive him and excuses 'his' behavior as a joke (916–17 cf. 682). Even this is not enough (rightly so!), and Jupiter only saves himself through the rich irony of a metatheatrical curse, which the kindhearted Alcumena rushes to avert (933–5):

JUPITER. id ego si fallo, tum te, summe Juppiter,
quaeso, Amphitruoni ut semper iratus sies.
ALCUMENA. a, propitius sit potius.
JUPITER. If I'm deceiving you, O Jupiter on high, invoke
thy curse upon Amphitryon forevermore!
ALCUMENA. No, no his blessing—let the great god bless you!

The real Sosia arrives and speaks with Jupiter, but no *Comedy of Errors* byplay ensues. He is merely dispatched to prepare for the sacrifice. Alcumena takes her departure (972), leaving Jupiter to address the unseen Mercury much as Prospero sometimes speaks to an unseen Ariel (974–83). Mercury is instructed to carry on with the play (980), while Jupiter departs to sacrifice—to himself (983)! I think there is more here than wonderfully narcissistic blasphemy. It is virtually a metaphor for the play: Amphitruo's delusion and Alcumena's virtue are Jupiter's offering to himself through the medium of the play. As actor within the play he enjoys the beautiful Alcumena, while as playwright/director, standing outside the play, he creates a farce of mistaken identity for both his own and the audience's pleasure.

Mercury, in keeping with the usual multiplicity of leading slave roles now enters in the role of *servus currens*. Indeed, he explicitly compares himself to this theatrical figure (984–7):

> MERCURY. concedite atque apscedite omnes, de via decedite,
>   nec quisquam tam au <i> dax fuat homo qui
>   obviam opsistat mihi nam mihi quidem hercle
>   qui minus liceat deo minitarier
>   populo, ni decedat mihi, quam servolo in comoediis?

> MERCURY. Look out everybody, no one block my way, clear
>   the street right out! By Hercules, why should a god
>   like me not have the same rights to harass the
>   people as a little slave in comedies?

Mercury reminds us that he has been called by Jupiter and ordered to delude (forms of: 997, 998, 1005) Amphitruo. This whole speech is made possible only by an acute consciousness of role and role-playing within the context of traditional Roman plots. When Mercury on entering compares himself to the *servus currens* he also reminds us of the stock situation in which the *servus currens* appears: to announce the safe arrival of a ship or warn of the approach of an angry *senex* (988). When he discusses his role as helper to the amorous Jupiter, he explicitly reminds us of his parasite role (993 *subparasitor*). Now he proposes to adopt the role (999 *adsimulabo*) of the drunken slave who abuses his master. Most importantly, he makes a direct appeal for audience involvement in the play. In his first explicit direct address to the audience since the original prologue, he promises them a good show (997–8):

> MERCURY. nunc Amphitruonem volt deludi meu' pater.
>   faxo probe jam hic deludetur, spectatores,
>   vobis inspectantibus.

> MERCURY. Now father wants to trick Amphitryon. And
>   he'll be tricked terrifically. Folks, I promise
>   that you'll see the trickery with your very eyes.

Then he acknowledges the need for the audience's help; once again (as in the prologue), his role is to act, while theirs is to listen (1005–6):

> MERCURY. sed eccum Amphitruonem, advenit; jam ille hic
>   deludetur probe
>   siquidem vos voltis auscultando operam dare.

> MERCURY. But look—Amphitryon's approaching! Here and now
>   he will be tricked terrifically—so everyone pay close attention.

Amphitruo returns, having failed to find Naucrates, and finds his own doors barred against him. Moreover, Mercury, in the guise of

Sosia, is guarding the gate and begins the promised scene of abuse. Here a well-known but frustrating lacuna in the text occurs. Attempts have been made to fill this gap, but even the most detailed reconstruction of events will not give us a very clear picture of the staging. The fragments only show us that as Mercury and Jupiter resist Amphitruo's attempt to enter, themes already established in the play (such as madness) recur.

When the text resumes, Jupiter's abuse of Amphitruo is just ending, and Blepharo the pilot, to whom Amphitruo appealed for proof of his identity, is retiring in disorder. Amphitruo finally suspects a supernatural origin (1043) for the problems of his house, but in his rage at being deluded (1041, 1047), he can think only immediate revenge and rushes the door.

It would be of the greatest value to know how the effect of Jupiter's thunderbolt was produced on the Roman stage, but we simply do not. The next scene opens with Amphitruo prostrate and the significantly named Bromia ('Bacchant'—another Dionysian name) bursting forth from the house with a report of the miraculous events within. She spots Amphitruo, revives him, and finishes her tale. Jupiter appears as *deus ex machina* to reassure Amphitruo and interestingly to dismiss from his mind the idea of consulting Tiresias or other sooth-sayers. On this rather abrupt note, the play simply ends.

At this point the connections between the *Amphitruo* and the *Bacchae* pointed out by Stewart should be clear. Both plays contain a god in disguise, and that disguise is repeatedly commented on. Verbal and visual ironies, flowing from this disguised god, permeate both plays. Both possess Theban heroes, who resist the invasion of their homes by what they characterize as foreign magicians. Finally and signifi-cantly, the language of both plays is dominated by themes of madness and drunkenness. Plautus has developed one other theme far more extensively: that of waking and dreaming. This theme is essentially confined to the inner, human play in the *Amphitruo*. While Mercury may threaten to drive the human protagonist mad (470–1) and play a drunken slave role himself (999), he and Jupiter never speak in the language of waking and dreaming. It is always the human characters who obsessively ask each other whether they are really awake (e.g. Amphitruo to Alcumena, 697) or protest their own wakefulness (most emphatically, Sosia, 623–4). Amphitruo in particular is eager to ascribe the supernatural events reported to him to the world of dreams (621). The use of this theme by Sosia and Mercury in the

opening scene foreshadows its structural functioning in the rest of
the play. Sosia fears that the unknown stranger before the house will
put him to sleep with his fists (298 *hic pugnis faciet hodie ut dormiam*).
Indeed that is just what Mercury proposes to do (313):

> MERCURY.   quid si ego illum tractim tangam, ut dormiat?

> MERCURY.   What if I touch him for a little while with my fists, so
> that he goes to sleep?

And in that sleep comes a dream of another man with his face, name,
and memories.

The confrontations of doubled characters in the *Amphitruo* form
powerful visual parallels to the Dionysos/Pentheus scenes in the
Bacchae. As Foley and others have pointed out,[2] Dionysos and
Pentheus are visual doubles of each other, possibly even to the extent
of themselves embodying the twin suns Pentheus says he sees
through their costuming in saffron robes. Both wore youthful, beard-
less masks which, while not identical, would closely resemble each
other and be set apart from other masks in the play. Certainly, there
are many other twins in Plautus (and other Roman comedies, to
judge from titles), but none are divine/human pairs for which the
Bacchae offers so powerful a visual parallel.

These visual similarities are undergirt by parallels of metatheatrical structure between the *Bacchae* and the *Amphitruo*. We will first
examine the functions of the prologues, then the roles of the gods as
directors of the play being produced, then finally the genre and structure of those plays that they create.

Both prologues have an expository function, but that is not their
first concern. The initial emphasis is on role and disguise and the
audience's expectations based on those roles. Foley notes that
Dionysos redundantly stresses his human disguise (4–5, 53–4) in the
play, as though fearful that the audience will not accept his rupture of
the stage conventions. Certainly the Greek audience expects that the
gods will confine themselves to the *theologeion* and not share the *skene*
with the mortal characters. Just so, Mercury seems deeply concerned
with overcoming his audience's similar expectations, and repeatedly
emphasizes his (and Jupiter's) human disguise. Where Dionysos
stretches the genre of tragedy, Mercury must transform the genre in
which he performs and his audience's expectations at the same time.

---

[2] H. P. Foley, *The Masque of Dionysos*, TAPhA 110 (1980), 107–33.

This he accomplishes through the slippery nature of his contract with the audience, as we have seen above.

Next, the gods of both plays set about the creation of a play. Foley shows how Dionysos functions as stage director of the *Bacchae*. He creates a play-within-the-play, whose tragic hero is Pentheus, victim of the illusions the theatre god weaves. Note that we as audience, despite our deep involvement in the tragedy of Pentheus, stand outside the illusion of this play-within-the-play. We can keep separate the divine and human characters, whereas the human participants are trapped inside the illusion. An example of this division between internal and external audiences of the play's events is the destruction of Pentheus' palace in the play. As Foley has shown, this was not done with primitive special effects. In a bold stroke, Euripides allows his audience to stand outside the illusion and experience the event only through the description given by the chorus, for whom it is real.

In the *Amphitruo* the role of stage director has been split in the process of multiplying the comedy. If we wish to continue the modern analogies, we might think of Jupiter as the producer and Mercury as the stage director working under him. Jupiter provides the outline of the plot from his own desires and supplies the power whereby those desires are fulfilled (e.g. the prolongation of night), but it is Mercury who oversees the details of stage business that create the play. Once again, we as audience stand outside the illusion of this play-within-the-play as exemplified by the tassel and wings by which we can distinguish divine and human doubles. Unlike the unfortunate Alcumena, we are never confused as to which is Jupiter and which Amphitruo.

Doubtless the play that Dionysos creates in the *Bacchae is* poetically richer. It is an explication through instruments, song, and dance of the theatrical nature of Dionysos worship. Plautus' play-within-the-play relies rather on the power of words and acting to create theatre. He celebrates the power of fiction in performance. Words spoken within the theatre space, in character, words that are in essence lies can create a new reality. Characters continually in this play accuse each other of lying (e.g. Alcumena on Sosia, 755 *falsum dicere*), yet the delicious irony is that the accused are nearly always speaking the 'truth'—the truth of theatre. In one or another fictional world all these things are true. It is theatre itself, we are led to conclude, that is the lie—but a good lie, an entertaining lie, a comic and refreshing lie.

It is this comic affirmation of the fictive power of lies to protect one

from reality that accounts for the diametrically opposed resolutions of
the *Amphitruo* and the *Bacchae*. Pentheus at first sees and believes the
fictions of Dionysos but is destroyed by the revelation of the truth.
Amphitruo, Pentheus' *echter Bruder*, sees the truth all along but res-
olutely refuses to accept it. This resolution protects his sanity and
makes possible the arbitrary happy ending—so long as Amphitruo
does not look beyond the inner human play. Plautus has inverted the
whole structure of the *Bacchae* in order to celebrate, not the god of
theatre, but theatre as god, as self-creating divinity.

It remains for us to account historically not only for the similarities
of narrative and setting of the *Bacchae* on the *Amphitruo*, but also their
concern with the nature of illusion and its audiences. The parallel but
comically transformed usage of the play-within-the-play motif argues
forcefully for a direct, not an indirect influence. Can we go beyond
Stewart and argue that Plautus indeed knew the *Bacchae* directly?

Recent work has considerably illuminated the Hellenistic background from which the archaic Roman theatre emerged. The dominant feature in the landscape of the Hellenistic theatre is clearly the
great actors' guilds, the Artists of Dionysos. The Artists and their performing tradition kept theatre alive in the Hellenistic period. It should
not, therefore, be considered chance that, as A.S. Gratwick notes,[3]
Plautus' taste in Greek plays was dominated by the three chief writers in the Artists' repertoire, Menander, Diphilus, and Philemon.
While most accounts of Plautus correctly portray him as a practical
man of the theatre, few have taken this picture to its logical conclusion. The handsome papyrus codices of Menander, designed for a
reading public, may lead us astray. One would not find these in the
prop baskets of a traveling theatre troupe. Publishers and performers
in the ancient theatre existed in a symbiotic relationship. Demand for
texts was stimulated by performance, and the texts that met that
demand depended on the performers' own copies of play texts. It
seems likely that Plautus saw many of the plays he chose to 'turn'
performed by Artists' companies, whether in south Italy, or on tour in
Rome. Whatever written texts he might have been able to obtain
would have been heavily influenced by the Artists' repertoire. The
Bacchae, one of the warhorses (along with most of Euripides' *oeuvre*)
of the Hellenistic theatre, ought to have been quite easy to obtain.

---

[3] A. S. Gratwick, Cambridge History of Classical Literature, vol. II, ed. E. J. Kenney
and W. V. Clausen (Cambridge 1982), 97.

A much wider ranger of possibilities should replace our usual picture (unconscious though it may be) of Plautus with a tidy, complete Greek text in hand. The close adaptation of some of Menander's *Dis Exapaton* in the *Bacchides* may suggest Plautus was working from a written script. But where had he obtained that script? It may have been the prompt book borrowed from one of the Greek touring companies or copied from such a prompt book. Alternately, like an Elizabethan publisher out to produce a 'bad quarto' of Shakespeare, Plautus may have induced a Greek actor to recite as much of the script as he could remember to a scribe or to Plautus himself. Finally, Plautus could simply have attended a performance, liked what he saw and heard, and used as much or as little of what he remembered in his own work. None of these models is *a priori* impossible.

The case for the direct influence of the *Bacchae* on the Amphitruo rests on the strong similarities of metatheatrical structure. If we no longer assume a specific Greek comedy behind every *comoedia palliata* then the following sketch accounts for the Euripidean influence in both substance and style better than any intermediate Rhinthonic farce or otherwise unknown New Comedy. Plautus had numerous opportunities to see the Greek repertoire performed by the Artists of Dionysos in south Italy. His most likely source for written copies of Greek plays was, directly or indirectly, these same Artists. I think it likely that he saw a performance of the *Bacchae*, not only because it was one of the most popular and therefore most available plays, but also because of Plautus' unique use of two playing levels in the *Amphitruo*, which is so visually dependent on tragedy. Moreover, the dearth of direct verbal echoes of the *Bacchae* (and possible parody of the *Heracleidae*) point to performance rather than text as the probable source. Plautus seems to have worked from his memory, rather than a written text, which, as the fragments of the *Dis Exapaton* have shown us, he could on occasion follow very closely. Plautus' treatment of the Amphitruo legend, then, is a comic response to the meta-tragic possibilities he saw in the *Bacchae*.

The virtue of seeing the *Amphitruo* as metatheatre is that it preserves the artistic integrity of Plautus' play while at the same time acknowledging a debt to Greek performance. If we recreate a hypothetical tragedy of the Amphitruo myth, Plautus' work is just a farcical accretion on a serious narrative. The concept of metatheatre allows us to see how Plautus has re-imagined the situation of the *Bacchae*, where a divinity creates a play-within-the-play for his own pleasure and worship: in the *Amphitruo* an inner human adultery comedy replaces the *Bacchae's* tragic *sparagmos*. In the *Bacchae* outer and inner plays finally collapse into one; in the *Amphitruo*, they remain separate. The *Amphitruo's* inner play can then be in one sense a perfect comedy, in that it allows the adultery and yet re-unites husband and wife with no regrets.

Thus the *Amphitruo* is far more than a parody of the *Bacchae*. The *Amphitruo* is a resoundingly comic and healthy response to man's dilemma in the face of the caprices of the gods. Plautus takes the dark despair of the *Bacchae* and converts it into a celebration of the powers of comic theatre. Jupiter has not replaced Dionysos as the object of worship and awe. We admire Jupiter for his potency, not his omnipotence. The object of this joyous celebration *is* the traditional Roman theatre itself, with its adultery plots, clever slaves, and mass confusion. Plautus dethrones Dionysos and puts in his place the benevolent genius of comedy.

IV
Terence

16

The Originality of Terence and His Greek Models

WALTHER LUDWIG

It is remarkable what different judgements about the poetical achievement of Terence can be found in modern scholarship. One finds him represented sometimes as a mere translator and adapter, sometimes as an original poet worthy to stand beside Menander himself. The best representative of the first view is Jachmann, who saw Terence's independence at work only in *contaminatio*. But the main tendency in Terentian scholarship of the last few decades has been to go in the other direction, to emphasize the originality of Terence as a poet and to discover that in remodeling the Greek comedies he created a new kind of drama and that he added important new elements of his own, even when he lost some of the beauties of his Greek sources. Norwood was the most extreme in this line—he granted Terence the liberties of a Shakespeare using Plutarch—and therefore his views have not been accepted by the majority of scholars. But a considerable number of German and Italian Latinists also depict Terence as a Roman poet in his own right. There are diveregencies, but on the whole they share a view of Terence remodeling and reworking the Greek comedies according to his own artistic ideals. Terence, in their view, aimed at a more realistic drama, avoiding the comedy of typical scenes and characters, eliminating actors' addresses to the public, shortening unrealistic long gnomic reflexions, strengthening the colloquial language and attempting to give his figures individual features. Likewise, according to these critics, he despised coarseness and vulgarity and deepened noble and humane sentiments, trying to show to his audience the right values. I may confess at the outset that I regard this picture in its essential points to be wrong and distorted, although I do not deny that some useful observations have been made; but, in my opinion, they have not been properly evaluated.

There seem to be three main reasons for this great range of opinion about Terence's originality. First, we lack complete agreement about the nature and extent of Terence's departures from his lost Greek originals, and in some cases it will never be possible to determine them with certainty. Second, even if we agree about a specific alteration made by Terence, it is still often difficult to state its motive. And finally, classical scholars often seem in the case of Terence more emotionally involved than usual. Those who see in him a highly original poet sometimes accuse their opponents of a romantic phil-hellenism, while they in their turn seem not entirely uninfluenced by a certain determination to vindicate the independence of Latin literature at any price, or even by a nationalistic Italian pride in the Roman past. Nevertheless we should not give up before the problem of the originality of Terence. The problem is and will remain important for the development of Roman literature. It can be solved only by taking into consideration the relation of Terence's plays to his Greek models, and this relation is by no means in every case so impossible to determine objectively that we must restrict ourselves to a neutral *non liquet*. Although we do not have space here to discuss in detail all relevant arguments, I should like to touch on certain points which seem to me of special importance.

It has always been noticed that Terence in choosing his Greek models was influenced by definite characteristics of his own interests and tastes. He limited himself to Menander and his follower Apollodoros of Karystos. He was careful about a certain morality, keeping within the bounds of what the Roman meant by *decorum*. A lovesick old man, who perhaps becomes his son's rival for a *hetaira*, is not to be found in his plays. Menander's *senes* are all quite respectable, well-intentioned and serious fathers, who are as sincerely concerned as their wives for the happiness of their children. His slaves do intrigue, but are not too unscrupulous about it. He did not enjoy presenting frivolous *meretrices*. The respectful prostitute aroused his interest. He avoided the low and the fantastic, putting on stage domestic affairs such as could happen every day. He also preferred an action rich in characters, if possible with two pairs of lovers and a correspondingly double happy ending. There is normally a moving recognition of someone long lost. Finally, he is attracted not least by psychologically subtle delineation of humane and sensitive characters, by the representation of problems of interpersonal relations and of those concerning the proper behavior by the older generation towards the younger.

But it would be rash to suppose not only that these interests determined the choice of his models, but that in adapting the Greek comedies he deliberately emphasized and expanded these elements and
thus was working on his own in the direction we have described. It
can easily be shown that the opposite was often the case.

For three of his six plays Terence used a second Greek original. As
he himself explains in a prologue (*Eunuchus* 7 ff.), he was convinced
that it was not enough to translate a good Greek play in order to write
a good Latin one, and so took the liberty, where he thought it in place,
to work scenes or parts of scenes from a second Greek play into the
primary model, the practice called *contaminatio*. What considerations
guided him in the choice of his secondary models?

In the *Adelphoe* he inserted a scene from the *Synapothneskontes*
(comrades in death) of Diphilos, in which a young man appears who
has just stolen a girl out of a brothel and who now has the *leno*, who
pursues him with insults, brought to reason by the blows of his slave.
In Menander's *Adelphoi* the carrying off of the girl was only narrated,
probably by the young man, and the *leno* appeared on stage later to
negotiate for the damages. Terence thought it fitting to substitute a
lively slapstick scene in place of the narrated event. Thus he strengthened the part of the *leno* and introduced a cudgeling scene, both contrary to the intentions which guided him in the choice of his primary
model.

He evidently found that thus enlivening the *Adelphoe*, otherwise
distinguished by its ethical and psychological interests, would not
harm the play. His intentions therefore entail a certain compromise.
On the one hand he wanted to get away from the traditional and, in
his view, vulgar jokes of a Plautus to the cultivated and meaningful
drama of Menander; on the other hand he apparently felt that you
could have too much of a good thing. In his opinion the play could
only gain by a bit more color. He overlooked or chose to ignore the fact
that the omitted narration of Aeschinus contained an indication that
Aeschinus was stealing the girl not for himself but for his brother.
Such an explanation however was extremely important for the
understanding of the speeches of the two fathers, since only thus
does a proper judgement of the attitude of the mild Micio and the
strict Demea become possible, and this is the whole point of the play.
In the *Eunuchus* we can observe an analogous situation. Here Terence
inserted monologues and dialogues from Menander's *Kolax*. The
proven sure-fire types of the parasite and the *miles gloriosus* were

meant to enliven the action even more (perhaps because the dramatist had indifferent success with the more staid *Hecyra*). In Menander's
Eunuchos in place of the parasite there stood only a slave, in place of
the *miles* a less colorful rival. Both roles were less prominent there. So
in the second act of the *Eunuchus* Terence inserted an effective
bravura scene from the *Kolax*, the entrance speech of the parasite
Gnatho. But this also shifted the emphasis of the scene. In Menander
a slave had brought Pamphila, the girl to whose recognition the play
leads, across the stage to the house of the *hetaira* Thais. This an event
full of consequence for the whole drama, for it is in the house of Thais
that the rape will take place, because of which the happy ending of
the play is seriously endangered. Pamphila appears on stage only in
this scene. She does not speak a word. But although two slaves carry
on the dialogue, she remains by her very silence the center of attention. In Terence the parasite upstages her. For the sake of a momentary comic effect the careful disposition of the action is somewhat
obscured.

At the end of the *Eunuchus* the soldier and the young Athenian
agree to share the *hetaira* Thais. The parasite draws a commission.
Such arrangements occurred in Menander's Athens. But this can not
have been the conclusion of the Menandrian *Eunuchos*. It is in contradiction not only to the goal of the external action of this play, but
also to the completion of its inner dramatic development. Thais has
revealed herself in the course of the play—contrary to what one
would have expected first—as a *bona meretrix*. She has solved all difficulties and behaved in a truly humane fashion. As a reward she has
got a rich old Athenian as a patron and is finally united with the
young man whom she loves. For her then to be treated as an article of
merchandise is irreconcilable with the external and internal structure of the Menandrian *Eunuchos*. Terence's ending seems to have
been composed in imitation of the *Kolax*, where the *hetaira* was not
free but the property of a *leno*, and where such an arrangement, in
which the parasite too gets his cut, suits excellently the young man's
repeatedly emphasized lack of money and the wealth of the proud
and stupid officer. Terence may have added this conclusion in order to
gain one final comic effect. That is, the *miles* is led around by the nose
once more through the agreement (his share will consist mostly of
paying the bills) and the lucky parasite is the only real winner. For the
sake of such effects Terence has destroyed the unity of the play, which
he had maintained so far. He has weakened the unconventional

theme of the *bona meretrix*, which he had chosen, by adding two traditional comic types.

A quick look to the *Andria*: the origin of the parts which concern Charinus, the second lover of the play, is controversial. I follow the view of those who regard these passages not as an independent addition by Terence but as essentially a borrowing from the *Perinthia*. In any case, Terence preferred in this play too the fuller double plot and chose as a primary model not the coarser *Perinthia* but the psychologically refined *Andria*. He took from the *Perinthia* only what seemed to him suitable to enliven and enrich the *Andria*, for instance the motif of the drunken midwife, although this involves a slight inconsistency in her character.

Thus Terence chose in each case a psychologically complex Menander play as his primary model. But he enriched it and strengthened its farcical elements from cruder plays of Menander and Diphilos, doing some damage thereby to the balanced organization of his primary models. If one observes this compromising tendency of Terence, one is in no danger of accepting the widespread idea that he is responsible for a fundamental humanizing and deepening of his models and that his use of *contaminatio* was guided by a humane aesthetic ideal.

Further consideration of the way in which Terence combined parts of a second Greek play with his primary model may save us from another error. It is frequently assumed that *contaminatio* was often in effect a dissolution of the primary model and meant a new conception of the play as a whole. In the *Adelphoe*, to be sure, no one could fail to see that only one or two scenes were replaced by the scene from Diphilos. But in the *Eunuchus* a fundamental remodeling of the middle part has been generally assumed. In my opinion the additions from the *Kolax* are limited to four separate scenes. There are no elements which would give the action an essentially new direction. Only the conclusion, about which we have already spoken, does not fit into this picture. Here Terence actually made a decisive change and destroyed the original conception of the play. But here too he was influenced not by a new conception of the play as a whole, but rather by the desire for an effective conclusion, which led him into the dénouement taken from the *Kolax*. The earliest play of Terence, the *Andria*, is the most deeply affected by *contaminatio*—the whole plot. But an analogous plot with two lovers was probably already to be found in the *Perinthia*, and Terence was generally able to insert scenes from the *Perinthia* at corresponding places in the *Andria* and so had to compose independently only the short final scene, in which Charinus is informed of the happy solution.

In no case was a radical alteration of the construction of the primary model necessary in order to work in the desired parts of the secondary model. Terence was able to get by with a few omissions, the addition of suitable transitions, retouchings to remove obvious contradictions and similar devices; and in this he succeeded quite well. The additions are far more carefully inserted than in Plautus, where marked inconsistencies and contradictions often become apparent.

Terence altered his originals in still other ways. The listing of a few examples suffices to show that it is misguided to explain these alterations, as has been done, from principles such as 'progress towards realistic drama', 'humanising and ennobling of the characters' or 'a will to the universally valid'. The desire for comprehensive syntheses and the wish to find deep meanings everywhere have often led to exaggerations and forced interpretations, or to the overlooking of contrary instances.

When Terence omits the name of an Athenian suburb and instead writes *in his regionibus*, it is certainly paying too much honor to this modification to see in such an avoidance of a reference too specifically Greek a search for the universal. Naturally Terence left out Greek place-names and customs which meant nothing to his public, as far as he could do so without harm to the intelligibility of the action. Unlike Plautus he consciously avoided for the most part allusions to anything specifically Roman. It was his principle to keep the Greek milieu of the plays except for certain details which seemed to him pointless and could only make comprehension more difficult.

Thus, for instance, it was a specifically Greek custom to cut one's hair short as a sign of mourning. Apollodoros, the author of the original of the Terentian *Phormio*, had a barber report to the young men waiting in his shop that he had just cut the hair of a poor and beautiful girl who had lost her mother. The young Antipho decides to visit her and falls in love at once with the girl, who at the end of the play is fortunately recognised as the daughter of a well-to-do citizen—and they live happily ever after. In Terence, too, the young men are sitting in the barber's shop, but the barber as narrator must disappear, to eliminate the non-Roman custom of cutting the hair in mourning. Instead Terence has a weeping young man enter who has just seen the unfortunate girl and describes her with emotion. The barber will probably have told the story without tears. Terence then would have also sentimentalized the scene. But it is certainly out of place to speak on that account of a deepening of emotional and spiritual content. In terms of the rest of the play this change, though it makes the scene itself more moving, creates difficulties later, because the agitation of the weeping young man is more than his merely intermediary role calls for. The spectators' interest in him is aroused and in his further connection with the poor girl, an interest which is not satisfied later on. For the young man immediately disappears into the wings, and, as in Apollodoros, only Antipho matters.

There are other instances of a certain sentimentalizing. This tendency however is not in undisputed command. Thus, to take one example, Terence does not allow an unhappy lover to think, as in Menander, of suicide, but only of emigration. A feeling for the limits of Roman common sense seems to have been at work here.

Still another tendency becomes apparent when we consider the negro slave girl who appears in the *Eunuchus*. Terence added her as a mute part, certainly for no other reason than that the audience would like to see this exotic figure. He sometimes kept minor figures on stage longer than in the original, or had them appear earlier. In these cases he gives them a few unimportant lines; otherwise they stand around rather purposelessly. His aim was to enrich the appearance of the stage.

But the playwright gives evidence of a more creative ability when he transforms a narrative monologue into a dialogue by introducing a second person, as he apparently sometimes did (Cf. Sosia and Simo in *An.* 11 and Antipho in *Eun.* 3. 4/5 (but this figure may have been in the original already, see *Philologus* 103 (1959) 32, n.1). There he enlivened the scene with poetical talent. But once, on the contrary, he eliminated a highly effective dialogue. The case in point is the dialogue of the *matrona* Myrrhina and the *hetaira* Bacchis in the original of the *Hecyra*. (Cf. Donatus *ad Hec.* 825). It was in this dialogue that the decisive recognition took place. The reason for the elimination of this scene and the substitution of a short narration of the event is difficult to see. Scholars have supposed that Terence wanted to avoid recognition on stage as too worn a theatrical motif. But this is improbable. Terence knew very well that comedy to a certain degree consisted of conventional *topoi* and that all depended on their variation in the particular situation (Cf. *Eun.* 355 ff.) The recognition scene in the *Hecyra* was quite unusual. Nevertheless Terence eliminated it. Why has he introduced the parasite and the *miles gloriosus* into the *Eunuchus*, why has he added a beating on stage to the *Adelphoe*, if he was in principle against typical comic figures and scenes? And why has he, contrary to Plautus, generally chosen recognition plays? One might consider another motive: perhaps the meeting of the respectable wife of a citizen with a prostitute, who saves the desperate lady, offended Roman morals. Roman *meretrices* seem to have had a worse social reputation than their Athenian counterparts. And it has already been noticed that Terence had a respect for proper behavior. Regard for Roman morality seems to have been at work, too, at the end of the *Adelphoe*, where the strict father Demea comes off better than in the original, in which the mild and humane Micio apparently was preferred. So in the *Hecyra* regard for Roman *decorum* seems to have worked against his general preference for dialogues.

But he was consistent in his refusal of a prologue in the form of a narrative monologue and gave the exposition always in dialogue. He could already find this form in Greek plays, he certainly sometimes substituted a dialogue of two persons for a Greek prologue spoken by a god. Expository material which he could not use here he skillfully distributed later in the play. One reason for avoiding exposition by monologue surely was that after a long personal prologue, which he regularly used for introducing the play, a second long speech could have been boring. Further, the suspense was heightened when the audience was not informed by a god about the ultimate solution (but at the same time certain dramatic ironies were necessarily lost). It is not impossible that the prologue-god was eliminated also to avoid a fantastic and unreal theatrical device.

But other instances which have been adduced to show the greater realism of Terentian drama often need correction. It is true that we have less breaking of the dramatic illusion in Terence than in Plautus (perhaps even less than in Menander), but Terence too kept the unreal convention of the speaking of asides which are not to be heard by the interlocutor but by the audience. And it is surely wrong to see in Terence's treatment of gnomic reflexions an attempt at greater realism. Terence did not at all avoid gnomic sentences; on the contrary he liked them in rhetorically brilliant form. Perhaps he cut off longer reflexions, but obviously not because of an inherent unreality of the scene, but simply because his public would not have favorably accepted too much philosophy.

Let me now remark briefly on the problems of Terence's translating from the Greek. Scholars have often attempted to show the special way Terence translated by a comparison between the few existing Greek fragments and their Terentian counterparts. But one should not try to discover in each slight deviation an important artistic principle, and the wish to balance each loss by an equivalent gain has sometimes prevented a just evaluation. Comparison of one-line fragments needs a cautious critic who does not burden our small material with too heavy deductions. But there is another way to investigate the translations of Terence which has not yet been used sufficiently. Papyrus discoveries have brought rather extensive fragments of Menandrian comedies to our knowledge. Although no play which served Terence as a model has yet been found, a general comparison between Menandrian and Terentian style has become possible. For instance, the relative frequency of colloquial and rhetorical elements, of stereotyped and individual expressions can be observed. It seems that Terence used more rhetorical figures than Menander. With them he aimed at stronger effects, sometimes at the price of specific nuances. He used more interjections; the intent was vivid colloquialism, but the result occasionally yielded a sort of cliché. On the whole we must be careful not to attribute to Terence what should be attributed to differences between Greek and Latin or to the traditional language of the Roman stage. Only from this background can the specific character of the Terentian way of translating be investigated.

But this kind of translating was at any rate a great achievement. It meant the creation of a new literary language in Latin with a purity, refinement and flexibility of diction that had not previously existed and that was capable of expressing complicated psychological processes. Even if Terence was stimulated by the urbane colloquial language of aristocratic Roman circles, the step to definite formation of a literary style was still a major one. It was brought about in the process of dealing with the texts of Menander and attempting to transpose the natural language of the Greek comedies into an appropriate Roman form.

Furthermore, Terence put before the eyes of the Romans in this new literary language subjects which had not been represented in Roman literature before. The psychological subtleties and problematical human situations of Attic comedy were reproduced with an understanding and a sympathy previously unknown. The Terentian conception of *humanum* is in my opinion such a reproduction of an analogous Greek idea. The term has neither been deepened, compared with the meaning of the corresponding Greek words, nor has it been filled with a specifically Roman mentality. But Terence was the first to open Roman comedy to this conception. With all this he helped unlock new realms to the Roman spirit, and this intermediary function is certainly not to be underrated.

Finally, Terence took an independent view of the question how Greek plays should be adapted in detail. On the one hand he strove, in reaction to the liberties taken by Plautus, for a closer imitation of the originals. On the other he kept to his own judgement and considered it his task not only to make the Greek plays accessible to the Roman spirit, but also as far as possible to improve them as stage plays. He worked, however, not by inventing new plot threads, and only occasionally by adding characters or freely rewriting speeches and dialogues. Terence found in the Attic comedies such a completely formed tradition of the well-made play that he knew his own attempts could not, as a rule, compete with it. As long as this reservoir was not exhausted, it probably seemed to him pointless to offer necessarily weaker creations of his own. He was able in general to confine himself to enriching the plays with additional Greek material where it seemed suitable. He hoped in this way to combine the advantages of two Greek plays. Where he found occasion to alter his models with inventions of his own, the result was normally not an essentially new creation. The changes are mostly of the sort that would be considered today as falling in the province of a director or producer, who does not feel bound to strict adherence to the script.

The tendency of his changes was especially towards a richer visual element, livelier plots and stage business, increase in suspense or emotional effect, regard for Roman morality or even simply consideration for the limited knowledge of his public—tendencies which sometimes worked against each other but to a certain degree converge in the basic aim of adapting the comedies in such a way that, while sticking as closely as possible to the Greek comedies, they might also be more effective on the Roman stage for the Roman public.

It is striking that precisely in his earliest play, the *Andria*, he made his most independent contribution with the invention of the *libertus* Sosia, and that the *contaminatio* is more extensive and more consequential in this play than later. One might imagine that Terence would have proceeded to freer and freer reworking of the originals. The contrary was the case. Terence deliberately bound himself in the course of the six years of his productive career closer to his models, even though he never adopted the principle of the absolute fidelity which his literary opponent Luscius Lanuvinus maintained. While the latter regarded addition from a second Greek play as well as independent interpolations as spoiling and defiling the beauty of the Greek original, Terence allowed himself alterations of this kind. But he willingly limited his liberties in reworking—a fact which can only be explained by his belief in the value of the Greek works which he wanted to bring to the Roman public.

Terence's deliberate adherence to his Greek models is basically different from the way in which Plautus used the Greek originals as raw material for his own creations, as well as from the way later Roman poets emulated the *exemplaria Graeca*. Terence was surely not the Virgil of Roman comedy, as Benedetto Croce has called him, and the picture of his literary development is totally distorted if we see him as a Latin poet who used the Menandrian comedies with the same liberty as, for instance, the Greek Apollodoros. The fundamental difference between Terence's achievement and that of a creative poet in the specific sense of the word (who may be very much indebted to literary predecessors) should not be obscured. Of course, we do not deny the kind of creativity which was necessary for the translating itself, nor do we see his activities restricted to the translating. But a warning against common misrepresentations of his poetical achievements may not be useless in order to gain a better view of the kind of originality which he did display.

17

The Dramatic Balance of Terence's *Andria*

SANDER M. GOLDBERG

Terence tells an old story in the *Andria*, old not only because he lifted his *argumentum* from Menander's *Andria* and *Perinthia*, but because his plot is simply a variation of the recognition motif so common in Greek New Comedy and the *fabula palliata*. Only an inexperienced spectator could fail to realize that the story of Glycerium's Attic citizenship dismissed by Davus as a fiction (*fabulae!* 224) is really the truth.[1] As Montaigne observed in his essay *Des Livres* (2. 10), '[Terence] fills the soul with so much grace that we forget the charms of the story'. The Roman playwright's appeal is certainly not in his plots, but a play needs something more than stylistic grace to be drama. Where lies the central strength and interest of the *Andria*? A. W. Gomme once faulted the play for not being about anything, and modern efforts to deduce lost Menander from extant Terence and to solve the riddle of *contaminatio* do little to absolve Terence of the charge.

But because his aim is not primarily to tell a story, Terence is free to use the established elements of his tradition to point his play in a different direction. He is interested not so much in action nor even in individuals as in the relationships among a set of characters, and his artistic strength lies in his sensitive portrayal of people caught up in webs of conflicting obligations. Each play uses the traditional material to focus on the resulting tangles. To do so Terence capitalizes on the fact that his dramatic situations are generated by a small number of roles in combination: the lover, the rival, the helper, etc. (a technique certainly not unique to Terence). By focusing on any one or a

---

[1] The plot of the *Andria* actually incorporates familiar folktale motifs as identified by S. Thompson, *Motif-Index of Folk literature* (Bloomington, Ind. 1957): L 162, 'Lowly heroine marries prince' and H 11.1, 'Recognition by telling life history'. The preparation for Crito's story is analyzed by E. Lefèvre, *Die Expositionstechnik in den Komödien des Terenz* (Darmstadt 1969), 13–16.

number of these roles as personified by his characters, he can alter our perspective on a stock situation and make it something new. Any character can become the focus of interest if the dramatist chooses to emphasize his role and his point of view. In the *Andria* Terence gives his old story new life by shifting the dramatic balance to put the *senex* at the center of his action. How he structured his play to create this balance and what he intended to achieve by doing so are the questions before us.

After a highly rhetorical appeal for the audience's good will, the play opens with the file of porters so common in the *palliata*.[2] By disposing of them at once, however, Terence lets pass the opportunity for laughter at their expense. They serve simply to initiate the action and make plausible the introduction of Simo and Sosia, whose dialogue provides the *Andria*'s true prologue. How Terence writes the dialogue between them to include the necessary exposition reveals much about his dramatic technique. In the course of this first scene all the major characters are named: Simo (41), Chrysis (85), Pamphilus (88), Glycerium (134), and Davus (159). The way in which these names are rationed out, though, is noteworthy. We learn that Simo has a son forty lines before we learn his name, and except for Sosia's somewhat contrived interjection of Simo's name at the end of line 41, they are fitted quite inobtrusively into the narrative. Chrysis, Pamphilus, and Glycerium are identified through reported conversations where the use of the names is entirely natural. Chremes and Davus are mentioned by name at appropriate places in the narrative.

The background information to be presented is carefully paced and related with considerable stylistic variation. Direct quotation enlivens the first long speech in which the existence of the Andrian woman and Simo's concern for her influence upon his son are revealed (69–102). Sosia's interspersed comments echo our own thoughts and draw us into the narrative while relieving the monotony of too long a recitation (73, 86, 103). When Simo comes to the second part of his account, the funeral of Chrysis and the discovery of Pamphilus' infatuation with Glycerium, the style changes (106–53). His sentences become shorter, and the marked asyndeton with which he describes the scene at the funeral pyre is highly dramatic, as befits an event of

---

[2] The rhetorical nature of the Terentian prologues is documented by H. Gelhaus, *Die Prologe des Terenz* (Heidelberg 1972). For the line of porters as a fixture of the *palliata* see J. Wright, *Dancing in Chains* (Rome 1974), 144–5.

great dramatic significance. In this way Terence introduces us to his characters and tells us of the past.

The bulk of this scene is taken up with character portrayal. Simo describes at length how he has raised Pamphilus, and he identifies Davus unmistakably as a *servus callidus*. But character is more suggested than explicitly described. Pamphilus comes to life as Simo reveals his character through his actions at the funeral and imagines how he would answer any reproaches his angry father might convey. Yet the character most thoroughly revealed by his words and actions in this scene is Simo himself. His language and his very way of constructing his narrative tell us a great deal about him. The indirect, pompous beginning reveals him as pedantic and a little self-important. The description of Pamphilus' education shows him to be an indulgent father, and his persistent inquiries about Pamphilus (note the repeated imperfects of 83–92) indicate a suspicious one. His initial tolerance of Pamphilus' sadness at the funeral because it suggests to him how excellent a mourner Pamphilus will be at his own reveals him as self-centered.

Simo also has an eye for a pretty face, for he emphasizes the attractiveness of Chrysis (72) and especially of Glycerium (119). His immediate anger at the discovery that Pamphilus has fallen in love with her, however, suggests what we now tend to call a double standard. His appreciation of the girl is an indirect indication of Pamphilus' good taste and the common ground between father and son. His disapproval because of a fatherly concern for *fama* is a plausible source of the tension between them (cf. 96–101). In short, Simo emerges as the single most important character in his own prologue. This discovery raises two important questions: Why did Terence choose to have Simo as the prologue speaker? Does this choice include an implicit statement about the dramatic focus of the *Andria*?

Although Simo alone is able to reveal that the intended wedding is a sham, he need not have done so in the first scene. The initial exposition might have been managed just as effectively by Pamphilus (as Menander has his *adulescens* do in the *Samia*), or by Pamphilus and Davus (as Plautus has young man and slave do in the *Pseudolus*). A love plot often makes us think of a romantic lead or, if we think mainly of the *palliata*, perhaps a *servus callidus* as the 'hero'. That the old man assumes the central position at the beginning of the *Andria* suggests that Terence may have decided to keep the traditional plot but change the dramatic focus. Simo's decision to test his son by demanding that he marry sets the action in motion, and he continues to hold the initiative throughout the play. In the very next scene, the first confrontation between Simo and Davus, Davus is immediately at a disadvantage. *Erus est*, he says, *neque provideram* ('It's master, and I didn't see him', 183). All the slave's schemes originate as reactions to situations created by his master. As Davus himself makes clear in the following monologue, Simo has put the challenge to him. He must respond. Pamphilus must do likewise. The confrontation between them in the forum is, at least as Pamphilus relates it, entirely at Simo's command. *Obstipui*, he says (256), 'I was stunned'.

Thus, after a preliminary scene that introduces all the characters and focuses on Simo, we see him in confrontation with the other two central characters, and in each of these meetings he puts a challenge to them. In the second act Davus attempts to wrest this initiative away from Simo and bring matters to a desirable conclusion for his young master. He shows his cleverness by deducing from the lack of preparations that the wedding is a sham (352 ff.), and he devises a way to foil Simo's scheme and please both Pamphilus and a second young man in love, Charinus. Simo is indeed fooled in Act 3, but not by Davus.

Simo outsmarts himself by thinking Glycerium's pregnancy and sudden labor an invention of Davus' *mala mens*. Davus, however, is entirely taken aback (*Mihin?* 476). Only after a few minutes does he recognize what has happened: *certe hercle nunc his se ipsus fallit, haud ego* ('By Hercules, he's deceiving himself now, not I', 495). The humor of the situation derives from Simo's excessive cleverness rather than from Davus', and from the conscious play upon the comic conventions of overheard remarks and speeches directed to characters offstage (474 ff., 490 ff.). Once Davus has recognized Simo's error he attempts to capitalize on it, as befits a *servus callidus*, but, significantly enough, when Davus attempts to gain the initiative Simo still has the last word. He orders Davus offstage and ends the scene with his own short monologue (523 ff.). The rest of the act is concerned with Simo's successful effort to win Chremes over to the marriage, and by doing so he once again determines the action of the play. In the last scene, when Pamphilus berates Davus for his failure, Davus must admit his abuse is justified:

> PA. an non dixi esse hoc futurum? D.A. dixti P.A. quid meritu's?
>   DA. crucem.
>   sed sine paullulum ad me redeam: iam aliquid dispiciam.
>
> (621–2)

PA. Didn't I say this would happen

DA.   You did.

PA.   What you deserve?

DA.   The cross

DA. (*shamed and defeated*).
     But let me collect myself a little. I'll think of something in a
       second.

This last appeal is granted, but again it is not Davus who ends the scene. The last thing we hear is Pamphilus' complaint that he cannot afford the time to punish him. Act 4 provides a fine example of Davus' *calliditas* but Chremes rather than Simo is its victim. Davus succeeds in manipulating Mysis and tricking Chremes, by no means the two most formidable intellects in the play, and he does so not with a scheme but with the truth. He wins only a tactical victory that we quickly perceive will come to little. For the arrival of Crito at the end of the act signals the true solution to the problem. Here Davus finally gets the last word in a scene, but it refers to Simo: *nolo me in tempore hoc videat senex* (819), 'I don't want the old man to see me at this moment'. As always, Simo is the force to be reckoned with.

The last act brings Davus his punishment. Simo has the slave carried off to the mill for telling the truth—when the old man thought he was laying a trap. It is a double joke on Davus, though he gets no time to discover it as Dromo whisks him away at Simo's order. To bring the action to a happy conclusion, however, Simo's opposition must be overcome. This is accomplished not by tricks, but by an additional truth. Chremes and Crito win the old man over not by outwitting but persuading him. After the reconciliation, Davus gets his freedom. He is manumitted not at Pamphilus' urging, but at Simo's command (955–6). Other characters still depend upon Simo's will.

In the romantic comedies such like the *Andria* a *senex iratus* is frequently the obstacle that the play's action must overcome. Terence has not so much changed that identification as altered our perspective on it. By making his *servus* ineffective and resolving the plot entirely with the appearance of a stranger from Andros, the playwright highlights the impact of the old man's opposition on others and makes that the cause of successive events in the play. The dramatic impetus comes entirely from Simo, whose opposition stems from elements in his character revealed in the first scene. The climatic confrontation between Simo and Pamphilus in Act 5 (872–903) is written with the artistry to compel the sympathy of any father and any son who have ever been at loggerheads. The dialogue is composed with great sensitivity, and it is true to the characters of Simo and Pamphilus: the father's outbursts are the erruption of the suspicion and irritation he has felt all along, and the son's efforts to cope with them reveal the deference with which Simo had credited him in the introductory scene. In fact, this deference is the first cause of Simo's outburst.

> SI. Ain tandem, civis Glyceriumst? PA. ita praedicant.
> SI. 'ita praedicant'? o ingentem confidentiam!
>   num cogitat quid dicat? num facti piget?
>
> $(875-77)$

> SI. Can you be saying that Glycerium's a citizen?
> PA.   So they claim
> SI. So they claim? What great audacity! Does he know what he's
>   saying? Has he no shame for what he's done?

When confronted by Simo with his alleged misdemeanour, Pamphilus tries to hedge—which is too much for Simo. In agony over the apparent realization of his worst fears, Simo then tries to dismiss Pamphilus entirely from his mind.

> SI. quor meam senectutem huius sollicito amentia?
> an ut pro huius peccatis ego supplicium sufferam?
> immo habeat, valeat, vivat cum illa. PA. mi pater!
> SI. quid 'mi pater'? quasi tu huius indigeas patris.
>
> $(887-90)$

> SI. Why get upset at this lad's thoughtlessness? Am *I* to be punished
>   for *his* wrongdoing? No, he can have her and begone, let him
>   live with her.
> PA.   My father!
> SI. Why 'my father'? as if you need *this* father.

The father's lapses into the third person at 877 and again here at 889 are efforts to divorce Pamphilus from his thoughts and his responsibility—to put distance between himself and his son. The words convey a bitterness and resignation which Pamphilus tries to soften with honesty, and even Chremes is moved (895).

Pamphilus' confession is a masterful combination of filial piety and loyalty to Glycerium.

> PA. tibi, pater, me dedo: quidvis oneris inpone, impera.
>   vis me uxorem ducere? hanc a mittere? ut potero feram.
>
> $(897-98)$

PA. I give myself over to you father. Load on any burden, command
me. Do you want me to get married? To put her aside? I shall
suffer it as best I can.

His surrender is nearly total; only the *ut potero* reminds us of his still
divided loyalties. The humility and respect of Pamphilus' short
speech prevents the fuming father from being absurd. Pamphilus
takes him seriously, and therefore the audience does, too. Simo's willingness to hear this confession suggests a genuine hesitation to make
the breach with Pamphilus complete, though the fact that he
answers *Chremes'* appeal for him to listen rather than Pamphilus'
suggests that the bitterness remains (902). Simo still tends to speak of
his son in the third person.

This touching and emotional scene is kept from high drama only
because what Pamphilus says is the truth and Simo's objections are
beside the point. Irony makes their confrontation comic. Terence
deliberately introduced the *senex* Crito at the very end of Act 4 to keep
a growing realization of the true situation fresh in our minds.
Although he here writes a scene charged with emotion, he can temper and control its effect on the audience by playing the drama of a
threatened breach between father and son off against the happy reconciliation the audience fully expects. The solution hinted at all along
then becomes explicit with Crito's reappearance in the next scene.

Yet Terence keeps his characters true to their personalities, and
their movement from despair to joy is a realistic progression. Simo is
a difficult man to persuade, especially when angry. His bad temper
threatens the revelations,

SI. Sycophanta. CR. hem. CH. sic, Crito, est hic: mitte.
CR. videat qui siet.
si mihi perget quae volt dicere, ea quac non volt audiet,

(919–20)

SI. Con man!
CR.   Huh?
CH.   That's the way he is, Crito. Forget it.
CR.   He'd better watch himself.
If he keeps saying what he likes to me, he'll hear something he
won't like.

and his *fabulam inceptat* at 925 is an ironic echo of Davus' earlier
fabulae! (224). Pamphilus, too, responds to the news in a realistic way.

Only Chremes laces his speech with exclamations (930, 931). Pamphilus, as befits a young man who has just returned from the edge of an emotional abyss, is silent until the drift of Crito's account finally awakens his interest (933). He provides the last bit of information— Glycerium's true name—and thus makes the identification certain, perhaps a fitting reward for having listened so closely as his mistress told it to him 'a thousand times' (946). Even in his moment of greatest excitement, however, his kindness does not desert him. He takes the time to plead for Davus. In his exuberance he is willing to risk his father's renewed anger with a politely worded protest:

> PA. pater, non recte vinctust.
> SI.   haud ita iussio.
> PA. ivbe solvi, obsecro.
>
> (955)
>
> PA. Father, he's been wrongly bound.
> SI. (*wrily*).   That's hardly what I ordered.
> PA. Let him be freed. I beg you.

Simo's immediate agreement reflects the reconciliation between father and son that the truth has brought. The fatherly indulgence which caused his difficulties reasserts itself once the source of his opposition has been removed.

What Terence presents in the *Andria*, then, is a relationship between a father and son as it is revealed under stress. The stock comic plot is a device for creating that tension and is overshadowed by the psychological depth and the realism with which it is depicted. By focusing on Simo and rooting both his opposition and Pamphilus' response to that opposition in aspects of their characters described and enacted on stage, Terence turns a conventional dramatic situation into a distinctive study of human relations. The conduct of fathers toward their sons and the results of various theories of education were subjects of great interest for Terence, as they evidently were for Menander before him.[3] In the *Andria* he has concentrated on the relationship between a single father and son and depicted it with the sensitivity and skill that indicate the developing talents of a Latin Menander.

---

[3] See E. Fantham, 'Hautontimorumenos and Adelphoe: A Study of Fatherhood in Terence and Menander,' *Latomus*, 30 (1971), 970-98.

18

Terence's *Hecyra*: A Delicate Balance of Suspense and Dramatic Irony

DWORA GILULA

The main interest of the *Hecyra*, as given in the play's exposition, is the fate of the failing marriage. Who is responsible for its possible breakdown, and can it be saved? Since the play is a comedy, it is reasonable to expect that all will be resolved in the 'happy ending'—in this case, with the salvaging of the endangered marriage. All the complications of plot, the more intricate the better, contribute to the proper pleasure.

The plot centers on the mysterious return of Philumena, a recently married young lady, to her parents' house, a short while after the departure of her husband on a trip abroad. This unusual action hints at a possible breakdown of the marriage, and could even be interpreted as a motion for divorce. The true reason is explicitly mentioned, but the audience is deceived into disbelieving it.

The puzzling situation is presented by Parmeno, the husband's slave who reports that Philumena had developed a deep hatred of her mother-in-law, Sostrata (177 ff.). He adds that initially relations between the two women had been excellent until suddenly Philumena began to avoid Sostrata. Finally pretending to be invited by her mother to take part in a sacrifice, she went away and stayed away. Sostrata repeatedly requested her return, but was turned down on various pretexts, the last of which was that Philumena was taken ill. However, when Sostrata attempted to visit her, she was refused admittance to the house. Hence Parmeno's conclusion that Philumena's sickness is but the latest in a series of improbable excuses for keeping away from the hated Sostrata.

Parmeno's conclusion is of course only his opinion, for Philumena does not confide in him. This cleverly induces us to accept as a fact and we are led to expect that the *morbus* is but a pretext, although Parmeno himself voices some reservations. For in spite of his conclusion, he finds Philumena's behaviour baffling. There seems to be no other plausible explanation: 'mother-in-law' evokes stereotyped conceptions. As Laches puts it, 'everyone knows that all mothers-in-law and daughters-in-law absolutely hate each other' (201). The true reason for Pilumena's strange behaviour, i.e. her 'sickness', is not even considered as a possible possibility.

Parmeno is not the only character to misinterpret the situation. The entire household believes that the women hate each other. When the news of it reaches Laches, Sostrata's husband, in his country estate, he decides to go himself to Athens to arrange for Philumena's return. He, too, believes that Sostrata is at fault.

Nevertheless, Laches considers it his duty to question the young girl's father, Phidippus, about the girl's health (255). There is also a legal problem, for Philumena's abandonment of her husband's home for that of her former *kyrios*, her father, might be regarded as intent to dissolve the marriage.

Phidippus emerges from his home, finishing a discussion with his daughter who remains within (243–5)—and in fact never appears. He has tried to persuade her to return, but she has insisted that she cannot while her husband is away (268–9). The audience is persuaded to accept the accuracy of Phidippus' report. This undermines Sostrata's claim of innocence. The fault must, therefore, be hers.

But is it really? Left alone on stage, Sostrata complains of the common stereotypes and reiterates her declaration of innocence. This helps to dispel doubts as to her innocence. If she has in fact treated Philumena like her own daughter (279), and is herself completely puzzled by the young woman's conduct, then Philumena's accusation, as reported by her father, is suspect. Philumena's sickness might not, after all, be a feigned one. Thus, precisely when the speculations regarding Philumena's behaviour have seemingly ended, and the *odium* explanation has acquired credibility, the playwright proceeds to undermine and challenge it with the *morbus* pretext.

Yet a certain amount of lingering doubt prepares us for the subsequent reversal. When young Pamphilus returns to Athens and is informed of the situation, he finds himself in a position of judge, aware that he will hurt one of the women as well as himself (299–302).

Fortunately, he is spared the painful ordeal. Before he has the chance to 'announce' his arrival, alarming noises are heard from Philumena's house: sounds of uproar, cries of pain, and her mother begging the girl to stifle her moans. Only then does Parmeno remember to inform his master that there have been some rumours of sickness, which the unusual noises seem to confirm.

But although the 'sickness' has been definitely established, the *odium* notion is not totally abandoned by others. It does not seem surprising, therefore, that Parmeno prevents Sostrata from visiting her daughter-in-law (343–4). That Philumena is actually 'ill' does not absolve Sostrata from her guilt (349–51), because the slave regards her as guilty simply because she *is* a mother-in-law, and is, therefore, expected to behave according to type.

When he emerges from Philumena's house (361–408), Pamphilus reveals three things. The first categorically absolves Sostrata of any guilt, a reversal which has been carefully prepared from the very beginning.

Second, Pamphilus reveals that the 'sickness' is, in fact, pregnancy. Philumena's labour pangs are a prepared surprise, for we have already learned that her marriage was never consummated (143–56), and instead Pamphilus made daily visits to his mistress, the *meretrix* Bacchis (157). This is of course a plot device which Terence will exploit later.

The final piece of information—not foreshadowed within the play itself—is that Philumena had been raped before their marriage. Rape is a familiar element in Menandrian New Comedy, and is here introduced to explain the girl's strange behavior.

While Philumena is in labour, her mother Myrrina begs Pamphilus not to disclose that the child is not his. She promises to conceal the birth and to expose the baby without delay. She believes that by doing this it may even be possible for Pamphilus to take his wife back (391).

But why is secrecy necessary for the poor girl to return to her husband? Does the law prohibit the husband from cohabiting with his raped wife, as it would if she had been adulterous? Apparently, Myrrina thinks that what the community does not know about need not be considered, so that as long as everything is kept secret, Pamphilus can disregard the law, take his wife back, and no harm will be done. Pamphilus' moral convictions, however, seem to be those of Athenian law and morality, for he feels that taking his wife back would not be *honestum* (403). Although he still loves her, to his mind she is no longer fit to be his wife, for even if nobody else knows about it, the assault had contaminated her. Therefore, he decides not to take her back (*nec faciam*, 404), although he does agree to comply with Myrrina's request that he keep the matter a secret.

The immediate result of Pamphilus's promise is the comic trans-formation of Parmeno from a know-it-all to a know-nothing. Because he is his master's confidant, and (except for the protatic cour-tesan Philotis) he is the only one who knows that Pamphilus' mar-riage has not been consummated, it is imperative to prevent his discovery of Philumena's condition, especially since he has been characterized as a gossip (109–12). Thus the stock-character of the running slave who possesses vital information unknown to others, and who, by his schemes advances the plot and is marginilized. The removal of the stock know-it-all running slave from the center of affairs, and maintaining of his ignorance because of his constant *running* are funny. Yet, in the end, despite his ignorance, he is credited unwittingly with doing a great deal of good (879–80).

When the audience finally learns the true reasons for Philumena's strange behaviour, there is a kind of irony. The erroneous *odium* explanation is cleverly and subtly used to reveal characters and to further the plot. The audience finally knows more about the true state of affairs than do some of the characters.

The question 'Can the troubled marriage be saved?' must, for the time being, be answered in the negative. Therefore it is still convenient for Pamphilus to offer the *odium* explanation as a pretext for his refusal to take his wife back (477–81). In their eagerness to bring about the reconciliation of the young couple, the older generation, in a pleasing inversion of comic convention, attempts to deceive Pam-philus by pretending that Phidippus had ordered his daughter to come to his house for a short visit (466). Whereas the young man, conventionally portrayed in comedy as deceiving his elders, is here cast as the object of their deception.

Eager to establish his innocence, Pamphilus stresses that his proper behavior towards his wife has given her no cause for complaint. It is she who cannot live in peace with his mother, so one of them must go. And yet as dutiful son he shows *pietas* for his mother; it is only right that he should first and foremost seek to preserve his mother's happi-ness. Only now can the audience appreciate the irony. What can be cleverer than invoking filial piety when appealing to the older gener-ation? It is unlikely that either father would attempt to refute it.

Convinced of the antagonism between mother-and daughter-in-law, it is easy for Laches to accept Pamphilus' explanation. Formerly, he had predicted that Philumena's departure would anger his son (261–2), and now that he is sure that his prediction has come true, he cannot refrain from telling Phidippus, 'See: I told you my son would take it hard!' (497–8). This is clearly ironic, for the audience now knows that Pamphilus' intransigence does not stem from anger at Philumena's departure. Laches, in much the same way as Parmeno, adjusts previous beliefs to present facts. He assumes that Philumena's conduct has angered Pamphilus, but is convinced that the young man's refusal to take his wife back is the result of maternal pressure. *Consilio* (514) ironically reveals Laches' stubbornness, for Sostrata is not even aware of her son's decision.

Laches' intention of punishing Sostrata greatly is a fine observation of human nature. Moreover, since the audience now knows that the attack which he is planning is unjustified, it becomes clear that all his previous insults have been equally unjust. His relationship with his wife is thus revealed as the true reason for his staying away in the country estate. Laches' failure to comprehend his wife's motives and actions dramatically prepares the way for the introduction of a parallel misunderstanding between Myrrina and Phidippus, who, in contrast to Laches, is portrayed as a mild and gentle man.

When he discovers that a baby has been born, Phidippus abandons *odium* and shifts the responsibility for Philumena's departure to his own wife. He concludes that Myrrina wants to expose the infant to terminate her daughter's marriage. He is convinced that Pamphilus's continuing relations with Bacchis are at the bottom of Myrrina's antagonism. Thus, the abandonment of erroneous *odium* generates a second set of misunderstandings. This time, however, the audience is aware of Phidippus' delusion, and does not share it.

In order to assure the comedy's 'happy ending', it is necessary at this point to save the child, and Phidippus departs to issue strict orders not to expose it, 'lest comedy turn to tragedy' (Donatus ad 563). For the time being, however, his interference greatly complicates the situation, since the survival of the child will automatically lead to Pamphilus' rejection of Philumena. This is an artful moment for Myrrina to explain why she is so afraid of being forced to raise the baby. Not only is the child not Pamphilus' but worse, it is of unknown paternity. The rape of Philumena took place in darkness and, contrary to convention, she was unable to snatch anything from the assailant that might have helped to identify him. Quite the contrary: it was the rapist who made off with *her* ring. This will be instrumental in the dénouement.

The two fathers, by a comical coincidence, have reached the

equally false conclusion that Bacchis is the cause of it all. Exhorted by Phidippus to take action, Laches summons the courtesan in order to effect her separation from Pamphilus by plea or by threat (717–8). In a confrontation abounding in irony, Laches not only demands that Bacchis sever her ties with his son, but is convinced that his efforts will be rewarded. By contrast the courtesan, when confronted by Laches, can react with sincere indignation, for she has no present relations with Pamphilus and is ignorant of his current difficulties.

In order to extricate herself from her unpleasant role as villain, Bacchis must somehow absolve herself by performing an act which would effect the reconciliation of the young couple. Indeed, she is aware of how unique she is and says so: *etsi hoc meretrices aliae nolunt* ('What other courtesan would act this way?', 834). But doing merely what Laches has requested is not enough, since she does not know who has made the girl pregnant. Yet unexpectedly Myrrina notices the ring on Bacchis' finger—it is the one which the rapist snatched from her daughter! Is it possible that Pamphilus himself could be the culprit? We suddenly discover the hero is also the villain. Far-fetched as it may seem, it is completely suitable for comedy and solves the central problem of the play. Mother, father and baby will now live happily ever after.

In sum, we may say that in the *Hecyra*, the elements of suspense and irony are artistically combined. In the first part, characters and audience are equally unaware of the true reason for Philumena's withdrawal. The audience, however, has the advantage of an overall view of the action. This enables them to draw conclusions based on the continual bits of new evidence as well as the reassessment of past events. In the second part, where the true reason for Philumena's conduct is revealed to several characters (and to the audience), the situation is ripe for dramatic irony—while maintaining tension. Thus Terence has entertained us with a delicate balance of suspense and irony, from which he has created a totally satisfying work.

19

Problems of Adaptation in the *Eunuchus* of Terence

J. A. BARSBY

It may be as well to begin by declaring some basic principles. In addition to the occasional external evidence presented by Donatus, it seems reasonable to presume adaptation by Terence of a Menandrian original, when (i) we find a practice which we can declare to be Terentian rather than Menandrian, on the basis of a general examination of their surviving corpuses, (ii) when we find puzzles or anomalies in Terence which can be most easily accounted for as resulting from the process of adaptation, and (iii) when we can reconstruct a convincing account of what the Menandrian original actually was. Also, we must not ignore the possibility that some of Terence's alleged anomalies have in fact been taken over from Menander, though Menander's surviving plays are relatively free from such things.

As far as the beginning of Terence's *Eunuchus* is concerned, Ludwig in his article queried the prevailing view that Menander had an expository prologue, which Terence chose to omit with consequent recasting of the opening scenes, but in his 1973 *Nachtrag* he withdrew his opposition.[1] The argument here turns mainly on the general practices of the two dramatists. Terence's six plays all begin with an extra-dramatic prologue, in which a prologue figure addresses the audience, outlining the quarrel between Terence and his critics and usually explaining something about the Greek original of the particular play. After this artificial prologue, Terence normally begins the play proper with a dialogue into which the basic expository material is incorporated, though in one case, *Adelphoe*, the play proper begins with a monologue, spoken by one of the characters of the play. Either way, the exposition is conveyed entirely through the human charac-

---

[1] W. Ludwig, 'Von Terenz zu Menander', *Philologus* C 19 103 (1959), 1–38, repr. with addenda in E. Lefèvre (ed.), *Die römische Komödie: Plautus und Terenz* (Darmstadt, 1973), 354–408 [page refs. are to the latter] 380, n. 59, 391 n. 86: cf. 404–5.

ters, who may or may not be in possession of all the relevant facts of the situation. If they are not, some of the facts remain unknown also to the audience, allowing Terence to exploit the possibility of surprise in the subsequent development of the plot.

Menander has no extra-dramatic prologues of the Terentian type; but he does have, in all the plays where the opening scenes survive, set-piece monologues conveying the basic expository material. These 'prologue-monologues' may be uttered by divine speakers (Pan in *Dyskolos*) or by human speakers (Moschion in *Samia*), and they may open the play (as in the two examples just quoted) or be postponed until after an opening scene of dialogue (as in *Aspis*, where the prologue speaker is Chance, or in *Perikeiromene*, where the speaker is Ignorance). Divine speakers are particularly used to reveal a hidden identity or to correct some other misconception of the situation, thus putting the audience in possession of facts of which the on-stage characters are ignorant and creating opportunities for dramatic irony.

Here then there is a clear distinction in general practice between the two dramatists, and a reason for supposing that Menander's *Eunouchos* did have an expository prologue which Terence omitted. Since there is a hidden fact in the situation, namely that the slave girl Pamphila is actually a true-born Athenian, it would seem to follow that the speaker of this expository prologue was divine, and this has been the generally accepted view. But, as Terence's play shows, the fact of Pamphila's citizen birth, and even the family to which she belongs, can be so strongly hinted by the human characters that we do not need a divine prologue to confirm it beforehand. So the view is beginning to gain ground that Menander's *Eunouchos* did not have a divine prologue; if it had a prologue at all, it was a human prologue, spoken by the courtesan Thais, who has correctly surmised the truth of Pamphila's birth and is in possession of all the other relevant facts, and it was probably a delayed prologue, coming after the opening scene between the lovesick Phaedria and his slave Parmeno (I. 1) and the following three-way dialogue between these two and Thais (I. 2).

At this point, a general observation about hypothetical expository prologues may be in order. It is hard to believe that Menander would have written an expository dialogue, followed by (or, for that matter, preceded by) an expository monologue which went over much of the same ground. In the *Aspis*, the one play of his where the sequence expositor dialogue plus expository monologue survives intact, there is almost no overlap between the postponed prologue-monologue of Chance and the preceding Daos–Smikrines dialogue. The dialogue gives the immediate situation as seen through one pair of human eyes; the monologue corrects a false assumption about the present and fills in the details of the past. In the case of *Eunouchos*, the basic exposition in Terence is carried by the three-way Thais–Parmeno–Phaedria dialogue of his second scene (I. 2). In practice, it would be difficult to reconstruct for Menander an expository mono-logue, whether for a deity or for Thais, of any length at all without dismantling Terence's second scene to such an extent that it would lose all its point. And, if all we are going to reconstruct for Thais is a slightly longer exit monologue than the one given to her by Terence at the end of this scene, it seems rather misleading to dignify this with the name of 'prologue'.

In short, of the uses suggested above to which Menander put his divine prologues, (i) the hidden identity of Pamphilia is more or less known by Thais and does not need divine revelation; and (ii) the only misconception of the situation is that Thais is a typical mercenary courtesan (the view exhibited by Phaedria and especially by Parmeno), which Thais herself can correct, as in Terence, in a simple exit monologue.[2] So, in terms of the exposition section of the play, there is no positive need to assume a divine prologue in Menander, or indeed a human prologue of any greater length than the exit mono-logue which Terence gives to Thais at the end of I. 2.

But it is not just a question of what is needed for the exposition of the play; we need also to consider whether there are any puzzles or anomalies in Terence's version which might have arisen from the expunging of a prologue from the Greek original. At first sight the answer is no; in fact, most scholars would agree that Terence's expos-itory Thais–Phaedria–Parmeno dialogue (I. 2) follows very neatly from his opening Parmeno–Phaedria scene (I. 1), and is itself per-fectly coherent; furthermore it is skillfully written, conveying not only the facts of the background but a vivid impression of the three char-acters involved. The only puzzle comes near the end of I. 2, where Phaedria and Parmeno appear to go off stage (196) while Thais delivers her exit monologue to the audience and then return at the

---

[2] There is a close parallel for the latter in the exit monologue of the 'lenient father' Micio at the end of the first act of Terence's *Adelphoe*, which similarly corrects the impression given in the earlier scenes (in this case that Micio is not much concerned at the exploits of his son Aeschinus).

beginning of II. 1 (207) without any indication of where they have been or why. Such dramatic awkwardnesses are not uncommon in Terence, but are hard to parallel in Menander.[3] However, it is not difficult to deduce a more 'logical' staging for Menander and to supply a reason for Terence's departure from his model.[4] In Menander Parmeno will have left the stage at 189 to fetch his master's gifts for Thais as instructed ('huc fac illi adducantur' / 'maxume'). Phaedria will have left at 196 to go to the country ('rus ibo', 187) after his farewells to Thais ('vale', 190), who has asked him to keep out of the way for two days while she obtains possession of Pamphila from her other lover. Thais will have delivered her exit monologue (197–206), declaring that her love for Phaedria is true and explaining that she has tracked down Pamphila's brother, and gone back into her house to await developments. Then, probably after an act-break, Parmeno will have returned (207), soliloquising about Phaedria's character and behaviour. What Terence has done is simply to replace this monologue of Parmeno's by a Phaedria–Parmeno dialogue, in keeping with a common practice of his, with the object in this case of enhancing the presentation of Phaedria's character. In doing so, he has blurred Menander's staging and created an awkwardness which, as he must have felt, would pass readily enough in the theatre. But (and this is the significant point) the change has nothing to do with the presence or absence of a formal prologue, divine or otherwise, in the Greek original. In short, this problem is soluble by what might be called micro-analysis, namely the identification and satisfactory explanation of a small-scale alteration, and we may here hazard the principle that, where the anomalies of a Terentian play (or the majority of them) can be solved by micro-analysis, there is no justification for supposing larger-scale adaptation. The corollary of this principle is, of course, that, where there are a number of anomalies which do not yield to micro-analysis, complex alterations can reasonably be suspected.

But more serious problems have been perceived, in fact three of them, in fitting the exposition to the rest of the play. First, there is the 'Parmeno problem', which is that, having heard Thais say in the course of I. 2 that Pamphila may be of citizen birth, Parmeno conspicuously

---

[3] For Terence see D. Gilula 'Exit Motivations and Actual Exits in Terence', *AJP* 100 (1979), S19–30.

[4] For convenience I use Terence's character-names and line numbers; in Menander's *Eunouchos* Parmeno, Phaedria, and Thais were called respectively Daos, Chairestratos, and Chrysis.

fails to mention this fact in II. 3 when trying to dissuade Phaedria's younger brother Chaerea from using the eunuch disguise to gain access to her (37 ff.). Since the rape of a citizen girl would be an outrage and a criminal offence, the mention of the possibility that Pamphila was in fact a citizen migh have been enough to deter Chaerea from his intention. But there is a perfectly adequate solution to this problem: Parmeno was clearly portrayed in I. 2 as highly sceptical of Thais' whole story, and we can easily imagine him to have dismissed her account of Pamphila's supposed birth as a fiction. And it has perhaps been too easily assumed that it is specifically rape from which Parmeno is trying to dissuade Chaerea; Donatus, at least, suggests that Chaerea himself did not begin to envisage rape until he saw the painting of Zeus seducing Danae in Thais' house, and Parmeno may have been thinking more of the outrage against Thais in invading her house than of what was likely to happen to the girl.

The second alleged problem, the similar 'Phaedria problem', is even easier to explain away. When Phaedria returns later in the play (IV. 3) and the rape is reported to him (643 ff.), he fails to exclaim 'Oh dear, and they say she must be a citizen'; but in fact this response would have been quite inappropriate in the particular scene, where he is trying to calm down the angry Pythias, the maid of Thais' who was supposed to be guarding the girl.

But the third problem is a very real one, the problem of Chremes, the supposed brother of Pamphila, who arrives in the middle of the play (III. 3) describing a previous visit to Thais' (507 ff.), whereas she, at the end of the expository scene with Phaedria and Parmeno (I. 2), has given the strong impression that she has not yet met him. What Thais says there is that she hopes she has now found the brother and that he has agreed to come to see her that day:

> nam me eiu' fratrem spero propemodum
> iam repperisse, adulescentem adeo nobilem;
> et is hodie venturum ad me constituit domum.
> concedam hinc intro atque expectabo dum venit.
>
> (203–6)

> I have high hopes that I've
> already found her brother.
> A very noble chap indeed. He'll
> come and see me at the house today.
> I'll go inside to wait for him.

It is difficult to interpret these lines as implying, or even allowing for, a previous visit. There is a further minor awkwardness in that Thais, having here declared that she is going to wait for Chremes to come (206), in fact chooses to go off to dinner with her soldier-lover instead, but this is covered by her need to maintain good relations with the soldier if she is to retain possession of Pamphila and by the instructions that she gives to Pythias to deal with Chremes' arrival (500–6).

The obvious approach to the Chremes problem is to suppose that Terence has for some reason meddled with the Greek original at either or both of the conflicting passages (Thais' monologue at the end of I. 2 and Chremes' speech in III. 3). It was long ago suggested that the latter was perhaps an addition by Terence, compiled from details given in a hypothetical divine prologue of Menander's or even from the later scene where Thais and Chremes first meet on stage (IV. 6 in Terence's version). This suggestion involves some complicated assumptions about Terentian adaptations of the middle of Menander's play, a question which is better left for the middle section of this paper; but in any case it fails to explain why Terence should have created an inconsistency out of what was presumably consistent material in the Greek original. Brothers, also assuming an opening divine prologue in Menander, supposed that Thais' monologue in I. 2 was based on a passage from this prologue; but the discrepancy with Chremes' later speech remains unexplained. Gratwick and Lowe suggest that Terence may have transferred material from a longer Thais monologue at the end of I. 2 to fill out Chremes' speech in III. 3, but we still lack a convincing motivation for this rewriting or an explanation of why Terence did not take the trouble to make the two passages cohere.[5]

Turning to the middle of the play (which we can define for convenience's sake as Acts II to IV), we immediately find various pointers to Terentian adaptation. This part of the play has three scenes involving more than three speaking characters; these cannot have stood in that form in the Greek original, since Menander observes a three-actor rule. Two of these scenes involve Thraso and Gnatho, the soldier and parasite imported from Menander's *Kolax*, as do two further scenes, so that we have a total of five scenes where Terentian adaptation is

---

[5] H. Drexler, 'Terentiana', *Hermes*, 73 (1938), 75; S. A. Gratwick, Review of Lefèvres *Expositionstechnik*, CR 22 (1972), 29–32, at 31; J. C. B. Lowe, 'The *Eunuchus*: Terence and Menander' CR 33 (1983), 428–44, at 441.

assured by these external considerations. In addition, there are a fair number of anomalies or puzzles in Terence's version, which raise questions on purely internal grounds; some of these anomalies may be more apparent than real, but they have cumulative weight, and they have to be considered, at least potentially, as evidence of adaptation.

It may be helpful to give a brief summary of the middle section of Terence's play. After Phaedria has gone away to the country, Gnatho arrives with Pamphila and hands her over to Thais as a gift from Thraso (II. 2). Chaerea, who has fallen in love with Pamphila in the street, takes up Parmeno's suggestion of the eunuch trick to gain access to her in Thais' house (II. 3). Gnatho returns with Thraso and, after watching Parmeno deliver Phaedria's presents to Thais (including Chaerea as the false eunuch), they persuade Thais to accept an invitation to dinner (III. 1–2). After Thais has left for this dinner, Pamphila's supposed brother Chremes arrives, and is told to go and find Thais at Thraso's (III. 3). Chaerea emerges from Thais' house, having raped Pamphila, and tells the story to a friend Antipho, who takes him off to join their military comrades at dinner (III. 4–5). Then a succession of people arrive back from the soldier's dinner party with news of a quarrel there between Thais and Thraso, who has taken Chremes to be a rival lover of Thais'. The first is Thais' maid Dorias (IV. 1); she is followed, after an interlude in which Phaedria, returning from the country, is confronted with news of the rape and drags the truth out of the real eunuch Dorus (IV. 2–4), by Chremes (IV. 5), and then by Thais herself (IV. 6), with news that Thraso and Gnatho are on their way to take Pamphila back. Thraso and Gnatho duly arrive with a motley army but they are beaten off by Thais and Chremes (IV. 7).

The central question, obviously, is how closely all this follows the plot-line of Menander's *Eunouchos*, and in particular how far Terence's plot has been affected by the introduction of the two characters from the *Kolax*. On this point the ground is largely still occupied by Ludwig, who argued that the 'contamination' from the *Kolax* affected only the particular scenes of Terence's in which the two *Kolax* characters appear. At first sight, it has to be admitted, this seems an unlikely conclusion: it seems improbable that two characters can be transferred from one play to another without bringing with them at least some element of plot. The question is complicated in this case by the fact that the soldier and the flatterer are stock characters, as Terence himself goes on to say in his prologue 35–41). How does transferring two stock characters from one play differ from transferring those same two stock characters from another play? It cannot be a matter of transferring their characteristics, because these are stock. It cannot be a matter of transferring their names, because in any case Terence has changed their names (Thraso and Gnatha were Bias and Strouthias in Menander's *Kolax*). So, unless we can interpret Terence to mean that he has merely transferred some plot-free dialogue from the *Kolax* (which is Ludwig's view, though this is scarcely the natural interpretation of Terence's words), there must be some transfer of plot.

It is obvious from the summary of *Eunuchus* given above that, if we delete Thraso and Gnatho from Terence's play, we delete a good many of the elements of the plot. Without Thraso and Gnatho, there would be no rival for Phaedria and no motive for Thais to shut him out (I. 1–2); there would be no Pamphila because there is nobody to present her (II. 2); there would be no dinner-party or any of the scenes connected with it (III. 1–2; IV. 1, 5–6); there would be no siege scene to try to recover Pamphila (IV. 7), and (to look ahead for the moment) there could not be the present ending of the play which involves Thais keeping Thraso as well as Phaedria (V. 7, 9). This leaves us in theory with two possibilities. Either all these plot elements have come from *Kolax* together with the two *Kolax* characters, in which case they have obliterated the plot line of Menander's original *Eunouchos*; or they were already present in the original *Eunouchos*, in which case that play must have already had characters analogous to Thraso and Gnatho. E. K. Rand, in an urbane article written in 1932 which is still well worth reading, actually argued that there was no Thraso-equivalent in Menander's *Eunouchos*, that is, that the Phaedria character there did not have a rival at all for the attentions of Thais. But the consensus today is that there *was* a rival lover of Thais in Menander's play, who *was* assisted by some sort of servant, who did present a girl to Thais, who did have a quarrel with Thais at a dinner party, who did come to claim the girl back, and so on; in other words, that the plot lines of Terence's and Menander's plays were practically identical.

This immediate problem with this view is how we are to envisage this rival lover in Menander's version. There are a number of scholars on either side. Either the rival was already a soldier, in which case transferring Thraso to the play actually means adding the characteristics of the swaggering soldier to an originally non-swaggering type, and transferring Gnatho means adding the characteristics of the flattering parasite to some less colourful soldier's servant. Or he was not a soldier but some other sort of rival, say a merchant, attended by a slave, and Terence has transformed this pair into a soldier and a parasite. Of the two, the soldier is the more plausible suggestion. The rivals of young men in love in New Comedy (Greek and Roman) are typically either soldiers or lustful old men (usually the youths' own fathers): merchants do not figure in the list. But, whether the original rival was a soldier or a merchant, there are still some difficulties in envisaging a Menandrian original which was identical in plot with Terence's but had purely colourless 'blocking' characters, and indeed in accepting that, when Terence says he has transferred characters from outside, he merely means that he has transformed characters which were already in the play. Scholars have tried to meet the latter point in two ways, by suggesting either that the soldier was a mere off-stage figure in Menander's *Eunouchos* whose interests were represented in the play by his servant or, conversely, that the soldier did play a role on stage but was not accompanied by a parasite. In either case Terence has 'added' only one of the characters, but this still does not quite square with his statement that he has transferred both.[6]

All this has been *a priori* argumentation. We now need to look at Terence's play and focus on the signs of adaptation in the middle section. The obvious approach is to see how many of these respond to what I have called micro-analysis, particularly (but not only) in terms of extended 'contamination' from *Kolax*. The following summary identifies the major anomalies, together with the other Terentian alterations which are guaranteed by the presence of four-actor scenes or the Thraso and Gnatho characters.

II. 2. Gnatho delivers a lengthy monologue on his skills as a parasite and indulges in a spirited dialogue with Parmeno on the merits of their respective gifts to Thais. The monologue, which is almost entirely plot-free, must be from *Kolax*. The dialogue contains a crucial plot element, namely the handing over of Pamphila to Thais' on behalf of Thraso. This must have had a counterpart in *Eunouchos* (unless we choose to believe that the girl was already in Thais' house), with the girl handed over either by the rival or his servant: in either case it looks as if Terence has remodelled the dialogue to fit the parasite character, using material from *Kolax*.

---

[6] For discussion see Ludwig op. cit. 387–9, 405–7.

III. 1. Gnatho indulges in some exaggerated flattery of Thraso, overheard by Parmeno. The first two-thirds of the dialogue are again almost entirely plot-free, and presumably come from *Kolax*, though Parmeno's asides may be Terence's addition. But at the end of the scene (441–3) Gnatho urges Thraso to summon Pamphila to entertain them if Thais ever invites Phaedria to a party; this foreshadows what happens at Thraso's dinner party in Terence's play, and (unless it is Terence's invention) must come from whichever Greek play had a corresponding dinner party.

III. 2. Parmeno delivers the false eunuch to Thais, amidst disparaging remarks by Thraso and Gnatho, and Thais accepts Thraso's invitation to dinner. This is a five-actor scene (it also involves Thais' maid Pythias), and as such is an interesting test case. If Thraso and Gnatho replace existing characters from Menander's *Eunouchos*, their presence should not in itself create scenes of more than three actors. Where such scenes are found, either (i) both Thraso and Gnatho were not originally present or (ii) Terence has added some other character for his own purposes.

This scene looks very much like a combination of *Eunouchos* (the delivery of the false eunuch) and *Kolax* (the Thraso-Gnatho banter). If the plot-line follows that of the original *Eunouchos*, the three characters in Menander's scene must have been Thais, the rival, and Parmeno; and, if the rival was not accompanied by a servant here, it follows either that the servant was sent away at the end of III. 1 or that III. 1 had no counterpart in *Eunouchos* at all. As for Pythias, who enters only at the end of the scene, she must be simply an addition by Terence, using the extra speaking actors available on the Roman stage. The movements of Pythias are in fact the first of the awkwardnesses in this part of the play. In the absence of any indication in the text that Pythias returns to the house as Thais departs with Thraso (506), we have to assume that she remains on stage silent and unseen during the following twenty-four-line monologue by the newly arrived Chremes, and that when he knocks at the door (530) she approaches him from the street. This would be a novel and even striking staging, but the suspicion is that Terence, so far from intending it, has failed to write in the movements of his extra character with sufficient care.

III. 3. Chremes' account of his earlier meeting with Thais, as we have seen, does not seem to square with Thais' account of her dealings with him in I. 2. At the end of this scene, there is a further anomaly: Pythias summons another maid Dorias to escort Chremes to the soldier's (538), though she had been expressly told by Thais to escort him herself (503) and no reason has been given for the change of the plan. There is the first of several indications that the whole Dorias character has been added by Terence.

III. 4–5. Chaerea emerges from Thais' house flushed with the success of his escapades and expresses great satisfaction that there are no busybodies around to pester him with questions as to why he is so happy, why he is dressed as a eunuch, and so on. Antipho approaches, asks him precisely those questions, and is greeted by Chaerea not with dismay but with effusive delight. It is tempting to connect this apparent contradiction with Donatus' statement (ad 539) that Antipho was invented by Terence to avoid a long monologue by Chaerea. Chaerea's opening remarks would have been a perfectly appropriate prelude in Menander to a monologue telling the story of his exploit; they are not so appropriate to the dialogue which ensues in Terence. Terence has certainly adapted Menander in this scene, but we should not be too eager to convict him of carelessness. Antipho was, after all, not a busybody but a good friend and a very suitable recipient of Chaerea's tale. The change in Chaerea's attitude is thus perfectly plausible.

IV. 1–3. Dorias returns from the soldier's party with news of the quarrel over Chremes. This is superfluous, since Chremes and Thais are soon to return with what amounts to the same news; if there was a counterpart in Menander, the speaker would presumably have been Pythias. Moreover, Dorias, having delivered this monologue, remains on stage unspeaking and unseen during the next scene (IV. 2), a monologue by the returned Phaedria, and for thirteen lines of the following scene (IV. 3), a dialogue between Phaedria and Pythias; it is something of a surprise to the reader of the text when Dorias suddenly joins in this dialogue (656). This awkwardness seems to confirm that Terence has added Dorias to the plot and has not been too careful about her stage movements. Terence has provided a motive for Dorias' early return, but this again leads to another awkwardness of staging. When the quarrel broke out at the soldier's party, Thais gave Dorias some gold (*aurum*) to take away, presumably jewellery for safe keeping; in fact Dorias stands around on the stage with this for three scenes, before Pythias finally tells her to take it inside (726).

IV. 4. This is a four-actor scene, involving Phaedria, the real eunuch Dorus, and both Pythias and Dorias, which furthers the suggestion that the Greek original did not have both Pythias and Dorias. The characterisation at the end of the scene (718–26) is also strange. After Phaedria has extracted the truth from Dorus, Pythias asks Dorias whether they should tell Thais about the rape or hush it up, and accepts her advice without question ('ita faciam' 724). In the rest of the play, Pythias, who is clearly the senior of the two, is also much the stronger character, and it is surprising to see her deferring to Dorias at this point. In Menander Pythias would have been left alone and have delivered an exit monologue.

IV. 5. Chremes now arrives back from the soldier's, explaining that he had left the party after Thais and wondering how he has got back before her. Terence thus calls attention to this oddity, but offers no explanation of it, leaving us to wonder why he created it in the first place. It is no doubt preferable dramatically for Chremes to arrive back first, but why could he not have left the party first? It is also the case that Chremes is drunk, which does not particularly suit his character as so far portrayed, a rather earnest, suspicious young man. We can rationalise his drunkenness as the inability of the naive rustic *adulescens* to handle the temptations of wine at a party, but there are further problems: how did he get drunk, since as an uninvited unwelcome guest he was scarely likely to be plied with wine by his host, and how does he manage to sober up completely by the beginning of the next scene? All this raises the question whether Chremes actually went to the dinner party in Menander or has been slotted into it by Terence.

IV. 6. Thais returns and warns Chremes that Thraso is on his way to reclaim Pamphila. There is another minor awkwardness here in that Chremes now fully accepts that Pamphila is his sister, even though when we last saw him (III. 3) he was very suspicious of Thais' questions and, as Terence has expressly told us (620–6), there was not much opportunity at Thraso's party for Thais and Chremes to discuss the matter further.

IV. 7. The siege scene, in which Thraso comes to reclaim Pamphila, involves five speaking characters, Thais and Chremes defending the house, and Thraso, Gnatho, and a cook called Sanga (plus some further mute characters) attacking it. If the scene has a parallel in Menander's *Eunouchos*, with the rival coming to demand the return of the girl, the Greek version can have had only three speaking characters, presumably Thais, Chremes, and the rival. If it comes from *Kolax*, on the other hand, the three characters there would be Thraso,

Gnatho, and a single defender (whoever has possession of the girl at the time). The obvious assumption is that there was a 'reclaiming' scene in both plays, and what we have here is an amalgamation of the two using the extra Roman actors: that is, that Terence has enlivened the plainer *Eunouchos* scene by adding Gnatho and some parts of the dialogue from *Kolax*.

V. 3. To these examples from Acts II to IV, we may add one from the fifth act. V. 3 is a curiously perfunctory scene in which Chremes, who has gone to show Pamphila's tokens to the old nurse Sophrona, returns with the nurse, and the two scarcely have time to exchange a word with Pythias, who is still on stage after her dialogue with Thais, before disappearing into Thais' house. This raises the suspicion that Menander may have dealt with the recognition in a different manner, perhaps involving a larger part for Sophrona. Moreover there is an awkwardness of staging at the end of the scene. Pythias specifically says that she will go into the house to confirm the recognition (921); but we then find her commenting on Parmeno's entrance monologue (941) without any indication that she has returned to the stage.

This is a fairly long list of anomalies and alterations. Many of those relating to Thraso and Gnatho do in fact respond to micro-analysis, along the line suggested. So do those relating to Dorias: we can be reasonably certain that Dorias was an independent addition by Terence, though it is not self-evident that the play has gained a lot by the addition.

More interesting are the number of the anomalies which relate to Chremes (who, as we have seen, causes problems in the exposition) and to the dinner party. These cannot on the whole be solved by micro-analysis, so that we have to consider the possibility of major adaptation. There are a lot of puzzles about the character of Chremes. As we have seen, he is called *adulescens* by Thais (204) and this description duly reappears in the cast list of the MSS, but his character has little in common with the normal *adulescens* type. In fact it is difficult to see a coherent characterisation in his case (though Donatus ad 507 suggests that rusticity was his hallmark in Menander's version). It is interesting that the name Chremes occurs elsewhere in comedy (*Andria*, *Heauton*, *Phormio*) as the name of an *old* man, and is so regarded by later writers such as Horace (*Epod.* 1. 33, *Sat.* 1. 10. 40), and also that the role of recognition agent which Chremes here plays is more often played by an elderly relative (Crito in *Andria*) or by a nurse. In fact, since we have Sophrona in *Eunuchus* to confirm the identity of Pamphila, we do not actually need Chremes as a recognition agent at all. And the role of potental *prostates* for Thais, for which Chremes is set up as Pamphila's brother, also turns out to be superfluous; in the end it is Chaerea's father who assumes this role.

We cannot speculate that Chremes did not figure as a character in Menander's *Eunouchos*: we have Donatus' express testimony that he did in the passage just mentioned. But should we entertain the possibility that Chremes did not go to the dinner party in Menander's version (the obvious person to excite the rival's jealousy there was not Chremes but Phaedria, and it is specifically Phaedria's presence which is foreshadowed by Gnatho in Terence's play at 439–45)? Or even that there was no dinner party in Menander's *Eunouchos*? Can this have come, like the siege scene to which it leads, from *Kolax*? Can it be that Terence has had problems in dovetailing Chremes, a *Eunouchos* character, into what is (at this stage of the play) essentially a *Kolax* plot?

The whole question of 'contamination' from the *Kolax* would be much simpler to answer if we had independent evidence for Menander's plot in either play. Unfortunately, neither Donatus nor the few surviving quotations from *Eunouchos* allow us to reconstruct its plot independently of Terence. But for *Kolax*, things are rather better; we do have fragmentary selections of the play on papyrus amounting to over hundred lines, and one major significant difference from *Eunouchos* can be established, namely that in *Kolax* the girl for whom the youth and soldier are rivals is a young slave-girl in the power of a pimp. The fragments also present, on the one hand, a pimp who is worried that someone (? the youth) may come with sixty comrades like Odysseus and threaten him, who decides not to sell the girl (?to the soldier) because she is capable of bringing in a sizeable income, and who fears that 'they' may kidnap her in the street and force him to go to law (*Kol.* 120–32 Sandbach), and, on the other, a cook conducting a sacrifice at the festival of the Aphrodite Pandemos (*Kol.* fr. 1 K-T).

There is no direct evidence for a siege scene in *Kolax*, but scholars have had no difficulty in reconstructing one, with the soldier and parasite coming to reclaim the girl either from the pimp or the young man in love with her. There is no direct evidence for a dinner party either, though one might naturally be associated with the celebration for Aphrodite Pandemos; Webster thinks that this may have been held at the house of the young man, and that the pimp or the girl or

both may have been invited, but there are clearly several other possibilities.[7] Can we reconstruct a dinner party for *Kolax* involving a quarrel over the girl which might have acted as a model for Terence? Could
the younger man, for example, have successfully invaded a celebration of the festival to Aphrodite at the soldier's house (or the pimp's)
and made off with the girl,[8] leading to the siege scene and the attempt
to recapture? This scenario would have required considerable adaptation by Terence (including the involvement of Chremes), and it would
not be surprising if the problems of the adaptation had led to anomalies of the kind which we find in *Eunuchus*.

All this is pure speculation; none of it quite fits; and it may all be
wide of the mark. In the end, the problem with any supposed transfer
of plot elements from *Kolax* to *Eunuchus* is that the situations are just
too different. Since there is no Thais character in *Kolax*, there cannot
have been the same sort of quarrel at any dinner party, and there
cannot have been a counterpart to the Thais–Chremes–Thraso dialogue (IV. 7) at any siege scene. We thus seem to be forced to Ludwig's
conclusion, that all that comes from *Kolax* (in this central section at
least) are the stretches of plot-free dialogue which involve the flattering parasite and the boastful soldier. But this still does not explain the
anomalies, and in particular those relating to Chremes. And the
anomalies continue to nag, together with the feeling that there is
more here than meets the eye. Ludwig may in the end be right, but
can we totally reject the possibility of more far-reaching adaptation
by Terence in the central part of the play, by independent composition
rather than by transfer from *Kolax*, even if we cannot pin down precisely what he has done?

Scholars have had much less difficulty in accepting that Terence has
radically departed from Menander's *Eunouchos* in his finale, and to
this we may now turn. Terence's play ends with Phaedria agreeing to
share Thais' favours with Thraso, which is a surprising conclusion, at
least to modern taste. The last three scenes involve the two *Kolax*
characters Thraso and Gnatho, and the last two require four speaking
actors. There is thus strong *prima facie* evidence for Terentian adaptation and for influence from *Kolax*. In fact, three different views of the
ending have been held. Some believe that Terence's ending is derived

---

[7] T. B. L. Webster, *An Introduction to Menander* (Manchester, 1974), 158, 160.
[8] The stealing of Sannio's girl by Aeschinus in *Adelphoe* offers a parallel of a sort.

from Menander's *Eunouchos*, warning that what seems unacceptable to modern taste may not have seemed so to ancient, and pointing to the ending of Menander's *Dyskolos*, where the ragging of the semi-reformed Knemon has similarly offenced modern susceptibilities; others that Terence has somewhat inappropriately chosen to replace the original *Eunouchos* ending by the *Kolax* ending; and others again that Terence's ending does not come directly from either of these two Greek models but is essentially his own creation.

Terence's finale proceeds as follows. Thais finds out the truth of the eunuch trick from Pythias (V. 1), and forgives Chaerea when he declares his love for Pamphila and his willingness to marry her (V. 2). The old nurse Sophrona arrives with Chremes to confirm the identity of Pamphila (V. 3). Pythia teases Parmeno with the story that Chaerea is to be castrated as an adulterer, and Parmeno blurts out the truth to the boys' father (V. 4–6). Thraso returns to throw himself on Thais' mercy (V. 7). Chaerea announces that his father has not only consented to his own wedding with Pamphila but has also agreed to take Thais under his protection (V. 8). Phaedria, who now seems to hold all the cards, threatens Thraso if he dares to set foot in the street again. Gnatho, however, persuades Phaedria and Chaerea that they should allow Thraso continued access to Thais, because he is stupid enough to pay for Thais' expensive tastes and too absurd to be a serious rival (V. 9).

This conclusion has seemed to many readers of Terence's version to go against the characterisation that he has developed in the course of the play. To take Thais first, it is true that she has exacted gifts from both Phaedria and Thraso; but the idea that she is simply the typical greedy and expensive courtesan, though repeated here (1075), has ben repeatedly scotched in the course of the play. It has become quite clear that she does have some genuine feelings both for Phaedria and for Pamphila, and that her ultimate motive is to obtain status, not gifts. She has also been shown to be an independent-minded and resourceful woman, well able to manage the men with whom she has to deal, so that it is strange to see an arrangement for her future being concluded behind her back and without her consent. Secondly, Phaedria has been portrayed as the jealous lover, unable to tear himself away from his mistress and unhappy to think of anyone sharing her favours, so that it comes as a surprise that he is willing to accept the soldier as a semi-permanent rival. It is by no means clear that he is as short of money as the traditional young man of comedy, though this too is alleged here (1075); he was able to purchase the eunuch and an Ethiopian slave girl for Thais before, and, in any case, his father, having become Thais' patron, will presumably be willing to give her adequate financial support. As for Thraso and Gnatho, their basically unsympathetic characterisation is maintained in the final scene, so that there seems no need to make concessions to them in the end, even granted the traditional 'inclusiveness' of the comic finale. The case of Thraso is not too much of a problem, since it can be argued that the final settlement is not so much a concession to him as a deserved humiliation, even if he himself does not perceive it as such.[9] But the treatment of Gnatho is a puzzle. Though some parasites (such as Phormio in Terence's *Phormio*) are resourceful endearing rogues whose triumphs the audience can share, Gnatho has been merely the slick self-serving flatterer: why then should the play end on a note of victory for Gnatho?

Some scholars have seized on the victory of Gnatho as a key to the interpretation of Terence's play. It is a play about the selfishness of human motives and the need to defer to others in order to achieve one's goals, or, to put it another way, about the impossibility of human independence; the victory of the parasite epitomises both the necessity of deferring to others and the rewards of exploiting them. Whether or not this is valid for Terence, Menander's *Eunouchos* cannot have ended on the same note, since, however we interpret Terence's prologue statement, Menander's version did not have a flattering parasite or a gullible soldier for the parasite to exploit. Menander *may* have ended with the youth agreeing to share the courtesan's favours with the rival, but it will have been a different sort of rival aided by a different sort of helper. And the ending will have had a different sort of moral or motive. If the rival was an unsympathetic 'blocking character', he might have been humiliated and 'humanised' before being finally 'reintegrated' by being allowed continued access to Thais, according to a recurring comic pattern which is exemplified in *Dyskolos* and has been traced in other plays of Menander's. On the other hand we could hypothesise for Menander a more sympathetic rival who deserved a share in the courtesan's favours (say, another young man or a friendly merchant) and a more sympathetic helper whose triumph we could share (say, a parasite like Phormio or an irrepressible trickly slave of

---

[9] Donatus (ad 446) takes a more sympathetic view of the characterisation of Thraso.

the Plautine type), and the problem of the 'including' of the rival would loom less large. But we would still have the problem of Thais and Phaedria. We could go on and hypothesise for Menander a totally mercenary courtesan and a totally feckless young man, for both of whom the sharing arrangement would have been appropriate (Plautus' *Truculentus* ends with just such a courtesan playing off just such a young man against a soldier and indeed a third rival). But common sense suggests that it is time to cry halt. There must be a limit to the reconstructing of Menander's play to suit Terence's ending; it is much more economical, and more plausible, to suppose that Terence has changed Menander's ending, over and above the different slant provided by the two *Kolax* characters. In fact, if we simply subtracted the *Kolax* characters from Terence's ending, we would be left with a rather unsatisfactory scene involving the Phaedria and Chaerea characters and the rival, but this would lack punch without Gnatho's contribution. So we have to admit the possibility of a quite different ending for Menander's *Eunouchos*. even involving Thais, which Terence has replaced, either by the ending of *Kolax* or by one of his own invention.

Unfortunately we have no independent evidence for the ending of *Kolax*. It *may* have ended with the parasite gaining some sort of settlement for himself and the soldier, but equally it may not. At first sight some such ending does seem more appropriate for *Kolax* than for *Eunouchos*, since the young man in the former play *was* impecunious (*Kol.* 5–7 Sandbach) and, as we have seen, the *meretrix* was not an independent courtesan but a slave in the power of a pimp, whose fate might well have been decided behind her back. We should again have to hypothesise a rather feckless young man with no great claim to our sympathies and to invoke the principle of the inclusiveness of the comic finale to allow the soldier to retain access to the girl. But on closer inspection doubts begin to appear. Some have held that the girl in *Kolax* turned out to be a citizen and hence marriageable, so that there could be no question of sharing her between the young man and the soldier. Again there is no clear evidence: it is true that the young pimp-owned girl of comedy often turns out to be a freeborn citizen, but this seems unlikely in *Kolax* where the girl is no longer a virgin but is already practising as a *meretrix* (*Kol.* 128–30 Sandbach). But there are problems in the 'sharing of favours' conclusion as applied to a slave-girl owned by a pimp, who would be expected to share her favours anyway; such a conclusion actually fits an independent courtesan rather better.

This last question is worth another look. In what circumstances in comedy does a *meretrix* share her favours between two men? In Plautus' *Truculentus*, as we have seen, Phronesium plays off three lovers against each other. Like Thais she is an independent courtesan and a strong-minded one; but unlike Thais her only aims are mercenary and she herself makes the decision to share. In Paululus' *Bacchides*, the two sisters seduce the fathers of their respective lovers. Again they are independent courtesans, and again they share their favours of their own free will; but they have a different object than either Thais or Phronesium, namely to secure the fathers' consent to their sons' affairs. In Plautus' *Asinaria*, after one young man has bought the services of Philaenium on a year's contract, a parasite acting for a rival young man proposes that the two *adulescentes* should share the contract on a night by night basis (918). We are not told whether this proposal is accepted, since the play ends with the exposure to his wife of the first young man's father, who has insisted on 'a night and a dinner' with the girl (736) as a reward for his help in the purchase of the contract. The proposed sharing is potentially an arrangement being made behind the girl's back, but only potentially, and Philaenium is not an independent courtesan, nor again a girl in the possession of a pimp, but the daughter of a *lena*. In fact there seems to be no real parallel in comedy either for an independent courtesan having her future decided behind her back or for a girl owned by pimp sharing her favours on a continuing basis between a steady lover and another man. If the latter *was* the ending of *Kolax* we might have to assume that the girl was first purchased from the pimp, though again there is no hint how the impecunious *adulescens* might have found the money.[10]

In the end we cannot rule out some influence from *Kolax* on Terence's 'sharing of favours' ending. Equally we cannot rule out the possibility that it is his own independent composition. Scholars have been willing to see independent Terentian modification of the ending

[10] There were no doubt all sorts of sharing arrangements in real life (see P.W. Marsh, *AJPh* 58(1937) 286), though the range represented in comedy is relatively small. The most interesting real-life case is that of Neaera ([Dem.] 59), a slave *meretrix* who, having been purchased by two lovers, bought her freedom with contributions from further lovers, and finally after a legal arbitration was declared free and independent but compelled to share her favours night by night between two men who had claims on her.

of Menander's *Adelphoi* without recourse to any theory of 'contamination' from a second play. Ths is not the place to analyse Terence's possible motive in changing Menander's *Eunouchos* ending or to evaluate the interpretations of the Roman play alluded to above. But the simplest explanation may be the right one. In *Eunouchos* as in *Adelphoe* (at least according to some views of the latter play), Terence has gone for the surprise conclusion, the arresting ending, the *coup de théâtre*, as a calculated move to win his audience's approval; in both cases he has been willing to sacrifice consistency for dramatic effect.

20

The Intrigue of Terence's
Self-Tormentor

J. C. B. LOWE

The complex machinations of the slave Syrus occupy a prominent position in the plot of Terence's *Self-Tormentor.* Any analysis must begin with them. Indeed the key to the play lies in distinguishing between Syrus' real schemes against Chremes and his pretended schemes against Menedemus. Whereas those against Menedemus are necessarily spelt out for Chremes' benefit, Syrus is secretive about his real intentions; and this has led to some confusion.

Syrus' initial strategem, devised before his first entrance, involves bringing Bacchis to Chremes' house together with Antiphila, who has been sent for by Clinia (191). His intention is to pass her off instead of Antiphila as Clinia's girl (332 f.), taking advantage of the fact that Chremes would not know the difference. His purpose is to secure for his young master Clitipho the company of Bacchis—really his mistress (321 f., 328)—and somehow to obtain money with which to satisfy her demands (329 f., 584). He has managed to persuade her to come with the promise of 10 *minae* (724). Antiphila is to be kept out of the way with Clitipho's mother Sostrata. The underlying dramaturgic justification for this is to bring about her recognition as Chremes' daughter, but a superficial reason is that, unlike Bacchis, she is not a *meretrix*—even if thought to be a non-citizen—and therefore belongs in the women's quarters.

Clinia, fearful of his father's anger and uncertain what to do (188 f.; cf. 433–5), apparently feels he has no alternative but to go along with Syrus' plan (359 f.). Obviously Syrus must have some story to explain why Antiphila has come with Bacchis, but he does not at first reveal it, *longumst, Clitipho, si tibi narrem quam ob rem id faciam* ('It's a long story, Clitipho', 335 f.). This is the first instance of a technique which is used several times in the play, to avoid repetition, to keep the audience in suspense and to emphasize the cleverness of the scheming slave; Syrus declines to give details of his plan and invests it with an air of mystery.

Nor does he give any hint of how he means to obtain the needed money, but it is clear that his intended victim is Chremes. It is normal in New Comedy that money needed by a young man in love is extracted from his father through the machinations of a slave. Syrus would not think of Menedemus as a potential source of money, and neither he nor Clinia knows of Menedemus' new willingness to disburse money for his son (189, 402, 526), because Chremes has deliberately suppressed this fact (199, 436). When Syrus soliloquizes 'a trick must be played on the old man' (513)intendenda in senemst fallacia, this can only refer to Chremes. *Senex* without qualification in the mouth of a slave naturally refers to his master (cf. 690, 697, 746); and Syrus' expression of fear in 516 that Chremes may have overheard him is confirmation enough (cf. 530 f.). Syrus' preceding words indicate, however, that he has not in fact yet devised a way of tricking Chremes out of the required 10 *minae* (512 f.).

Chremes observes early on that Syrus is up to something; he notices Syrus and Dromo whispering together with their young masters (471–4, 514–16). Since, however, he believes that it is Clinia who loves the expensive Bacchis and knows nothing of his own son's affair, he naturally assumes that any intrigue on the part of the slave is aimed at Clinia's father, Menedemus. Having conceived the devious notion that Menedemus should not follow his instinct and lavish money on his restored 'prodigal' son but rather allow himself to be tricked out of it (466–89), Chremes accordingly encourages Syrus to use all his ingenuity to help the dull Dromo (515, 545) to bring this about. The result is a highly amusing scene (512–58) in which Syrus, who is planning to deceive Chremes, is surprised and delighted to be lectured on how it is sometimes the duty of a slave to trick his master. From now on Syrus is playing a double game, pretending to Chremes that he is scheming against Menedemus but in reality scheming against Chremes himself.

After a diversion in which Clitipho nearly gives the game away by allowing Chremes to see him fondling Bacchis (562–94), Syrus expounds to Chremes a 'scheme' to extract money from Menedemus (596, *fallacia*). He begins with what he claims to be a statement of the facts regarding Antiphila's relationship with Bacchis, related 'in order' (598). This is presumably the 'long story' which Syrus declined to reveal to Clitipho in 335 f. How far this is Syrus' fabrication is not entirely clear. It is based on fact; Antiphila's reputed mother was an *anus Corinthia* and she had recently died (96 f., 271 f.). It is at least partly false, however, since Syrus knows that the Corinthian was not in fact Antiphila's mother (270); and Bacchis' alleged shameless request to Clinia for a loan on the security of Antiphila is clearly fiction, based on the pretence that Clinia is Bacchis' lover (519 f., 605 f.). What then of the loan which Bacchis is alleged to have made to the Corinthian and for which Antiphila is said to be the security (603, *arrabonist*)? The legality in Athens of a loan on the security of a person has often been questioned, but in the present argument this is a side-issue, since, whether true or false, Syrus' story should not blatantly conflict with Athenian law; it is possible that the law only applied to Athenian citizens, or that Terence has slightly altered the wording of his Greek model in speaking of an *arrabo* (in 791, after her recognition as a citizen, Syrus speaks simply of a debt which Antiphila owes to Bacchis, *argento quod ista debet Bacchidi*. It is conceivable that Bacchis had in fact lent money to the Corinthian, but it is much more likely that the 'debt' is entirely fictitious; it cannot be accidental that the sum involved exactly coincides with the 10 *minae* Syrus has promised Bacchis.

In any case the important point is that Chremes is expected to and does accept all this story as fact, and this crucially affects the development of the plot. Only after this introductory account of what purports to be the facts of the situation does Syrus proceed to offer his 'scheme' to extract money from Menedemus; he proposes to tell Menedemus that Antiphila is a captive from Caria, of a rich family, and that her purchase would be a profitable investment (*magnum inest in ea lucrum*, 608 f.). To this proposed 'scheme' Chremes objects that Menedemus would not agree to pay for the girl (610 f.); Chremes knows this to be untrue but it accords with the negative conception of Menedemus' attitude which he encourages in Syrus (cf. 535, *difficilem . . . senem*). Syrus replies that this does not matter, implying that he has other strings to his bow (611 f.)—once again the slave exudes confidence, but mysteriously refuses to give details ('you'll soon find out', 612). Now the dramatist knows that the recognition of Antiphila as Chremes' daughter will in the event wreck this 'scheme' but will present Syrus with new opportunities. At this point, however, the audience is surely intended to understand Syrus as hinting that the *fallacia* to deceive Menedemus is unimportant because he is really scheming to extract money from Chremes, even if he does not yet know how this will then be; another example of the irony which constantly characterizes Syrus' exchanges with Chremes.

The discovery of Antiphila as Chremes' daughter completely changes the situation. As Syrus listens to the dialogue between the old man and Sostrata in 614–67, he expresses mounting alarm at the new development (cf. 654, 659, 663). After the others have gone inside, he reflects on the problem now facing him. He fears that he will be in serious trouble unless he can devise some way of preventing Chremes from finding out that Bacchis is Clitipho's mistress (670 cf. 690). He correctly anticipates that, if Antiphila is discovered to be a citizen, the way will be open for Clinia to marry her and he will be unwilling to maintain the pretence that Bacchis is his girl.

In the following scene, after the recognition has been confirmed, the overjoyed Clinia is intent only on approaching his father and arranging a marriage as soon as possible (691, 699, 713 f.); he is with difficulty persuaded by Syrus temporarily to maintain the pretence and to allow Bacchis and her entourage to move over to Menedemus' house. Syrus further fears that he now has no hope of achieving his ultimate object of obtaining money for Bacchis, but will be lucky if he can escape a beating (671 f.); he laments the cruel fate that has suddenly snatched 'such a haul' from his grasp (673), but he does not explain precisely how his plans have been thwarted. Obviously the story about the Carian captive cannot be maintained after the recognition of Antiphila, but, as argued above, that belongs to the pretended stratagem to obtain money from Menedemus, not Syrus' real (though unspecified) scheme to obtain money from Chremes. Thus it appears that the one thing Syrus fears as a direct result of the recognition of Antiphila is that Chremes should learn of Clitipho's affair with Bacchis, as mentioned explicitly in 670; his hopes of obtaining money, by whatever means, depend on maintaining the deception of Chremes.

Syrus continues his soliloquy by exhorting himself to think up a new plan to meet the new situation (674 f.). After rejecting three unspecified ideas (676 f.), he finally thinks of one with which he is more satisified, *euge habeo optumamand*, by which he is confident of capturing the elusive money (677 f.); what this plan is emerges in the following scene. Clinia has to be persuaded, in the interest of his friend, to maintain the pretence that Bacchis is his girl, not to leave her in Chremes' house but to take her with him to his father's (695–8). To Clinia's inquiry as to what he is to say to his father, Syrus replies that he should tell him the entire truth (709–12). The brilliant feature of Syrus' new ploy, as he himself proudly boasts, is *vera dicendo ut eos ambos fallam* ('to deceive both by telling the truth', 711). Chremes will not believe it when Menedemus tells him the truth, because he will take it as a *fallacia* concocted to extract money from Menedemus; his neighbor will be persuaded, at least temporarily, that Chremes is right. If the immediate object of transferring Bacchis to Menedemus' house is to maintain the deception of Chremes, Syrus' ultimate object is still to obtain money for Clitipho and Bacchis, as he tells Clinia in 717 and assures Bacchis in 737 f. and 740 f., without giving any details; and his intended victim is still Chremes, as he makes clear in 746 f., where he predicts that the removal of Bacchis and her entourage, apparently a relief, will in fact cost Chremes dearly.

On meeting Chremes again Cyrus proceeds to put his plan into effect. He presents Clinia's statement that Bacchis is Clitipho's girl and request that he should himself marry Antiphila as all a *fallacia* designed to obtain from Menedemus money for Bacchis. Since Chremes has been urging Syrus to devise a scheme against Menedemus, he readily accepts this as a new scheme and thus, as Syrus predicted in 709–12, takes to be fiction what is really fact. Chremes objects to Syrus' second 'scheme' to deceive Menedemus, as he had done to the first (610 f.). As Clinia had anticipated, he has no intention of agreeing to the marriage of his newly discovered daughter to Clinia, whom he believes to be attached to Bacchis, and he is unwilling even to co-operate with the new 'scheme' by pretending to agree (779–85). Syrus expresses mild regret but accepts Chremes' decision and agrees to think up something else (788–90). He now suddenly changes tack and reverts to the supposedly factual account with which he had prefaced his first 'scheme' against Menedemus, the story of the money owed Bacchis by Antiphila.

Although abrupt, his new proposal follows naturally enough from Chremes' rejection of the second 'scheme'; if Bacchis is not immediately to receive money by the deception of Menedemus, it is only reasonably that Chremes should make himself responsible for the repayment of a supposedly genuine debt owed by Bacchis by his newly discovered daughter. Some have criticized the gullibility with which Chremes agrees without question to Syrus' suggestions and thus allows the wily slave to achieve his aim. Perhaps by some standards Chremes is implausibly gullible, but this is a comedy, not real life. One psychological factor which can perhaps be seen as con-

tributing to Chremes' deception is a certain sense of guilt with regard
to the daughter he had rejected in infancy; he speaks of the 10 *minae*
he pays on her behalf as in lieu of what it would have cost him to rear
her (835 f.). Moreover Syrus' flattery of him as one who would not use
the letter of the law to escape a moral obligation to pay his daughter's
debts would have its effect (792–8).

Above all, however, we should observe the care with which the
dramatist has depicted Chremes as caught off guard. Thanks to Syrus'
ingenuity, Chremes still has no inkling of his son's affair with Bacchis;
and his preoccupation with 'intrigues' to deceive Menedemus makes
it more plausible that he should fail to recognize that Syrus is really
scheming against him. That Chremes is the key instrument of his
own deception makes the situation more comic still.

The final touch in Syrus' deception of Chremes is to persuade
him to give the money to Clitipho so that he can personally give it
to Bacchis; Chremes believes he is furthering a 'scheme' against
Menedemus, adding verisimilitude to a *fallacia* (799–802), whereas he
is in fact furthering Syrus' *fallacia* against himself. The irony of the
situation is expressed in Syrus' ambiguous comment, *et simul confi-
ciam facilius ego quod volo* ('and at the same time I shall bring about
what I want', 803). This provides a direct link between the 'scheme'
against Menedemus and Syrus' real duping of Chremes. The one
provides the essential background which makes possible the other.
[In hiding the true situation from Chremes under the guise of ficton
it achieves its purpose. It is wrong to describe it as a separate, real
scheme to obtain money from Menedemus which 'founders on the
rock of Chremes' refusal to co-operate' and has to be replaced by a
new scheme. Rather, Syrus' real scheme against Chremes is cun-
ningly embedded in the 'scheme' against Menedemus; the whole
forms a single complex *fallacia*, conceived in 677, of which the key feature is telling the truth, *vera dicendo fallere* (711).]

It will be clear by now that the intrigue of the *Self-Tormentor*, for all
its complexity, shows a unity of design that argues strongly for a single author. That was surely Menander, creator of the original plot. In
two other Menandrian plays, the same motif of 'deceiving by telling
the truth' occurs. In *Bacchides* 692–912 Chrysalus' second scheme
against Nicobulus is based on a letter which he gets Mnesilochus to
write informing Nicobulus to regard as Mnesilochus' fabrication. In
Andria 459–513 the excessively suspicious Simo takes the signs that
Glycerium has given birth to a baby to be a *fallacia* of Davos. Davos

then exploits Simo's misunderstanding for his own ends ('soon the boy will be brought outside', 507; cf. 721 ff., 834 ff.). There seems no reason to doubt that Menander conceived his *Self-Tormentor* as primarily a play of intrigue, of which the principal character was not Menedemus but Chremes. The recognition strand is secondary, which explains why it occurs unusually early in the play. That is not to say that Terence did not make any changes to his Greek model; but a drastic transformation of the basic plot is highly improbable.

21

Phormio *parasitus*: A Study in Dramatic Methods of Characterization

W. GEOFFREY ARNOTT

The garbled pages of the commentary deriving from Donatus suggest that in the *Phormio* Terence made few alterations of any import to his Greek original, and very few alterations indeed of one type that is characteristic of his universalizing method: the deletion or blurring of specifically Greek images, references, and proverbs. The *Phormio* provides perhaps three examples only of this type of alteration: at 49, where Terence cuts out the specific references to Samothrace which he original names as the scene of the initiation ceremony; at 91, where Terence suppresses his original's allusion to the Greek custom of having the hair cut short as a token of mourning, and consequently makes the barber's shop scene less relevant; and at 661, where Terence deletes the more vivid Greek proverb. Against this trio, however, can be instanced a sextet of places where Terence has faithfully retained a Greek proverb, image, or vivid turn of phrase.[1] The multiplicity of proverbs and of other tropes is one of the *Phormio*'s more remarkable features, and requires closer investigation. Their presence is one element in the play's domination by Phormio the parasite.

Phormio's language marks him out from the other characters with whom he speaks at the time. As an important feature of his characterization, it helps partly (not wholly) to explain the curious spell that Phormio casts over the other characters not only when he is on the stage but at other times also. In fact Phormio stalks along the stage for a mere third of the play (353 lines out of the play's total of 1055), and yet one has gained the impression that Phormio is in it from start to finish, an illusion created by . . . By what? By a variety of factors:

---

[1] 186, 506, 562, 575, and 587, which are all discussed by Donatus, ad 78, who does not give the well-known Greek version of the proverb.

obviously the circumstance that Phormio is the well-spring of ideas
and actions in the plot, that he is at the focus of several scenes where
he is not actually on the stage (122–36, 459–78, 591–711), that he is
given a part in which he is able to defeat his opponents by superiority
in argument. But this is not all—important too is the presentation of
the character, the first impression that an audience receives of him on
his first entrance. After what the audience has previously been told
about his impudent brilliance, Phormio has a reputation to live down.
He must show himself a more lively and interesting character than
anybody else with him on the stage. How is this accomplished?

Before Phormio makes his first entrance at 315, we have already
learnt that he is a damnable self-confident parasite (122 f.) who had
enabled Antipho to marry the orphan Phanium by an ingenious
abuse of the Athenian law of *epidikasia*, designed to keep the property
of any orphaned heiress within her father's family by compelling her
to marry her male next-of-kin. It is clear that Terence here is fully
reproducing the original concept of Apollodorus' *Epidikazomenos*, his
Greek model. Phormio had seen to it that a claim to Phanium's hand
had been deposited with the relevant archon by Antipho (125 ff.), by
virtue of Antipho's 'alleged' relationship to the girl's father. Phormio
had spun a fragile web of false pretences with complete success.

An intelligent audience would have been expectantly curious to see
whether on his first appearance Phormio displayed abilities commen-
surate with his reputation. It is always a challenge for any dramatist
to portray convincingly genius or success, dominance and over-
mastering unscrupulousness. Here the difficulty was increased for
Apollodorus (we must remember that the play's basic *hypothesis* was
his, not Terence's) by his first presenting Phormio not in a situation
built for his creative spirit, but simply in one of restatement and reaction. In his initial scene Phormio is given no opportunity to organize
and mount a new attack, like the one mounted against the old
codgers in the play's final scenes: he can only react to Demipho's own
attack. How can such a situation earn real glory for Phormio? The
answer of the playwright (Terence only? Or also Apollodorus? We
shall see later) is ingenious: Phormio's part on first entry is gor-
geously enriched with figurative language.

Yes: parasites like Gnatho in the *Eunuchus*, for example, do lace
their speech with pert and witty buffooneries. This is a leading characteristic of comic parasites, and Gnatho's main function in the
Eunuchus is decorative, to add an amusing gloss to the military scenes

by polished witticism, ironic *double entendre*, and so on. But Phormio is not just another Gnatho. He is the dominator, not the hanger-on, and must be shown: first with Geta, whom he accompanies on to the stage at 315, and then with the deputation of Demipho and Co. at 348 ff. For the first thirty-five lines or so Phormio's part is descriptive, preliminary to the confrontation beginning at 348; these introductory lines are carefully written, in order to establish at the outset Phormio's intellectual and imaginative supremacy over his companion Geta. To this end Geta's part is just as carefuly toned down as Phormio's is enlivened. Geta has a succession of unimportant, unimpressive phrases: 'Quite', 'Help us', 'You're a brave man and a friend as well': phrases that provide the *basso continuou* to Phormio's virtuoso melodies.

But in addition to this deliberate decolorization of Geta's remarks between 315 and 347, the language in the second part of the scene immediately preceding Phormio's first entry (253–314) has also, and with the same purpose, been effectively neutralized, so that it could serve with all the gloss removed as the necessarily dull antecedent against which the colours of Phormio's own imagery would glow in emphatic contrast. In that previous scene, from Phaedria's greeting of Demipho at 253 right up to 314, the line before Phormio's entry, the conversation between Demipho, Phaedria, and Geta is conducted in unadorned, virtually image-free phrases. Such tropes as can be instanced there are few in number, altogether unremarkable, and even then limited to the earlier part of the passage in question; after 287, apart from Geta's one mildly amusing sally at 299 ('We don't need a plan, we just need money') we hear nothing but dull statements unemphatically expressed, right up to the moment of Phormio's entrance—or rather, to be more precise, up to the word immediately preceding that entrance. For as Demipho goes off, he ends that scene with the words 'so I won't be unprepared if Phormio should show up'. This placing of Phormio's name as the last word in the scene is clearly a deliberate dramatic link with the scene that follows. Whether Terence here scrupulously copied the word order of his original Apollodorus or devised the link himself, we do not know; but the device itself is Greek, and particularly Menandrean.

Phormio comes on stage in mid-conversation with Geta, debating his imminent confrontation with the returned Demipho. But if his entrance is not obviously dramatic, his language is. His exhortation is peacock-feathered, gorgeous with metaphor and image. 'It's to you alone, Phormio, that the supreme command returns. You made the pudding, now it's yours to eat. Gird yourself for battle', he says immediately at 317–18. Donatus notes that the choice of metaphor is 'appropriate for a parasite, because it is about food'; it is easy to overlook, among the gallimaufry of Phormio's characteristics, the subtle allusions to his basic interest in food. At 321 *instructa* is a military metaphor, at 323 *deriuem* a metaphor from irrigation. There follows Phormio's confident *apologia pro uita sua*, full of image, hyperbole, and metaphor. I should be surprised if *periclum* there (326) was not deliberately chosen for this context because of its legal overtones. From law court to the open road: 'now I see the way to escape: all metaphorically', as Donatus comments. In 327 'beat to death' allies metaphor to hyperbole. At 330 'the parasite speaks by allegory' (Donatus), with the fable of the hawk and the kite.

How much of the detail is Terentian and how much Apollodoran is hard to estimate. The actual choice of metaphor, which depends on the particularity of the Latin language, must be original to Terence. Alliteration, too, is a hallmark of earlier Latin poetic style; this, rather than the reference to debt-slavery itself, may make the idea of *ducent damnatum domum* ('they're bringing back a bloke to bankrupt you') at 334 wholly Terentian.

Thus in thirty-one lines, Phormio's powers of imagination are vividly stamped on the audience by his choice of language alone. His lively mind is thereby established. And the poet for future scenes will need less of this kind of embellishment; Phormio's talents will now be shown in action and in the matter more than in the dress of his ideas. The heightened language, so carefully placed at key points in the scene, is now merely one detail in the mosaic of Phormio's characterization as the clever, dominant manipulator. The demonstration of Phormio's superior intellectual methods has become more important.

Demipho is no fool, no weakling: a worthy opponent for Phormio rather, strongly drawn with subtle detail. It is a gross oversimplification to dismiss him simply as a typified *homo auarus*, as too many commentators do; he is more precisely a hard-headed businessman, portrayed by his creator with many of the ancillary qualities that accompany or further business success: toughness, determination, and resilience, common sense and the ability to detect weakness in other people's arguments and character, a knowledge of the law and a readiness to use it for his purposes, and finally—an important detail which in the end helps to undermine Demipho in the final battle with Phormio—complete predictability in action and reaction. Such men are yet always difficult to defeat, especially when in cool command of the circumstances governing their life.

As a result of his legal shenanigans, Phormio has the initial advantage over Demipho of partial control of the present situation; but that is not nearly enough against an opponent of Demipho's calibre. Demipho must be made to lose total control, not only of the situation but of himself. Geta's remark that Demipho *iratus est* acts as a launching-pad for Phormio's plan. Demipho's anger must be turned against Demipho himself, increased to an uncontrolled fury unable to counter Phormio's thrusts. 'I'll deal with him in a moment', says Phormio (351); the game begins, with Phormio and Geta staging for Demipho's benefit (or rather, discomfiture) a little quarrel, ostensibly oblivious to their surroundings. In this feigned quarrel Phormio looses three shafts at the unsuspecting Demipho in order to attract his attention and increase his fury.

The first is a simple statement of Demipho's refusal to acknowledge Phanium's kinship (352); for emphasis this statement is repeated with a changed order of words (353), an idiom particularly characteristic of New Comedy's colloquial Greek;[2] Demipho's attention is aroused. The second and third shafts are aimed at Demipho's choler: a sly side-kick at his *auaritia* (357 f.), and the repeated accusation that he has neglected a kinswoman (365 f., 371; cf. 373). The success of Phormio's game is shown by the mood of Demipho when he first approaches Phormio at 378 ff.; an icy, sarcastic politeness to cloak the seething rage beneath.

The author of this virtuosic play now produces a daring stroke that would not have disgraced Menander himself. With malicious irony against his audience, who by now have been led to expect in Phormio an infallible, invincible intriguer, the dramatist gives him a touch of human imperfection and makes him forget the vital name of Stilpo which he has mentioned unprompted, when it did not matter, a moment before (356). Terence's refusal to take over the narrative prologue of his originals has resulted here (as elsewhere) in the unnecessary blurring of what in the Greek model may have been one of its author's most delightful ironies. 'Stilpo' was the name used by Chremes for his bigamous liaison in Lemnos, and so the name by

---

[2] Cf. e.g. Menander's *Girl With Her Hair Cut Short* (*Perikeiromene*), 256 f.

which Phanium knew her father. Readers aware of the dangers of the documentary fallacy will not waste their time on guessing either how Terence envisaged this transfer of information or how Apollodorus described it in his prologue. Such guessing is irrelevant; what is important is the dramatic use of the Stilpo name in this scene. By forgetting it at 385 Phormio shows that he is human after all, not an infallible automaton; it is in fact a neat psychological observation of the way a person's memory (particularly of names) lets him down at important moments.

Inevitably this lapse loses Phormio the initiative for a few lines, and it is not regained without some quick thinking on Phormio's part— another sly dig at Demipho's *auaritia* (393) and some forceful reiteration of legal arguments. Phormio is not only human, then, but also intellectually quick and resilient, not easily thrown off balance. Not only human, but also humorous: Phormio's discomfiture and delaying tactics while Geta supplies the forgotten name are richly comic. And there is yet another dramatic factor involved in this play of names; by having Stilpo mentioned three times in a memorably comic two lines (389 f.), the author imprints this name indelibly on the audience's mind in preparation for the play's later developments, which begin with the confrontation of Sophrona and Chremes at 740. The ability to juggle with half a dozen balls at once seems to have been an endowment of the author of this plot, as it was of Apollodorus' greatest predecessor and influence, Menander himself.

After Phormio's minor discomfiture the ebb and flow of the argument is maintained at a consistently high mark: Phormio here is not going to win an intellectually easy victory, as he does later in the blackmail of Chremes. Victory now has to be fought for every inch, acute questions parried or answered with rapier thrusts. Demipho's shrewd question about Phanium's precise relationship to himself (396 ff.) could easily have occasioned difficulties: Phormio parries it with equal acumen, taking his stance on the argument that the lawsuit was decided and no appeal against the verdict possible. Apollodorus' Athenian audience and Terence's Roman one were well aware that it was normally illegal in both Athenian and Roman law to make a second investigation on the same charge against the same person.

The Greek playwright, however, was faced with a difficulty at this point in constructing the fabric of his plot. In Athenian law a special exception to the rule debarring retrial was allowed in such cases of *epidikasia* where a rival claimant to the girl's hand could be produced. There was thus a ready solution for a real-life Demipho who had been caught in such a web of intrigue. But a play is not real life, and the complicating exception was conveniently suppressed by Apollodorus and neglected by Demipho. It is in fact unlikely that Terence made any sweeping changes here to adapt the situation to the more rigorous Roman law, since the whole concept of *epidikasia* is Greek and the Greek procedure is carefully outlined by Terence for the benefit of his Roman audience in the exposition of his adaptation (125 ff.). Even so, Demipho's counter to Phormio's cocksure legal aplomb is as shrewd and knowledgeable as ever; he gives Phormio five minas to take the girl off his hands, 'the exact amount of dowry the law prescribes' (409 f.). One wonders whether Terence's Roman audience could have enjoyed these legal arguments as much as the original Athenian one, many of whom would have been trained in the law by personal experience as dicasts. Demipho's offer is based on an Athenian law quoted in the speech against Makartatos in the Demosthenic corpus (xliii. 54):

As regards all orphan heiresses who are classified in the lowest social class, if the next of kin does not wish to marry such an heiress, let him give her in marriage with a dowry of 500 drachmas [= 5 minas] if he be of the first social class, of 300 drachmas if of the second, and of 150 drachmas if of the third, in addition to the girl's own possessions.

Apollodorus' play was produced less than a century after the Makartatos speech, and his audience doubtless appreciated the legal exactitude of Demipho's offer; doubtless also their excitement was whetted to see how Phormio could wriggle out of the corner into which his knowledgeable and determined opponent had put him.

First, slight delaying tactics, to increase the audience's expectations. Phormio laughs with an air of superiority; as Donatus acutely notes (on 411), 'with a laugh he destroys what the old man alleges'. The destroying argument follows: was it, Phormio asks, the purpose of the Athenian *epidikasia* law to allow a poor *epiklēros* to be treated like a *meretrix*, who is cast off with her wages when you've enjoyed the best years of her life, or was its purpose instead to safeguard her interests as a free citizen, who ought not to be forced into dishonorable conduct just on account of poverty? The terms of this question are extravagantly rhetorical, and its language is loaded emotionally with moral and social overtones.

Yet despite the rhetoric and the emotive weighting, Phormio's argument contains one point that—at least to Terence's Roman audience—would appear unanswerable. Phanium was no longer a virgin; if Demipho now had his way and effected her remarriage, she could never have inscribed on *her* tombstone 'Having been chosen for one man I guarded my chastity every faithful'.[3] In an important paper Gordon Williams has clearly shown that the ideal of marriage to one husband only was zealously cherished by Roman *matronae*, but that 'there is nothing in Greek to correspond to this ideal'.[4] Thus it is to Terence's credit that here he has seized so well the opportunity of reinforcing Phormio's argument and rendering it invincible in Roman eyes.

The rest of this scene can be dealt with more briefly, for Demipho has now exhausted his stock of new arguments. He has only threats (419 f., 420, 425) and the repetition of arguments already dismissed (418, 396 ff.): the weapons, that is, of an angry (426) but beaten man, worried and afraid. Phormio quickly realizes that he has gained the whip-hand (428 f.), and half-seriously, half-contemptuously offers friendship on terms of the *status quo* (429 ff.). This offer, together with Phormio's subsequent insulting reference to Demipho's age (433 f.), is precisely calculated to goad a frustrated Demipho to impotent rage. Demipho has been transformed into Phormio's pet bear, forced to dance sullenly to Phormio's fiddle. Phormio goads Demipho to fury, then quietly asks him to be calm (435). He goads Demipho to a final threat that he'll eject Phanium, with an impressive clausula *dixi, Phormio* that may well be translated verbatim from the Greek original. In Menander's *Epitrepontes*, at any rate, the corresponding verb *eirêka* is used in just such a way by Syros and Daos to reinforce the conclusions of their arbitration speeches (116, 176; cf. 117).

But Demipho does not have the last word. Phormio caps his opponent's final outburst, by the mimicry first of a counterthreat expressed in even more forceful language ('I'll sue you for everything you've got', 439), and secondly of an echoing clausula (*dixi, Demipho*) which sounds twice as sinister, twice as emphatic by virtue of its repetition of the *dixi* and the rhyming vocative. So Phormio sweeps off home, undisputedly the victor in a battle that was partly intellectual,

---

[3] Cf. *Carm. Epigr.* 1523 Bücheler = *CIL* ix. 2272.

[4] 'Some Aspects of Roman Marriage Ceremonies and Ideals', *Journal of Roman Studies*, 48 (1958), 22 ff. Cf. his later *Tradition and Originality in Roman Poetry* (Oxford, 1968), 378.

partly psychological. It was not merely superior argumentation that achieved victory, but also Phormio's powers of revival after being temporarily nonplussed, and his calm centrality: he was the still centre round whom the others lose their self-control.

Of all the extant plays of Greco-Roman comedy only the *Hecyra* and the *Phormio* reveal just this amount of calculated, detailed planning—and both stem from Apollodoran originals. Terence's other plays and the extant work of Menander are delicately constructed, but without quite this incessant concentration on a prolixity of realistic detail and structural complexity that we may accordingly infer to have been a special characteristic of Apollodorus' work. Thus at 574 Chremes explains his long absence in Lemnos as due to illness, and old men are often ill: 'Old age is itself an illness' (*senectus ipsa est morbus*) says Chremes (575) in words translated exactly from the Greek, as Donatus here shows. It is a small, even a trivial, detail: but by lighting on illness as the reason why Chremes was so long away, Apollodorus has realistically explained why Chremes was unable to contact his menage in Lemnos, and at the same time has satisfactorily accounted for a lapse of time sufficient to enable Phanium's family to leave Lemnos, her mother to die in Athens, and all the actions in the subsequent love affair to occur. Here care over a small detail has produced a masterly effect; but in the scene beginning at 606 the presence of Antipho (Phanium's husband, Demipho's son) serves only to multiply the complications, when he accidently overhears Geta's plan for the transfer of Phanium from Antipho to Phormio, about which he has not been warned.

One more example to illustrate this obsessive concern with detail will be sufficient. For the sake of the plot Geta must secretly overhear that Phanium is the daughter of Chremes (Demipho's brother) (861 ff.). To prepare for this dramatically, the author creates a complex little structure of commands and countercommands, beginning at 718 ff. when Chremes asks his brother to tell Nausistrata, Chremes' wife, to explain to Phanium about the necessity for Phanium's divorce; at 776 f. accordingly Demipho goes off to speak to Nausistrata, preparing Geta to tell Phanium that Nausistrata will be coming, at 782 f. Geta goes off to see Phanium and to explain that her divorce is a pretence; at 784 ff. Demipho actually asks Nausistrata to see Phanium, and Nausistrata is on the point of so doing when Chremes forestalls her in that delightfully comic scene (796–815) about the problems of communication; at 815 accordingly Nausistrata returns home without accomplishing her mission. This interplay is certainly more mesmerizing to a reader in his study than to an audience in the theatre; it is clear that the author carefully worked out in advance this perhaps unnecessarily complicated structure (there is no real need for Demipho to give Geta the order at 776 f.) and then enjoyed the precise insertion of the required details into his dialogue.

Careful planning, however, may go for nothing if it is not accompanied by lively writing. In several scenes of this play Terence achieves the fine synthesis of exposition, preparation, characterization, and amusing or vital dialogue which is known to have informed Menander's own best work and may be confidently postulated for Apollodorus as Menander's imitator. The comic vitality of scenes like that in which Chremes attempts to communicate his news about Phanium's identity in front of Nausistrata by incoherent hints needs no emphasis from a commentator; here perhaps it will be preferable to illustrate the liveliness by concentrating particularly on the characterization of Chremes, who first appears on stage in the interval between Phormio's two appearances (567), and must be swiftly established as a distinct personality in preparation for his important part in the second half of the plot.

The bold outline of Chremes' characterization, as a weak-kneed husband with a guilty secret that he wishes to keep at all costs from his domineering wife, has long been clear to commentators, who well note his contrast with the tougher businessman Demipho. But this bold outline is shaded in with a multitude of subtle details that turn a type figure into an individual. For example, Chremes' speech to Demipho just after his first arrival on stage (578–87) is outwardly an attempt to explain to his brother the logical reasons for his worry about his nephew's marriage; the way he expresses those reasons, however, reveals clearly three important aspects of his personality: fear of scandal (579–80), fear of his wife (585–7), and self-pity (587); in ten verses an individual emerges.

During the following scenes, the details which contrast him against his brother Demipho are gradually sketched in: Chremes' willingness to pay any sum, however extortionate, for the preservation of his secret—a fact that makes him the ideal blackmail victim (664, 670 f.); the combination of his weakness and tortured fears that make him press for haste in the earlier putative healing with Phormio (716 f.); and the self-revelations of 718–26, perhaps the subtlest lines in the play. They expose Chremes' need to lean on the stronger Demipho in

difficult dealings with his own wife, his willingness to go to absurd
lengths of self-justification, which so often characterizes the guilty
(722–5), his concentration on the external appearance rather than on
the inner motivation of human actions (especially 724), which
becomes ever more relevant later as he makes his ineffectual attempts
to conceal the bad smell of his guilt. Joined to this interconnected
alliance of unattractive traits is one that is essential to the rounded
portrait, but often missed—a basic obtuseness which contrasts
strongly with (for instance) Demipho's cleverness at getting his own
way with Chremes' own wife first by flattery (784) and secondly by
tact (793 f.). This obtuseness is established by a series of delicate
nuances, two of which may serve here by way of illustration.
Chremes' emphasis on the size of the proposed dowry at 722–3 (a pal-
liative to his own bad conscience, as we have already seen) shows a
lack of delicacy and *savoir-faire* which the sensible Demipho is quick
to notice (*quid tua, malum, id refert?*, 723). The other touch is brilliantly
funny as well as relevantly illuminating: Chremes' question at 753 f.,
quid? duasne uxores habuit? This is the recognition scene between
Chremes and Sophrona, the servant of his bigamous wife; and
Sophrona has just explained that Antipho has married Chremes'
Lemnian daughter. Slow wits and a mind that runs in a very limited
number of grooves are the psychological explanation of Chremes'
question; his own condition as a bigamist blinds him to the obvious
deduction from Sophrona's news. Having established Chremes'
obtuseness by such nuances, the playwright can now capitalize on it
for the rest of the play, in Chremes' comically ineffectual attempts to
transmit the information about Phanium to Demipho without
Nausistrata's knowledge, at 795 ff., for example.

When Phormio returns to the stage at 829, vaunting his success
and launching an early metaphor (*uicissim partis tuas acturus est*,
835), an audience may well expect the re-establishment of his
character and dominance by a display of peacock language similar to
that which irradiated his earlier appearance. But nothing of the sort
happens. Instead, for over forty verses (841–83) Phormio is removed to
the periphery while Geta appropriates all the heightened language for
the prelude to his dramatic announcement that Phanium is the
daughter of Chremes. Geta spouts vivid metaphors (*commoditatibus .
. . ope . . . hunc onerastis diem*, 841 f.; *odio tuo me uinces*, 849; *delibutum
gaudio*, 856), and indulges in word play (*onerastis diem | nos exonerastis
| umerum onero*, 842–4) and concundrum structure (851) in a way

that reminds us of Plautus. This surprising reversal of dramatic expectations was partially dictated by the play's organization. By deferring the second emphatic dominance of Phormio these forty verses or so, and turning the linguistic spotlight meanwhile on Geta, the playwright succeeded in combining a pretty symmetry of structure with eminently practical considerations. Audiences are best not bludgeoned, or fed a diet of fanciful language incessantly. If after Geta's scene the author had immediately restored Phormio to the limelight with a renewal of images and metaphors, the effect would have been blunted by Geta's own preceding virtuoso performance. Instead, right up to 938—over a hundred lines after his re-entry—Phormio has virtually no verbal fireworks (the image at 890 is a very damp squib), and achieves his dominance by argument over Demipho, the opponent who had previously shown his worthy mettle. But from 938 on to the end of the play a hundred or more lines later, the fireworks crack and sparkle again in a succession of vivid metaphors.[5] With the metaphor goes lively abuse (948 f.), Phormio's mimic summary of his opponents' apparent vacillations (950 f.), and the amusing *double entendre* on *dormis* (1007). By enlivening only the second part of Phormio's final appearance with such verbal pyrotechnics, the playwright enables the audience first to recover from the preliminary appetizer of Geta's scene before digesting Phormio's feast of metaphor, and secondly to leave the theatre at the end of the play with Phormio's majestic language still buzzing in their ears.

When Phormio re-enters at 829, the money for the purchase of Phaedria's *citharistria* has already (if only temporarily) been secured by his off-stage machinations. There seems to be no immediate need for further chicanery. But Geta's arrival with the information about the skeleton in Chremes' cupboard changes the perspective, by offering Phormio an early opportunity to retain permanently the thirty minas he had previously gained on swindler's loan, as it were.

---

[5] 939 *patrocinari*; 954 *inieci scruplum*; 964 *gladiatorio animo ad me adfectant uiam* (like *prouinciam* in 72 and *subcenturiatus* at 230 a particularly Roman image, and so obviously the brainchild of Terence); 973 *lautum precatum tuum* (cf. Donatus' explanation of the metaphor, *ut labem uel maculam*); 974 f. *hisce ego illam dictis ita tibi incensam dabo ut ne restinguas, lacrimis si exstillaueris* (where the image is cleverly sustained by embroidery more typical of Plautus); 994 *friget*; 997 *delirat* (the metaphor being still alive perhaps in Terence's day); 1015 *uerba fiunt mortuo* (where the proverbial expression refers simply to the wasted labour of telling tales to a corpse, and is almost certainly translated verbatim from Apollodorus' Greek); 1026 *exsequias Chremeti . . . ire*; 1028 *mactatum . . . infortunio*; 1030 *ogganniat*.

Battle is joined directly between a Phormio confident of his ability to hold on to the money (888–9) and a Demipho equally intent on getting this money back (896–8). Without beating about the bush both Phormio and Demipho come straight to the point; Chremes is also present, but until his ears prick up in 940 he is little more than a sleeping partner to Demipho. Phormio has the initiative right from the start of this conflict, easily and simply because, having the money, he is in the position of control; it is Demipho who must use all his skill in argument to try to winkle Phormio out of his entrenched position.

Demipho's arguments are not subtle, but they are not at first feeble, either; he wants the money, and will use any and every argument to get it. A good instance of this less scrupulous side of Demipho's character is at 910–15; the excuse pleaded there by Demipho for his change of front is an indication of this businessman's intention to get his way (and the money) at all costs, whatever pleas or inconsistencies of posture this may necessitate.

Phormio, on the other hand, is in a strong position, with the appearance of the right on his side; clever rogues, the playwright has well realized, are never more dangerous, never more effective than when they can speak of reliability (*fides*, 904), rectitude (*aceuom*, 927), and dignity (*uestri honoris causa*, 928). For the demonstration of Phormio's intellectual superiority, however, competent parrying of Demipho's thrust is not enough; accordingly the author organizes the struggle in such a way that Phormio's superior talents can achieve total intellectual victory in twenty-five lines. Phormio is made to control the direction and the terms of the argument right from his early remark that he is already engaged in the necessary preparations for his marriage to Phanium (901 ff.). By getting in first with his statement of involvement in the transaction from which Demipho and Chremes want him deflected, he makes it all the harder for the brothers to counter convincingly. On the other hand, when Demipho a little later introduces the question of his possible loss of face before people in general (911 ff.), Phormio is able to counter devastatingly with a reference to his own loss of face before his imaginary 'spurned bride' (915 ff.). By 918 Demipho has run out of arguments, and requires to be prompted by the feebler Chremes; by 924 he acknowledges intellectual defeat (*quid igitur fiet?*), and is forced to resort to angry expostulation and sarcastic questions (930 ff.; 932 f.; 933 f.).

The contrast between the ice-cool, self-assured Phormio, who issues his ultimatum to Demipho with the same mastery of detailed precision that has characterized him throughout (924 ff.), and the blustering Demipho has great dramatic point. The defeated Demipho has only one card left, and he plays it in 963: 'go sue me.' Demipho is an experienced, not unintelligent man, but like an old dog he is reluctant to learn new tricks. Tactics that have served him successfully in one situation will be adopted by him again in a similar one. In the *Phormio* this complete predictability of Demipho's reactions and techniques is displayed particularly in his conversations with Nausistrata. He knows—as her husband Chremes apparently does not know—how to flatter her, cajole her, persuade her. But he always uses the same arguments, the same sort of language: thus 1020 in substance repeats 784, 1019 repeats 965 ff. Similarly in his dealings with Phormio, Demipho will settle—or try to settle—matters by strictly legal means. At 407 ff. (cf. 411–12) he proposes the legal remedy; at 936 he calls Phormio to court. Phormio now has enough evidence to predict that if in any future situation Demipho is driven into a similar corner, he will resort to a similar *in ius ambula*; the use that Phormio makes of this predictability will be demonstrated at 980 ff.

For the moment, however, Phormio simply trumps Demipho's last card by revealing his knowledge of Chremes' bigamy. At this point the dramatic writing is calculated to the last, fine detail in the interests of good theatre. Some of the strokes may be obvious, but no less effective for all that: Phormio's menacing switch from *indotatis* to *dotatis* (938–40), for example, which brings Chremes into the centre of the stage for the first time in the present scene, or the sadistic skill with which Phormio reveals his knowledge about the bigamy, trickle by trickle, both at 941 ff. and later (1004 ff.) in the repeat for Nausistrata's benefit. It is probable that Terence here is mimicking exactly the technique of his Greek model, just as it is that Apollodorus was thereby refining a device already known to Menander, who employs it in the dream narrative of *Dyskolos* 409–18. But some more subtle strokes are easily missed by the reader, insulated as he is from the atmosphere of the theatre. Two of these may be instanced: the sinister emphasis of Phromio's *enim uero* (937: cf. the later counterpart at 958), as he sets in train his savage denoucement, and the deliberate vagueness of *illi* in 944, where even the sex of the person indicated is left indistinct. So Phormio toys with his victims.

By 947 Phormio's revelations have achieved their immediate objective; the 30 minas are his unreservedly. The game appears to be over.

But if the play had ended at this point there would have been several untidy loose ends to mar the typical happy or bitter-sweet ending demanded by Greco-Roman comedy. The use to which Phormio had put his ill-gotten gains would have remained an uncomfortable secret, and the future of Phaedria's liaison problematical. Chremes would have escaped punishment for his infidelity at the hands of the person most justified in inflicting it, his wife. And Phormio would have secured no personal reward for his efforts. To those structural and moral (or immoral) reasons for continuing the play a further scene or two, may be added another, more purely dramatic one. If the play had ended at 947 or thereabouts, the dramatist's portrait of Phormio would have been unsatisfactory and incomplete.

At 954 ff. Demipho attempts to rally his brother with the sensible advice that an immediate confession by Chremes to Nausistrata would be the most effective way of foiling the blackmailer. To prevent the implementation of this suggestion Phormio launches against the two old men a verbal assault (968 ff.) designed to make them lose their tempers and thereby the initiative. To this end Phormio's speech is loaded with insolent, emotional language:

> uni quae lubitum fuerit peregre feceris
> neque huius sis veritus feminae primariae,
> quin novo modo ei faceres contumeliam,
> venias nunc precibus lautum peccatum tuom.

> You came to a foreign country behaved as you pleased,
> and submitted a high-class woman, without any qualms,
> to cruel and unusual treatment,
> and now you want to wash your hands of your outrage.

This is certainly strong language, since Chremes had previously referred to this as *meam neclegentiam* ('my oversight'). The speech achieves its effect of enraging Demipho (976 ff.) and leaving Chremes helpless (978 ff.): the one remedy that the ever-predictable Demipho can now suggest is legal action ('let's go to court', 981), and this offers Phormio the chance at which his calculated insults had been aimed. In order to secure Phormio's arrest, force is required, but since Demipho and Chremes are old, while Phormio is an able-bodied *adulescens* (378), they need the assistance of Chremes' slaves. This gives Phormio time enough to ensure that his cries reach Nausistrata; it also ensures that when Nausistrata does finally emerge at 990, Phormio will hold both the initiative, as the person invoking help, and also the sympathy of Nausistrata, as the apparent victim of aggression. In fact by 990 Phormio's total victory is guaranteed, and the remaining lines of the drama merely play out the inevitable consequences of Phormio's successful legal maneuvres. Demipho, it is true, strives manfully and with considerable cunning to soften Nausistrata's wrath by palliating Chremes' offence (thus his description of the events at 1016 ff. gives a rather different impression of what happened in the Lemnos affair from the various earlier hints and accounts), but Phormio intervenes with his usual impeccable timing before Chremes can be granted his pardon, in order to ensure recognition for Phaedria's liaison and a dinner invitation for himself.

ACKNOWLEDGEMENTS

1. Bernard Knox, 'Euripidean Comedy,' From Alan Cheuse and Richard Koffler (eds.), *The Rarer Action: Essays in Honor of Francis Fergusson*, copyright © 1970 by Rutgers, The State University. Reprinted by permission of Rutgers University Press. Reprinted with revisions and footnotes omitted by permission of the author and publisher. Those referring to this essay for scholarly purposes are requested to consult the original version.

2. E. W. Handley, 'The Conventions of the Comic Stage and Their Exploitation by Menander,' in *Entretiens Fondation Hardt*, 16 (1970), 3–26. Reprinted with revisions and footnotes omitted by permission of the author and publisher. Those referring to this essay for scholarly purposes are requested to consult the original version.

3. David Wiles, 'Marriage and Prostitution in Classical New Comedy', *Themes in Drama 11: Women in Theatre* (Cambridge, Cambridge University Press, 1989), 31–48. Reprinted with revisions and footnotes omitted by permission of the author and publisher. Those referring to this essay for scholarly purposes are requested to consult the original version.

4. P. G. McC. Brown, 'Love and Marriage in Greek New Comedy', *Classical Quarterly*, 43 (1993), 189–205. Reprinted with revisions and footnotes omitted by permission of the author and publisher. Those referring to this essay for scholarly purposes are requested to consult the original version.

5. N. J. Lowe, 'Tragic Space and Comic Timing in Menander's *Dyskolos*', *Bulletin of the Institute of Classical Studies*, 34 (1987), 126–8. Reprinted with revisions and footnotes omitted by permission of the author and publisher. Those referring to this essay for scholarly purposes are requested to consult the original version.

6. Erich S. Gruen, 'Plautus and the Public Stage', in *Studies in Greek Culture and Roman Policy* (Leiden, 1990), 148–57. Reprinted with revisions and footnotes omitted by permission of the author and publisher. Those referring to this essay for scholarly purposes are requested to consult the original version.

7. Gregor Vogt-Spira, 'Traditionen improvisierten Theaters bei Plautus', in B. Zimmerman (ed.), *Griechisch-römische Komödie und Tragödie*

(Stuttgart, 1995), 70–93. Reprinted with revisions and footnotes omitted by permission of the author and publisher. Translated by Leofranc Holford-Strevens in an abridged form for this collection. Those referring to this essay for scholarly purposes are requested to consult the original version.

8. William S. Anderson, 'Plautus' Mastery of Comic Language,' excerpted from *Barbarian Play: Plautus' Roman Comedy* (Toronto, University of Toronto Press, 1993), 109–118. Reprinted with revisions and footnotes omitted by permission of the author and publisher. Those referring to this essay for scholarly purposes are requested to consult the original version.

9. Erich Segal, 'The *Menaechmi*: Roman Comedy of Errors,' *Yale Classical Studies*, 21(1969), 77–93. Reprinted with revisions and footnotes omitted by permission of the author and publisher. Those referring to this essay for scholarly purposes are requested to consult the original version.

10. Holt Parker, 'Crucially Funny, or Tranio on the Couch: The *Servus Callidus* and Jokes about Torture', *Transactions of the American Philological Association*, 119 (1989), 233–46. Reprinted with revisions and footnotes omitted by permission of the author and publisher. Those referring to this essay for scholarly purposes are requested to consult the original version.

11. David Konstan, '*Aulularia*: City-State and Individual', from *Roman Comedy* (Ithaca and London, Cornell University Press, 1983), 33–46. Reprinted with revisions and footnotes omitted by permission of the author and publisher. Those referring to this essay for scholarly purposes are requested to consult the original version.

12. A. R. Sharrock, 'The Art of Deceit: *Pseudolus* and the Nature of Reading', *Classical Quarterly* 46 (1996), 152–74. Reprinted with revisions and footnotes omitted by permission of the author and publisher. Those referring to this essay for scholarly purposes are requested to consult the original version.

13. Timothy J. Moore, *The Theater of Plautus: Playing to the Audience* (Austin, University of Texas Press (1998) 166–80. Reprinted with revisions and footnotes omitted by permission of the author and publisher. Those referring to this essay for scholarly purposes are requested to consult the original version.

14. Florence Dupont, 'Significance comique du double dans *Amphitryon* de Plaute', *Révue des etudes Latines*, 54 (1976), 129–41. Reprinted with revisions and footnotes omitted by permission of the author and publisher. Translated by Leofranc Holford-Strevens in an abridged form for this

collection. Those referring to this essay for scholarly purposes are requested to consult the original version.

15. Niall W. Slater, '*Amphitruo, Bacchae,* and Metatheatre', *Lexis* 5–6 (1990), 101–25. Reprinted with revisions and footnotes omitted by permission of the author and publisher. Those referring to this essay for scholarly purposes are requested to consult the original version.

16. Walther Ludwig, 'The Originality of Terence and his Greek Models', *Greek, Roman and Byzantine Studies,* 9 (1968), 169–82. Reprinted with revisions and footnotes omitted by permission of the author and publisher. Those referring to this essay for scholarly purposes are requested to consult the original version.

17 Dwora Gilula, 'Terence's *Hecyra*: A Delicate Balance of Suspense and Dramatic Irony', *Scripta Classica Israelica,* 5 (1979). Revised and footnotes omitted by permission of the author and publisher. Those referring to this essay for scholarly purposes are requested to consult the original version.

18 J. A. Barsby, 'Problems of Adaptation in the *Eunuchus* of Terence', in B. Zimmermann and N.W. Slater (eds.), *Beiträge zum antiken Drama und seiner Rezeption 2: Intertextualität in der griechisch-römischen Komödie* (Stuttgart 1993), 160–179. Reprinted with revisions and footnotes omitted by permission of the author and publisher. Those referring to this essay for scholarly purposes are requested to consult the original version.

19 Sander M. Goldberg, 'The Dramatic Balance of Terence's *Andria*', *Classica et Medievalia,* 33 (1981–2), 135–143. Reprinted with revisions and footnotes omitted by permission of the author and publisher. Those referring to this essay for scholarly purposes are requested to consult the original version.

20. W. Geoffrey Arnott, 'Phormio *parasitus*', *Greece & Rome,* 17 (1970), 32–57. Reprinted with revisions by permission of the author and publisher. Those referring to this essay for scholarly purposes are requested to consult the original version.

GLOSSARY

adulescens: the youthful romantic hero in New Comedy. He—and his slave—are destined to defeat their rival, often a *senex*, sometimes a *leno*

agapê: brotherly love, charity (*sc.* chaste) the opposite of *eros*

Agnoia: ignorance, specifically of a character's true identity. Sometimes she appears as a personification, as in the prologue to Menander's *The Girl Who Gets Her Hair Cut Short* (*Perikeiromene*)

agroikos: rustic, the country bumpkin—one of the types described by Theophrastus (q.v.) in his famous *Characters* (no. 4)

a*ischrologia*: the obscenity characteristic of Old Comedy as opposed to the *hyponoia* or innuendo of Middle and New Comedy. The distinction is made by Aristotle, who far prefers the more subtle type (*Nicomachean Ethics* 1128a23)

alazôn: boaster, charlatan, blowhard. Described by Theophrastus, *Characters* (no. 23). Plautus drew his *The Braggart Soldier* (*Miles Gloriosus*) from a play of that name

alumnus: foster son

amans et egens: 'in love and in debt,' an apt description of the young hero who typically lacks the financial means to pursue his beloved, usually a *meretrix*.

anagnôrisis: Aristotle's famous description of the moment of recognition, the tragic hero's final painful discovery of his true identity. This in contrast to the *cognitio*, the analogous moment at the conclusions of Greek or Roman comedies, the hero—or heroine's—joyful discovery that he or she is, after all, socially marriageable. Menander's *Sicyonian* is but one of many examples. Here, in Shakespeare's words, 'the catastrophe is a nuptial'. The term was popularized by Northrop Frye in his influential *Anatomy of Criticism* (Princeton, 1957)

apologia: a speech of defence

architectus doli: 'architect of trickery', used often by Plautus to describe the *servus callidus*. A rich example is *The Braggart Soldier* (*Miles Gloriosus*) which employs this sobriquet to describe the slave Palaestrio

argumentum: plot, storyline often sketched by a prologue

astikos: urbane, 'city man' as opposed to *agroikos*, a hick, a simple 'stupid' country man

autarkeia: self-sufficiency

bona meretrix: 'virtuous' prostitute, Terence's twist on the traditionally venal 'fancy woman' *calliditas*: cleverness

chrêstos: good, noble. Often used of an extraordinary hetaira.

chiasmus: any ABBA arrangement, i.e. in the shape of the Greek letter *chi* (X) e.g. Coleridge's 'flowers are lovely, love is flowerlike'

cognitio: the recognition—usually before the finale. The comic equivalent of *anagnôrisis*

contaminatio: literally 'spoiling', the fusing of two Greek models into a single new Roman comedy. This was not regarded as proper practice. This accusation is hurled at Terence by the *malevolus vetus poeta*, 'the nasty old playwright', in, for example, the prologue to *The Self-Tormentor* (*Heauton Timorumenos*)

embolima: a 'thrown-in' song or interlude having little or nothing to do with the plot of the play. This is a first step towards the ultimate disintegration of the chorus as used in Old Comedy

epidikasia: a family obligation to marry an orphan girl relative

êremia: quietude, reclusiveness

eros: sexual desire, later to be construed in Christian literature as the direct opposite of *agapê*

exemplaria Graeca: the Greek models adapted by Roman playwrights. The term is Horace's (*Ars poetica* 268), where the aspiring playwright is urged to study the 'Greek examples' carefully as a key to Roman success

fabulae Atellanae: a type of improvisatory comedy named from the Campanian village where it probably originated. Its influence is visible in the farcical aspects of Roman (Plautine) comedy

fabula palliata: 'play in Greek dress'. In this type of Roman comedy the characters are allegedly 'Greek', playing on the common perception that the decadent denizens of Athens were the precise moral and social opposites of the citizens of Rome. A good vehicle for ironic 'in-jokes'—anti-Roman quips. For example in *The Haunted House* (*Mostellaria*) (828), the clever slave quips: *non enim haec pultiphagus opifex opera fecit barbarus* ('no porridge-eating barbarian workman could make a thing like this')

fabula togata: 'play in Roman dress', set in the familiar social world of Rome. The genre did not catch fire and seems to have had no real influence on the comic tradition

fama: reputation, or rumour. Interestingly, depending upon the context, it can mean either a *good* name or a *bad* one

fescennini: rustic abuse in bantering verse, typical of Roman wedding and harvest celebrations. The word is possibly related etymologically to the Roman *fascinum*, (the male member)—an element never far from the comic genre

fortuna: chance or fortune, sometimes personified; corresponding to the Greek *tychê*

furtum: the 'robbery' by a Roman playwright of scenes from a Greek play that had previously been Latinized. It might even have been a coinage merely for comic purposes. After all, the ancients had no copyrights

geôrgos: farmer

hetaira: 'companion', sophisticated prostitute—corresponding to Latin *meretrix*

hetaireia: brotherhood or companionship, particularly political

histrionia: the dramatic art

humanitas: a concern with human nature characteristic of Terence which corresponds to the notion of *philanthropia* in Menander. The opposite of this trait is epitomized in describing the crotchety old hero of *The Grumpy Man* (*Dyskolos*) 6: *apanthrôpos tis anthrôpos*, 'of all the humans he's most inhumanly inhumane'. In later ages the phrase which first appears in the opening scene of Terence's *Self-Tormentor* (*Heauton Timorumenos*), (77); although taken out of context, became the watchword of Renaissance Humanism: *homo sum: humani nil a me alienum puto*—'I'm a human being. Nothing of humankind is alien to me'

hyponoia: the innuendo characteristic of Middle and New Comedy, as opposed to the obscenity (*aischrologia*) of the Old

imago: appearance, mirrored reflection, twin, ghost, image

in medias res: a story which begins 'in the middle of things', recounting earlier events through flashback. The *Odyssey* is a perfect example

kômos: wild, no holds-barred revel, with which Aristophanic comedies typically concluded

kyrios: lord or master

latifundia: large Roman factory farms worked by slave labour

leno: pimp, usually the villain of the peace, since he has what the hero cannot afford to buy. Hence he is the perpetual antagonist

libertus: freedman. To become one was allegedly the aim of every Roman slave—but in the joy of the conclusion all but a few seem to forget this ambition

locus classicus: a passage typically cited as the best illustration of something

ludi Romani: the Roman harvest festival

malitia: wickedness, malice, trickery. Sometimes, when used by the clever slave, it can mean 'cleverness'

maritus: husband

matrona: the mother of a Roman family was normally revered. But in their comedies she is typically an opponent of the festivities planned by father or son—in collusion with the clever slave. The wife Cleostrata in Plautus' *Casina* is a perfect example

medicus: doctor, a stock comic figure from earliest times, typically a boastful quack

meretrix: an upper-class prostitute as opposed to a *scortum*, (slut), a stock comic figure

miles gloriosus: braggart soldier, the title of a play by Plautus which presents the ultimate ridiculing of this figure—again, as with *matrona* the opposite of the everyday Roman ideal

oikos: household—extended family

paedagôgus: teacher, tutor

palliata: see *fabula palliata*

paterfamilias: the male head of a Roman family and household

patria potestas: the father's absolute power of life and death over his dependents

peculium: administrative power (but not ownership) over assets, granted by a *paterfamilias* to a son or slave. Often used by the bondsman to purchase his freedom

persona: character (literally actor's 'mask')

philanthropia: sympathetic concern for human nature exemplified by many of Menander's characters

philia: love, friendship, affection—again the opposite of *eros*

Phlyax: a tradition of popular farce said to have originated in Magna Graecia, particularly Tarentum (Greek *Taras*). Many choice scenes from these playlets are depicted on surviving vases. Their influence on Plautus is evident

pietas: perhaps the cardinal Roman virtue; heros are admired for their observance of moral and familial propriety. The quintessential example is *pius Aeneas*

pornê: a brothel slave, of inferior social status to the *hetaira*

redende Namen: 'speaking names', which do not designate a person but reveal his personality. For example Pseudolus—a phoney trickster.

senex: old man—often even a senator—who in comedy has grandiose libidinous ambitions but always fails in the end

senex iratus: the 'angry old man' who often blocks the romantic designs of the *adulescens*

servus callidus: the clever, scheming slave who engineers the duping of the blocking character on behalf of the *adulescens*

servus currens: running slave

skênê: a wall at the back of the stage with doors for exit and entrance

storgê: affection—of parents to their children

technitai: craftsmen; the '*technitai* of Dionysus' were professional acting companies. Comedy was a skilled profession

theologeion: a higher part of the stage used for divine appearances, very common in Euripides

Theophrastus: late third-century BC polymath who is now best remembered for his *Characters*—short and interesting sketches of various comic types which had much influence on later comic theory and practice

tibicen: the *tibia* or flute player in Roman comedy

to automaton: chance, often the presiding deity of comedies (and especially of the later 'tradgedies' of Euripides)

topos: a literary trope or conceit (lit. 'place')

tragicomoedia: an imaginary genre concocted by Plautus to describe the tragicomic *Amphtruo*. In the prologue the god Mercury, explains that this hybrid coinage is necessary because the play contains both gods and mortals on the stage together. A similar term was used for the mimes of Rhinthon of Tarentum (early third century BC) *Hilarotragoedia*—'merry tragedy'.

Tychê: chance, fortune, sometimes personified. For example, as when she speaks the prologue to Menander's *The Shield* (*Aspis*). Many of his characters meditate on the brevity of human good fortune

uxor dotata: the rich, henpecking *matrona* who thinks that her large dowry entitles her to make her husband's life a misery

vortere: *vertere*, the process of Roman adaptation of a Greek play. The verb literally means to 'turn'. See, for example, the Prologue to the Asinaria (line 11): *Demophilus scripsit Maccus vortit barbare*, 'Demophilus wrote it, but Plautus turned it in to a barbarian entertainment'.